WORK, INDUSTRY AND CANADIAN SOCIETY

WORK, INDUSTRY AND CANADIAN SOCIETY

HARVEY J. KRAHN
GRAHAM S. LOWE
University of Alberta

NELSON CANADA

© 1988 Nelson Canada,
A Division of International Thomson Limited, 1988

Published in 1988 by
Nelson Canada,
A Division of International Thomson Limited
1120 Birchmount Road
Scarborough, Ontario
M1K 5G4

Canadian Cataloguing in Publication Data

Krahn, Harvey
　　　Work, industry and Canadian society
Bibliography: p.
Includes index.
ISBN 0-17-603414-5

1. Work — Social aspects — Canada. 2. Industrial
sociology — Canada.　　　I. Lowe, Graham S.　　II. Title.

HD6957.C3K72 1988　　　　306'.36' 0971　　　C88-093562-6

Printed and bound in Canada
　3 4 GP 92 91

CONTENTS

Acknowledgements   ix

Introduction   1

1. INDUSTRIALIZATION AND THE RISE OF CAPITALISM   7

Introduction   7
The Origins of Industrial Capitalism   8
  Work in Feudal Society   9
  Work in Early Capitalist Society   10
Canada's Industrialization   14
  Work in Pre-Industrial Canada   14
  The Beginnings of Industrialization   15
  The Decline of Craft Work   16
  Working in the Resource Industries   17
  Corporate Concentration and Modern Management   18
Industrial Capitalism and Social Theory   21
  Karl Marx and the Exploitation of Labour   21
  Smith, Babbage, and Durkheim on the Division of Labour   24
  Max Weber and the Spread of Bureaucracies   26
  The Rise of Corporate Capitalism and the "Managerial
    Revolution"   28
  The "Logic of Industrialism" Thesis   30
  Lenski: Technology and Stratification Systems   31
  Perspectives on "Post-Industrial Society"   32
Conclusion   34

2. CHANGING LABOUR FORCE TRENDS: WHO WORKS WHERE?   38

Introduction   38
Labour Force Participation   39
Canada's Changing Industrial and Occupational Structure   41
Changes in the Canadian Class Structure   46
Regional Variations and Single Industry Communities   48
Time Spent at Work   53

The Growth of Part-Time Employment   54
Unemployment Trends   55
Future Trends   61

3. THE SOCIOLOGY OF LABOUR MARKETS   67

Introduction   67
Good Jobs and Bad Jobs   68
  Income   68
  Fringe Benefits and Job Security   70
  Occupational Status   71
The Human Capital Model of Labour Market Operations   73
Occupational Allocation: Choice, Chance, or Destiny? 74
  Educational Aspirations   75
  Occupational Aspirations   76
  Other Influential Variables   76
Social Mobility and Status Attainment Research   78
  How is Occupational Status Attained?   79
  Differences by Gender and Immigrant Status   81
  "Deskilling" and the Future of Status Attainment   82
Labour Market Segmentation   84
  Dual Economies   85
  Segmented Labour Markets   85
  Internal Labour Markets   87
  Barriers to Primary Labour Market Entry   88
  The Changing Nature of Labour Market Segmentation   90
Labour Market Segmentation or the Human Capital Model? 92

4. WORK ORGANIZATIONS   98

Introduction   98
What's Wrong With Bureaucracy?   99
Key Issues in Organization Theory   101
Management and the Quest for Control   103
Scientific Management   104
The Human Relations Movement   106
The Informal Side of Organizations   110
Organizational Culture   112
The Labour Process Debate   114
Conclusion   118

5. WOMEN'S EMPLOYMENT   123

Introduction   123
Women's Economic Role in Historical Context   123
Rising Female Labour Force Participation   125
Work and Family   127
Occupational Sex Segregation   129
Trends in Occupational Sex Segregation   130
Gender Stratification Within Occupations   133
The Wage Gap   135
Explanations of Work-Related Gender Inequalities   138
Toward Workplace Equality   142

6. SUBJECTIVE EXPERIENCES OF WORK   147

Introduction   147
Work Values and Work Orientations   148
   The Changing Meaning of Work   148
   The Protestant Work Ethic   150
   A Declining Work Ethic?   151
   Work as Self-Fulfilment   154
   Orientations to Work   155
Job Satisfaction and Dissatisfaction   159
   The Prevalence of Job Dissatisfaction   160
   Job Satisfaction and Individual Characteristics   161
   Job Satisfaction and Work Content   163
   Consequences of Job Satisfaction and Dissatisfaction   167
Work and Stress   168
Work and Alienation   169
"The Long Arm of the Job"   172

7. UNIONS AND INDUSTRIAL RELATIONS   181

Introduction   181
Theoretical Perspectives on the Labour Movement   182
Power, Conflict, and Cooperation   183
What Do Unions Do?   186
The Emergence of the Canadian Labour Movement   187
The Role of the Canadian State in Industrial Relations   190
Union Membership Growth Trends   192

The Current State of Unions in Canada 194
Women and Unions 199
Management Opposition to Unions 201
The Future of Union–Management Relations 202

8. INDUSTRIAL CONFLICT **208**

Introduction 208
From Individual to Collective Action 208
What are Strikes? 211
Canadian Strike Trends 212
Explaining Strikes 216
Worker Militancy and Class Politics 217
The Future of Worker Militancy 221

9. WORK IN TRANSITION **225**

Introduction 225
Work Humanization Through Job Redesign 225
Industrial Democracy 230
Industrial Democracy in Action: The Case of Sweden 232
Work and Well-Being 236
Achieving Safe and Healthy Workplaces 239
The Micro-Electronics Revolution 241
Industrial Restructuring 249
Conclusion 251

References *259*

Index *303*

LIST OF TABLES AND FIGURES

Table 2.1 Labour Force Participation by Sex, 1901-1986   40

Figure 2.1 Percent Distribution of Labour Force, Major Occupational Groups, 1901-1981   43

Table 2.2 Employment by Occupation and Sex, Canada, 1986   45

Table 2.3 Labour Force by Industry and Region, Canada, 1986   50

Table 2.4 Occupations Expected to Contribute Most to Employment Growth in Canada, 1986-1995   62

Table 3.1 Average Earnings by Occupation and Sex, Canada, 1975 and 1985   69

Table 5.1 Female Participation Rates in Nine Industrialized Countries, 1960, 1970, and 1981   126

Table 5.2 Employment Concentration of Women, Canada, 1984   131

Table 5.3 The Five Leading Female Occupations, Canada, 1901 and 1981   132

Table 5.4 Occupations with the Highest Male Average Employment Income ($30,000 or more) for Full-time, Full-year (49-52 weeks) Male Workers and Number of Men and Women and Average Employment Income in these Occupations, 1980   136

Table 7.1 Union Membership Growth in Canada, 1911-1986   193

Table 7.2 Union Membership Density and Growth in Selected Industrial Countries, 1961-1981   194

Table 7.3 Union Membership and Unionization Rates by Industry and Sex, Canada, December 1984   196

Table 7.4 Union Membership and Unionization Rates by Occupation and Sex, Canada, December 1984   197

Table 7.5 Ten Largest Unions, Canada, 1986   198

Figure 8.1 Strikes and Lockouts in Canada as a Percentage of Total Working Time: 1919-1983   213

Table 8.1 Strikes and Lockouts in Selected Industrial Countries, 1975-1984   215

ACKNOWLEDGEMENTS

The creation of this book has been very much a collective enterprise. The project was launched with the encouragement of Peter Milroy at Methuen. He convinced us of the value of following our reader in the sociology of work and industry, *Working Canadians* (Methuen 1984), with a textbook in the same area. Peter's sound advice and tolerance of several delays helped nudge the book toward completion. A number of colleagues and students made valuable contributions, and the final product is much improved as a result. Tim Williams' diligence as a research assistant deserves special thanks. Linda Abbott assisted in the preparation of tables and figures. Laura Hargrave used the University of Alberta computer to produce the final page proofs. Dale Cunningham helped by proofreading the text. The following individuals offered thoughtful comments on drafts of various chapters: Jed Fisher, Bob Hinings, Alf Hunter, Barb Marshall, David Mills, Lindsay Redpath, Julian Tanner, Tim Williams and the publishers' two anonymous reviewers. While we must take the ultimate responsibility for what appears in print, we have tried to incorporate the useful suggestions and critical comments provided by these readers. A final note of appreciation goes to our families, whose support and understanding made the project go much more smoothly.

HARVEY J. KRAHN
GRAHAM S. LOWE

Edmonton, July 1987

INTRODUCTION

In many ways, work can be seen as the most essential form of human activity. From the perspective of individuals in society, work is necessary for survival, and may be a source of personal fulfilment. Alternatively, taking a far more general viewpoint, the kind of economy and society we now have in Canada is a product of the combined work efforts, over the years, of millions of men and women. In short, work is a central life activity for most people, and also one of the primary foundations of society.

This book explores a broad spectrum of questions about the changing nature and content of work, and about the consequences of different types of work arrangements for both the individual and society. As the title suggests, a sociological analysis of work must be grounded in the industrial context — hence our emphasis on the underlying economic forces that have shaped particular work options. Equally important for achieving a comprehensive picture of the work world, we must take the larger society into account. There are important links between a person's work and his or her social relationships, social position, and social identity. In brief, this book is about work, its industrial or economic context, and its fundamental importance for both the individual and Canadian society.

Let us identify more sharply the subject matter of the text. The sociology of work and industry is not a neatly delineated area. More than most sociological sub-areas, it crosses into related disciplines. Organization theory, organizational behaviour and organizational psychology, industrial relations, labour economics, political economy, labour history, women's studies, stratification and mobility research, social policy — these are some of the diverse literatures upon which we draw. Because of this broad scope, our coverage of literature is far from exhaustive. Instead, we selectively discuss the literature in ways that will highlight key themes, problems, and issues in the sociology of work and industry. Our objective is to introduce students to the many interesting questions in this field, to show ways in which they may be approached theoretically, and to consider how these explanations stack up against available empirical evidence.

A few brief definitions may help to orient the reader to how we approach the study of work. First, *work* refers to activity that provides a product or service used or valued by others in society. More abstractly, through our work we actively transform raw materials as

1

diverse as iron ore, trees, and information into something that is socially desirable or necessary. The ability to transform the natural world is what distinguishes humans from other species. The emphasis in this definition is on activity; action verbs such as cook, hammer, clean, drive, type, teach, sculpt, or serve are what we typically use to describe work. Obviously, such a definition is very broad, including paid and unpaid work, activities ranging from the legal to the illegal, from the highly esteemed to the undesirable and despised.

In this study, however, we have narrowed our focus to *paid employment*, and therefore do not examine in any detail housework, the major form of unpaid work in society. Volunteer work is also not considered, nor is work in the expanding "informal" economy, or work in the traditional hunting and gathering economies that still exist in Canada. The omission of these non-wage forms of work is not meant to suggest that they are unimportant but, instead, that they warrant careful study in their own right. Nevertheless, having recognized that we cannot equate work with only remunerated activity, the fact remains that Canada is an advanced capitalist society in which paid employment is the dominant form of work activity for the vast majority of individuals.

In fact, the relationships between employers and employees are at the core of sociological theory and research in the area of work. Several of the book's central themes reflect such concerns. The study of work structures and relations is rooted in classical sociological preoccupations with *inequality, power, conflict,* and *social integration.* Are there inherent conflicts of interest between employers and employees that define the employment relationship? A basic problem in all societies involves the distribution of wealth, power, and prestige. Paid work is central to this dilemma of distribution. More concretely, *who* gets the well-paying, interesting, and high-status jobs? Who is most vulnerable to unemployment? Conversely, even casual observations of contemporary workplaces reveal that a considerable degree of cooperation is required to provide a service or make a product. How does cooperation among employees and between management and employees occur? To what extent are employees really integrated into their work organizations? How much do consensus and cooperation reduce the potential for conflicts over the control of work and the distribution of its rewards?

An equally important theme juxtaposes social structure and individuals by contrasting *macro-* and *micro-*levels of analysis. At the macrolevel, we focus on labour markets, occupations, bureaucracies, industries, and a variety of institutions that "structure" or create predictable patterns of work activity in society. But a complete reliance on this type of structural analysis risks losing sight of the individuals who comprise a society. Hence it is essential to examine the continual interplay between social institutions and individual actors. A micro-level analysis investigates how people actively interpret, create, and recreate their social world, constrained, of course, by existing social structures. The dynamic interactions between individual employees and the work organizations and institutions they encounter is at the heart of the sociological study of work and industry.

This basic insight leads us to pose some crucial questions: How do individuals actually experience different work situations? What leads to work satisfaction, or to dissatisfaction and alienation? What attitudes do different social groups hold about work? And what are the diverse ways in which people either accept or attempt to change their work situations? In general terms, how do we account for variations in the work-related behaviours and attitudes of individuals?

The marriage between macro- and micro-levels of sociological analysis is necessary in yet another respect. People are not prisoners of their work situations. Alternatives to present work arrangements do exist. Thus, there is nothing inevitable about the daily work routines of individuals in advanced capitalist societies. The work structures we have inherited from the past need not sweep us into the future according to some inner logic of development. We will argue that work can be a dissatisfying or a self-fulfilling activity. Whichever form it takes is, in large part, a result of the aspirations and actions of ordinary employees. In the following chapters, we do not advocate some utopian vision of work. Rather we highlight the possibilities, challenges, and pitfalls of more humanized, egalitarian, and democratic forms of work. Approaching the study of work from a reformist perspective, we recognize the impossibility of complete detachment from the subject. Nevertheless, we believe that sociologists can, through rigorous empirical research, contribute to the process of workplace reform.

With such an orientation to the subject matter, we are clearly not presenting a strict Marxist explanation of work as exploited labour. Similarly, we do not adhere solely to a Weberian approach, giving undue emphasis to employees' own understandings of their work situations. And we certainly do not advocate a neo-functionalist or Durkheimian model of the work world, allowing the processes of social integration and stability to take on a larger-than-life presence. To varying degrees, we have been influenced by all of these theoretical orientations, although our starting point is, more than anything, located within a "conflict" perspective. The recent growth of Marxist sociology, as articulated in the "labour process" literature, has helped to shape the book's themes of power, conflict, and control. Weberian sociology sensitizes us to the centrality of the individual in sociological analysis. And, to a lesser degree, the Durkheimian tradition reminds us of the importance of social integration, consensus, and stability within work organizations. In our reviews of the literature on various topics below, we attempt to draw out the strengths and weaknesses of these and other theoretical perspectives.

This book is designed, then, to provide broad coverage of the work and industry area from a Canadian perspective. We evaluate the applicability of various concepts and theories in light of the Canadian situation. At the same time, we have incorporated a comparative dimension where possible, noting the similarities and differences between Canada and other major capitalist societies. The changing nature of work in Canada can be better understood with some knowledge of other societies. The discussion is aimed at the second- and third-year undergraduate level, although the book could also be used profitably by advanced undergraduate and graduate students seeking a general assessment of the literature from a Canadian perspective. We have provided an extensive guide to sources, allowing students at all levels to find their way into the literature in pursuit of answers to their own research questions.

We begin with an overview of the industrialization process and the rise of capitalism in Chapter 1. This discussion provides a backdrop against which subsequent questions can be addressed. In the Canadian case, resource extraction during the colonial era gave way to an agricultural economy and then infant industrialization in the late nineteenth century. The twentieth century brought huge corporations (often multinational) in mass production industries, and a booming service sector. Each stage transformed the work conditions and experiences of Canadians.

Chapter 2 traces the main labour force trends in Canada historically, showing how the industrial and occupational distribution of employment has changed dramatically with the development of the economy. Labour markets are central institutions in the contemporary work world. Chapter 3 examines how they actually operate by focusing on a comparison of two leading labour market theories. Chapter 4 shifts the focus to how work activities are typically organized in large bureaucracies. Here we consider theories and research on work organizations from a range of competing perspectives, including the various schools of management and the critical "labour process" literature.

Chapter 5 deals with what until recently was a rather neglected issue, namely, women's employment. The movement of women out of the home and into paid employment is clearly one of the most remarkable social changes of the twentieth century. The chapter charts the transformations in women's economic roles, emphasizing the ways in which gender has become a source of entrenched divisions within the labour market and within work organizations. This, in turn, has led to inequalities between men and women in terms of job rewards and career opportunities.

We shift to a micro-level of analysis in Chapter 6, exploring individuals' subjective experiences of work. In particular, the chapter assesses current debates surrounding work values and the work ethic. The prominent issue of job satisfaction — or dissatisfaction — is examined, along with related concerns of job stress and alienation. The chapter emphasizes the necessity of combining people's perceptions of their immediate work situation with a more structural analysis of its "objective" features.

A pair of chapters probe the always controversial areas of unions, industrial relations, and industrial conflict. Chapter 7 examines the nature of trade unions, their development in Canada, and the creation of an elaborate legal framework for regulating union–management relations through institutions of collective bargaining. We then ask about the conditions under which employees might reject an individual relationship with their employers in favour of collective action. Industrial conflict is a logical extension of this discussion. Chapter 8 focuses on strikes, the most visible form of industrial conflict. But we also point out that conflict can materialize in different ways. The chapter concludes with a discussion of why industrial conflict has not developed into political challenges to capitalism by the working class.

In the final chapter, the theme of "change" is further amplified with an extensive discussion of the future of work. A handful of recent trends are likely to have an enormous impact on the workplace as we head into the twenty-first century. Work humanization through job redesign, industrial democracy, occupational health and safety, the micro-electronics revolution, and the forces of industrial restructuring all hold out possibilities for creating a better workplace. But these are promises only. The directions such trends take are not predetermined. Ultimately it will be public debates about work democratization, new technologies and industrial development strategies, and the collective efforts of working Canadians to change their own work organizations that will determine the future of work in this country.

1

Industrialization and the Rise of Capitalism

INTRODUCTION

We begin our examination of work and work organizations in Canadian society with a look back in history. With some understanding of the nature of work in earlier times, we may be able to see more clearly the unique features of present patterns. We will also be better equipped to judge the significance of changes we are currently observing. And, if "improving" work or workplaces is among our goals, an awareness of the many past attempts to make such improvements can perhaps help us to avoid some mistakes.

There is another important reason for opening this study with a short historical overview. As in other areas of the discipline, the sociology of work and industry contains a large and important theoretical literature, much of it influenced by the writings of Karl Marx, Emile Durkheim, Max Weber, and other classical sociologists. These writers developed their theories out of observations of the world they inhabited. To better understand their concerns and conclusions, it is useful to know something about the times they were describing. Thus, this chapter begins with a historical account of the origins of industrial capitalism in Europe. It is followed by a parallel discussion of the Canadian industrialization experience. With this descriptive background, we can begin to consider the various theoretical explanations of these events, as well as a number of attempts to predict the future of industrial capitalist societies.

We are already using concepts that should be more clearly defined. Exactly what do we mean by the terms *industrialization* and *capitalism*? Industrialization refers to the technical aspects of the accumulation and processing of a society's resources. Capitalism is a term describing the social organization of the productive enterprise. Thus an industrial society would be one in which inanimate sources of energy such as coal, oil, hydro-electricity, or atomic energy fuel a production system relying heavily on complex mechanical technology for the processing of raw materials. Most discussions of industrial society,

7

including the one that follows, begin with comparisons to agricultural societies from which the industrial form evolved. But labelling a society "industrial" tells us very little about the relationships among the individuals involved in the productive process, that is, about how the whole system is organized. A capitalist system of production would be one in which some society members own the productive technology and others, without ownership rights, are hired to work for them.

These are hardly complete definitions, and we will return to them shortly. However, identifying both Canada and Russia as industrialized countries, and, at the same time, calling Canada a capitalist society and Russia a communist society is a more concrete way of distinguishing between the two concepts. Both countries have an industrial economy, but in Russia the state claims complete ownership of the productive system.

THE ORIGINS OF INDUSTRIAL CAPITALISM

Some accounts of the transformation of European society during and following the seventeenth century emphasize the Industrial Revolution, but largely ignore dramatic changes in the social organization of production which were also occurring. Other studies describe this era as a time of transition from feudalism to capitalism, with industrialization presented as a subtopic.[1] It is perhaps more accurate to view these two processes of change as occurring together and influencing each other. However, most historians discuss the development of capitalism in terms of two basic periods — mercantile or commercial capitalism, which began in the 1500s, and industrial capitalism, which evolved somewhat later. In the mercantile period, European merchants accumulated huge fortunes by trading around the world in a variety of goods, including spices, precious metals, sugar, cotton and, somewhat later but equally important, slaves. This trading activity, and the pillage of other cultures (slaves from Africa, for example, and huge amounts of gold and silver from Central and South America) provided much of the wealth that would subsequently fuel the growth of industrial capitalism in Europe.[2] In this sense, capitalism did precede industrialization.

The development of capitalism was a process that encompassed a broad range of social, economic, and political changes. Unlike other more specific historical events, we cannot pinpoint precisely where and when it first appeared. In fact, it evolved slowly and unevenly in several European countries. Its roots can be traced back to the sixteenth century when merchants, bankers, and monarchs in Spain, Holland, England, and France began to search the globe for gold and other valuables that could be brought back for trade in Europe. A very elaborate trading network evolved, linking Africa, Asia, and the American colonies with Europe. But at this time Europe itself was still immersed in feudal society, and the Industrial Revolution had not yet broken loose. A very small minority, living in a few trade-oriented cities, participated in and benefited from such global adventuring. But most of the population of these countries still lived in the country, where, as had their ancestors, they continued to work the land, supporting with their labour the landowning families who controlled rural life.

The class structure of these pre-industrial societies was composed of the aristocracy and the merchant classes, mainly resident in the cities, and the landowning and peasant classes in the country. Over time, the merchant class grew in strength as it shifted much of its energy into industrial production. And as urban industrial production began to replace agriculture's dominance of the economy, the rural landed class became relatively less powerful. With the evolution of industrial capitalism, many rural peasants left the land for the cities, forming a huge class of urban wage labourers. These changes occurred over centuries, with a different pace and pattern in each country. But while the precise details of capitalist development differed internationally, and across regions within countries, the underlying processes and causal forces were similar. The results were monumental changes in how, where, for whom, and under what conditions individuals worked.

Work in Feudal Society

Basic work relationships in this feudal era involved peasants farming small portions of land they did not own. The landowning families received rent in the form of a specified number of days of labour each year or, more frequently, in the form of produce from the land. Labour mobility was rare, and the frequently impoverished peasants lived and died on the same feudal estates, as did their children since the landlord–serf relationship was passed on from generation to generation. There was little question about who had power and who was born to obey.

Virtually everything used and consumed on the manor was also produced there. Some objects (metal tools, for example) might be made by craftsmen in the villages and medieval towns. The organization of this non-agricultural work, including how much assistants were paid, the choice of technology, the level of production, and the cost of the finished product, was carefully regulated by the guilds. Practitioners of the different crafts would each belong to their respective guilds, essentially the forerunners of the trade unions that appeared centuries later. To the extent that markets for goods and services existed, they were local and controlled by these organizations of craft workers. Money was not as essential to these exchange relationships as it is today. In fact, very little agricultural produce was sold for cash. This was largely a pre-market economy in which the producer was also the consumer. It was also a pre-industrial economy. Agricultural technology was simple, and animals and family members were the sources of energy.

Equally important, this was a pre-capitalist economy. Wage labour was virtually non-existent, and the merchant class had not yet come into power. The landed class accepted rent and expected service. In turn, they allowed historical tenancy relationships to continue and provided some protection, if necessary, for their tenants, upon whom they depended for their rents. Typically, landowners did not directly involve themselves in the agricultural activities of their tenants. So long as the annual contributions in labour and in produce were made to the landlords, serfs could more or less determine how and when they did the work. This might not have been a large consolation, but it was something to which future generations of urban wage labourers would not be entitled.

Feudal society was thus built upon a system of mutual rights and obligations, reinforced by tradition. It was, consequently, a relatively stable society, but also one that stifled economic progress. For several centuries, social and economic changes were very gradual, technical and social innovations were infrequent, and the standard of living did not rise. But in time feudal society declined and new patterns of social organization emerged. Did the decay of feudalism lead to the rise of capitalism, or was it the other way around? This question has been the focus of much scholarly debate. One side argues that factors internal to feudal society, such as growing rural populations, deterioration of land, and landlords demanding more rent, forced people off the land and into the cities where they could become an urban working class. The counter argument holds that as mercantile capitalism developed in urban areas, and as the market economy slowly began to make an impact on rural life, cities began to look more attractive to the landless serfs in the countryside. Consequently, they began to leave their manors and their traditional employment relationships and head for the city. A final answer in this debate is probably impossible since the two processes were surely influencing each other. Whatever the causal direction, the eventual outcome remains the same — a very different type of society.[3]

Work in Early Capitalist Society

Signs of industrial capitalism began appearing in the early 1700s. Skilled artisans, working independently or in small guilds, had historically been the producers of finished goods. But by the beginning of this century, an alternative system, in which merchants "put out" the work to be done by peasants in their own homes, had become an important form of non-agricultural production. Long hours and low pay perpetuated rural poverty for the unorganized workers but, at the same time, produced large profits for those coordinating the production and selling the goods. In France, production by individual artisans and the "putting out" system were giving way to larger workshops. By the beginning of the 1700s there were over 400 "manufactories" operating. Some of these larger workplaces produced metal, cloth, glass, and other finished goods. They were staffed by craftsmen who had been convinced to work under one roof for a single employer who would supply the raw materials and market the goods. Others were run by forced labour. For example, the French government forced many unemployed citizens to work in these primitive factories as a way of stimulating the country's relatively weak manufacturing base.[4]

England too was witnessing the appearance of new forms of industrial production. Craft work and the "putting out" system were common there as well. By the latter part of the 1700s, however, a variety of inventions were beginning to revolutionize production techniques. James Hargreaves' spinning jenny — a hand-operated spinning wheel that could handle several threads at one time — was altering the nature of work in the textile industries by the 1770s. Used in combination with Richard Arkwright's new water-frame, which could harness the energy of running water, this technological innovation led to a huge increase in textile production.

New techniques for the processing of iron led to the appearance of iron rails and other previously unavailable products. During these same tumultuous decades, inventors were discovering additional ways of harnessing water and steam. James Watt's steam engine put immense amounts of energy at the disposal of those who could find a way of using it. The technical/social innovation growing out of these earlier inventions was the industrial mill. It was a technical breakthrough since it involved harnessing many machines to a single source of inanimate energy; but it also had immense social implications, for it forced large numbers of workers to congregate under one roof where their labour could be carefully controlled.

By all descriptions, work in these mills was not pleasant and many, particularly artisans who had previously worked at home or in small workshops where they had controlled the labour process, resisted this trend. In some cases, angry demonstrations by unemployed craftsmen called "Luddites" culminated in the destruction of new textile machinery. While not widespread nationally, outbreaks of factory-wrecking took place between 1811 and 1816 in a number of central

British communities. These displaced workers are often remembered as undisciplined and unthinking opponents of technological change. In fact, they were highly skilled workers intensely frustrated by rapidly changing economic and social conditions that were making their skills redundant. In the end, their rebellions were unsuccessful. The power of the state was invoked, and individuals involved in machine destruction were handled harshly. Some were jailed or deported, and others were hanged.[5]

It was only a matter of decades before factory methods of production completely dominated industrialized capitalist societies. The wage-labour force for these factories and mills was drawn, in part, from the ranks of the former craftsmen. It also included transients and others forced to work. Child labour was very common. In some cases, this was forced labour, particularly if families were receiving some form of aid from the parish. In other situations, men would hire children — their own or others' — as apprentices to serve under them in the mill.[6]

An additional source of factory labour were the many migrants from rural areas. The feudal era in agriculture — traditional landlord–serf relationships — had by now largely given way to a more diverse pattern of agricultural employment practises.[7] Some peasants still maintained tenancy relationships with landlords, but wage labour had also become very common in rural areas. This was useful for large landowners, allowing them to purchase labour only at those times in the agricultural cycle when it was most needed. However, this shift to wage labour, and the growing poverty that resulted, created other problems for the wealthy. The "poor rates," taxes used to provide some assistance for the poor, were rapidly increasing in the decades before and after 1800.[8]

Many peasants also managed to grow produce or raise a few animals on small bits of land they owned or rented, or on common land that historically had been shared by local residents. These common rights, a legacy from an era when private property was not as institutionalized, were important for the livelihood of rural residents in some regions of the country, although in other areas the tradition did not exist.[9] The chance to graze a few animals and collect some fuel could supplement the unsteady income provided by agricultural wage labour. In the eighteenth century, however, many rural residents were forced off the land and into urban areas by the "enclosure" movement. Rural landlords were beginning to shift their efforts to large-scale crop production and animal breeding, most frequently sheep. The elimination of small tenant holdings frequently resulted, as did the arbitrary enclosing of common land for use by only the local wealthy families. Historical rights and the obvious hardships being imposed on the rural poor were generally ignored.

The mechanization of industry and the movement to factory-based production proceeded even faster in the 1800s, with a number of European countries and the United States joining the race. Canada, as we shall see, was a late starter. Agriculture became secondary to industry in terms of the value of annual output. Industrial production in Britain, for example, increased by 300 percent between 1820 and 1860. The proportion of the labour force employed in agriculture in Britain, France, Germany, the United States, and other industrializing countries declined, while the proportion in manufacturing and service occupations soared. Hence, the populations of the large manufacturing cities increased in the same dramatic manner. By the end of the nineteenth century, industrial capitalism was clearly the dominant system of production in the Western world.

Karl Polanyi has written about "the great transformation" that occurred in Europe as the *market economy* (or what we have called industrial capitalism) grew into prominence.[10] He describes how virtually no aspect of social life was left untouched by this process. The struggle for democratic forms of government, the emergence of the modern nation-state, the rapid growth of cities — all of these can be directly linked to the major economic changes we have only briefly highlighted. To summarize these changes, the Industrial Revolution brought with it more advanced forms of technology. It involved the replacement of human and animal sources of energy with inanimate sources. A production system that had seldom seen the separation of producers and consumers was replaced by a market-based system in which money and trade were essential ingredients.

Equally important were the changes in the manner in which work was organized. In time, relatively stable non-monetary relationships between landlords and serfs were replaced by wage-labour relationships between industrialists and their factory labourers. Employers paid for a set amount of work, but felt no further responsibility for their workers. However, it was assumed that the payment of wages also carried with it the authority to determine exactly how, and under what conditions, the work should be done. Previously independent artisans were slowly brought into the factory system. Some broadened their scope and actually became part of the class of capitalists, hiring others to work for them. But many others did not. Having long had control over how they did their work, they frequently resisted this new set of authority relations. On the other hand, rural migrants entering the factories had little choice but to accept membership in the class of wage labourers. In the end, the result was a higher standard of living for most residents of the industrialized countries. But the interrelated processes of change to capitalism, industrialism, and a market economy also led to new problems of control, coordination, and management of work — all of which are central themes in this book.

CANADA'S INDUSTRIALIZATION

The process of industrialization in Canada can be traced back to the mid-1800s. Canada was a late industrializing nation, lagging behind both Britain and the United States.[11] Canada's role as a British colony had been to provide raw materials rather than to produce finished goods that would compete on world markets with those of the mother country. Therefore few attempts were made by British industrial interests to promote manufacturing. In addition, Canadian individuals and families who might have undertaken such efforts themselves seemed more interested in the continuation of economic activities of the past — that is, in collecting staple products such as timber and furs for sale on world markets, and in developing transportation networks (particularly railways) that could link the resource producing regions of the country with the port cities involved in export trade.[12]

Work in Pre-Industrial Canada

The first half of the nineteenth century, then, was a pre-industrial economic era in the history of Canada. It could also be described as a pre-market economy since much of what was consumed in rural households was also produced there.[13] In fact, given the peculiarities of colonial development, even land itself was not really a commodity. Huge portions of available agricultural land had previously been given to land companies or individuals in favour with the French (and later British) crown. But by the mid-1830s, less than one-tenth of the land received by these individuals and companies had actually been developed. Speculation in land required less effort but could still be very profitable.

At the same time, immigration from Europe had been increasing. Shortages of land for small farmers, potato famines in Ireland, and generally dreadful working conditions in many of the urban factories of Europe were fueling the successive waves of immigration to the New World. Large numbers of immigrants landed in Canada, but were confronted with a shortage of urban factory jobs and a parallel shortage of cheap agricultural land. Many simply continued on their way. It has been estimated that as many as two-thirds of the immigrants arriving in Canada during this time sought employment in the United States, where the process of industrialization had already begun.[14] As we noted earlier, historians have not been in agreement about the causes of the transition from feudalism to capitalism in Europe. The explanation that a demand for labour in the growing trade and manufacturing cities attracted migrants from rural areas has been countered by the argument that the presence of an underemployed urban labour force led to the growth of industrial capitalism. In Canada at this time, the cause and effect seem much clearer. Because of immigration from Europe, there was a class of (frequently un-skilled) workers available for industrial employment, but the factory jobs had still not appeared.

Nevertheless, some of the immigrants who stayed in Canada were fortunate enough to obtain land and take up farming, while others found employment in various urban sectors of the economy. A large number were employed in the construction of the Welland and Rideau Canals, both of which were dug in the first half of the nineteenth century. This provided work for up to 10,000 labourers at one time. Unfortunately, two or three times as many unskilled workers were arriving in Canada during some of these years. Hence there was a great demand for these seasonal jobs, which often involved fourteen to sixteen hours a day of very hard and poorly paid work. Poverty was widespread. In the winter of 1844, the *St. Catherines Journal* reported that:

> . . . the greatest distress imaginable has been, and still is, existing throughout the entire line of the Welland Canal, in consequence of the vast accumulation of unemployed labourers. There are, at this moment, many hundreds of men, women, and children, apparently in the last stages of starvation, and instead . . . of any relief for them . . . in the spring . . . more than one half of those who are now employed must be discharged.[15]

Thus, by the 1840s, Canada's economy was still largely agrarian. But the labour force necessary for industrialization was available, and the transportation infrastructure, which would aid central Canada's movement in this direction, was being put in place.

The Beginnings of Industrialization

It is interesting, given Ontario and Quebec's present dominance of the industrial economy, that some of the first factories in the country were set up in Nova Scotia. Sizeable glass and clothing enterprises were operating profitably in this region, as was a major shipbuilding industry, before the Maritime provinces entered into Confederation in 1867.[16] But with Confederation came the centralization of manu-facturing in Ontario and Quebec and the deindustrialization of the Maritimes. The building of the railway systems, linking the Maritimes to central Canada, soon had the effect of reversing the flow of manufactured products that had previously come from the Atlantic regions to central Canada. Once this process of concentration of production in one region began, it was almost impossible to stop. A larger population base, easy access to United States markets, and railway links to both eastern and western Canada ensured that the regions around Montreal and Toronto would remain the industrial heartland of the country.

At the time of Confederation, 50 percent of the Canadian labour force was still to be found in agriculture, but things began to change rapidly. The period between 1870 and 1890 witnessed the most rapid industrialization, with the total number of factories in the country increasing from 38,000 to 70,000 and production output climbing dramatically. In 1900, Canada ranked seventh in terms of output among the manufacturing countries of the world. By then it was outproducing both Japan and Sweden, two other late starters in the process of industrialization.[17] The large urban factories which had begun to appear some decades earlier in the United States and some generations earlier in Britain, were now coming into existence in Toronto, Hamilton, Montreal, and other central Canadian cities. In fact, many of them were being built by American firms, beginning a pattern of direct foreign investment in Canada that has continued to the present.

With these economic changes came rapid growth of the central cities and some of the urban social problems for which the European and American industrial revolutions gained notoriety. Labour law was underdeveloped, allowing employers to hire women, men, and children for low pay in return for long hours of work in often very unsafe conditions. While factory work was tough, the subcontracting of work to be done in workers' homes often produced even more unhealthy conditions. Whole families might be employed under one small roof for very low pay. Housing for the urban working class was of inferior quality. Neighbourhood conditions were generally unsanitary and health and social services were largely absent. In short, as economic production increased incrementally in the decades following Confederation, poverty remained the norm for much of the working class in the major manufacturing centres.[18]

The Decline of Craft Work

Skilled craft workers had historically been somewhat better off than the unskilled workers, being able to determine their own working conditions, hire their own apprentices, and frequently set their own prices for their services and products. Some had worked individually, while others had worked in small groups in the manner of European craft guilds. While most were still in some way in the employment of the owner of a "manufactory," they had considerable control over their own work. But as Canada moved into its era of rapid industrialization, these patterns began to change.

Factory owners were little influenced by arguments of tradition, but extremely conscious of the increased productivity American industrialists were obtaining with new technology and modern systems of factory management. Characteristic of most of these innovations was the reduced need for highly skilled workers. A job previously begun and completed by the same person could be separated into several jobs, each requiring less knowledge of the overall process. This meant that the work could now be performed by less skilled and lower-paid employees. The substitution of machines for workers could further cut costs while increasing productivity. Hence, such systems were rapidly put into place in Canada, leading to a considerable reduction in individual workers' autonomy on the job. The outcome of this clear conflict of interests between skilled workers and their employers was a great deal of labour unrest. Between 1901 and 1914, for example, over 400 strikes and lockouts occurred in the ten more industrialized cities of southern Ontario.[19]

Some might find it tempting to see in such accounts of conflict between skilled workers and their employers evidence of a brewing working-class revolution that, for whatever reasons, never fully developed. It is probably more appropriate to interpret these conflicts as the product of a somewhat more privileged group of workers encountering attempts to reduce their occupational power. It is also tempting to conclude that this era of rapidly changing technologies and forms of production meant that most workers were being deprived of previously held autonomy in their work. There were, undoubtedly, large numbers of craftsmen such as these. The "crisis of the craftsmen"[20] was real enough for them. But there were also, as noted earlier, thousands of workers whose only employment had been as unskilled manual labourers. Substitution of twelve hours of low-paying work in a factory for the same number of hours of work digging a canal probably made little difference in terms of pride over work. Both were clearly preferable to unemployment, which was also very common during this era.

Working in the Resource Industries

In addition, there were thousands of workers employed in the resource extraction industries throughout Canada, and many others working on the construction of railways. In his book *The Bunkhouse Man*, Edmund Bradwin estimated that up to 200,000 men living in around 3,000 work camps were employed in railway construction, mining, and the lumber industry during the first years of the twentieth century. Many of these workers were immigrants from a variety of European countries. They were considered good candidates for such work since, thankful for any job and unable to communicate with workers of other nationalities, they were unlikely to collectively oppose their bosses, even when low pay and difficult working conditions made their lives intolerable. Most of the time, this assumption was supported, but such a hiring strategy did not always ward off collective action: immigrants were sometimes the most radical members of the working class.[21]

The building and operation of the transcontinental railway led to a large demand for coal. Mines were opened on Vancouver Island, and a string of coal-producing towns appeared in the Alberta Rockies. Immigrants quickly arrived to take the new jobs. In the absence of an organized working class and any real labour legislation, mine owners and managers were able to extract a lot of work for relatively little pay. If necessary, the military could be brought in to control unruly workers. In addition, working conditions in both provinces were very unsafe. It has been estimated that at the beginning of the 1900s, every one million tons of coal produced in Alberta took the lives of ten miners. Similar statistics for British Columbia revealed twenty-three dead for every million tons of coal. The North American average at this time was six deaths per million tons.[22]

Thus, in spite of the hiring of mixed-race work forces, and in spite of the ability of mine owners to deal harshly with labour unrest, these conditions did lead to strikes, union organization, and even political action. In 1909, Donald McNab, a miner and socialist, was elected to represent Lethbridge in the Alberta legislature. The same year, the Revolutionary Socialist Party of Canada elected several members to the B.C. legislature and for a short term became the official opposition.[23] Earlier we questioned whether the skilled craftsmen of central Canada, angrily opposing the introduction of new technology and management systems in their places of work, were to be remembered as a quasi-revolutionary, working-class group. In many ways, these less privileged workers in the mines and forests of western Canada exhibited more radical behaviour. But their successes, including terms in the legislature, were usually short-lived. While the labour movement did manage to take root in the resource industries, it never became the revolutionary movement that some of its more radical leaders had envisioned. We will return to a discussion of labour radicalism, in Canada's past and in the present, in a subsequent chapter.

Corporate Concentration and Modern Management

In 1890, Canada boasted around 70,000 manufacturing enterprises; by 1920, the number had shrunk to around 22,000. However, this was not a case of declining production, but the very opposite. It was an era of "concentration of production." Many corporate mergers were occurring in the first decades of this century as larger manufacturing enterprises swallowed up smaller ones.[24] In addition, many factories were expanding to increase their economies of scale and to produce more for growing national markets. Western Canada was being opened for immigration. A wheat boom at the beginning of the century made the West a more promising market for manufactured goods from central Canada. Industrialization was also being observed in parts of the hinterland. Winnipeg, for example, was expanding its manufacturing potential. In 1891, the average manufacturing enterprise in that city employed eight people and had about $10,000 in assets. By 1911, the average Winnipeg manufacturing firm employed over sixty workers and was worth close to $150,000.[25]

Thus, the decades surrounding the First World War (up until the Depression years) were a time of consolidation and growth in the Canadian industrial structure. Many of the large firms that now dominate the national economy were being formed then. In terms of the work experiences of Canadians, this was a time when both government and the private sector were expanding and creating new jobs, a time when wage labour was becoming the norm. Craft workers who had dominated the industrial scene only half a century earlier were now becoming a minority. Agricultural workers made up only 40 percent of the labour force in 1901, despite the fact that agriculture was expanding in the West during this time. By 1921, agriculture's share of the Canadian labour force had shrunk to about one-third.[26] Canada had become an industrial nation.

As business enterprises and government departments grew in size, finding more efficient methods of organizing production or the provision of services became a major concern of managers. Record-keeping requirements in both the private and public sectors were growing exponentially. A massive increase in the number of office workers was one of the consequences.[27] Clerical workers made up 3.2 percent of the total Canadian labour force in 1901. By 1921 this had increased to 6.8 percent. In absolute terms, there were over 216,000 office workers in Canada in 1921, up from about 57,000 in 1901.[28] The rapid growth of the clerical sector also involved a very important shift in its composition. Clerical work had historically been a male domain. As the number of such jobs grew, the proportion of women in this field increased substantially. In 1901, women made up 22 percent of the clerical labour force, but by 1921 this had almost doubled to 42 percent. Thus, the administrative revolution of the early twentieth century signalled two fundamental labour force changes: the emergence of the white-collar sector and the movement of women into the paid labour force.

Probably the most logical explanation for the exodus of men and the movement of women into this field involved the reduced status and rewards of these newly created office jobs. This, in turn, can best be attributed to the growing division of labour in the government and private sector offices. A contributor to the *Monetary Times* in 1920 showed a good understanding of the process when observing that:

> The construction of the modern office grows constantly more like the construction of the factory. Work has become standardized, long rows of desks of uniform design and equipment now occupy the offices of our large commercial and financial institutions. With the increasing division of labour each operation becomes more simple. The field in which each member of the staff operates is narrower.[29]

Thus, the division of labour that had drastically altered production work quickly became a standard feature of clerical work as well. While many more individuals were involved in the process, each worker had a reduced area of responsibility in which fewer skills were required. Overall, this typically meant greater efficiency and productivity; for individual workers, it usually meant lower status and reduced work rewards.

Increasing efficiency also meant obtaining greater control over all aspects of organizational activity, including the specific jobs being done by employees. Management's concern with the problems of controlling large work forces was growing. This led to the frequent adoption of "modern" management techniques in Canada, a subject to which we return in Chapter 4. As had been the case for new manufacturing technologies, these methods of organization and management were frequently first observed in the United States and then imported into Canada. "Welfare work" was one such managerial innovation introduced in larger enterprises. Employers attempted to improve the work and home lives of their employees by providing a variety of benefits, and by making working conditions more comfortable and safe. Welfare work can be viewed, appropriately enough, as a liberal response to the excesses of rapid industrialization. But it was also an attempt to gain greater control over one's work force. If expression of concern over the welfare of workers could lead to a reduction in management–labour disputes, it would be worth the effort.

A second influential management approach that became popular during this era was "scientific management." Frederick Winslow Taylor's advice to managers in the United States, regarding methods of linking payments to effort and matching workers to specific tasks, also appealed to some Canadian managers. This approach (as we will see in Chapter 4) was based on a very different premise about human nature. But both were new techniques designed to motivate and control the now much larger and diverse work forces found in Canadian firms and government agencies. By the late 1920s, these modern management techniques were in place along with modern methods of production, including the assembly line. Over the next decades, there would be further changes in the technical and social aspects of work, but these would be more gradual than the changes that had transformed work for the majority of Canadians in the first decades of the twentieth century. The Depression would constitute a major setback for many Canadian businesses and, particularly, for thousands of families left without a source of livelihood for almost a decade. But as Canada's industrial structure revived with the on-slaught of World War II, there would be a continuation of the trends begun at the start of the century.

INDUSTRIAL CAPITALISM AND SOCIAL THEORY

Karl Marx and the Exploitation of Labour

Karl Marx spent a lifetime critically examining the phenomenon of industrial capitalism. His assessment of this new type of society was presented within a very broad theoretical framework. He called the overall system of economic activity within a society a *mode of production,* and he identified its key ingredients as the *means of production* (the technology, capital investments, and raw materials) and the *social relations of production* (the relationships between the major social groups or *classes* involved in production). In earlier modes of production, different technologies had been paramount, and different relation-ships had existed between social classes. Feudal societies and societies built around the institution of slavery were among the earlier modes of production discussed by Marx. In both examples, he focused on the manner in which the ruling class controlled and exploited the subservient class, and on the *class conflict* between them.

Class conflict was the key factor in Marx's theory of social change. He argued that previous modes of production had collapsed and been replaced because of conflicts among class groups within them. Feudalism in Europe, for example, had given way to capitalism as a result of (1) the growing power of the merchant class relative to the traditional alliance of landowners and the aristocracy, and (2) the deteriorating relationship between landowners and peasants. This capitalist revolution had been gradual and only occasionally violent. But, Marx argued, capitalism would itself eventually be replaced by a socialist mode of production. The impetus for this massive change would again be widespread class conflict. Marx's vision of the future portrayed a revolutionary upheaval in which the oppressed working class would destroy the institutions of capitalism and replace them with a socialist society based on collective ownership of the means of production.

Marx separated industrial capitalist society into two major classes — the capitalist class or *bourgeoisie,* which owned the means of produc-tion, and the *proletariat* or working class, which exchanged its labour for wages. He also identified a smaller *petite bourgeoisie* class of inde-

pendent owners and producers, and small business owners. But this
third group was of lesser significance in Marx's scheme of things. In
fact, he expected it to largely disappear as capitalism matured and
drew members of the petite bourgeoisie into the two major classes. Of
much greater significance was the relationship between owners and
workers.

Marx argued that the value of a product sold on the market was a
function of the labour needed to produce it. Since, in a capitalist
system, wage labourers produced more than the amount needed to
pay their wage, *surplus value* was being produced. Consequently, the
relationship between capitalist and worker was exploitative since the
worker who produced the profit was not receiving it. This form of
exploitation was not like that of slaves or of serfs tied to a manor. These
were, after all, "free" labourers being hired to work in the factories.
However, by virtue of acting as the purchaser of labour, the capitalist
class gained control over the labour process itself. The working class
had little choice but to accept the arrangement, and had no control
over how they actually did their work. A final consequence, according
to Marx, was the feeling of *alienation* from their work that labourers
in a capitalist society experienced. Having no control over the labour
process and over the products they were creating, workers felt separated (or alienated) from their work. We will return to a discussion of
alienation from work in Chapter 6, but for now it is sufficient to note
that Marx believed that, in time, the working class would react to this
alienation and exploitation, and eventually revolt.

Few people would disagree with Marx's claim that the industrial
working class of his time was being exploited. This was a time when
wages were typically at a level just high enough to keep a worker's
family from starving — a time when child and female labour was
ruthlessly exploited in factories because it could be obtained cheaply.
The working class of Marx's day had to accept long hours of work, very
unhealthy working conditions, and often harsh and arbitrary treatment from factory owners. Labour laws limiting the excesses of
capitalism had yet to appear. The craftsmen forced into the industrial
mills were, according to one commentator: "subjected to inflexible
regulations, and driven like gear-wheels by the pitiless movement of
a mechanism without a soul. Entering a mill was like entering a
barracks or prison."[30] In short, the nineteenth century was an era in
which the accumulation of massive fortunes in Europe and in North
America was based on widespread working-class poverty.

In 1845, Friedrich Engels documented this exploitation and poverty in his classic book, *The Condition of the Working Class in England.*
Describing one of London's many slum districts, and noting that
other manufacturing cities of the day were much the same, Engels
wrote:

St. Giles is in the midst of the most populous part of the town, surrounded by broad, splendid avenues in which the gay world of London idles about. . . . It is a disorderly collection of tall, three or four-storied houses, with narrow, crooked, filthy streets . . . . The houses are occupied from cellar to garret, filthy within and without, and their appearance is such that no human being could possibly wish to live in them. But this is nothing in comparison with the dwellings in the narrow courts and alleys between the streets, entered by covered passages between the houses, in which the filth and tottering ruin surpass all description. . . . Heaps of garbage and ashes lie in all directions, and the foul liquids emptied before the doors gather in stinking pools. Here live the poorest of the poor, the worst paid workers with thieves and the victims of prostitution indiscriminately huddled together . . . and those who have not yet sunk in the whirlpool of moral ruin which surrounds them, sinking daily deeper, losing daily more and more of their power to resist the demoralizing influence of want, filth, and evil surroundings.[31]

It was from such first-hand observations of industrializing Europe that Marx developed his critique of capitalism.

Marx generated a torrent of scholarly and political writings debating the validity of his theories and the accuracy of his predictions. Indeed, much of twentieth-century sociological theory has been, according to Irving Zeitlin, a debate with the ghost of Marx.[32] For our purposes, there are several key themes originating in Marx's analysis of industrial capitalism that have influenced debates and research agendas in the sociology of work and industry. First, Marx emphasized the degree to which the profit motivation of capitalism is in direct opposition to the interests of the working class, that is, better wages and working conditions, and a higher standard of living.[33] Viewing workplace relationships in this manner involves taking a *conflict* perspective, one which is very different from *consensus* approaches, which assume that the interests of these two groups are actually much more congruent. In Chapter 4, we will be examining a variety of management theories that are based on assumptions of such a consensus of interests.

Second, Marx pointed out that the wage-labour production relationships of capitalism led to workers losing control over how they actually did their work and to widespread alienation from work. Many industrial sociologists, including some with little affection for Marx, have subsequently looked for ways of redesigning work organizations in order to correct such problems. Some of these innovations will be discussed in Chapters 4 and 9. Third, Marx predicted that in time the working class would begin to organize itself and more actively oppose the ruling capitalist class. We have witnessed the growing importance of labour unions in the past century, and it is now impossible to study the sociology of work without considering the role they play. In Chapters 7 and 8, we will focus directly on the issue of industrial conflict, examining the Canadian labour movement and asking, among other questions, whether it is evolving in the direction Marx predicted.

Linking these three themes is the most obvious but perhaps also most important observation Marx left with us. The relations of production in industrial capitalist society are organized in a hierarchy, with owners (and their representatives) having more power, status, and wealth. Almost all of the debates about better ways of organizing workplaces and managing employees, about the need for unions and labour legislation, and about the future of work in our society stem from this basic inequality.

Smith, Babbage, and Durkheim on the Division of Labour

The independent, highly skilled craftsmen who were largely replaced by the factory workers of the Industrial Revolution are often remembered as representing the *ideal* of working life. C. Wright Mills, for example, emphasized the personal satisfactions derived from being involved in all aspects of the creation of some product, being free to make decisions about how the work should be done, and being able to fully develop one's skills and abilities.[34] Obviously not all workers in the pre-factory era were fortunate enough to be craft workers, but it is clear that such opportunities became less common with the growth of industrial capitalism. Part of the change was due to the loss of control over work that accompanied the transition to widespread wage labour. Equally significant was the separation of work sequences into simpler and smaller tasks, each done by an individual worker.

Human societies have always been characterized by a basic *division of labour*. In primitive societies, work roles were assigned mainly according to age and sex. But with economic development these roles became more specialized, and the arrival of industrial capitalism further intensified this process. Once a certain scale of production was reached, it was much more efficient to break complex jobs into their component tasks.

In his highly influential book *The Wealth of Nations*, Adam Smith identified the extensive division of labour as one of the secrets of economic succcess. Using the example of a pin factory, he described how productivity could be multiplied many times by assigning workers to specific tasks such as stretching wire, cutting it, and sharpening it. Whereas individual workers might, at best, produce 20 pins a day, with a well-defined division of labour, ten people could make 48,000 pins a day. The greater productivity, Smith reasoned, came from the increased dexterity a worker could master in repeating a single task over and over again, the time saved in not having to shift tasks and tools, and the added savings obtained from designing machines that workers could use to repeat the single task.[35] Obviously the advantages of this form of production would only be realized if one were to produce large quantities of the product in question, which is precisely the goal in industrial capitalist systems of production.

In 1832, Charles Babbage translated Smith's principles into some practical cost-cutting advice for entrepreneurs. By subdividing the tasks, he argued, less skill was required of any individual worker than had previously been the case. Consequently, one could also get away with paying less for the labour involved. Even if a group of workers with specific limited tasks could produce only as much as an equivalent group of craft workers, the overall cost to the capitalist factory owner coordinating the work would be less. Workers with fewer skills simply cannot demand as high a reward for their work.[36] The early history of industrialization is full of examples of this basic economic principle at work. The advent of factories with detailed divisions of labour almost always involved the replacement of highly skilled craft workers with minimally skilled factory workers who were paid less. And as we have noted in our examination of Canadian history, the same process occurred in the administrative revolution when clerical workers encountered the division of labour.

Neither Smith nor Babbage are remembered for negative comments about the division of labour, although Smith clearly recognized the bleaker side of this process.[37] But returning to Mills's description of the ideal of craft work, we can easily see some of the problems. A central feature of craft work was the degree to which one individual was involved in all aspects of the creation of some product. The pride resulting from this personal act of creation was one of the first casualties of industrialization. Furthermore, the extreme subdivision of tasks demanded by an efficient factory system inevitably led to repetitious, boring work. It is little wonder, then, that many craft workers actively resisted the movement toward factory-based production — they were being paid less for more work that was less enjoyable.

Marx focused directly on these negative consequences in his discussions of alienated work. His was a radical critique, for it identified capitalism itself as the source of the problem. The division of labour was simply a technique employed to create greater profits from the labour of the working class. Emile Durkheim, a French sociologist writing at the beginning of the twentieth century, provided the alternative conservative assessment of the division of labour. He noted that modern societies contain very diverse populations in terms of characteristics such as race, ethnicity, religion, occupation, and education. In addition, there is a great diversity in beliefs and values. Such differences could very easily generate disruptive conflict among different groups — conflict over how scarce resources should be distributed, over rights and privileges, and also over different beliefs. Looking back over the history of industrialization in Europe, Durkheim had little difficulty in finding evidence of such conflicts. But rather than place the blame on the division of labour, he viewed it as a major source of societal cohesion, as a factor that would reduce the potential for conflict.[38] He reasoned that individuals and groups engaged in different tasks in a complex division of labour would recognize not only their own importance but also the importance of others involved elsewhere. This recognition of mutual interdependence would, in turn, generate greater tolerance and a more harmonious society.

How is this general theory of society and social change relevant to our study of work? Durkheim was arguing that individuals in modern society are forced to rely on each other because of the different occupational positions they fill. In simple terms, lawyers need plumbers to fix their sinks, while doctors may need lawyers to fight malpractice suits. Both lawyers and plumbers may at some time require the services of the physician. Taking this argument to a broader level of analysis, capitalists and their employees are interdependent. Without some degree of cooperation between these two groups, the economy would grind to a halt. Thus we can see Durkheim's positive assessment of the division of labour underlying many of the management theories that assume a congruence of interests in the workplace. While Marx's critical response to industrial capitalism has influenced conflict perspectives on work in modern society, the conservative assumptions of Durkheim's general model are really the backbone of the consensus approach.

Max Weber and the Spread of Bureaucracies

Having observed the process of industrialization in Europe, Marx recognized that such massive societal changes involved more than just the adoption of new technologies and energy sources. Equally important was the replacement of earlier social relations of production with capitalist wage labour relationships. Max Weber, a German sociologist writing in the early twentieth century, was also conscious of this important difference. But in his writings he addressed yet another major change flowing out of the process of capitalist industrialization. Weber noted that Western societies were becoming more rational in both the technological and social spheres. One of the critical aspects of this social change was the degree to which *bureaucratic* work organizations were becoming the norm. Small, informal relationships among workers, and between workers and employers, were being replaced by more formal, impersonal work relations in large bureaucracies. Rules rather than relationships were now determining one's behaviour at work. Weber's account of this trend was not totally positive — he regretted the loss of more intimate interpersonal relationships — but he felt that the greater efficiency (hence profit) provided by this new form of work organization made it inevitable. The rise of bureaucratic forms of work organization was, to Weber, synonymous with capitalism. Industrial capitalism was a system of rationally organized economic activities; bureaucracies provided the most appropriate organizational framework for such activities.

Weber identified what he saw to be the key characteristics of bureaucratic organizations. Most important was a well-defined division of labour and an equally well-defined hierarchy of authority. Each office or work role had its own duties and responsibilities, and each was part of a chain of command in which orders could be passed down and rewards and punishments used to ensure that they were followed. But the power of the employer could not extend beyond the bureaucracy. The contract linking employer and employee was binding only within the work relationship. Necessary for the continued smooth operation of the organization were extensive written files containing records of decisions made and transactions completed. Recruitment into and promotion within the bureaucratic work organization were based on competence, performance skills, or certifications such as educational credentials. Individual employees would make careers within the organization as they moved as far up the hierarchy as their skills and initiative could carry them. However, the office holders remained employees only. Their contract with their employers assured them a position so long as they were needed and could satisfactorily carry out the functions of the office. It was not a permanent position, and they could obviously not pass it on to one of their children. In short, rationality, impersonality, and contractual relationships defined the bureaucratic work organization.

Bureaucracies were not, strictly speaking, inventions of the nineteenth century. A somewhat similar form of centralized government had existed in China centuries earlier, and European societies had been organizing their armies more or less in this manner for some time. What was unique, however, was the degree to which workplaces in the nineteenth century took on bureaucratic characteristics. The organization of agricultural and craft work in feudal and early industrial Europe (and also North America) had been very different. Early factories, still partially controlled by organizations of guild workers, operated with a division of labour and a hierarchy of control, but with none of the formal rules and chains of command Weber was describing. With the maturing of capitalism at the beginning of the twentieth century, however, increased competition and the development of large, complex manufacturing systems demanded rationalization of production techniques and worker control systems. Large bureaucratic work organizations would become the norm throughout the industrial capitalist world. We have looked briefly at the Canadian experience in this regard, but such a form of organization would also become the norm (perhaps even more so) in industrialized communist countries. Recognition of this fact forces us to remember that, while totally intertwined in the history of industrial capitalist societies, bureaucracy and capitalism are, in fact, separable phenomena.

The Rise of Corporate Capitalism and the "Managerial Revolution"

We have identified several distinctive features of this new industrial capitalist mode of production: an increased division of labour, the growth of a wage-earning class, and the appearance of large bureaucratic work organizations. One additional factor deserves comment. As the nineteenth century drew to a close, the pattern of extensive competition among many small entrepreneurs was beginning to give way to a system in which fewer but much larger firms were active. At the beginning of the twentieth century, large corporations began to dominate the economy, particularly in the manufacturing sector. We have already noted the frequency with which these organizations took on a bureaucratic form, but some further important characteristics of the modern firm should be highlighted.

Traditionally, manufacturing enterprises had been owned and controlled by individuals or families, the exceptions being those owned by small groups of individuals who, while not related, still knew each other. The twentieth century, however, introduced the joint-stock companies in which hundreds or thousands of investors would receive a share of the ownership and the profits. Such a diverse group of owners obviously could not directly control the giant corporation in which they had invested; hence, a class of managers to run the enterprise became essential.[39]

As this pattern became more pronounced, observers began to question the Marxist model of industrial capitalism, which had portrayed the relations of production as a simple two-class system — capitalists who owned and controlled the means of production in conflict with workers who had little choice but to exchange their labour for a wage. An alternative model became popular. It predicted a new era of reduced conflict and greater harmony in the workplace as a result of this *managerial revolution*. The argument hinged on the assumption that managers, who were salaried workers and not owners, would be likely to consider more than just profit in their decision making. The good of the company and the good of the workers would be equally important considerations. Since ownership of the firm was now diffused over many individuals, who would seldom be able to get together to insist on their ownership rights, power and control of the enterprise had essentially shifted to a new class of presumably neutral managers.

Several decades of debate and research later, it is generally agreed that this new perspective on industrial relations in capitalist society probably exaggerated the degree of change.[40] First, family ownership patterns may be less common, but they have certainly not disappeared in most industrialized countries. Furthermore, while ownership of corporations may be spread across more individuals, many corporations are still controlled by small groups of minority shareholders. Rather than totally diffusing the power invested in ownership, the rise of the joint-stock company has created situations in which individuals or families can control a firm without having to own a majority of the stock. An additional post-war trend has been toward corporate ownership of shares. In other words, concentration of ownership has increased as a few large holding companies replace the many individual owners whose shares were purchased.

Canada's situation is much like that of other industrialized capitalist nations. The prominence of names like Labatt, Molson, and Bronfman support research findings that document the remaining strength of family ownership patterns. In the case of corporations in which single families do not have majority control, ownership still remains concentrated among a small number of stockholders. A recent Canadian study concluded that only a very small number of the largest Canadian corporations did not reveal such concentration of ownership. Other research focusing on the individuals who serve as directors of major corporations has clearly demonstrated the degree to which they are joined in a network of cross-cutting relationships. Many directors sit on the boards of several major corporations simultaneously. Thus, the belief that the relatively small and very powerful capitalist class described by Marx has largely disappeared is unsubstantiated by current evidence.[41]

Advocates of the managerial revolution thesis must also demonstrate that, compared to the capitalists of an earlier era, the new breed of managers is less likely to be influenced by the "bottom line" of profit. Research suggests that senior managers and corporate executives think and act in much the same way as do capitalist "owners." They share a similar world view or ideology. In fact, they tend to come from the same social backgrounds as do owners, and they often hold large blocks of shares in the corporation, where they frequently serve as directors as well. In summary, the optimistic predictions of a new era of industrial harmony brought on by new patterns of corporate ownership and management have proved to be largely unfounded.

However, the fact remains that a much larger majority of Canadians today are employed in very large corporations, and that a large managerial class responsible for coordinating and controlling their work has come into being. Indeed, we have become accustomed to discussing "labour–management" relations, as if these were the two main partners in the economy. Given the evidence discussed above, it is clearly important to remember that the concept of management cannot be divorced from the concept of ownership. The management and control of workers in large corporations (and also in government bureaucracies) is a central topic in later chapters.

The "Logic of Industrialism" Thesis

Our quick excursion into Canadian history has demonstrated that not all countries went through the industrialization process in the same way the Western European societies did. However, there are underlying dynamics and processes that do appear to be similar. In industrialized countries, which tend to be highly urbanized, production is typically organized on a very large scale, technologies are complex, and workplaces are frequently large and organized in a very formal manner. Most citizens are reasonably well educated and there appears to be some correspondence between the level of education and training obtained and the status and rewards of the occupation. Industrial societies typically have a large middle class of white-collar workers.

Recognition of such similarities in the social and economic structures of the more industrialized countries has led to observations like the following: "The world is entering a new age — the age of total industrialism. Some countries are far along the road, many more are just beginning the journey. But everywhere, at a faster pace or a slower pace, the peoples of the world are on the march towards industrialism."[42] This is the *logic of industrialism* thesis, a very deterministic and unilinear argument about the immense and inevitable effects of industrial technology. In brief, it contends that industrialism is such a powerful process that any country, whatever its characteristics at the outset, will eventually begin to resemble the other industrialized countries. The logic of industrialism dictates these changes, and eventually all societies will be affected by it. Furthermore, their individual paths of development will begin to converge — hence, another name for this argument is the *convergence* thesis.

This theory is further elaborated by focusing on how industrialism is based on the use of complex technology and new sources of energy in the transformation of raw materials into finished goods. A skilled work force is required to work with the new technologies. The "needs" of the technology, therefore, demand that societies develop a sophisticated education and training system that will support and sustain the industrial process. In order to maintain the system, those most educated — and hence most valuable to the system — must also be paid more than the less trained and less important members of the society. Legal and political systems allowing the free movement of labour, accumulation of capital, and so on must also come into being. "The iron hand of technology tends to create uniformity in job structure, compensation differentials and technical training."[43]

This is a very broad technology-based theory of social and economic change. It argues that all countries, including both communist and capitalist varieties, will eventually become very similar in structure. Like many other attempts to explain large parts of the social world, the predictive value of this theory remains high so long as one does not get too close to the subject matter. However, an examination of production structures and work patterns in different countries reveals some important differences that are not about to disappear. For example, unemployment rates have been kept much lower in some countries than in others. We find that innovative forms of work organization have been introduced in a number of countries, leading to considerably less industrial strife and a more productive economy. In some industrialized countries, unions have become part of the social fabric, while in others they are currently fighting just to stay in existence. Some industrialized countries have continued to retrain workers made redundant by the introduction of new forms of technology, while others leave such workers to cope on their own. Some of these cross-cultural differences will be examined in more detail in later chapters, in order to illuminate unique characteristics of work and work organizations in Canadian society.

Lenski: Technology and Stratification Systems

Gerhard Lenski paid special attention to some of these same factors in his analysis of the link between technology and a society's stratification system.[44] In simple hunting and gathering cultures, he argued, the few resources of the society were distributed primarily on the basis of need. But as societies became more complex, privilege, or the control of the society's surplus resources, came to be based on power. Ruling elites received a much larger share of the resources. In agrarian societies, some form of governing system had evolved, giving the privileged class, through control of this political system, access to even more of the society's resources. An example of this would be the extreme contrast between the wealth of the ruling families and the poverty of the masses in agrarian societies such as pre-colonial India. Thus, in Lenski's theory, the technological base of the society largely determines the degree of inequality or the structure of the stratification system within society.

However, the arrival of the industrial age reversed this "age old evolutionary trend toward ever-increasing inequality."[45] Lenski's explanation of this abrupt halt to a historical pattern hinged on the complex nature of industrial technology. Owners of the means of production could no longer have direct control over production. In the interests of efficiency, they would have to delegate some authority to subordinates. This would lead to the growth of a middle level of managerial and technical workers, who would have to be highly educated — the technology demanding this — and who would expect greater compensation for their training. Education itself would also broaden the horizons of this class of workers, introducing them to ideas of democracy, as well as making them more articulate and capable of using the political system to press their demands for a larger share of the profits produced from their labour.

In short, Lenski's theory proposed a link between complex industrial technology, the higher education of workers, and their insistence on sharing in the growing wealth of an industrial society. But why would employers give in to this demand? Because, argued Lenski, the industrial elite needed educated workers; the productive system could not operate without them. In this sense, Lenski's theory incorporates some of the features of the managerial revolution thesis discussed earlier. Equally important, the much greater productivity of industrial societies meant that the "elite can make economic concessions in relative terms without necessarily suffering any loss in absolute terms."[46] Because the economic pie was so much bigger, everyone could have a larger share.

Perspectives on "Post-Industrial Society"

The convergence theorists described *industrial society* and argued that other differences among societies would come to be of lesser importance. Other observers have focused on continuing changes in industrial capitalist societies and have labelled yet another newer type — *post-industrial society*. Most representative of this group is Daniel Bell, who was among the first to note an important shift in the U.S. occupational structure.[47] The Industrial Revolution had seen jobs in the manufacturing and processing sectors replacing agricultural jobs. By the middle of the twentieth century, jobs in the service sector were becoming much more prominent. Factory workers were being replaced by employees in the areas of trade, finance, education, health, entertainment, government, and a variety of other business sectors. White-collar workers were beginning to outnumber blue-collar workers.

Whereas industrial societies had involved the majority of their citizens in the production of goods, Bell argued that post-industrial societies would come to involve many more in the production and dissemination of knowledge. Professionals, technicians, and scientists would become a much more important class in this new society, and their presence would begin to reduce the conflict between polarized classes that had typified the arrival of the industrial age. Thus, while the managerial revolution thesis hypothesized that the growth of a new class of managers would reduce industrial conflict, Bell proposed that a different group would evolve to fill this role. Power would no longer merely reside in the ownership of property, but in access to knowledge and in the ability to think and to solve problems. Thus, while industrialization brought with it an increase in productivity and in the general standard of living, post-industrial society was ushering in an era of reduced concentration of power.[48]

A more recent proponent of a similar position is John Naisbett. By including occupational groups as diverse as secretaries, data entry clerks, lawyers, and librarians in his category of "information workers," he concludes that a majority of the work force in the United States today is employed in the information sector. Among other things, Naisbett argues that knowledge, unlike property, cannot be accumulated in the hands of a small elite. Since a majority of the population is involved in the creation, processing, and distribution of information, society must be moving into a new, more democratic era. "The new source of power is not money in the hands of a few but information in the hands of many."[49] In an equally optimistic vein, Naisbett predicts that traditional bureaucratic workplaces will give way to more flexible, less hierarchical, and less alienating work organizations. His reasoning is that bureaucracies were necessary inventions of the industrial age, needed to keep track of people and the products they produced. The computer can link people and process information without having to rely on such archaic organizational forms.

These are but a few of the more recent attempts to explain how industrialization has affected the nature and quality of work, and of life as a whole, in the twentieth century. The logic of industrialism perspective may have overreached itself in its predictions of an ever greater convergence in the characteristics of industrial societies. Closer examination soon reveals that class structure, state policies, racial and ethnic characteristics, and cultural legacies can all influence the direction in which a society evolves. But the convergence thesis did highlight the fact that technological innovations have an impact as well. The discussions of post-industrial society have moved the analysis forward, drawing our attention to the growth of the service sector and to the resulting changes in occupational opportunities. But once again, an undue emphasis on technological determinism, and a failure to look closely enough at the empirical evidence, must be corrected.

This is perhaps most important for our examination of relationships of power and control within work organizations. Lenski argued that the technology of the industrial era had led to a reduction in inequality in the distribution of wealth and power in society. Theorists of post-industrial society have carried on this theme, suggesting that because information has become the primary commodity of the late twentieth century, traditional class-based hierarchies are crumbling. We would argue that this conclusion is somewhat premature. Discussions in subsequent chapters will focus on very prominent continuing inequalities within work organizations, and on methods of control used to maintain these workplace hierarchies. In addition, we will examine how the introduction of new information-processing technology may be eliminating jobs and so creating a much larger class of unemployed workers, an outcome never addressed by overly simplistic analyses (Naisbett's, for example). Our intent is not to downplay the monumental impact of industrialization or of the transition to an "information age." Instead, we will argue as we have already done that industrialization is only one of several massive transformations that have had an impact on our society. Other factors, such as capitalism, the growth of large corporations, and the spread of bureaucracies must also be considered.

CONCLUSION

We have covered a lot of territory in this chapter, both historically and theoretically. In our examination of the origins of industrial capitalism, we highlighted some of the key social and economic changes which occurred in Europe in the seventeenth and eighteenth centuries. As feudalism gave way to capitalism, the marketplace grew in importance. A new class structure evolved, and a largely rural society became an urban society. Factory-based wage labour became the norm, while craft work declined. Larger workplaces demanded new organizational forms and, in time, bureaucracies evolved to fill this need. And while industrial innovations led to substantial increases in productivity, it was some time before the standard of living of the working class began to reflect this increase.

All of these dramatic changes left their mark on the theories of sociologists like Marx, Durkheim, and Weber. Marx focused on the exploitation of the new wage-labour class, predicting that this would in time lead to the downfall of the capitalist mode of production. Durkheim, on the other hand, emphasized the positive functions of the division of labour. These two assessments of early industrial capitalism have provided the underpinnings of the conflict and consensus approaches to industrial sociology, alternative perspectives to which we will frequently return in this book. We will also come back to consider the merits and problems of bureaucracy, issues Max Weber addressed decades ago as he outlined the characteristics of this new organizational form of the twentieth century.

In our overview of the Canadian industrialization experience, we moved closer to contemporary times. The advent of modern corporate capitalism has involved massive growth in the size of firms, the appearance of a managerial class, and rapid expansion of the white-collar work force. Again, such changes have generated a variety of social theories. We focused in particular on explanations of the linkage between technology and social inequality, and on predictions that expansions of the managerial or the white-collar groups might reduce industrial conflicts.

Finally, our focus on Canadian history allowed us not only to note cross-national similarities in the industrialization process but also to identify some of the unique features of the Canadian case. Canada was a late starter, due largely to its history as a New World colony. This also meant that its resource industries played a larger part in its economic development, and have continued to do so. In addition, Canada has experienced a relatively high level of foreign investment in its manufacturing sector. These and other more specific features of Canada's industrial and occupational structures are considered in the next chapter.

NOTES

1. Michel Beaud's (1983) history of capitalism is our major source. See also Hilton (1976) on the transition from feudalism to capitalism, and Miller and Form (1980: 38-63) on pre-industrial and early industrial work patterns.
2. Beaud (1983, chapter 1). See also Amin (1976) and Worsley (1984): 1-16.
3. Hilton (1976) presents much of this debate. See also the later collection of papers in Aston and Philpin (1985).
4. Beaud (1983): 39.
5. See Beaud (1983: 65) and Jones (1982: 20) on the reactions of skilled craftsmen to the use of new technologies.
6. Beaud (1983): 66-67; Burawoy (1984).
7. Malcolmson (1981): 22-47.
8. See Piven and Cloward (1971, chapter 1) who link together the growth of wage labour, the spread of poverty, and the state's response during this era in Britain.
9. Malcolmson (1981): 34-35.
10. Polanyi (1957).
11. Laxer (1985).
12. Naylor (1972).
13. Rinehart (1987): 26.
14. Teeple (1972).
15. Bleasdale (1981): 13. See Wylie (1983) on the building of the Rideau Canal.
16. Veltmeyer (1983): 103.

17. Rinehart (1987): 34-35. See Laxer (1985: 312) for comparisons with Japan and Sweden.
18. Copp (1974) discusses the life of the working class in Montreal at the turn of the century, while Piva (1979) does the same for Toronto.
19. Heron (1980). See also Heron and Palmer (1977).
20. Heron (1980). See also Rinehart (1987): 43-44.
21. Bradwin (1972). See Rinehart (1987: 46) and Avery (1979) on radical behaviour among immigrant workers.
22. Mine accidents that took the lives of many miners at one time are mainly responsible for these high averages. For example, 189 miners died in a mine explosion in Hillcrest in 1914. See McCormack (1979: 9) on British Columbia, and Caragata (1979: 16-21) on Alberta coal miners during this era.
23. Marchak (1981): 106; Seager (1985).
24. Rinehart (1987): 45; Smucker (1980): 85-89.
25. McCormack (1977): 3.
26. Marchak (1981: 112). Although Canada was a late starter in the industrialization process, it went through this period of concentration of production at much the same time as did Britain, France, the United States, and other industrializing countries. Beaud (1983: 136) reports that between 1880 and 1918, 655 British companies merged into 74 larger companies.
27. See Lowe (1987) for a more detailed discussion of this process.
28. Lowe (1986): 103.
29. *Ibid.*, 100.
30. Paul Mantoux, quoted by Beaud (1983): 66.
31. Engels (1971): 63 [1845].
32. See Zeitlin (1968) and Coser (1971) for overviews of Marx's theory of social change and the responses of some of his critics.
33. Hill (1981): 1-14.
34. Mills (1956): 220.
35. Smith (1976 [1776]). See Braverman (1974: 76) for additional discussion.
36. Braverman (1974): 79-83.
37. Weiss (1976).
38. Durkheim (1960) did allow that a "forced" division of labour, where individuals had no choice over how they participated in the productive system, would not lead to increased social solidarity. But he argued that this, and other abnormal forms of the division of labour, would disappear as industrial capitalism matured further.
39. Berle and Means (1968).
40. See Hill (1981: 71-76) for a more extensive discussion.
41. See Antoniou and Rowley (1986) on family ownership patterns, Dhingra (1983) on concentration of ownership, and Carroll et al. (1982) on cross-cutting directorship ties.
42. Kerr et al. (1973): 29.
43. *Ibid.*, 48.
44. Lenski (1966).
45. *Ibid.*, 308.
46. *Ibid.*, 314.
47. Bell (1973). See Hunter (1986: 40-42) for a discussion of post-industrial society theories.

48. Bell (1973): 358-67.
49. Naisbett (1982): 7.

2

Changing Labour Force Trends: Who Works Where?

INTRODUCTION

In the last chapter, we discussed the emergence of an industrial capitalist mode of production, both in Europe and in Canada. We continue that theme here, closely examining some of the specific changes that have occurred in the Canadian labour market. In general terms, a *labour market* can be defined as the economic arena in which employers search for qualified workers, and in which potential employees attempt to find satisfactory jobs. In the next chapter, we will examine some of the processes through which individuals are "matched" to jobs. We will also ask how inequalities in the distribution of better jobs are maintained.

But before attempting to explain how these patterns evolved and are perpetuated, we need a good sense of the structure of the Canadian labour market. In this chapter, we begin by focusing on changes in labour force participation and in the occupational and industrial structures. We then shift our attention from the jobs people hold to the class structure of Canadian society. The chapter concludes by considering two issues currently receiving much public attention — unemployment and the shift to part-time work.

In Chapter 1, we relied heavily on descriptive historical data. This more detailed look at how individual Canadians participate in the work force, and at how such patterns have changed over time, is based primarily on statistical data. One major source is the Canadian census, a survey of the complete population of the country undertaken every ten years by Statistics Canada. The next Canadian census will be completed in 1991. The huge effort and cost involved in collecting information on the millions of people in the country means that only a limited number of questions can be asked about each household and the individuals within it. Furthermore, because such an exercise cannot be conducted every year, census results are not completely up to date.[1] Despite this, the census provides the most complete and accurate picture of the Canadian industrial and occupational structures at specific points of time, and allows us to accurately plot changes historically.

A second source of information on patterns of work is the monthly Labour Force Survey. Unlike the census, which attempts to cover a range of areas, this sample survey is designed to collect only work-related information, and so provides much more detail. Because the survey is done every month, information is very up-to-date. In order to get precise estimates of the labour market behaviour of Canadians aged 15 and older, a large sample is needed. Approximately 48,000 households (containing about 100,000 individuals) are included in the randomly selected sample.[2] Households remain part of the sample for six months before being replaced. The Labour Force Survey provides the data for monthly estimates of unemployment rates, labour force participation rates, and so on. Frequently, more detailed surveys, designed to study specific work-related topics, are also "piggy-backed" on the monthly Labour Force Survey. Examples of such topics include occupational mobility patterns, involuntary part-time work, and job-search behaviour. Many of the statistics cited in this chapter are obtained from this useful source.[3]

LABOUR FORCE PARTICIPATION

Labour force participation, according to the official definition used today, is determined from the perspective of paid employment. Whether relying on census or monthly survey data, calculations of labour force size or rates are based on the number of individuals 15 years of age or older who are working for pay (including the self-employed and those employing others), or who are looking for such employment. Thus the unemployed (those out of work but having actively looked for work in the past four weeks) are included as part of the labour force, but individuals choosing to work within their homes are not. Rather, they are counted among those unable or unwilling to undertake paid work.[4] It is important to remember this fact since it has contributed to a downgrading of the status of unpaid household work within our economy.

Official labour force participation statistics probably also omit some Canadians working in the *hidden economy* or, as it is sometimes called, the *underground* or *irregular* economy. This might involve illegal activities such as selling drugs, prostitution, or gambling. More often, however, it would be legal work done for cash or in exchange for some other services. Mechanics working out of their homes, carpenters doing extra renovations on weekends, and a lawyer drawing up a will in exchange for an artist's painting would be typical examples. Some members of the "non-criminal" group would be represented in labour force surveys through their "real" jobs; but others, if surveyed, might report themselves unemployed or out of the labour force in order to avoid detection by tax authorities.

There is very little research on the subject, since there is no direct way of systematically studying behaviour which people do not wish to be publicly documented.[5] But the research that does exist suggests that a sizeable number of Canadians are engaged in work they are not reporting to tax authorities. Using several different methods of assessing the extent of such work, economists have suggested estimates ranging from 5 to 20 percent of total economic activity in Canada.[6] A recent discussion of "concealed employment" — legal but unreported work — in western industrialized countries concluded that up to one in five adults might be involved at some point in a given year (although, for most of these individuals, this would reflect relatively few hours of work).[7] In short, official statistics probably underestimate the number of working Canadians. Recognizing this, it is still useful to see how participation in the "paid labour force" has changed over the years (Table 2.1).

Table 2.1
Labour Force Participation by Sex, 1901-1986

Year	Both Sexes	Female	Male
1901	53.0%	16.1%	87.8%
1911	57.4	18.6	90.6
1921	56.2	19.9	89.8
1931	55.9	21.8	87.2
1941	55.2	22.9	85.6
1951*	54.3	24.2	84.1
1961	55.1	29.1	80.8
1971	58.0	39.9	75.4
1976	60.0	45.0	75.5
1981	64.8	51.8	78.3
1986	65.7	55.1	76.7

* Includes Newfoundland.
Sources: 1901-1981 from Chen and Regan (1985): 135; 1986 from Statistics Canada, *The Labour Force* (December 1986, # 71-001, Table 55), p. 84.

In 1901, 53 percent of Canadians (15 years of age and older) were participating in the labour force. This had increased to over 57 percent by 1911, but the rate didn't really go much higher until the 1970s. By 1981, almost 65 percent of the eligible population was working or seeking work. The 1986 Labour Force Survey estimates of a 65.7 percent participation rate show that this total figure has changed little since the last national census. In terms of actual numbers, 1,783,000 Canadians were considered part of the labour force in 1901. This number had more than doubled by 1931

(3,927,000) and again by 1971 (8,631,000). Labour Force Survey results reveal a total of 12,870,000 labour force participants in 1986, representing a participation rate of 65.7 percent.

An examination of the rates for both sexes combined masks the really significant changes that have occurred. Table 2.1 also displays female and male labour force participation rates over the same eighty-five-year period. In 1901, only 16.1 percent of women aged 15 or older were in the paid labour force. However, this rate increased with each ten-year census. By the post-World War II period, the size of these increases was substantial. Between 1961 and 1971, female labour force participation jumped from 29.1 to 39.9 percent, and the following decade saw an even larger increase from about 40 to almost 52 percent. The landmark year was 1980, the first in which a majority of Canadian women were part of the officially defined labour force.[8] The rate has continued to climb since then (up to 55.1 percent in 1986), but not quite as quickly as in the previous two decades.

While female participation rates have gone up over the decades, male rates have declined (although not in as dramatic a fashion). Between 1901 and 1931, male participation rates remained close to 90 percent, dropping to the mid 80 percent range in the pre- and post-World War II decades. The 1970s and 1980s have brought an additional drop. In 1986, 76.7 percent of Canadian men aged 15 and older were in the labour force. Thus, the general increase in total rates of participation in the paid labour force is a product of very substantial increases for women and less significant decreases for men. The latter change is due, in part, to earlier retirement (as compared to the turn of the century) and longer periods of time spent in school. The causes of growing female labour force participation, which are more complex, are discussed in Chapter 5.

CANADA'S CHANGING INDUSTRIAL AND OCCUPATIONAL STRUCTURE

There are several ways in which we can label or categorize the work done by labour force participants. We can, first of all, discuss the *industry* in which they are employed, thus directing our attention to the major type of economic activity occurring within their workplace. In the broadest sense, we can distinguish the *primary sector* (including agriculture, mining, forestry, and other resource extraction industries) from the *secondary sector* (manufacturing and construction), where goods are produced from the raw materials supplied by the primary sector, and the *tertiary sector,* where services rather than products are provided. These general industrial categories can be further subdivided into more specific industries. The service sector, for example, includes (among others) the finance, education, retail trade, government, and health service sectors.

While the industrial classification system is based on *what is being produced,* we can also separate labour force participants into different groups on the basis of their *occupation.* Occupational distinctions are determined by the *kind of work* an individual typically performs — the actual tasks he or she completes. Thus we find people working as secretaries, managers, or accountants (occupational titles) in mining companies, automobile manufacturing establishments, and government bureaucracies — that is, in the primary, secondary, and service sectors of the economy. Some other occupations, however, are more likely to be found only within specific industrial sectors. Teachers, for example, are an occupational group seldom found in the primary or secondary sectors. Similarly, most barbers would be employed in the "personal services" sector. In other words, the two classification systems parallel each other to an extent but also overlap considerably.[9]

With the aid of these technical distinctions, we can now look more closely at the extensive changes in Canadian society over the past century described in Chapter 1. In 1891, the primary industries accounted for 49 percent of the people in the labour force, the secondary sector for 20 percent, and the service sector for the remaining 31 percent.[10] In the following decades, the primary sector (particularly agriculture) became less dominant, while the manufacturing industries came into greater prominence. At the same time, the service industries were growing even more rapidly. Hence, by 1981, only 7 percent of the Canadian labour force was to be found in the primary industries, while 26 percent was located in the secondary sector. But the service sector had more than doubled in this ninety-year span, now accounting for 67 percent of the labour force. In terms of its percentage contribution to the total value of goods and services produced in the Canadian economy, the service sector's growth was similar. These few statistics clearly demonstrate that we are now living in a service economy. A similar pattern of change has been observed in other industrial capitalist societies such as the United States, Japan, and Germany. Compared to these nations, however, manufacturing has played a less important role in Canada's development.

The rise of the service sector can be attributed to a combination of factors. Productivity gains due to new technologies and organizational forms in manufacturing (and also in the resource industries) have meant that fewer people could produce much more. Thus, expansion of production in these sectors has not been accompanied by a proportional demand for more employees. (This phenomenon is discussed in Chapter 9 with respect to the effects of recent developments in the areas of robotics and micro-electronics.) However, the pattern was already apparent at the beginning of the century during the period of rapid industrial expansion.[11] Industrial expansion and productivity gains over the years led to higher incomes and increased amounts of leisure time. These factors, in turn, fueled the demand for a wide range of services, particularly in the last few decades when the recreation, accommodation, and food service industries grew rapidly. In addition, the expansion of the role of the state as a provider of health, educational, and social services has contributed significantly to the growth of the service sector.

Figure 2.1
Percent Distribution of Labour Force, Major Occupational Groups, 1901-1981

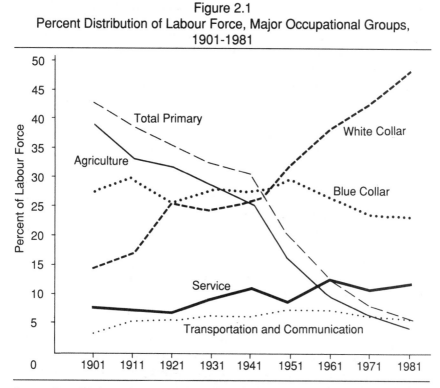

Source: Based on Sylvia Ostry, *The Occupational Composition of the Canadian Labour Force* (Ottawa: Dominion Bureau of Statistics, 1967), Table 2 [for 1901-61]; 1981 Census, *Population: Labour Force — Occupation Trends* (# 92-920, vol. 1) [for 1971-81].

Figure 2.1 shows changes in the occupational structure over the past eight decades. Our claim that the majority of Canadians are employed in the service industries seems to be contradicted by this graph. However, recalling the definitions of industry and occupation can help clarify the issue. Most employees in the service sectors would be located among *white-collar* workers, a broad category including managerial, professional, clerical, and sales occupations. Using more detailed occupational titles, the white-collar category would include secretaries, nurses, teachers, lawyers, artists, cashiers, sales clerks, telephone operators, and many other occupational groups. Thus, in this graph, the massive expansion of the service sector industries is reflected primarily in the "white collar" line, which shows a huge increase from 15 percent of the labour force in 1901 to 49 percent in 1981. A very large proportion of these new white-collar jobs have been filled by women. Thus Figure 2.1 is really highlighting three of the most significant changes of this century in the Canadian labour market: the expansion of the service sector, the growth of white-collar occupations, and the movement of women into the paid labour force.

The decline of primary sector occupations (mainly agricultural jobs) is the other side of the picture. In 1901, 45 percent of labour force participants were employed in agricultural occupations, but by 1981 this had shrunk to 5 percent. *Blue-collar* occupations (manufacturing and construction jobs) climbed to around 30 percent of the labour force during the industrial expansion eras at the beginning of the century and again during the 1950s, but appear to have been losing ground since then (24 percent of the total in 1981). Transportation and communication occupations have increased only minimally, relative to the total occupational distribution, as have the strictly "service" occupations.[12]

These broad occupational groupings demonstrate that we now live in a service economy, and that fully half of the labour force members are employed in white-collar occupations. Table 2.2 adds to our understanding of the contemporary occupational structure by providing 1986 data, in somewhat finer categories, separately for women and for men. In this case, we are examining only a subset of the total labour force — the currently employed.[13] Considering first the total distribution (female and male combined), we can see the range of occupations encompassed by the broad category "white collar." Managers, professionals in various fields, clerks, and sales workers would all be included. Obviously, there is a great deal of variation among these occupations. Not all white-collar workers are well paid, and not all white-collar occupations have high status. The differences in job characteristics and job rewards within this large category are probably as great as differences between white- and blue-collar work. Separation of the latter into its manufacturing, construction, and transportation components highlights even further the fact that only a small minority of the Canadian labour force is actively engaged in the processing of raw materials into finished goods.

How does Canada's contemporary occupational structure compare to that of other industrialized nations? In 1981, 8.2 percent of Canadian labour force participants were to be found in managerial and administrative occupations, compared to 10.8 percent in the United States but only 4.9 percent in Japan, 3.0 percent in West Germany, and 2.3 percent in Sweden. Also, in 1981 a total of 28.6

Table 2.2
Employment by Occupation and Sex, Canada, 1986

Occupation	Number (1000s)			Percent		
	Total	Female	Male	Total	Female	Male
Managerial/administrative	1,390	471	919	11.9	9.5	13.8
Natural sciences	403	66	337	3.5	1.3	5.0
Social sciences	191	108	83	1.6	2.2	1.2
Religion	35	8	27	0.3	0.2	0.4
Teaching	511	311	201	4.4	6.2	3.0
Medicine and health	574	451	123	4.9	9.1	1.8
Artistic and recreational	192	81	111	1.7	1.6	1.7
Clerical	1,928	1,537	390	16.6	30.9	5.8
Sales	1,119	483	636	9.6	9.7	9.6
Service	1,572	882	690	13.5	17.7	10.4
Agriculture	488	125	363	4.2	2.5	5.5
Fishing/hunting/trapping	36	—*	34	0.3	—	0.5
Forestry and logging	53	—	50	0.5	—	0.8
Mining and quarrying	61	—	60	0.5	—	0.9
Processing	357	74	283	3.1	1.5	4.3
Machining	235	15	221	2.0	0.3	3.3
Product fabricating/ assembling/repairing	985	223	762	8.4	4.5	11.5
Construction	639	11	628	5.5	0.2	9.4
Transportation	434	30	403	3.8	0.6	6.1
Materials handling	272	58	214	2.3	1.2	3.2
Other crafts/equipment operating	159	37	122	1.4	0.7	1.8
Total	11,634	4,977	6,657	100.0%	99.9%	100.0%

* Statistics Canada does not publish estimates of less than 4,000 because of concerns about the reliability of such (relatively) small estimates from sample survey data.
Source: Statistics Canada, *The Labour Force* (December 1986, # 71-001, Table 71), p. 105.

percent of Canadian workers were in traditional blue-collar occupations (manufacturing, construction, transportation) compared to 32.9 percent in the United States, 34.9 percent in Japan, 37.3 percent in West Germany, and 33.3 percent in Sweden.[14] In other words, compared to other industrial capitalist societies, Canada has a relatively small manufacturing base. On the other hand, we have a high proportion of managers (as does the United States) in our occupational structure, a fact that should not be ignored when comparing Canadian productivity levels to those of the Japanese and other industrial nations.

Chapter 5 focuses directly on the unequal employment experiences of women and men, so we will comment only briefly at this point on the male and female occupational distributions in Table 2.2. It is apparent that men are distributed more evenly across the occupational structure, with somewhat more than 10 percent in management, service, and product fabricating occupations, but smaller percentages in the remaining categories. Women, however, are more concentrated in several occupational groups, with over 30 percent in the clerical category and almost 18 percent in the service category. In fact, almost six out of ten women in the paid labour force are to be found in the clerical, sales, and service occupations, which tend to involve lower status, lower-paying types of work. Women are also somewhat concentrated in the teaching and health professions, while men are more likely to be employed in the traditional blue-collar occupations. As for managerial and administrative occupations, 9.5 percent of employed women compared to 13.8 percent of employed men are found here. This substantial gap would be even wider if upper-level management positions were considered separately. In the same way, while many more women than men are found in the medical occupations, much of this can be accounted for by distinguishing nurses (a traditionally "female" job) from doctors (a traditionally "male" job).

CHANGES IN THE CANADIAN CLASS STRUCTURE

Studying where and under what conditions Canadians work also helps to illuminate the class structure of our society. The term *social class* is employed in a variety of ways by social scientists. Frequently, it is used interchangeably with *socio-economic status* to refer to higher or lower positions in a social hierarchy, as determined by one's occupation, education, and income. We will return to this concept of socio-economic status (SES) in a later discussion of social mobility. For now, we will focus on social class as a term specifying power relationships among groups directly engaged in the productive process.[15]

In his analysis of industrial capitalism, Marx focused primarily on the relationship between the class of capitalists who owned the means of production and the proletariat. The latter class owned no production-related property, and so had little choice but to exchange labour in return for a wage. But Marx also discussed the middle class of small business owners (the petite bourgeoisie) and predicted that, in time, it would largely disappear; small businesses would be swallowed by larger competitors and self-employment in agriculture would gradually be replaced by wage labour. Canada, like other industrial capitalist societies, has clearly moved in this direction. In 1946, "paid workers" represented 67 percent of all those employed. By 1981, this had risen to 90 percent.[16]

A large part of this major shift can be explained with reference to changes in the agricultural sector in the twentieth century. Back in 1911, almost 75 percent of those employed in agriculture were owner-managers. By 1971, this had shrunk to 50 percent. In addition, the actual number of farms in Canada declined from a high of around 700,000 between 1911 and 1941 to only 369,000 in 1976. The total number of people employed in agriculture fell from almost 1.2 million in 1946 to less than half a million in 1981. In short, while wage labour became more common in agriculture, a reduction in the number of family farms also meant relatively fewer self-employed individuals and unpaid family workers. By 1984, the 476,000 Canadians employed in agriculture consisted of: paid workers (28 percent); unpaid family workers (16 percent); owners who employed others in their enterprises (13 percent); and self-employed — without any paid employees — (only 43 percent).[17]

Self-employment has also declined over the decades in the secondary and tertiary sectors of the Canadian economy. However, a slight increase has been observed in the first part of the 1980s, probably due to the economic recession. The percentage of self-employed who did not employ others increased from 6.9 to 7.6 percent between 1979 and 1984, and the percentage of paid workers shrank accordingly.[18] With many firms laying off employees and others failing to expand their hiring, traditional job prospects have been reduced. Thus the increase in self-employment might reflect a response of the unemployed to the recession. However, a recent overview of self-employment in western industrialized countries (including Canada) suggests that the majority of the self-employed come from the ranks of wage earners. Furthermore, managerial, professional, and technical workers are much more likely to become self-employed than are clerical and manual workers (the groups most affected by unemployment). In short, self-employment is unlikely to be a major solution to Canada's unemployment problem.[19]

Our discussion so far has relied on rather crude categories. While an individual whose store has three employees is classified as an employer, his or her responsibilities and power are hardly comparable to the president of a corporation employing thousands of workers. Similarly, while both a senior manager in a large corporation and a sales clerk in a retail store may be paid workers, their work experiences and rewards are probably very different. A variety of attempts have been made to incorporate such clearly important distinctions into discussions of social class position. One of the more widely used approaches has been developed by Eric Olin Wright.[20]

In his classification of labour force participants, Wright takes into account ownership, the employment of others, supervision of others, and control over one's own work. He distinguishes between *large* and *small employers*, two groups that have legal ownership and also employ others, and the *petite bourgeoisie* (or traditionally self-employed), who own their business (or farm) but do not have others working for them. Large employers (the group most closely resembling Marx's class of capitalists) are separated from small employers with only a handful of employees, since the latter typically would be directly involved in the productive process (working alongside their employees). The large class of paid employees is separated by Wright into: *managers* who, while not owning the enterprise, would be involved in decision making along with (or in the absence of) the legal owners; *supervisors,* who are not involved in planning and decision making but who nevertheless exercise authority over others; and *workers,* who have no ownership rights, decision-making power, or authority over others. One final class grouping, *semi-autonomous workers* (e.g., social workers, university professors, and other salaried professionals), are identified by the relatively greater control they retain over their own work.

Census and labour force survey data do not contain the detail necessary to classify the Canadian labour force in this manner. However, a national survey designed to collect this information was completed in 1982. Analysis of data obtained from 1,756 randomly selected labour force members suggests the following Canadian class distribution: large employers (0.9 percent); small employers (2.8 percent); self-employed (12.3 percent); managers (14.6 percent); supervisors (10.9 percent); semi-autonomous workers (16 percent); and workers (43.4 percent).[21] While the small sample size (compared to monthly Labour Force Surveys) means that these estimates may not be highly precise, these data do demonstrate that the large class of "paid workers" contains several very distinct types. Some Canadian workers clearly have better jobs than others. In the next chapter, we will look more closely at variations in working conditions and job rewards.

REGIONAL VARIATIONS AND SINGLE INDUSTRY COMMUNITIES

So far we have treated Canada as a single economic entity, thus ignoring important regional differences. Anyone who has ever driven across Canada will have a clear mental image of its regional diversity. The fishing boats and lumber mills of the West Coast are left behind, replaced by oil wells and grain elevators as one begins to head east across the Prairies. The flat landscape disappears a few hours beyond Winnipeg, where one is faced by the rocks, forests, and water of the Canadian Shield. The smokestacks of Sudbury and other mining communities in northern Ontario are reminders of the natural resource base of that region, but they eventually give way to the old grey barns of Ontario, symbols of an agricultural economy older than the one observed several days earlier. But this is unlikely to be the dominant memory of the trip through Ontario and into Quebec. The huge Highway 401 pushing its way through miles of warehouses and suburban factories will probably leave a stronger impression as it takes one through the industrial heartland of the country. Then, repeating the pattern observed in the West (but in reverse, without the mountains and on a smaller scale), the farming economies of Quebec and the Maritime provinces begin to merge with a forest-based economy. Eventually, one returns to a region where fisheries are once again important. In short, regional diversities are also economic diversities.

This description of major economic activities in the various regions of the country is an obvious over-generalization. There are farms and high technology firms found in the Fraser Valley, factories in Calgary and Winnipeg, and oil wells off the East Coast. Still, we must remember the size of the country, and the concentration of specific industries in different regions, when considering work opportunities and life chances available to Canadians. A brief comparison of industrial distributions across provinces highlights these variations (Table 2.3). For example, in 1986, 13.5 percent of the labour force in Manitoba and Saskatchewan was employed in agriculture, compared to less than 3 percent in all of the regions further east. Larger than average concentrations in "other primary industries" reflect the presence of the fishing industry in the Maritimes and British Columbia, forest-based industries in the Maritimes, Alberta, and B.C., and the oil industry in Alberta. On the other hand, 22.3 percent of labour force participants in Ontario in 1986 were employed in manufacturing, compared to only 7.8 percent in Alberta. In terms of probability, a resident of Ontario would have been almost three times more likely to have a factory job than would someone living in Alberta. Even labour force participation varies across regions. In 1986, the province with the highest participation rate was Alberta (72.1 percent) while Newfoundland had the lowest rate (53.0 percent).

Canada is not unique in having some regions in which primary industries are most important, and others in which manufacturing is concentrated. But its economic history is characterized by a distinctive reliance on the export of raw materials such as furs, fish, timber, wheat, coal, natural gas, and oil. Canada was expected to serve this function while still a colony but, as an independent industrializing nation, it has continued to play this role in the global economy.

The work of Harold Innis and his successors documents the economic, political, and social consequences of this dependence on the export of unprocessed staple products. Known as the "staples theory of economic growth," it argues that over-commitment to extraction and export of a single or few resources makes a nation or region vulnerable in world markets. The relative absence of secon-

Table 2.3
Labour Force by Industry and Region, Canada, 1986

Industry	Maritimes	Quebec	Ontario	Man./Sask.	Alberta	B.C.	Total
			Percent				
Agriculture	2.2	2.8	2.8	13.5	7.0	2.6	4.0
Other primary	5.8	1.7	1.2	2.3	6.3	4.3	2.7
Manufacturing	12.6	19.5	22.3	8.8	7.8	11.7	17.2
Construction	7.3	5.2	5.9	5.4	6.7	6.2	5.9
Transportation/ communication	7.7	7.4	7.0	8.2	7.9	8.8	7.5
Trade	18.3	17.8	17.1	17.6	18.4	18.3	17.7
Finance/insurance/ real estate	3.7	5.1	5.8	5.0	4.9	6.1	5.3
Service	31.1	32.6	31.4	31.3	33.2	34.8	32.2
Public administration	9.0	6.8	6.1	7.4	7.2	6.2	6.7
Unclassified*	1.3	1.1	0.4	—**	0.6	1.0	0.8
Total	99.0%	100.0%	100.0%	99.5%	100.0%	100.0%	100.0%
(N, 1000s)	(996)	(3,221)	(4,897)	(1,028)	(1,271)	(1,457)	(12,870)

Note: Small samples in some of the smaller provinces lead to less reliable estimates for some less prominent industries. Since Statistics Canada does not publish estimates of less than 4,000, the four Maritime provinces have been combined as have Manitoba and Saskatchewan.
* Unemployed persons who, while considered part of the labour force, have never worked for pay and those who last worked more than five years ago.
** Provincial estimates of less than 4,000. These omissions, and several for P.E.I. (in the Maritimes column), lead to total percentages of less than 100 percent.
Source: Statistics Canada, *The Labour Force* (December 1986, #71-001, Table 66), p. 100.

dary (manufacturing) industries means that unusually large proportions of the work force remain employed in lower-skill primary and tertiary sector jobs. In addition, a weak manufacturing sector does not encourage large amounts of research and development, and does not generate additional spin-off industrial activity. These limitations, along with dependence on a limited number of foreign markets, eventually leave a nation or region few development alternatives other than continuing to operate within the "staples trap."[22]

With respect to Canada, it is clear that reliance on the production of raw materials is a matter of degree; after all, we discussed the era of Canada's rapid industrialization in the last chapter. However, much of this shift to factory-based production took place in southwestern Ontario and in the Montreal region. The legacy of a history of staples production is much more apparent in the hinterland regions of the country where wheat, oil, hydro-electricity, coal, and timber are still the economic mainstays. One of the clear signs of this fact is the speed with which local and regional economies can shift from vigorous economic growth and labour shortages to situations of economic stagnancy and high unemployment. Edmonton and Calgary's growth in the 1970s and recession in the 1980s, in response to the expansion and contraction of the international oil market, are but one example of the "boom and bust" consequences of over-reliance on a single natural resource.

Another indicator of the regional economies' resource-extraction base is the number of *single industry communities* scattered across the country. These towns and cities, often situated in isolated areas, exist only because the harvesting of some raw material requires a resident labour force. The local economy is dominated by this major activity (e.g., oil in Fort McMurray, Alberta or nickel in Sudbury, Ontario), such that if the market for the staple were to disappear, so would the economic base of the community. Mine shutdowns in 1982 in Uranium City, Saskatchewan and Schefferville, Quebec provide the most recent examples. One critic has suggested that ghost towns are the most appropriate symbol of Canada's resource development policies.[23] A brief look at work opportunities and occupational structures in such resource towns is useful, then, in order to correct the impression that almost all Canadians work in large firms or government agencies in the more heavily industrialized cities of Canada. While work in the service sector in Elliot Lake, Ontario or in a government agency in Thompson, Manitoba may, in most ways, resemble work in equivalent jobs in Hamilton, Vancouver, or Quebec City, single industry resource towns also have some unique characteristics.

Over the decades, the prospects of better jobs and higher incomes have led many thousands of individuals and families to "go down the road" to the industrial cities of central Canada. But many have also been attracted to the resource towns of the hinterland for the same reason. Such communities have historically provided work for unemployed or underemployed migrants from other regions of the country. However, the unusual life cycle of resource towns, as they move through fairly predictable stages of development, means that work opportunities for residents and migrants do not remain constant.[24]

A pre-discovery stage is typically characterized by a small indigenous population (frequently native Canadians) surviving on a combination of hunting and trapping, and limited wage labour. Some of the mining towns in northern Canada were still in this stage a decade or two ago, but most other Canadian resource towns are somewhat older. The discovery and exploration stage pushes the local economy further toward a wage-labour mode of production as additional seasonal workers are brought in. If the resource appears to be sufficiently profitable, a construction stage follows. The building of a mine or mill and of a community to house the new arrivals attracts a large, migrant labour force and dramatically alters the local occupational structure. This preponderance of construction jobs quickly changes, however, as the community moves into its operations phase, which may continue for a considerable length of time. Skilled and semiskilled construction workers are replaced by a slightly more diverse work force of mill operators or miners. A final stage for some towns will be one of decline when the depletion of the resource or the collapse of a world market make the community itself obsolete.[25]

During the construction era, labour demands and turnover are frequently very high as the community may be overrun by an influx of young male unskilled workers. When construction is complete, a new labour force may be imported for the operations phase. Some original residents of the area may be fortunate enough to find work in construction or operations, but generally they have benefited less from the development of these types of towns since they do not possess the occupational skills needed. Native Canadian groups resident in northern mining and mill towns have been most disadvantaged in this respect.[26] As the labour force and occupational structure stabilize in the operations phase, job openings become less frequent. Thus it is primarily at expansion stages in the community's economic history that the opportunities exist for unskilled and semiskilled migrants from other regions of the country. Fort McMurray, Alberta, for example, grew from a small village in the 1960s to a large city in the late 1970s and, in the process, provided well-paying jobs for thousands of immigrants fortunate enough to find employment with the major oil companies.[27] These work opportunities are no longer available, since the major oil companies are no longer expanding; dropping oil prices in the 1980s have meant, instead, increased layoffs in this boom-and-bust community.

The occupational structures of resource towns during their operations phase are somewhat different from those of multi-industry urban centres. Because of the dominance of the local economy by a single industry, there are fewer middle-level clerical and service jobs available. This, and the fact that mining and other "blue collar" industries have historically been male occupational preserves, means that women often have trouble finding satisfactory employment. The over-representation of women in lower-paying, lower-status jobs is a topic we explore more fully in a subsequent chapter, but it is important to note that this pattern is even more pronounced in many of Canada's resource towns.

Another unique feature of the occupational structure of such communities is their "truncated class structure." Ownership of the dominant industry is almost always from outside (of the town, region, and often the country), and the low level of industrial diversification also means that the managerial class is smaller than usual. The implication of this for individuals resident in the community is that opportunities for upward occupational mobility may be limited. There are fewer jobs in the middle levels of the occupational ladder through which one can move in a career path. [28] Finally, as noted at the outset, economies built around the demand for staple products are always more precarious than manufacturing economies. Hence, an ever-present reality in single-industry resource towns is the threat that the mine or mill may shut down in response to low prices or lack of demand, leaving the majority of local residents out of work.

TIME SPENT AT WORK

On average, employed Canadians worked 37.8 hours per week in 1984, down from an average of 39.0 hours in 1976. The parents of these labour force participants probably put in similar hours a generation ago, since a roughly 40-hour work week has been the Canadian norm for a full thirty years. Using data on standard hours per week (the number beyond which overtime would typically be paid to full-time employees) from the manufacturing sector, we can go back much further to 1870 when 64 hours per week was the norm. [29] This incredibly long (by contemporary standards) work week was reduced because of trade union pressures, the details of which we will discuss in Chapter 7, and also through the introduction of new industrial technology. By 1901, 58.6 hours per week was standard in manufacturing. By 1921, 50 hours per week was typical, but this stayed relatively unchanged until after World War II. Between 1946 and 1949, the manufacturing standard dropped from 48.7 hours per week to 43.5 hours. It then fell to 40 hours by 1957, fluctuated slightly around this point for the next few decades, and dropped to around 39 hours per week by the mid-1970s. Thus, compared to the situation one hundred years ago, Canadians spend considerably less time at work. But the biggest reductions in hours per week occurred in the decades immediately before and after the turn of the century, and in the decade following the Second World War. Little appears to have changed in the last twenty years. However, shorter work weeks have been negotiated in a number of European countries in the last few years, and the Canadian labour movement is clearly interested in promoting the same idea.

A closer look at the 1976 to 1984 drop of 1.2 hours per week does, however, reveal a very important change in Canadian work patterns. We find that *full-time* workers were putting in an average of 42 hours per week compared to an average of 15 hours per week for *part-time* workers. These averages have not really changed since 1976. Hence, the decline in the overall average can only be attributed to an increase in the number of part-time workers. In fact, the pattern of working hours has been shifting over the last decade, with a substantial increase in the proportion working short hours and a somewhat smaller increase in the proportion working unusually long hours.[30] Thus the average Canadian work week conceals a great deal of variation in the number of hours worked, and this variation appears to be increasing. To the extent that more hours per week mean higher incomes, this change could lead to greater income disparity within the Canadian labour force.

THE GROWTH OF PART-TIME EMPLOYMENT

The recent decline in standard hours worked per week in this country is, we have seen, due almost entirely to the growth of part-time employment. But this shift in employment patterns is a relatively recent trend. In the years following World War II, the number of full-time jobs increased rapidly as the Canadian economy expanded. Thus, in 1953, only 3.8 percent of employed Canadians were working part-time (less than 30 hours per week). However, the last two decades have seen a slowing down in the creation of full-time jobs, while growth in part-time jobs has been maintained. Between 1966 and 1973, the average annual increase in full-time employment was 2.7 percent compared to 6.9 percent for part-time jobs. The years 1973 to 1979 saw average annual increases of 3.3 percent in full-time and 4.0 percent in part-time jobs. However, between 1979 and 1983, Canada experienced average annual increases of 6.1 percent in part-time employment and no increase in full-time employment.[31]

Women have traditionally been overrepresented among part-time workers. In 1966, 17 percent of women compared to only 3.4 percent of men in the labour force were classified as part-time workers. Twenty years later, 25.9 percent of female labour force participants and 7.8 percent of males in the labour force (a total of 1.3 million women and 520,000 men) were to be found in part-time jobs. Looking at this in a slightly different way, we find that more than seven out of ten part-time workers are female. High-school and college students are a second group frequently found to be working part-time. Students may find part-time work attractive since it allows them to earn some money while continuing their education. Among non-students, some women may also prefer part-time employment because it can be balanced with child-rearing responsibilities they are maintaining in the home. It is important to remember, however, that part-time employment is frequently not by choice. In 1986, 28.4 percent of the 1.8 million part-time workers reported that they were working part-time because this was the only job they could find. Most of these *involuntary part-time workers* were either women or youth. A decade earlier, in 1975, only 11 percent of part-time workers considered themselves underemployed in this manner.[32] Because part-time jobs have been created much more rapidly than full-time jobs over the past few years, many Canadians have had little choice but to accept part-time work.

About 90 percent of the part-time jobs created in the past two decades have been in the service-producing industries.[33] The restaurant, entertainment and recreation, and retail sales industries are examples of areas in which part-time employment has expanded most rapidly. Employers are shifting to part-time labour as a way of cutting costs and achieving greater flexibility in the utilization of labour. This trend appears to have increased substantially in the last few years, no doubt as a response to the economic recession of the early 1980s. The shift to part-time work may take the form of operating with a skeleton staff during slow times in the day (between rush hours for transit workers, for example) or during the week (Monday mornings in a retail store), and then bringing in extra employees for peak periods. It may also involve hiring extra part-time staff during busy periods of the year (Christmas in the retail sector, or summers in the tourism industry). Labour costs are reduced not only because of the shorter hours of employment but also because part-time workers seldom receive the same (costly) fringe benefits to which full-time workers are entitled.

Looking at it from the worker's perspective, the part-time job is also, typically, a less secure job and invariably one with few career advancement opportunities. In fact, many part-time jobs are also only "part year" jobs.[34] Although the flexibility of part-time work may appeal to some labour force participants (particularly students and young parents), the fact that fringe benefits, job security, and career potential are typically limited, and that many part-time workers would prefer full-time employment, suggests that the larger beneficiaries of this major shift in the Canadian labour market are employers.[35]

UNEMPLOYMENT TRENDS

An *unemployment rate* is calculated by dividing the number of individuals out of work and looking for work by the total number of labour force participants (including the unemployed). Statistics from the early part of this century, while not as accurate as contemporary estimates, nevertheless give us a sense of how the unemployment rate has varied over time in Canada. In the 1920s, unemployment rates moved between 4 percent and 9 percent with an average of about 5.5 percent. During the Depression they rose rapidly to a high of about 27 percent around 1932 and 1933, but averaged about 18 percent for the decade. Compared to these hard times, the war years of the 1940s and the post-war 1950s were times of relatively low unemployment (under 5 percent). Post-war economic expansion meant that jobs were being created about as fast as demand for them was increasing. Even in the 1960s, unemployment rates seldom went above 5 percent — but they have never been that low since. The number of jobless Canadians began increasing rapidly in the 1970s, and by the early 1980s unemployment rates had reached 10 percent. The rates continued to rise, peaking in 1983 at 11.9 percent. By 1986, the annual average was somewhat lower (9.6 percent), but this still represented 1,236,000 unemployed workers. This decline, although a welcome one, is probably not the start of a significant trend; some estimates suggest that unemployment rates near 10 percent will remain until the end of the 1980s.[36]

National unemployment rates conceal a large amount of variation across regions of the country. In 1986, Newfoundland's unemployment rate was 20.0 percent, compared to 14.4 percent in New Brunswick, 11.0 percent in Quebec, 7.0 percent in Ontario, 9.8 percent in Alberta, and 12.6 percent in British Columbia. The Maritime provinces, particularly Newfoundland, have had higher than average rates of unemployment for decades, while the manufacturing provinces of Ontario and Quebec have typically had the least problem with unemployment.[37] Manitoba and Saskatchewan have remained somewhat below the national average for the last decade; both had 1986 unemployment rates of 7.7 percent. The economies of the most western provinces, dependent as they are on a few resource-extraction industries, have been less predictable. During the 1970s, for example, Alberta's oil industry fueled a huge economic boom and the province's unemployment rates were among the lowest in the country. Dropping world oil prices in the 1980s reversed the situation and pushed unemployment rates well above the national average.

Unemployment also tends to be concentrated within specific occupational groups and industrial sectors. Seasonal work like fishing and logging, and construction (which also declines during the winter months) lead to frequent periods of unemployment for individuals working in these areas. Such seasonal work patterns account for some of the concentration of unemployment in the natural resource-dependent regions of the country.[38] Given these substantial variations, it is important to look beyond national rates of unemployment when discussing causes of and responses to unemployment. The small decline in Canadian unemployment rates in 1985 and 1986, for example, really reflects an economic upturn in central Canada only. The country-wide recession in the early 1980s led to widespread unemployment, even in the manufacturing regions of central Canada where factory shutdowns and layoffs were common.[39] Ontario appears to have recovered from this recession, at least in terms of unemployment rates, but economic restructuring (most visible when factories shut down) is clearly continuing in the Canadian economy. We will return to this topic in Chapter 9.

Although precise estimates are unavailable, it is clear that native Canadians have experienced unusually high rates of unemployment over the past decades. In larger urban centres with sizeable Indian and Métis communities (Winnipeg, for example), native Canadian unemployment rates in the neighbourhood of 30 percent have been suggested. These figures are low compared to some of the rates estimated for northern Manitoba, Saskatchewan, and Alberta.[40] Part of the problem, in some of these communities, may stem from the fact that Indians, Métis, and Inuit engaged in traditional hunting, trapping, and fishing are considered "unemployed" since they do not have a wage-paying job. In other words, the labour force measures of an industrial society may be inappropriate for those operating within a non-industrial mode of production.[41]

But for many inhabitants of native communities, unemployment and the poverty that follows are very real. The roots of the problem are diverse. The absence of employment opportunities in some cases is directly attributable to the isolated locations chosen for reservations when treaties were signed in the nineteenth and early twentieth centuries. In addition, both provincial and federal governments have long ignored native communities when attempting to stimulate job creation. However, large oil reserves and mineral deposits in the North have attracted the interest of both government and industry, and the number and range of available jobs in northern centres increased during the 1960s and 1970s. Unfortunately, the majority of these new jobs did not go to those who needed them most.[42] Low levels of education, limited work experience other than in short-term low-skill jobs, minimal access to information about jobs and to those doing the hiring, and discrimination in hiring have all resulted in few appreciable changes in the high unemployment rates of native groups. Similar factors are also largely responsible for the continuing unemployment problems of Indians and Métis living in southern Canadian communities.

As more women have entered the labour force over the past decades, they have also come to represent a larger proportion of the pool of unemployed workers. In fact, female unemployment rates have traditionally been a bit higher than male rates, except in those occupations where male unemployment is high and few women are employed. Since women are typically employed in lower-status and part-time jobs, and frequently have less seniority, they are often among the first to be laid off. With the exception of the public sector, unionized jobs which should be more secure are more often held by men. Nevertheless, when the problems of unemployment are documented by the media, or when governments intervene in the economy to save jobs, it is usually male unemployment that is being considered. The large factory shutdowns that attract attention generally involve primarily male work forces. Equally important, women losing their jobs may be more likely to drop out of the work force or resort to part-time employment.[43]

Young Canadians have been another group facing more severe problems of unemployment, with the very young and least educated having the most difficulty finding work. Youth unemployment rates (ages 15 to 24) have been higher than adult rates for a long time, but became particularly apparent when they doubled between 1973 (9.7 percent) and 1983 (19.9 percent). The largest part of this increase was observed in the early 1980s. In the last few years, we have seen a small decline: the national youth unemployment rate was 15.2 percent in 1986. This downward trend has been explained with reference to the baby boom of the 1950s and 1960s, the argument being that the last of the children born in that era of high birth rates have by now left school and made their way into the labour force. Some commentators conclude that the "problem" of youth unemployment is, consequently, about to disappear. Others suggest that as this large cohort of "baby boomers" matures, we will simply be faced with more severe problems of young adult unemployment. Given the other emerging patterns in the Canadian economy and labour market, this is a probable scenario.

But a third and perhaps more accurate view is that the traditional patterns of transition from school to work, and from dependence on parents to independence, have been changing. For example, jobs that used to provide an entry point into the labour force are disappearing, and educational institutions are struggling with the question of how best to prepare students for the employment world. Consequently, in the absence of substantial responses to changing economic realities, present and future cohorts of Canadian youth will continue to experience unemployment problems.[44]

The official definition of unemployment identifies a state of being without paid work, while being available for work and actively looking for work. This definition excludes students, individuals working in the home, the disabled, and the retired, all of whom are considered outside of the labour force. It also excludes potential labour force participants who, believing there is no work available in their community or region, have not actively looked for work in the previous four weeks. The debate over the size of this group of *discouraged workers,* and over whether they should be included in counts of the unemployed, has not been resolved. On one side, we see arguments that if discouraged workers and other "hidden unemployed" (such as involuntary part-time workers) were added to those officially unemployed, the rates would be much higher. One estimate suggested that the 1983 Canadian unemployment rate would have been around 16 percent (compared to the official rate of 12 percent) if these groups had been included. Critics of this position reply that "discouraged workers" often have little real commitment to finding work— surveys show that many had not looked for any work in the previous six months.[45]

In a 1982 report, the Economic Council of Canada steered a middle course through this debate. The Council concluded that at least some of those withdrawing from active job search were doing so because they had tried but could not find work. Furthermore, the report argued, the problem of "discouraged workers" was usually more pronounced in regions where unemployment rates were higher (the Maritimes, for example), and that groups such as women and youth, which typically experience labour market difficulties, would be more likely to contain individuals who had given up the job search because of a belief in the absence of jobs.[46] In short, when looking at unemployment rates it is best to remember that they are probably underestimates of the real size of the unemployment problem, although it is impossible to be precise about the number of "discouraged workers" who have left the labour force.

We have already hinted at some of the causes of unemployment in the Canadian economy. Obviously, there is a demographic factor to consider here. A large increase in the birth rate in the years following World War II resulted in a similar increase in the labour force several decades later. In addition, the increased proportion of women entering the labour force led to greater demand for jobs. But people working for pay are also people with money to spend, and the growth in labour force participation itself led to substantial job creation. We must, therefore, look beyond this single explanation.

Some observers emphasize "voluntary" unemployment, suggesting that many of the unemployed could be working if only they would be willing to accept the less attractive jobs that are available. No doubt this argument accounts for some of the unemployed in Canada, but it is simply not strong enough to explain the whole problem. In many communities, the total number of jobless far exceeds the total number of available jobs, whatever they might be. Furthermore, many of the jobs that may be available (and even hard to fill) are part-time, low-paying, and unlikely to lead to career improvements. The large number of part-time workers who report that they would prefer full-time work suggests that the unemployed often do take such work. But many could simply not survive (let alone take care of their families) on low-paying, part-time work. Accepting such work would be an irrational economic act, for it would force the individual to attempt to survive on an amount no greater than that provided by government social security agencies, while discontinuing an active search for a better job.

This suggests a third popular explanation of unemployment — the laziness of the unemployed in combination with the generosity of the government. This argument is often supported with anecdotal evidence, since there is little other evidence that would be relevant. It is hard to believe that more than a few Canadians would prefer the very low level of government assistance to a higher and more secure income. It is also hard to believe that somewhere in the 1970s (when unemployment rates began to rise), unusually large numbers of Canadians were suddenly overcome by laziness. In addition, research on Canadians' work values (discussed in Chapter 6) suggests that very few would prefer the economic hardships and the stigma of unemployment to a regular job.

In short, demographic changes and voluntary unemployment are only a part of the answer. Canada, like other industrialized nations, also faces a problem of structural unemployment. The global economy has been changing rapidly in the past decade, with major corporations shifting their activities to countries and regions where labour costs are lower, and where government legislation regarding labour relations, worker safety, and environmental protection is less developed. Some of Canada's resource-extraction industries (oil, wheat, and lumber, for example) have encountered very unstable world markets. New technologies are displacing workers in a variety of industries. Government agencies at the national, provincial, and municipal levels are responding to fiscal problems by cutting full-time employees. Changes in the industrial and occupational structures, as a consequence of these national and global trends, have had a large impact on the steady increase in unemployment rates over the years.[47]

How do Canadian unemployment rates compare to those of other industrialized countries? In mid-1987, the Canadian rate was 9.1 percent, compared to 14.0 percent in Holland, 10.4 percent in Britain, 14.0 percent in Italy and 11.0 percent in France. It is apparent that some other industrialized countries are facing similar problems. But if we compare our performance with that of West Germany, Sweden, and Japan, for example, our unemployment rates in the past decade have been almost twice as high. What is their secret?

There is no single answer. A policy of lifetime employment, at least within the largest corporations, has kept some Japanese workers employed. In addition, early retirement policies are common. West Germany has both encouraged early retirement and introduced shorter work weeks to increase the number of jobs in some industries. But it has also "exported" some of its unemployment. Back in the 1970s, when workers were scarce and jobs were not, West Germany allowed thousands of "guest workers" to enter the country. When jobs began to disappear in the 1980s, they were sent back to Turkey and Yugoslavia. In Sweden, shorter work weeks (an average of around 30 hours per week), strong unions that have fought layoffs and plant shutdowns, and a government involved in providing many services have all led to continued low rates of unemployment. Could Canada borrow some of these ideas? Most of them would be difficult to transplant, but the idea of reducing working hours to create more jobs has been recently suggested.[48]

FUTURE TRENDS

Over the last century we have observed pronounced changes in how, where, and for whom Canadians work. The decades at the end of the nineteenth and the beginning of this century were times of rapid industrialization and of workplace rationalization. The years following saw further growth in white-collar occupations, expansion of the service sector, and a decline in self-employment. By the 1960s, the Canadian work world had been largely transformed. But, as our examination of more recent statistics has shown, changes are ongoing. Female labour force participation has increased further. The shift to predominance of the service sector has continued, while manufacturing industries have declined in importance.[49] Over the last three decades, we have seen a steady decline in the contribution made by manufacturing industries to total employment growth in Canada.[50] Average weekly hours of work have dropped below forty hours a week, largely due to a substantial increase in part-time employment, and unemployment rates have risen dramatically in the last decade.

We have discussed some of the factors responsible for service sector growth and increased part-time work. But we should also note that some of these trends, particularly growing joblessness and the relative decline of employment in the manufacturing industries, are related to global economic crises affecting Canada. Dropping oil prices and very unstable world markets for some of Canada's staple products have had a devastating effect on the economy, particularly on some of the areas most dependent on primary industries. Continuing high rates of unemployment in these regions are the result. Increased competition from countries like Japan has led Canadian manufacturers (and multinational firms operating in Canada) to respond in ways that affect employment opportunities. Some firms have rationalized their operations by simply shutting down Canadian plants and moving to countries where the absence of labour legislation and a lower standard of living help to cut labour costs in production. Others have increased productivity by replacing workers with automated manufacturing systems. Robots may be costly to design and construct but once put in place their operating costs are low. They don't need pension plans or vacation pay, and can work around the clock; thus, equivalent or higher productivity can be obtained with fewer employees. Canada's economy, then, is not insulated from global economic forces, and many working Canadians are directly affected by these larger patterns of change.

So what can we expect to see in the future? There is little disagreement among observers about the continuing shift away from the secondary manufacturing sector to the service sector, both in Canada and other western industrialized countries.[51] We have already noted that most economists are in agreement about continuing high rates of unemployment, at least some of which is attributable to the decline of manufacturing.[52] There is also consensus about the further growth of part-time employment. We would, however, be somewhat more cautious when considering projections of employment growth and decline in specific occupations, given the large number of unknown and unmeasurable variables that cannot be included in computer-generated scenarios of the 1990s. Recognizing the limitations of such future predictions, it is still instructive to look at the types of jobs that are expected to increase.

Table 2.4
Occupations Expected to Contribute Most to Employment Growth
in Canada, 1986-1995

Occupational title	New growth in employment
Salespersons, commodities	91,000
Food service	80,000
Bookkeepers	56,000
Secretaries and stenographers	54,000
Chefs and cooks	47,000
Cashiers and tellers	47,000
Janitors and cleaners	40,000
Truck drivers	33,000
Sales management	26,000
Barbers and hairdressers	26,000
Motor vehicle mechanics	25,000
Nurses	24,000
Financial officers	22,000
Supervisors; food and beverage preparation	19,000
General office clerks	18,000
Labourers, services	17,000
Services management	16,000
Receptionists and information clerks	15,000
Carpenters	15,000

Source: *Globe and Mail* (23 March 1987), p. B15.
Original source: Employment and Immigration Canada; based on cops *1986 Reference Scenario.*

Some projections of job growth are calculated in *percentage change* terms. For example, in making the argument that many new service sector jobs are really better than the manufacturing jobs being replaced, one recent U.S. prediction noted that computer service technicians would double in number by 1995. Building custodians, on the other hand, would show a smaller increase of less than 30 percent. This is somewhat deceptive since it ignores the *number* of individuals currently employed in each of these occupations. In fact, when considering actual numbers of jobs expected to appear in the United States by 1995, the predictions were for an additional 53,000 computer service technicians, but a huge increase of 778,000 building custodians.[53]

Equivalent Canadian predictions of growth in the number of jobs up until 1995 are presented in Table 2.4.[54] Salespersons, food service workers, bookkeepers, secretaries and stenographers, chefs and cooks, cashiers and tellers, and janitors and cleaners top the list. While there are a few exceptions in the table, the "growth" occupations tend to be white-collar service sector jobs, typically held by women and amenable to part-time employment. In other words, the patterns of the past few decades appear to be pushing us into the next century. Finally, it is interesting to note that these projections challenge the argument (discussed in Chapter 9) that office automation will lead to substantial reductions in clerical and office employment.

NOTES

1. An additional census is done at the middle of the 10-year span between major census years, but fewer questions are asked and only 20 percent of Canadian households are included.
2. Excluded are residents of the Yukon and the Northwest Territories, residents of Indian reservations, full-time members of the armed forces, and prison inmates.
3. All 1986 estimates are from the annual averages, compiled by Statistics Canada from these monthly surveys (*The Labour Force,* cat. no. 71-001, December 1986, various tables).
4. See Chen and Regan (1985:17-21) for a more detailed discussion of labour force participation definitions.
5. Methods of studying work in the irregular economy include unofficial surveys (assuming one can gain the confidence of respondents), examination of law enforcement records (in an attempt to estimate amounts of illegal economic activity), assessments of the amount of cash in circulation in an economy (compared to taxation reports of the total amount of reported income), and so on. See the 1986 *OECD Employment Outlook* (chapter 3, p. 68) for a discussion of such studies.
6. Mirus and Smith (1985).
7. *OECD Employment Outlook 1986* (chapter 3, p. 68).
8. Armstrong and Armstrong (1983): 6.
9. For a more precise discussion of these distinctions, see the *Standard Occupational Classification Manual* produced by Statistics Canada (1980): 11-12.

10. Matthews (1985): 36.
11. Pomfret (1981: 123) describes how, in the latter half of the nineteenth century, productivity per worker doubled despite a reduction in hours worked.
12. As already noted, most service sector employees would be considered white-collar workers. This residual *service* occupation category includes occupations located primarily within service industries, such as police officers (protective services), waitresses (food services), and hairdressers (personal services).
13. Inclusion of the 1.2 million unemployed labour force members would alter the table slightly. The percentages in the administrative and professional occupations would decrease, with corresponding increases in the other occupational categories where unemployment rates are higher.
14. Ornstein (1983a): 252; data from 1980 is reported for the U.S., West Germany, Japan, and Sweden.
15. Such an approach does not consider individuals who work (without pay) in their homes, students, the retired, and the disabled, although a broader analysis of household class position, and of class position prior to leaving the paid labour force, would include these groups. For further discussion of differing conceptions of social class, see Ornstein (1983a), Hunter (1986), and Curtis and Scott (1979).
16. Riddell (1985:9) provides these estimates by distinguishing between employers, the self-employed, unpaid family workers (someone working, without formal wage arrangements, in a family-owned business), and "paid workers."
17. See Johnson (1979:94) on owner-managers in agriculture, Ornstein (1983a: 246) on the number and size of farms, Riddell (1985:8) on numbers employed in agriculture, and Statistics Canada (1985b:15) for 1984 data.
18. Statistics Canada (1985b): 9. In this special report, Statistics Canada notes that the percentage of self-employed actually increased from 12.0 to 13.5 percent over these five years. This larger figure is obtained by reclassifying as self-employed individuals who own business enterprises and who also employ others. While these individuals are obviously not employed by others, such a classification does not correspond to our typical use of the term "self-employed."
19. OECD *Employment Outlook 1986* (chapter 2, p. 60).
20. Wright et al. (1982).
21. Black and Myles (1986): 162.
22. See Watkins (1963, 1982) for discussions of this "staples theory."
23. See Lucas (1971), Himelfarb (1976), and Bowles (1982) for discussions of Canada's single industry communities, and Watkins (1977:90) on the ghost town as a symbol.
24. See Clark (1971), Forcese (1986:30), and Marchak (1981:106) on migration to Canada's resource towns. Lucas (1971), Himelfarb (1976), and Gertler and Crowley (1979:255) discuss stages of resource town development.
25. The construction of such resource towns may soon become a thing of the past. Many mining companies, for example, are moving toward a fly-in rotation system in which shifts of workers are flown into an isolated site for several weeks, and then flown back to their homes in a more central city while a second shift of workers replaces them. The costs of airlifting whole shifts are offset by the savings resulting from not having to construct a completely new community with homes, schools, roads, and other community necessities. (Institute for Research on Public Policy, 1986).
26. Lucas (1971): 130; Stymeist (1975): 66; Elias (1975): 8; Loxley, (1981): 152.

27. Krahn and Gartrell (1983).
28. Forcese (1986: 32) discusses the absence of middle-level jobs, and Marchak (1975: 33) comments on the truncated class structure of resource towns. See Lucas (1971:95), Clement (1981:58), and Luxton (1981:176) on the relative absence of jobs for women.
29. See van Cleef (1985:87) for average hours in 1976 and 1984, and Reid (1985: 146-50) for standard hours since 1870. Reid argues that standard hours in manufacturing are quite similar to those for all industries, but uses manufacturing data because of the longer time-series available.
30. van Cleef (1985) reports that the group working more than 50 hours per week increased from 11.7 percent of the employed in 1976 to 12.3 percent in 1984.
31. Weeks (1980:69) provides 1953 data. Kaliski (1985:86) discusses job creation rates over time. Zero percent average annual growth does not mean that no new full-time jobs were created. Instead, on average, as many full-time jobs disappeared as were created.
32. Armstrong (1984:203) for 1966 data, Boulet and Lavallee (1984:12) for 1975 data, and Akyeampong (1986:144) for characteristics of the involuntary unemployed.
33. Kaliski (1985): 86.
34. In 1985, a majority of those employed part-time were only employed for a portion of the year (Veevers 1986). Since women are vastly overrepresented among part-time employees, they are also overrepresented among part-year workers.
35. See Weeks (1980) for an excellent discussion of the "business view on second-class jobs" for women.
36. Jones (1983:30) provides unemployment rates (1920-40) for ten industrialized countries, including Canada. The Economic Council of Canada (1982:5) charts Canadian rates since 1960, and Parliament (1987) continues the series.
37. See the Newfoundland and Labrador Federation of Labour (1978) on unemployment in that region, and Phillips (1982) for a general discussion of regional disparities in Canada.
38. Riddell (1985): 31.
39. Grayson (1985).
40. See the Economic Council of Canada (1982:11) and Ponting and Gibbins (1980: 50-54) on native Canadians in the labour force.
41. This became a central issue during the Mackenzie Valley Pipeline Inquiry in the 1970s. Corporate groups promoting the construction of the pipeline argued that unemployed native Canadians would benefit from this huge project. Native groups responded by noting that the traditional way of life, which might be destroyed by widespread oil exploration and development in the North, was still economically viable. See Berger (1977) and Asch (1977) for extensive discussions of this debate.
42. See Grant (1983) for several case studies of corporate and government attempts to increase native Canadian participation in their work forces.
43. Armstrong (1984): 59, 84, 97.
44. See Foot and Li (1986) on the link between the baby boom and present high rates of unemployment, and Marsden (1986) on the breakdown of social institutions facilitating the transition from youth to adulthood.
45. The Social Planning Council of Metropolitan Toronto (1984) calculated the 1983 unemployment rates based on inclusion of discouraged workers. See *The Labour Force* (March 1984) from Statistics Canada for a discussion of job search behaviour

of discouraged workers.

46. Economic Council of Canada (1982): 53-58.

47. See Grayson (1985) on structural unemployment; and Kaliski (1985) and the Economic Council of Canada (1982:9-12; 47-61) for useful discussions of alternative explanations of unemployment.

48. Handy (1984:25) on Sweden, West Germany, and Japan; Reid (1985) on employment sharing to create jobs; *The Economist* (22 August 1987:91) for national unemployment rates for mid-1987.

49. See Picot (1987) for a recent overview of shifts in the relative strength of industrial sectors between 1951 and 1985.

50. Manufacturing industries were responsible for 23.7 percent of overall growth between 1956 and 1966, 15.9 percent between 1966 and 1973, and 12.2 percent between 1973 and 1979. The period between 1979 and 1983 saw manufacturing accounting for a negative change of 54.6 percent of overall employment growth in Canada (Kaliski 1985): 84.

51. See the *Washington Post* (30 November 1986, p. H1) on projected changes in the U.S. industrial and occupational structures; also Kirkland (1985) for a similar discussion in *Fortune Magazine* (10 June 1985).

52. Parliament (1987) analyzes the growth in "long-term unemployment" in Canada over the past decade.

53. Kirkland (1985): 40.

54. See Rinehart (1987:167) for a set of similar projections.

3

The Sociology of Labour Markets

INTRODUCTION

We have defined a labour market in general terms as the arena in which employers seek to purchase labour from potential employees who themselves are seeking jobs suitable to their education, experience, and preferences. In the labour market, workers exchange their skills, knowledge, and loyalties in return for pay, status, career opportunities, and other job rewards.[1] There are a number of other institutions that support or interact with the operations of the labour market. Schools and families prepare individuals for entry (or re-entry) into the labour market. Governments legislate rules governing some aspects of labour market operations, and government agencies play an active role in job training and other programs. Unions and professional associations have an impact on access to certain types of work opportunities and rewards. But of particular interest to sociologists are the distributive aspects of the labour market; in short, how it generates and perpetuates patterns of inequality in society.[2]

Our earlier discussions of the changing Canadian occupational and class structures noted that some jobs are clearly more desirable than others. This chapter begins by reviewing some of the dimensions on which society evaluates the desirability of jobs. We then consider the question of who gets the "good" jobs from the perspective of the *human capital* model of labour market processes. According to this theory, the allocation of jobs generally results in a close match between the demands of the work and the skills and abilities of the person in the job. The result, at the societal level, is a more efficient and productive economy. Those jobs requiring the most effort, training, and skill usually receive the greatest rewards. Such outcomes would satisfy our sense of justice, assuming there was an open and equal competition for the more rewarding jobs.[3] In reviewing some of the major findings of occupational choice, status attainment, and labour market segmentation research, we then attempt to demonstrate the degree to which the labour market does *not* operate in this

67

manner. In fact, there is evidence that the open competition assumptions of human capital theory need to be reconsidered, and that the labour market often operates in a manner that perpetuates social inequalities. Thus the study of labour markets is not only about who gets which jobs; it also addresses broader questions about social justice.[4]

GOOD JOBS AND BAD JOBS

How does one decide whether a particular job is a "good" or a "bad" job? The answer seems simple — you compare its rewards against your own needs and aspirations. While some people might choose a job on the basis of their subjective assessment of its value to the community or society, most people work with a set of assumptions about what is important to them personally. In general, these might be *extrinsic* concerns about pay, fringe benefits, job security, or prestige; or they might be *intrinsic* rewards of work, such as the degree to which the job allows one to be creative, to work independently, to develop friendships, and so on. These intrinsic rewards of work will be examined in Chapter 6 along with work orientations and work values. For now we will consider the material rewards, since these have a more direct impact on an individual's socio-economic status and life chances. However, we should mention that there is a relationship between the distribution of intrinsic and extrinsic job rewards. Frequently, better-paying jobs are also those that are more intrinsically satisfying.

Income

So which are the better-paying jobs? Table 3.1 displays average 1985 earnings in major occupational categories, as well as comparable statistics from a decade earlier. Managers ($30,196) and professionals ($24,638) clearly are paid more for their work than are individuals in clerical, sales, and service occupations. The lowest annual average earnings ($10,970) are reported in service sector occupations, the most rapidly expanding area of employment. In very general terms, then, Canadians employed in managerial positions make approximately three times as much as those in service jobs. The traditional blue-collar occupations have relatively high average earnings, ranging around $20,000 a year.[5]

Table 3.1 also highlights sex differences in earnings within each of these major categories. Comparing the average 1985 earnings (all occupations combined) of women and men, we find that women are receiving about 58 percent of what men are earning. This may be due partly to the larger proportion of women working in part-time or part-year jobs. When only the full-year, full-time employed are included, we find the male average (for all occupations) increases to $28,848 while the female average climbs to $18,736.[6] This translates into women receiving, on average, 65 percent of what men earn. The 1975 statistics in the table demonstrate that this female-male wage gap, to which we return in Chapter 5, is not a recent phenomenon.

Table 3.1
Average Earnings by Occupation and Sex, Canada, 1975 and 1985

| | *Average Earnings($)** | | | | |
| | *1975* | | *1985* | | |
*Occupation***	*Female*	*Male*	*Female*	*Male*	*Total*
Managerial	9,891	17,850	20,356	35,377	30,196
Professional	8,123	15,154	18,726	31,436	24,638
Clerical	5,852	9,455	13,274	20,388	14,688
Sales	4,130	12,056	10,075	21,176	16,416
Service	3,301	8,336	7,352	15,474	10,970
Primary***	2,839	7,946	7,022	12,634	11,687
Processing and machining	5,238	10,287	12,963	23,765	22,229
Product fabrication	4,870	10,586	11,693	21,810	19,540
Construction	—	11,110	—	19,765	19,691
Transportation	4,987	10,385	11,181	19,982	18,716
All Occupations	5,798	11,460	13,437	23,217	19,034

* Earnings (wages and salaries, and net income from self-employment) form the largest part of total income, which also includes investment income, government transfer payments, pensions, and miscellaneous income.
** Includes the currently employed (full-time and part-time) and those unemployed who have worked in the previous five years.
*** Primary sector occupations include those in agriculture, hunting and fishing, forestry and logging.
Source: Statistics Canada, *Income Distributions by Size in Canada* (# 13-207); 1975, Table 57, p. 103; 1985, Table 60, pp. 128-29.

If we were to present data on specific occupations within these broad categories, we would observe income differences much larger than a three-to-one ratio. A few selected examples will serve to make the point. Within the managerial group, for example, we would find senior managers in the federal and provincial government generally earning in excess of $50,000 a year. Senior managers in the private sector would typically be paid equally as well, or better, but seldom as much as the executive officers of major Canadian corporations, some of whom earn in excess of a million dollars a year.[7]

Among professionals, doctors earned an average of about $93,000 in 1982. Senior corporate accountants averaged around $85,800 a year in 1983, compared to top corporate lawyers with an average salary of $78,000. At the bottom end of the pay scale, we find cashiers in the food-service industry usually earned around $5.00 an hour in 1983.

Working full-time at $5.00 an hour would mean an annual income of less than $10,000, an amount below the official poverty line for a two-person household in a major urban centre.[8] Hourly rates in the blue-collar occupations such as construction or manufacturing are typically higher, but some of these jobs are seasonal and subject to frequent layoffs. The relatively higher blue-collar wages, in contrast to the white-collar service sector, can be largely attributed to two factors: the high proportion of women (who typically earn less than men) in the service sector, and the greater presence of unions (and men) in blue-collar manufacturing and construction jobs.[9]

Chapters 5 and 7 will look more closely at women's work and at the role of unions in our society. We introduce these topics here simply to underline the immense income disparities found in the Canadian labour market, which obviously influence individuals' standard of living and quality of life. Furthermore, these patterns have been remarkably stable over time. In 1951, the most advantaged 20 percent of households received 43 percent of total Canadian income, while the bottom 20 percent received 4 percent of all income. By 1981, average incomes were higher and the Canadian population had increased considerably. But the distribution of income was virtually unchanged — the poorest 20 percent of the population still received 4 percent of all income, compared to the 42 percent going to the wealthiest 20 percent.[10]

Fringe Benefits and Job Security

One should not ignore the indirect impact of fringe benefits on income distribution in Canada. It has been estimated that, on average, fringe benefits add about 33 percent to the pay for regular hours worked. The largest part of this indirect income comes from paid holidays and vacation, and from employer contributions to private pension plans.[11] Some Canadian workers also receive medical and dental plans (for themselves and other family members), life insurance, the use of company vehicles, interest-free housing loans, cash bonuses, and stock options, among other things. But such fringe benefits are not equally distributed. Part-time workers and others working near minimum-wage levels, as well as employees in small firms, seldom receive any additional benefits beyond those required by law.[12] On the other hand, high salaried managers and professionals and many unionized workers in the public sector or large corporations receive a wide range of fringe benefits.

Better-paying jobs often also provide more job security. Again, we can attribute some of this to unions obtaining such protection through collective bargaining. However, Canadians with the highest incomes (business managers and executives, doctors, lawyers, dentists, and some other self-employed professionals) are usually not union members. Hence, the correlation between pay and job security is probably not as strong as the relationship between pay and benefits packages. Members of professions, of course, can increase job security by regulating entry into their field. In sum, when we speak of "good jobs" we are referring to the likelihood of higher income and of generous benefits, and the lower probability of unemployment.

Occupational Status

Another "extrinsic" work reward useful for evaluating jobs is *status*. We seldom find doctors, lawyers, scientists, or professors blushing when, at a party for example, they are asked, "What do you do?" But for clerks, janitors, parking-lot attendants, and many others the same question might elicit an apologetic "I'm *just* a . . . ." In short, there is considerable consensus in our society about which jobs have higher status. While of lesser importance than income (which directly determines one's standard of living) and job security (which ensures continuity of that standard), occupational status is something we do consider when comparing different jobs. To a large extent our own self-image, and the respect and admiration of others, is determined by our occupation. Not surprisingly, there is a fairly systematic relationship between occupational status and income. On the surface, it might seem that higher pay and status are a direct result of the greater skill and responsibility demands of certain jobs. Generally, higher-status jobs require more education, cognitive ability, and skill.[13] But it is also possible that the higher status of some occupations comes about because of high incomes earned in these fields, or because some occupational groups are powerful enough to limit competition by restricting entry into their field.[14]

Evidence of the relationships among income, education, and occupational status have led to widespread use of *socio-economic status* (SES) scales in sociological research. In Canada, the most frequently used SES measures are the *Blishen scores*, named after the sociologist who developed them. Bernard Blishen began with the results of a mid-1960s national study which asked respondents to rank the "social standing" of almost 200 occupations by sorting cards containing these occupational titles into nine groups. He obtained, from census data, the average education and income of Canadian men employed in a subset of these occupations. Blishen then calculated the statistical relationships among these three variables, and used these calculations, along with census data on the average education and income of men in occupations not examined in the original study, to estimate SES scores for almost 500 occupational titles.[15] The resulting index ranges from very low status scores, such as 19.2 for newsboys and 23.0 for farmers, to very high evaluations of occupations such as nuclear engineer (74.7) and medical doctor (74.2). In between, we find occupations such as librarian (61.9), photographer (49.5), and truck driver (29.7).

Researchers have identified a number of problems with this particular SES scale, including the tendency to undervalue work in the primary sectors (farming, for example) and to exaggerate the status of clerical work. The latter problem can be traced to the use of only male data in the original calculations (men in clerical occupations, for example, would typically make more money than women in the same area).[16] A useful alternative occupational classification system consists of a 16-category typology developed from the occupational codes used in the 1971 census.[17] This set of rankings relies more on the nature of the work done by particular occupational groups, and on the skill and knowledge levels required. Self-employed professionals (doctors and lawyers, for example) are at the top of the list. Going down the rankings, we find categories such as semi-professionals, technicians, middle management, skilled clerical, semiskilled manual workers, and so on. This classification scheme parallels the Blishen scores.[18] The advantage of the categorical ranking is that the title assigned to the rank (e.g. semiskilled clerical, sales, and services) actually tells us something about the occupations included. Blishen scores remain numbers, with no real meaning in themselves, showing us only that some occupations are being awarded higher social standing than others.

Although SES scores are often loosely labelled as measures of social class, they clearly do not index class position as defined in the previous chapter. Furthermore, SES scales of this type overlook some important features of stratification systems within societies. A number of British sociologists have begun to use a *relational* approach for constructing occupational scales.[19] They argue that if our goal is to understand the nature and dynamics of the stratification system within a society, we must explore the shared experiences, day-to-day interactions, and basic lifestyle similarities among different occupational groups. Thus, in constructing their occupational ranking system, they asked survey respondents about the occupations of their friends and neighbours, and used statistical techniques to determine the degree of interaction among various occupational groups. The Canadian SES scales, like the U.S. scales on which they were modelled, do not measure such *stratification arrangements.* Nevertheless, they are still useful indicators of an individual's current location in the stratification system. And they clearly show that better-paying jobs are also accorded higher status in our society.

THE HUMAN CAPITAL MODEL OF LABOUR MARKET OPERATIONS

We have argued that, on a variety of dimensions, some jobs are better than others, while recognizing that some jobs require more skills and training. In a perfect world, we would expect that jobs with specific requirements would be filled by individuals most suited for such positions. If being suited for a particular job meant that one must first obtain an advanced education, then it would seem only reasonable that having done so one would be rewarded with a better job. Stripped to its essentials, these are the basic premises of *human capital* theory, a major explanation of how the labour market operates.[20] This theoretical perspective assumes that job rewards are basically determined by the contribution of that job to the economy. The model also assumes that labour force participants are all competing for jobs in a single, open labour market. Information about available jobs is widely circulated. All potential employees have equal access to job openings, except for those without the necessary qualifications. When it comes to choosing whom to hire, employers make only rational decisions, based on an assessment of an individual's skill, training, and initiative.

In order to compete for the better jobs and "get ahead," it makes sense for job-seekers to get more education and training. But this delaying of entry into the labour market means foregoing some potential earnings. Yet this is not a permanent loss because by obtaining more education one is investing in "human capital," which can later be "cashed in" for a better job. In short, the human capital model emphasizes the "supply" side of labour market operations, and largely overlooks the behaviour and characteristics of employers and work organizations. Substantial differences in pay, benefits, job security, and occupational status are attributed primarily to differences in the characteristics of workers themselves.

Moving from the theory to the real world of work, we find many instances of well-trained and highly motivated workers being paid much less than this theory would predict. Alternatively, a closer look reveals that many of the wealthiest members of our society are not that much more educated or skilled than the rest of us.[21] There is also evidence that fully equal access to rewarding jobs is largely a myth. Thus the relationships among education, occupation, and income are not nearly as consistent as this economic model would suggest. Supporters of the human capital approach might respond that a theory able to explain part of this pattern is better than no theory at all, and that the many discrepancies between education, training, and income are largely due to chance or luck.[22] This might be a convincing response if discrepancies were randomly distributed; however, research showing that specific groups are less likely than others to have benefited from their investments in human capital challenges the theory, as do observations that reasonable returns to education and training are obtained only in certain industrial sectors or only from some types of employers. In other words, assumptions about how the ideal labour market operates may only be applicable to limited portions of the real labour market. These basic criticisms of the human capital model are elaborated in the following review of research findings, which sets the stage for our introduction of an alternative explanation — the *labour market segmentation* model.

OCCUPATIONAL ALLOCATION: CHOICE, CHANCE, OR DESTINY?

The human capital model attempts to explain how people are sorted into different occupational positions by focusing on the characteristics and behaviours of individual workers. People with skills and abilities more valued by society, and who have invested more in education and training, will be leading candidates for the better jobs. The model also assumes that individuals choose among work options, eventually settling on the occupational niche that best suits them. But to what extent do people actually choose among the various occupations available? Perhaps occupational choice is largely illusory, with allocation occurring according to criteria over which individuals have little control. Or perhaps the match between individuals and jobs is mainly due to chance?

We probably know people who as children decided they wanted to be a teacher or a doctor, and then carefully pursued the educational route to this goal. Such behaviour and outcomes are consistent with human capital predictions. On the other hand, we probably also know a few individuals who accidentally ended up in their current job, with little planning, or who landed a great position by just being in the right place at the right time. Such examples notwithstanding, there is much more evidence of the pervasive influence of socio-economic background on career patterns. For example, it would probably be unthinkable to grow up as a Bronfman or an Eaton and aspire to be a bus driver. Similarly, many people who make their living as farmers would probably cite "growing up on a farm" as a major influence, and growing up in a working-class family in Windsor, Ontario would likely channel a youth into one of the local factories. Certainly, many women in today's labour force were constrained in their career choices by society's attitudes about appropriate female roles. Thus, for many working Canadians, family circumstances, social class background, and community of origin, along with personal attributes such as race, ethnicity, and gender, are important determinants of occupational position.

In the research literature on *occupational choice*, distinct approaches emphasizing choice, chance, or destiny can be clearly identified.[23] Studies in this area make the point that, to a considerable extent, factors other than skills and training influence occupational allocation. Such findings question the utility of the individualistic human capital model by highlighting some of the social structural factors that have important prior impacts.

Educational Aspirations

One of the most highly valued principles underlying our system of education is that of equality of access. If education is meant to be the major route to labour market success, then everyone should have an equal chance to obtain a good education. Over the years, numerous studies in Canada and other western industrial societies have investigated the degree to which access to higher education is equally distributed. Some have looked at the social class, racial, and ethnic origins of those with high levels of education. Others have examined reasons for differences in the educational aspirations of young people. An important Canadian study by John Porter and Bernard Blishen began with the premise that equality of educational opportunity means: ". . . making it possible for anyone, regardless of sex, race, ethnicity or social class background, to strive for the heights of the educational ladder, and from there, to aim for the high status, highly rewarded positions in the occupational world." [24]

A total of 9,000 Ontario students (equally split across Grades 8, 10, and 12) completed questionnaires in the first phase of this 1970 study, as did the parents of about one-third of this sample. The students were asked, among other things, about self-perceptions of ability, school experiences, and education and work plans. Parents also commented on expectations they had for their children. Several years later, the student participants in the study were recontacted to see how much education they had really obtained. The researchers concluded that social class origins have a strong influence on educational aspirations of the youth in our school system. Middle- and upper-middle class parents have had more education themselves and this provides a role model for their children. Middle-class children have higher assessments of their own ability, which translates into higher educational aspirations. In addition, middle-class parents have higher expectations regarding their children's education. Taken together, these factors make it much more likely that the offspring of parents in higher-status occupations would aspire to post-secondary education.[25]

These findings would matter little if the educational aspirations of high-school students did not have a bearing on their actual behaviour after graduation. In the follow-up phase of the study, the researchers discovered that (as we might expect) not all of those who had originally planned to go on to university had actually done so. Some might have been unable to afford it or make the entrance requirements, while others might have lost interest, or exaggerated their plans and abilities in the first place. What is more crucial than the initial class differences in aspirations is the close link between social class origins and *educational attainment*. Middle-class youth were more likely to obtain a university education, and lower-class youth were overrepresented among those who had aimed high but who had failed to carry through with these plans.

Occupational Aspirations

Although its major focus was on the question of equality of access to higher education, this Ontario study also examined the linkages between social class background, education plans, and *occupational aspirations*. It found what we might by now have predicted, and what other Canadian researchers have also confirmed — the higher the occupational status of the parent, the more likely the child is to aspire to a high-status job. Both educational and occupational aspirations appear to be significantly determined by social class origins.[26] But this only begs another question: Do higher occupational aspirations, influenced as they are by social class, really translate into better jobs?

The answer is, on average, yes. The major link between occupational aspirations and eventual location in the labour market is primarily via educational aspirations and attainment, a process we have already discussed. In another study of Ontario high-school students, Paul Anisef and his colleagues surveyed over 1,500 young people who, as graduating high-school students, had taken part in a similar survey six years earlier. The results showed that young people from higher socio-economic backgrounds were more likely to have completed "academic" programs while in high school. This became a major factor in their subsequent decisions about continuing on to university. And a university education significantly increased the chances of entering a higher-status occupation. The researchers concluded that post-secondary education "amplifies" or increases the impact of socio-economic origin and other background factors.[27]

Other Influential Variables

Both of these major Ontario studies also looked at the effects of gender on educational and occupational aspirations and attainment. The Porter and Blishen surveys revealed lower educational and occupational aspirations among female high-school seniors than

among males. In addition, parents held very low educational aspirations for their daughters. Hence, a major reason for the lower
aspirations of young women could be the traditional gender-role
attitudes encountered in their families. For young women from a
lower-class background, the likelihood of low aspirations was even
greater. Similarly, the Anisef study noted that young women were
much less likely to plan to go on to university than were young men;
and when they did go, it was usually into traditional "female" programs such as nursing or teaching. These educational patterns reinforced occupational segregation by sex and the female-male wage gap
mentioned earlier. Such findings suggest that gender and educational attainment may be even more important than social class origin
in determining initial labour market entry points for Canadian
youth.[28]

In addition, the Porter and Anisef studies examined the effects of
factors such as ethnicity and region of residence on educational and
occupational aspirations. In particular, they noted that rural youth
were less likely to plan on higher education. The Porter study
speculated that the more "limited horizons" of rural youth might be
due to their underexposure to attitudes favouring higher education.
The Anisef study noted that the absence of local institutions of higher
learning forces rural youth to leave their homes and communities to
go to university, making the transition to higher education more
difficult.[29]

How can these findings help us assess the human capital model of
labour market operations? The obvious importance attached to
education per se cautions us not to ignore its role in determining who
gets which jobs. However, this research is an important corrective to
the human capital model because it identifies several other variables
that greatly influence one's chances of obtaining a good education.
Gender is one of these variables, social class is a second, and region of
residence is a third. Thus, while higher education may be an important avenue to better jobs, access to higher education is itself not
equally available. This could mean that the most capable people are
not necessarily being sorted into the most important and rewarding
jobs. There is also evidence here that some groups, particularly
women, are less able to "cash in" their investments in education for
higher-paying jobs. Thus the human capital model may be more
relevant for some groups in the labour force than for others. Finally,
because the human capital view of the labour market focuses on
education and other characteristics of labour *supply*, it tends to ignore
how employers can determine the *demand* for certain types of labour,
thereby diminishing the potential levelling effects of education.[30]

While this research has highlighted the effects of variables like
gender, social class, and region of residence on education and work

opportunities, we cannot completely overlook the role of individual decision making. Nor can we simply ignore the impact of chance in the matching of people to jobs. In the end, the question of whether choice, chance, or destiny determines where one works — or if one is unemployed — becomes one of degree. Obviously all three factors enter the equation, but some are more important than others. Making the same point, but within a much broader historical analysis, Karl Marx once wrote: "Men make their own history, but they do not make it just as they please; they do not make it under circumstances chosen by themselves, but under circumstances directly encountered, given and transmitted from the past."[31]

SOCIAL MOBILITY AND STATUS ATTAINMENT RESEARCH

Status attainment research also demonstrates that background characteristics can have a substantial influence on one's education and work opportunities. However, this research makes more sense when we discuss it alongside the social mobility research from which it evolved. The term *social mobility* is a general one which could be used to describe how individuals or groups move from one position within a social hierarchy to another. For example, we might find immigrant groups that arrived in Canada several generations ago having a much higher status today than upon arrival. We might also reflect on our own careers, noting any movement (up or down) the occupational ladder over the years. Or we might document the misfortunes of a once wealthy and powerful family that had become downwardly mobile because of poor management in the family business. But in our society, social standing is largely influenced by occupational position, and therefore most social mobility research has involved the study of *occupational mobility*.

We can usefully distinguish between *intergenerational* and *intragenerational* mobility. The former involves comparisons between an individual's occupational status and that of someone in a previous generation, most frequently his or her parent (or grandparent). The latter addresses the issue of mobility within a generation, or comparison of a presently held occupation with one from some earlier point in an individual's work career. There is also an important difference between *structural mobility* and *circulatory mobility*. Chapters 1 and 2 documented massive upheavals in industrial capitalist societies over the past century: a huge decline in agriculture and a parallel expansion of the urban work force, the rise of large bureaucratic organizations, and extensive growth in the service sectors. These changes precipitated an enormous growth in white-collar occupations. Thus, simply by virtue of changes in the occupational structure, we would expect to find much larger proportions of labour force participants in middle-level occupations today than a generation earlier; your parents would have had fewer chances than you of finding white-collar employment. So when we examine the amount of intergenerational occupational mobility within a given society, we have to recognize that some of this is due to structural mobility, or increasing opportunities due to changes in the occupational structure.

Researchers have devised statistical techniques to determine precisely how much structural mobility has been occurring. This allows us to then address a potentially more interesting question: How much intergenerational mobility do we observe net of the effects of changing occupational structures or, phrased differently, how *open* is a given society to occupational mobility? As we have already noted, a core belief in democratic societies is that the "best" people end up in the more responsible and rewarding jobs. If this were the case, we would observe a large amount of circulatory mobility across generations, in contrast to a *closed* society in which occupational positions are inherited. Theoretically, circulatory intergenerational mobility occurs when those with more talent, skill, training, and motivation are able to move into the higher occupational positions, leaving others to take the lower-status jobs. According to this perspective, merit — not social origin — determines position. No society has ever realized the goal of becoming a true *meritocracy*. The question, then, becomes: To what degree are occupational position and social status "socially inherited" in our society? Equally interesting, are different societies more or less "open" in this regard? [32]

Early social mobility studies distinguished among three basic occupational categories — agricultural, manual, and non-manual work — and examined intergenerational mobility across these occupational boundaries. In 1959, Seymour Martin Lipset and Reinhard Bendix compared the United States with a number of European countries. Many might have predicted that occupational inheritance would be more pronounced in European countries with a feudal heritage, and less significant in the United States with its strong democratic values. However, few important differences in this respect were observed across industrialized countries. [33] Democratic traditions and ideals, it would seem, have little impact on social mobility opportunities. Lipset and Bendix went on to address other issues, such as the consequences of social mobility for both individuals and society, and the manner in which education influences social mobility opportunities in different societies.

How is Occupational Status Attained?

Pioneer researchers like Lipset and Bendix used crude occupational categories and simple statistical techniques. Methodological advances have led to more rigorous analysis of how much intergenerational mobility actually occurs in industrial capitalist societies, and whether or not some societies are more "open" than others.[34] But researchers began to address somewhat different questions following the appearance in 1967 of *The American Occupational Structure,* a study by Peter Blau and Otis Duncan.[35]

In their research, Blau and Duncan used occupational status scores rather than large occupational categories. Data from a survey of American men allowed them to employ statistical techniques that could isolate the unique effects of an individual's education on the status of his first job and present job. Blau and Duncan also examined intergenerational mobility (or the impact of social origin) by considering the impacts of fathers' education and occupational status. In short, rather than asking about how much occupational mobility was occurring, they tried to identify the major determinants of an individual's position in the occupational structure. "How is occupational status attained?" became the central question for researchers in both the United States and Canada. Blau and Duncan had used national survey data for their study; the first Canadian studies had to rely on surveys of individual cities or regions of the country. However, in 1973 a nation-wide Canadian Mobility Study was undertaken. Information on work and education was collected from a random sample of 44,000 Canadian households, providing the data necessary to replicate the ground-breaking Blau and Duncan study in Canada.[36]

The Canadian Mobility Study data plainly document how higher education translates into a higher-status occupation. The relationship between an individual's education and his or her current occupation is the strongest of all the relationships examined using the standard status attainment model outlined above. Taken alone, this finding lends support to the human capital model — investments in education translate into better jobs.[37] However, the intergenerational component of the status attainment model yields clear evidence of considerable status inheritance. Although these relationships are not as strong as those between an individual's own education and current occupation, we find that the higher the education of the parent, the higher the education of the child. Equally important, the higher the occupational status of the parent, the more education the child is likely to get and the higher the occupational status of the child's first and present jobs. Thus, while status attainment studies are supportive of the emphasis on education in the human capital model, they also highlight inequality in occupational opportunity through their demonstration of status inheritance.

Status attainment studies do not show us precisely *how* social origin affects labour market opportunities. We must look elsewhere in the sociological literature for insights. Obviously, wealthier parents can afford more (and better) education for their children. Having more education themselves and being situated higher in the occupational hierarchy, they may also be able to provide more information about the operations of the labour market. Moreover, family social networks and "contacts" may lead to better jobs.[38] In addition, they will have a substantial influence on the aspirations of their children, especially by providing a home environment in which education is encouraged and valued. In fact, some status attainment researchers have begun their research with younger subjects, collecting information on family background, academic performance, self-concept, and career aspirations in order to map out more clearly how status attainment occurs.[39]

Differences by Gender and Immigrant Status

These are but a few of the general observations made by students of status attainment in Canada. However, the research literature also contains more focused studies, including comparisons of the mobility opportunities of women and men, different ethnic groups, immigrants and those born in Canada, and also different generations of Canadians.[40] Researchers have noted that Canadian women working full-time are, on average, located in slightly higher-status jobs than are full-time male workers. Given what we know about restricted work opportunities for women, this seems to be a contradictory finding. However, it begins to make more sense when we realize that part-time workers (a majority of whom are women) are excluded from the comparison, and when we remember that some of the white-collar clerical jobs held by women may have an artificially high occupational status score.[41] Furthermore, women typically experience little intragenerational mobility. On average, Canadian men move up about five points on the Blishen and McRoberts occupational status scale over the course of their careers, compared to less than two points for women. Women who enter the paid labour force are more likely to be employed in occupations with limited opportunities for upward mobility. Thus, despite equivalent or higher educations, they are less able to "cash in" these credentials for jobs with career potential. Similarly, participation in a sex-segregated labour market means that the effects of social origin are less pronounced for women than for men.

Canadian researchers have also discovered few overall differences in the average occupational status scores of native-born Canadians and immigrants to the country. Once again, this challenges our assumptions about the inferior position of immigrants in the Canadian labour market. But examining the data in more detail, we find that immigrants tend to come from higher-status social backgrounds — a reflection of Canadian immigration policies over the last few

decades designed to favour well-educated and highly skilled applicants. But not all immigrants fit this description, and the less qualified
(usually from non-English-speaking countries) are much more likely
to be employed in lower-status and less rewarding jobs. Even for the
highly qualified, status attainment studies demonstrate that they are
less able than native-born Canadians to convert their higher education into high-status jobs. Licensing requirements in some professions, inadequate knowledge of the Canadian labour market, and
discrimination in hiring may all be factors responsible for such
differences.[42]

In summary, we have found some support for the human capital
model by identifying the central role education plays in determining
one's occupational status. However, this must be weighed against
evidence of considerable status inheritance, which suggests that, to
some degree, the issue of who gets the good jobs is class-based rather
than an outcome of a meritocratic labour market. By further examining the status attainment processes, we learned that the Canadian
labour market is not equally open to all labour force participants.
Some groups of workers are less able to "cash in" their education and
training for higher status and higher incomes. Stated differently,
there may be more than one labour market in operation, a possibility
not considered by the human capital model. Access to the preferred
jobs may, as we shall see shortly, depend not so much on skill, training,
and effort, as upon a range of other factors.

"Deskilling" and the Future of Status Attainment

As we have seen, opportunities for occupational mobility have increased in past generations because of major structural changes in
industrial capitalist societies. We also know that our industrial and
occupational structures are continuing to evolve. Can we, consequently, expect further changes in mobility patterns and opportunities?

In a provocative book, *Labor and Monopoly Capital: The Degradation
of Work in the Twentieth Century*, Harry Braverman argued that modern
capitalism was different from the mode of production Marx had
examined.[43] A relatively small number of huge, powerful corporations now controlled the national and international economies. The
role of the state in the productive process had expanded, new
technologies had evolved, workplace bureaucracies had spread, and
the labour process itself had become increasingly rationalized.
Braverman's analysis of the transformation of clerical work raises
interesting questions about social mobility prospects. He pointed out
how, in the past, clerical work had involved fairly high-status and
responsible jobs. Turn-of-the-century male clerks and bookkeepers

had been able to exercise considerable control over their work, and had been responsible for a wide variety of tasks. But this was no longer the case. What the feminization of the occupation masked was how an extensive division of labour in offices had narrowed the scope of the work done by any one clerk. Office work had been standardized and mechanized. Clerks essentially processed an endless stream of paper on a white-collar assembly line, their routine tasks devoid of much mental activity. In short, clerical work had been *deskilled* and degraded.

Braverman attributed these changes to management strategies designed to improve efficiency and gain more control over the office labour process. Thus, office workers had experienced the same "degradation of work" highly skilled craft workers had experienced in the nineteenth century when factory-based production was expanding. Many of the management principles introduced to the factory were now also in operation within private sector and government bureaucracies. In Braverman's opinion, these very same trends would soon affect the working conditions of many technicians, professionals, and middle-level managers. In other words, both low- and higher-status white-collar workers were descending into the same "working class."

As we shall see in Chapter 4, Braverman's thesis has been the target of many critics. With respect to his deskilling argument, critics claim that he generalized from scattered evidence in North America (where there indeed may be evidence of such a trend) to assert that this was a universal pattern in all capitalist societies. Important cultural differences in the labour process were consequently ignored. Furthermore, within societies, widespread deskilling was assumed rather than empirically demonstrated. Thus, Braverman ignored situations in which automation, work reorganization, and employee relations policies provide more autonomy and responsibility to workers. In short, creating deskilled and regimented work is sometimes the least effective means for management to gain employee cooperation and loyalty. Other critics have argued that Braverman had a conspiratorial image of managers (e.g., always looking for ways of exerting greater control) and that he therefore portrayed workers as largely helpless victims.[44]

The reason we have introduced Braverman and the deskilling debate within a discussion of social mobility and status attainment research is this: if Braverman is correct (and to some degree he is) real upward occupational mobility or status attainment may be substantially reduced. For example, a white-collar job in a bank or a store might still be assigned a higher status score, but in reality this status may be of little substance, given that both intrinsic and extrinsic job rewards are minimal.[45] As for middle-level technical, managerial, and professional jobs, they may still provide more material rewards and greater job security, but they may no longer involve as much diversity in tasks, or provide as many intrinsic satisfactions. In a way, Braverman was arguing that some of the middle rungs of the occupational ladder were weakening — an occupational hierarchy with distinct gradations was being squeezed in the middle to create a two-class, more polarized society.

LABOUR MARKET SEGMENTATION

Labour market segmentation researchers begin with the proposition that there is not a single, open labour market operating in our society. Instead, better and worse jobs tend to be found in different settings and are usually obtained in different ways. Certain types of labour force participants (women and visible minorities, for example) are concentrated in the poor jobs. Segmentation theories also highlight the slim chances of mobility out of the *secondary* labour market into jobs in the *primary* labour market. This is a key proposition, since the human capital model does not deny that some jobs are much better than others. It simply explains that those individuals with the most ability and effort, and with the largest investments in education and training, will be able to obtain the more demanding and rewarding jobs. However, the segmentation perspective highlights the substantial structural barriers that inhibit the free flow of many qualified individuals into the primary labour market. In fact, the persistent over-representation of women and minority groups in lower-status jobs originally led researchers to question the human capital model and to develop the segmentation perspective as an alternative.[46]

There are actually several labour market segmentation perspectives. They share the basic propositions listed above, but differ in their explanations of the origins of segmentation, and in the breadth of their analyses. The broader approach has evolved out of the work of Marxist scholars tracing the growth of dual economic sectors in industrial capitalist societies. Beginning with this type of structural analysis, they have gone on to study the different work experiences and work rewards in *core* and *periphery* sectors of the economy. The more narrow approach has grown out of studies of labour market dynamics within firms or government bureaucracies, and out of examinations of tactics used by various occupational groups to restrict entry into their midst. We will label the two approaches the *dual economy* and *internal labour market* perspectives, respectively.

Since these approaches focus on distinct divisions within the working class, these researchers also differ from Braverman and other Marxists who assume a large and homogeneous working class. In fact, some of the dual economy theorists have argued that the resilience of the capitalist mode of production results largely from the political impotence of a working class divided into distinct segments.[47] Rather than rejecting one or the other of these perspectives, we must recognize that they are asking somewhat different questions. Labour market segmentation researchers have placed much less emphasis on the broad implications of deskilling, focusing instead on material rewards, career opportunities, and job security.

Dual Economies

The dual economy model assumes that an earlier era of competitive capitalism has been succeeded in the twentieth century by an age of monopoly capitalism.[48] As industrial capitalist societies have matured, we have seen a few large and powerful firms come to dominate automobile manufacturing, the oil and mining industries, and the computer industry, for example. Similarly, the finance sector has come to be controlled by a handful of large banks, trust companies, and insurance companies. While not technically a monopoly situation (*oligopoly* would be more accurate), there is little doubt that in our economy key sectors are controlled by a small number of corporations. Limited in number, they can exert considerable control over suppliers and markets; and because of their size and power, they can manipulate their political environment. Examples of the power of these firms are easy to find, and would include recent incidents in which automobile manufacturers have been able to limit foreign imports and in which oil companies have influenced government policies.

Dual economy theorists go on to portray a parallel periphery sector comprised of diverse minor industries. Here we discover numerous smaller enterprises. Because they have less control over their environments, and because they face generally more intense competition, they typically have a much greater chance of failure. Many service sector businesses would be situated here, as would some firms in the retail and light manufacturing sectors. Such enterprises are typically less profitable since they cannot control their markets and suppliers, have low capital investments, and are generally more labour intensive. Compared to the core sector firms, these enterprises do not require the same degree of skill, education, and commitment from employees. Indeed, replaceable unskilled or semiskilled employees are often ideal.

Segmented Labour Markets

What can these industrial sector comparisons tell us about labour market processes? Briefly, the segmentation model proposes that the core sector contains the primary labour market with its better jobs, while the periphery sector is where we find the secondary labour markets. Capital-intensive core enterprises, by definition, require fewer workers to equal or exceed the productivity of more labour-intensive firms, although they frequently require more highly trained and educated workers. The large and bureaucratic nature of these enterprises means that there are generally good opportunities for upward mobility within the organization. The workers in these types of enterprises tend to be well paid, generally have good benefit packages, and enjoy a higher degree of job security. Because of these material advantages, they are in a better financial position when they retire.[49] They may also be managed in less authoritarian ways, a topic to which we return in the next chapter.

These are obviously very broad generalizations, leading a number of writers to distinguish between the *independent* and *subordinate* levels of employment within the primary labour market.[50] The subordinate tier contains primarily blue-collar, unionized industrial workers. The independent primary tier consists of a variety of managerial, professional, and craft workers whose jobs typically involve more general skills, higher educational credentials, and more individual control over work itself. In comparison to the secondary labour market, both of these tiers would contain good jobs, but the chances for career development and the possibility of higher incomes would be greater in the independent primary labour market. There is also merit in distinguishing, as some researchers do, the public or *state* sector — employment within the various levels of government — from the core and periphery sectors of the economy. The working conditions and work rewards within government bureaucracies are, however, often equivalent to those in the independent primary labour market.[51]

But why would core sector employers be willing to pay more than the going rates in the secondary labour market? Part of the answer lies in the collective strength of unions and professional associations, which have been much more active in the primary sector. As well, labour market segmentation theorists have argued that it would be too costly for core sector firms not to pay well. These enterprises have large capital investments and so would wish to avoid costly shutdowns due to labour disputes. High levels of labour turnover could lead to expensive retraining programs. Hence it is rational behaviour to offer job security (negotiated with a union, if necessary), provide generous wage and benefit packages, and attempt to improve working conditions. Besides, high profit margins make it relatively painless; these employers can afford to pay more, and would prefer to do so in order to maintain a stable, well-trained, and committed work force.[52]

In the peripheral sectors, in contrast, employers rarely provide high wages, extensive benefits, and long-term job security. Here, smaller profit margins, intense competition, difficulties in imposing increased labour costs on customers, and greater vulnerability to economic cycles place downward pressure on wages. In addition, labour turnover is less problematic for periphery sector employers. Low skill requirements and little on-the-job training make workers easily replaceable. Hence, low-paying jobs are common and labour turnover is high which, in turn, makes union organizing more difficult. The term *job ghettos* has frequently been used to describe work in such labour markets. Job insecurity, higher chances of unemployment, and irregular career earning patterns are a fact of life in secondary labour markets.[53]

Internal Labour Markets

In addition, there are fewer chances for career mobility within firms located in the periphery.[54] For example, an individual working in a carwash or as a mechanic in a small automobile repair shop seldom has promotion prospects simply because an elaborate bureaucratic hierarchy with career channels is absent. An employee of IBM or Shell Canada, however, does have such mobility opportunities. In contrast to the "dead-end" jobs of secondary labour markets, large corporations and government departments have well-developed internal training systems and career routes. These are called *internal labour markets*.

Researchers who focus on internal labour markets have side-stepped larger questions about the changing nature of capitalism and about dual economies, concentrating instead on restricted labour markets within firms or government bureaucracies. A central focus has been on *ports of entry*, which limit entry into bureaucratic work organizations; *mobility chains* (or career ladders), through which employees can pass; and *training systems* and *seniority rules*, which govern movement through the ranks.[55] In essence, the internal labour market concept elaborates in an interesting way Weber's theory of bureaucracy. The approach has also been used to study the manner in which craft unions or professional associations restrict membership in order to limit competition and to improve job security for their members.[56]

There is obviously some overlap between this internal labour market type of analysis and the broader dual economy perspective. Researchers have, on occasion, assumed that all core sector firms contain extensive and restricted internal labour markets. However, it is becoming more apparent that important exceptions exist. For example, many major corporations have elaborate career ladders, but these are open to only some of their employees. Clerical workers (usually women) are the group most often restricted from moving up through the bureaucratic ranks. Research has demonstrated that women are more likely to be found in jobs with short career ladders.[57]

Barriers to Primary Labour Market Entry

Returning to our original proposition that structural barriers restrict movement of potentially qualified individuals out of the secondary labour market,[58] we can now see how internal labour markets contribute to this process. Generally, there are only a limited number of positions in such systems, and entry is restricted to those with the proper credentials — a degree, a union card, or membership in a professional association. Often, superior credentials (an MBA from a prestigious university, for example) will further improve one's chances of getting into the system and moving through it.[59]

Information about vacancies within the primary labour market is not always widely distributed. In some cases, it may only be passed on through small and informal networks. Since research shows that at least one-half of all job-holders find their jobs through personal referrals, it is clear that access to information is extremely important.[60] Without "contacts" within the primary labour market, qualified applicants might never be aware of the job opening. Other examples would include the internal posting of government jobs, or the advertising of job openings only in union publications. If we were examining a situation in which access to credentials and information was tied to skill and ability, or in which access was simply randomly distributed, there would be little more to say. However, we have already discussed several research literatures that show how access to educational credentials is restricted and how status and power can be inherited. In brief, some groups of Canadian workers have better chances of gaining access to the advantages of primary labour markets.

Other barriers, such as employer discrimination in hiring, can block movement into primary labour markets. Direct discrimination may take the form of male employers or managers deciding that a female applicant does not have the personality necessary for the job or the career commitment that the corporation demands. Similar stereotypes can handicap women already inside a corporation or government department when they apply for promotions into better jobs. (We will address this issue more fully in Chapter 5.)

Discrimination may also surface when middle-aged workers, laid off in a plant shutdown and now applying for a core sector job, are rejected in favour of younger applicants. At a certain point in one's career, employers begin to view seniority and experience as negative assets. On the other hand, youth attempting to find their first permanent job may face *age discrimination* of the opposite sort. Finding employment in the part-time service sector is generally less difficult than gaining an interview for a full-time career position in a major corporation or a government department, even if one has the educational qualifications. "Lack of experience" is a term frequently heard by unsuccessful young job applicants.[61]

Recent Canadian research also shows that visible minorities continue to be excluded from employment opportunities. A 1984 study in Toronto compared the experiences of black and white subjects, with equivalent qualifications, applying in person for the same job. Blacks obtained fewer interviews or job offers. Instead, they were frequently told the advertised position was filled even though, in some cases, a white member of the research team was offered the job only minutes later. Some form of preference for white applicants took place in about 25 percent of the roughly 200 job openings tested. In another part of the same study, subjects with names and accents identifying them as members of non-white or immigrant groups telephoned for job interviews. Out of a total of 237 advertised positions tested, Indo-Pakistani subjects were told the job was no longer available 44 percent of the time, compared to 36 percent for black West Indians, 31 percent for white immigrant subjects, but only 13 percent for white non-immigrant subjects. In total, over one-half of the employers telephoned appeared to be practising some form of discrimination.[62]

It is noteworthy that many of the employers investigated in this study operated in the secondary labour market. Visible minorities and recent immigrants are often excluded from even low-status jobs. This may lead to high concentrations of these groups in a limited number of occupations — taxi drivers, janitors, parking lot attendants, security guards, or work in ethnic restaurants are obvious examples. In an earlier era, Canada actually had laws limiting the occupations in which some racial and ethnic groups could be employed. Peter Li has described how, in the early part of this century, Chinese immigrants in western Canada had no option but to work in an "ethnic business enclave." Because of widespread antagonism directed toward Chinese workers, jobs in Chinese restaurants were often the only work available.[63] Today, discrimination is less institutionalized and blatant, but the evidence cited above demonstrates it has not disappeared. Together with other barriers to equality of occupational opportunity, it is a source of labour market segmentation and one of the explanations of why some minority groups are overrepresented in marginal jobs.[64]

Barriers to mobility out of the secondary labour market may also be more subtle. For some individuals, a history of employment in the peripheral sector may itself act as a barrier. In some regions of Canada, the prevalence of seasonal work means that many people are forced into an annual cycle consisting of short-term jobs, unemployment insurance, and welfare assistance. Hence, a work record showing frequent layoffs or job changes may simply be reflecting the nature of the labour market. But it could also be interpreted as an indication of unstable work habits, locking an individual into a "bad job syndrome." [65] Thus, geography itself can limit one's work opportunities. A highly motivated and skilled individual living in rural New Brunswick or in northern British Columbia is clearly at a disadvantage. We have already suggested this in our earlier discussion of the occupational structure of single industry communities. There are simply fewer good jobs available outside of the metropolitan heartland of the country. In addition, residents of the outlying areas are less likely to have obtained the credentials necessary for participation in the primary labour markets.

A research team in Atlantic Canada has spent a number of years examining that region's employment opportunities. They argue that the high level of poverty and unemployment in the Maritimes simply cannot be explained with reference to inadequate education, training, or effort on the part of local residents. A "casualty" model of poverty does not fit the facts, while an explanation that focuses on the nature of the local labour market is much more useful. [66] In short, many Maritimers have spent their working lives in a *marginal work world* where low pay, few career opportunities, and little job security are a way of life. These researchers conclude, as do many other labour market segmentation analysts, that participants in the secondary labour market are trapped "in a succession of low wage, dead end jobs interspersed with spells of unemployment." [67]

The Changing Nature of Labour Market Segmentation

The appeal of the dual economy perspective lies in its account of labour market inequality against a backdrop of larger questions about the changing nature of class structure and conflict. One of the more important contributions to this literature is *Segmented Work, Divided Workers* by David Gordon and his colleagues. [68] In their detailed historical analysis of the rise of industrial capitalism in the United States, they document the development of dual economies and segmented labour markets. Their central thesis is that a consequence of labour market segmentation has been a dividing of the working class and a reduction of class conflict. Segmentation has meant that some workers have been "bought off" at the expense of others. In fact, the more advantaged workers may even see those in the secondary labour markets as competitors rather than as allies in a class struggle. Thus internal class divisions and inequalities have diminished the potential for collective action. This conclusion is at odds with Braverman's thesis that deskilling has produced one large, homogeneous working class, with considerable potential for militant class action.

Questions about class militancy and political action among Canadian workers will be taken up in Chapter 8. For now, let us concentrate on the development of industrial capitalism in the United States. Gordon, Edwards, and Reich separate the last century of American history into three major epochs, beginning with a period of *initial proletarianization* from about 1820 to 1890. During this time, wage labour was on the increase in the United States, and a large, relatively homogeneous industrial working class was emerging. While modern forms of capitalist management were still in their infancy, craft workers were beginning to lose control over the labour process. However, this trend did not develop fully until the era of *homogenization of labour,* which covered the end of the nineteenth century up until the Second World War. This period saw extensive deskilling of labour and mechanization, the growth of large workplaces, and the rise of a new managerial class within American capitalism. The period following World War II has been one of *segmentation of labour* in which distinct primary and secondary labour markets have developed.

Canada, as we have already seen, began to industrialize later and has always remained more of a resource-based economy. Thus we cannot assume that the same three stages describe our history, although our discussions of the Canadian industrialization experience do reveal some similarities.[69] However, the emphasis on *change* in this overview encourages us to ask the next logical question: Are further changes in labour market segmentation occurring today? The answer may be "yes" since, in the last few years, we have begun to see signs of a "disappearing middle class" in North America. If we take the term "middle class" to mean those in the relatively well-paying and secure white- and blue-collar jobs, we may be witnessing a shrinking of the primary labour market.

The industrial and occupational structures of both Canada and the United States have experienced dramatic alterations in the past decade. Factory closures due to increased competition from overseas and the movement of corporate activities to low-wage countries have led to what Barry Bluestone and Bennett Harrison have labelled the "deindustrialization of America."[70] The introduction of computers and robots has allowed other industries to maintain production levels with fewer employees. A similar situation has developed in Canada's resource industries where technological innovations have led to substantial layoffs.[71] And the last few years have also seen major layoffs in the public sector as governments have tried to cut deficits by "downsizing" their bureaucracies.

A consequence of all of these trends has been increased unemployment, but, contrary to common   stereotypes of the unemployed, frequently among previously advantaged middle-class workers. A recent *Globe and Mail* article stated that "the middle class is under pressure and losing ground as the rich get richer and the poor get more numerous."[72] This is not simply a problem of a short-term economic downturn. What we appear to be experiencing are fundamental realignments in industrial and occupational structures across North America. As we saw in Chapter 2, most new employment is generated in the service sector, characterized by a prevalence of part-time and low-paying work. Thus, even if unemployment rates do drop significantly, our occupational structure will have been altered. Some of the well-paying, middle-level jobs may be gone for good — a loss, as we said above, that basically reflects a shrinking primary labour market.

LABOUR MARKET SEGMENTATION OR THE HUMAN CAPITAL MODEL?

Labour market segmentation theories have not escaped criticism.[73] Researchers in this tradition have often assumed the existence of primary labour markets within core sector establishments, without actually demonstrating this one-to-one relationship. There is disagreement about the most appropriate unit of analysis: Should researchers concentrate on comparing industrial sectors, occupational groups, corporate enterprises, or individual local establishments? There are ongoing debates about the boundaries between core and periphery economic sectors. While researchers have extensively studied the differences between jobs in the various labour markets,[74] there has been less work documenting the exact nature of barriers between labour markets and the processes by which women and visible minorities are initially "sorted" into less rewarding jobs. The political consequences of segmentation, and the degree to which the labour movement has influenced the history of segmentation are just beginning to appear on research agendas. Similarly, we have only recently begun to see studies of cross-cultural differences in internal labour markets.[75] But despite these criticisms and research gaps, it is clear that this approach helps explain stable patterns of inequality in the workplace.

The labour market segmentation model offers a stronger explanation of the distribution of better jobs than does the rival human capital model. The human capital model cannot adequately account for the many examples of qualified and highly motivated individuals working in low-status and unrewarding jobs. The segmentation approach, however, distinguishes between primary and secondary labour markets, and demonstrates the variety of ways in which access to the former is frequently denied. The segmentation model also allows us to make more sense of status attainment research results showing limited career mobility for women, and for non-native-born labour force participants. For a variety of reasons, these groups are over-represented in the secondary labour market where career mobility opportunities are very limited. The emphasis on internal labour markets within this literature adds to our understanding of work and careers by drawing on our knowledge of bureaucratic work organizations. Finally, the dual economy emphasis in segmentation research provides an additional attraction. With it, we are able to account for the origins of the different labour markets by referring to the changing nature of industrial capitalism. This, in turn, provides us with a fuller understanding of the implications of industrial restructuring for work and career opportunities in Canada.

NOTES

1. See Kalleberg and Berg (1987:48-49) for an elaboration of this definition.
2. See Porter (1985) who discusses the "societal context of occupational allocation."
3. See Jasso and Rossi (1979) for a study of what people consider to be a fair income, and how education, occupation, gender, and marital status influence these beliefs; Gartrell (1982) examines how comparisons to others' incomes influence perceptions of whether one is being paid fairly.
4. See Ashton (1986, especially chapter 1) on labour markets and social inequality; Hunter (1986, chapter 6) on education, occupation, and social inequality in Canada.
5. Hunter (1986:102-9) comments further on income differences across occupations in Canada; See Kalleberg and Berg (1987, chapter 4) for a discussion of income inequality as the key labour market outcome.
6. Statistics Canada, *Income Distributions by Size in Canada 1985*, Table 72, pp. 148-50.
7. In 1986, Canada's highest paid executive was Frank Stronach, chairman and chief executive officer of Magna International. He was paid $2.21 million, most of it through a profit-sharing scheme. In contrast, the highest paid U.S. executive was Chrysler Corporation chairman Lee Iacocca, who received more than $20 million in 1986, primarily through stock-options; *Financial Times* (13 April 1987): 1,11; *Globe and Mail* (18 April 1987): A7. See Hunter (1986:106) and Forcese (1986:62) for other examples of high executive incomes in Canada.
8. National Council of Welfare (1984b): 7.
9. Anisef and Baichman (1984) provide details on pay scales for specific jobs: managers in the civil service (p. 22); doctors (p. 203); accountants and lawyers (pp. 73-75); cashiers (p. 163).
10. Statistics Canada, *Charting Canadian Incomes 1951-1981*, provides national income distribution data over time.
11. Reid (1985): 165.
12. These would include statutory holidays, and employer contributions for unemployment insurance and to the Canada or Quebec Pension Plans.
13. Jones (1980) and Hunter and Manley (1986) examine the relationship between occupational status and skill levels.
14. See Coburn and Edwards (1976) for an interesting analysis of these relationships,

and how they affect individuals' perceptions of their own positions in the class structure.

15. Pineo and Porter (1967) conducted the original study of occupational prestige. Blishen and McRoberts (1976) provide the most recent socio-economic index for occupations.

16. Boyd (1986) demonstrates the biases created in the original scale due to the use of only male census information, and develops an improved scale based on both female and male data.

17. Pineo et al. (1977).

18. Jones (1980:181) reports a correlation of .80 between the Blishen scores and this alternative classification system, which means that occupations that would appear in the higher categories would typically also receive higher Blishen scores. See Pineo et al. (1977:98) and Hunter and Manley (1986:64) for more detailed comparisons of the two systems.

19. See Stewart, Prandy, and Blackburn (1980), especially chapters 1 and 2.

20. Becker (1964) is generally credited for having developed this theory, although its basic premises really underlie much of classical micro-economics; see Thurow (1975) for a cogent critique of these premises. Denton and Hunter (1982) summarize the model, and test its explanation of gender discrimination; Hunter (1986, chapter 6) and Ornstein (1983b) also discuss the relevance of the human capital model to the Canadian labour market. The human capital model, as we describe it here, also has many similarities to the functionalist theory of stratification (Davis and Moore, 1945); see Hunter (1986, chapter 2) for a good review and critique of the functionalist position.

21. See Thurow (1975) for an economist's critique of conventional "marginal productivity" explanations of income and wealth; chapter 6 examines the origins of huge fortunes.

22. Hunter (1986:107-8) comments on the "luck" argument.

23. Chen and Regan (1985:39-62) present a useful overview of this literature which they separate into the "fortuitous, rational decision making, and socio-cultural influences" approaches.

24. Porter et al. (1982): 8.

25. *Ibid.*, 311-19; see also *Does Money Matter?*, an earlier report on this study by Porter et al. (1979).

26. Porter et al. (1982): 114. See Breton (1972) for a national study, and Brinkerhoff and Corry (1976) for a study of Calgary high-school students, that reaches similar conclusions.

27. Anisef et al. (1980).

28. Porter et al. (1982) on lower educational aspirations (p. 56), lower occupational aspirations (p. 215), lower aspirations on the part of parents (p. 224), and the double jeopardy of social class and sex (p. 213); Anisef et al. (1980) on gender being more important than class (p. *xxix*) and on wage differences by sex (p. *xxxii*).

29. Porter et al. (1982): 67; Anisef et al. (1980): *xxiv*.

30. See Thurow (1975, chapters 4 and 5) on the demand side of job competition.

31. Marx and Engels (1962, vol. 1): 247.

32. Hunter (1986:161) uses the term "social inheritance" in a useful discussion of "social background and social inequality."

33. Lipset and Bendix (1959): 12.

34. See Matras (1980) and Tyree et al. (1979) for examples of multi-society comparative research of this type; Kerckhoff et al. (1985) return to the question of whether the U.S. or Britain allows more mobility and conclude, again, that there are few differences.

35. Blau and Duncan (1967). Goyder (1984) presents a useful discussion of changes in method and emphasis in mobility studies.

36. See Pineo (1981) and Boyd et al. (1985, chapter 1) for discussions of the 1973 Mobility Study, which was "piggy-backed" on one of the monthly Labour Force Surveys run by Statistics Canada. Earlier Canadian status attainment studies include Cuneo and Curtis (1975) and Turrittin (1974).

37. Knottnerus (1987) discusses the "image of society" underlying status attainment research, suggesting that it is, in fact, congruent with human capital and structural-functionalist theories of stratification; see also Horan (1978), Campbell (1983), and Goyder (1984): 336-38.

38. Although it is a very different type of study, Wallace Clement's (1975) examination of *The Canadian Corporate Elite* documents how the children of the wealthy and powerful frequently inherit similar positions in the social hierarchy. John Porter's earlier study, *The Vertical Mosaic* (1965), tells the same story.

39. See Looker and Pineo (1983) for a Canadian example of status attainment research based on this "Wisconsin model" with its emphasis on social-psychological variables. Status attainment researchers have also looked at the effects of education and social origin on current income. Ornstein (1983b), for example, examines Canadian workers' incomes, but carries the analysis further by demonstrating that social class position and gender have substantial additional effects.

40. See Boyd et al. (1985) for a collection of many of these studies.

41. Refer to the earlier discussion in this chapter of the construction of occupational status scores.

42. See Boyd et al., (1981:659-61) for a more detailed discussion of these gender and immigration status comparisons, as well as similar discussions of French-English and ethnic group differences in status attainment processes.

43. Braverman (1974).

44. See Zimbalist (1979), Wood (1982, 1987), Littler (1982), Littler and Salaman (1982), Penn and Scattergood (1985), Heron and Storey (1986a), and Lowe (1987) for contributions to the deskilling debate, which is well summarized by Thompson (1983, chapter 4). Many of the contributions to this debate are British; for empirical evidence on the U.S., see Spenner (1983) and Wallace and Kalleberg (1982).

45. See Boyd et al. (1985:6) for a short discussion of this argument.

46. See Bluestone et al. (1973), Hirsch (1980), Kreckel (1980), Clairmont et al. (1983), and Clairmont and Apostle (1986) for a variety of discussions of segmentation theory.

47. Edwards (1979); Gordon et al. (1982).

48. Averitt (1968); Edwards (1979); Hodson and Kaufman (1982); Gordon et al. (1982).

49. Leon (1985) examines the effect of labour market segmentation on retirement incomes and concludes that the segmentation model can better account for differences in retirement income than can the human capital model.

50. Piore (1975); Edwards (1979).

51. O'Connor (1973) and Hodson (1978) distinguish a third "state" sector; Boyd and

Humphreys (1979) and Denton and Hunter (1982) have separated public sector employment in their Canadian studies.

52. It is obviously difficult to obtain data proving that these are the motivations of those who control core sector industries. One recent study has demonstrated that core sector industries are "strike prone" while peripheral sector industries are "quit prone" (Cornfield 1985), which suggests that the greater presence of unions in the core sector is clearly an important factor in explaining wage, benefit, and job security differences.

53. Parker (1981). See Ashton (1986) for an informative discussion of segmented labour markets and unemployment.

54. See Wanner and Lewis (1983) for evidence supportive of this proposition.

55. Piore (1975), Spilerman (1977), Grandjean (1981), Smith (1983), Osterman (1984), Wholey (1985), and Jacoby (1985) are examples of this type of research.

56. See Althauser and Kalleberg (1981) who distinguish between "firm" and "occupational" internal labour markets; Ashton (1986, chapter 3) also discusses labour market shelters.

57. Bielby and Baron (1986). See also our earlier discussion of status attainment research.

58. D'Amico and Brown (1982), Tolbert (1982), and Jacobs (1983) have tested this proposition.

59. See Useem and Karabel (1986) for a detailed analysis of how an upper-class background and a degree from the "right" school can create "pathways to top corporate management."

60. Anderson and Calzavara (1986): 318.

61. Tanner et al. (1984): 28; Johnson (1986).

62. Henry and Ginzberg (1985).

63. Li (1982). See also Avery (1979) and Sunahara (1981) on the treatment of immigrant groups and visible minorities in Canada's past.

64. For additional discussion of racial and ethnic inequality in Canada, see Porter (1965, chapter 3), Hunter (1986, chapter 8), and Chen and Regan (1985): 149-61.

65. See Butler (1980) for a useful discussion of how work-welfare job histories can be a consequence of the local labour market.

66. Clairmont et al. (1980): 285.

67. Osberg et al. (1981): 388; see Clairmont et al. (1983), Clairmont and Apostle (1986), and Apostle et al. (1985, 1986) for additional discussions of the Marginal Work World research project.

68. Gordon et al. (1982). For an extensive critique, see Nolan and Edwards (1984).

69. See Heron and Storey (1986b) for an application of a modified version of this model to Canada.

70. Bluestone and Harrison (1982). See Grayson (1985) for a similar discussion of the Canadian situation, and Hill and Negrey (1987) for a more recent assessment of the northern U.S. economy.

71. Clement's (1981) case study of technological change at Inco documented the beginning of a trend in the Canadian mining industry, which still continues.

72. Steed (1986). See Kuttner (1983), Finn (1983), and Blackburn and Bloom (1985) on the "decline of the middle class." Levy (1987) uses data on the distribution of family income in the United States to argue that there has not been a major shift,

but suggests that the growth of two-earner families has offset the polarization effect.

73. See Hirsch (1980), Kaufman et al. (1981), Osberg et al. (1981), Zucker and Rosenstein (1981), Hodson and Kaufman (1982), and Clairmont et al. (1983) for some of these criticisms.

74. The largest body of research has focused on income differences. See Boyd and Humphreys (1979), Ornstein (1983b), and Apostle et al. (1985) for Canadian examples.

75. See Form (1985) on the political consequences of labour market segmentation, and Loveridge (1983) on "sources of diversity in internal labour markets."

4

Work Organizations

INTRODUCTION

We live in an organizational society.[1] Large bureaucratic organizations touch all aspects of our daily lives. Attending school, buying a hamburger at McDonalds, negotiating a student loan, or watching your favourite TV program — all these activities bring us into contact with formal organizations. Even more important, at least from the perspective of industrial sociologists, are the organizations in which people work. In this chapter, we examine work organizations, sampling selectively from an enormous literature on the sociology of organizations.

Work organizations are far from uniform, varying in size, function, and structure. And an individual's perceptions of a work organization will also differ, depending on his or her vantage point within it. While a manager or executive may assess a particular work organization in terms of efficiency or profitability, other employees may use totally different criteria. Given these variations in the objective and subjective features of work organizations, a number of interrelated questions can be asked.

First, what are the major factors that determine the structure — that is, the patterned regularities — of work organizations? Second, how are organizations transformed over time? To what degree is organizational change a response to a changing external environment? Third, how do power and conflict affect the processes of change and stability in organizations? And finally, how much do the actions and beliefs of managers, subordinate employees, and other groups such as clients influence the form, goals, and internal dynamics of an organization?

Managers have played a key role in constructing modern organizations, mainly because they make critical decisions about goals, structure, personnel, and technology. We therefore will examine various "schools" of management, as well as a new critical perspective on management found in the "labour process" literature. Our discussions of bureaucracy, the division of labour, managerial authority,

98

work groups, and the informal side of organizations also raise issues about possibilities for reforming work organizations. But that topic must await the concluding chapter.

WHAT'S WRONG WITH BUREAUCRACY?

As we saw in Chapter 1, a major step along the road to industrialization was the subdivision of craft work into simpler components. Each of these narrow tasks could then be performed more cheaply by unskilled labourers. But once all the parts of a craft worker's job had been simplified and reassigned to less skilled workers, coordinating and integrating these tasks became a problem. This helps to account for the importance of managers, who, since the late nineteenth century, have become central actors in most work organizations. Questions about how best to integrate and coordinate the activities of large numbers of workers within a single enterprise gave rise to early theories of management.

The organizational structure adopted by nineteenth-century businessmen was the *bureaucratic hierarchy*. As we have already seen, Max Weber considered bureaucracy to be the organizational form best able to efficiently coordinate and integrate the multitude of specialized tasks conducted in a large factory or office. Without bureaucracy, he predicted, "capitalist production could not continue."[2] Although he described the general features of bureaucracy, Weber did not intend to present a practical guide for managers on "how to organize." Nevertheless, his description has become the model for a highly mechanistic type of organization. Gareth Morgan defines bureaucratic organizations as those "that emphasize precision, speed, clarity, reliability, and efficiency achieved through the creation of a fixed division of tasks, hierarchical supervision, and detailed rules and regulations."[3]

No doubt bureaucracies were an improvement over the tradition-bound "seat of the pants" methods of running most nineteenth-century businesses. Their predictability greatly increased the productivity of industrial capitalism. Furthermore, a bureaucracy is a system of authority. Its hierarchical structure, formal lines of authority, and impartial rules and regulations are designed to elicit cooperation and obedience from employees. And given that bureaucracies have a highly specialized division of labour, which can also lead to increased productivity, it would seem that bureaucratic work organizations are, in fact, the ideal.

But most sociologists would agree that bureaucracies have serious flaws. Organizational researchers have amassed considerable evidence showing that bureaucracies are often overly complex and difficult to manage, resistant to change, and unable to cope with uncertainties. Working conditions within bureaucracies are frequently dissatisfying.[4] In many respects, large bureaucracies are like dinosaurs: huge, cumbersome, slow to respond and adapt, and, some critics would predict, a dying breed. The turbulent economic environment of recent years has led even the most vocal champions of bureaucracy to search for better ways to manage organizations. For example, popular management books such as *In Search of Excellence* document how rigid, inflexible organizations are less able to survive, let alone grow and profit, in today's rapidly changing economy.[5]

One of the paradoxes of bureaucracy is that, far from achieving machinelike efficiency, it often unintentionally creates inefficiencies, a problem Weber largely overlooked.[6] This point is underlined in many of the classic studies of bureaucracy. For example, Robert Merton described how employees who slavishly obey the rules can undermine the efficiency of a bureaucracy.[7] The rules become ends in themselves, rather than means of achieving organizational goals. Officials acquire a *bureaucratic personality*, compulsively following procedural manuals to the last detail. Similarly, Peter Blau's field work in U.S. government agencies revealed how workers behaved according to their own unofficial rules.[8] In doing so, they were directly responding to organizational pressure to attain certain goals, such as handling a quota of clients or cases in a given period. Blau identified the tension between the official rules of the bureaucracy and workers' counter-rules. By striving to make their jobs easier, employees often erode bureaucratic efficiency.

A final example is Alvin Gouldner's classic study of an American gypsum plant.[9] It is inaccurate to assume, asserts Gouldner, that organizational life can be made as fully predictable as the bureaucratic model would suggest. Events such as promotions, layoffs, or dismissals are unpredictable. Moreover, argues Gouldner, we should remember *who* benefits from predictability; rules reducing uncertainty for management may be a major source of discontent among employees. In fact, Gouldner argues, the bureaucratization process often is implemented not for reasons of greater efficiency, but as a result of power struggles between workers and managers. In short, there is nothing inevitable about bureaucracy; rather, its many faces spring from variations in the balance of power between workers and managers within an organization.

The notion of bureaucratic efficiency rests, in part, on the assumption that employees will readily submit to managerial authority. In Weber's view, bureaucrats accept the legitimacy of the existing authority structure, abide by the rules, and obey their bosses because they believe the basis for such authority is impartial and fair. Underlying capitalist bureaucracies is a *rational-legal* value system. However, this assumption of general acceptance of goals is contradicted by the realities of employee–employer relations, which are punctuated by struggle and conflict.

In all modern industrial and service enterprises, the few command and the many obey, or at least they are expected to. Organizational goals are established by those in positions of power. These goals are therefore "rational" from management's perspective, but not necessarily from the perspective of workers; what is rational for them is what reflects their own interests — higher pay, a safer and more comfortable work environment, or more scope for making work-related decisions, for example. These goals are often in conflict with those of management. Hence conflicts over the distribution and use of decision-making power are normal.[10]

Weber's model of bureaucracy neglects employee resistance to such authority. Resistance can frequently be detected in workers' informal group norms and codes of conduct that run counter to the official systems of production. Not surprisingly, a major concern of management has been to find ways of gaining worker cooperation. Managers have gone to considerable lengths to convince workers to accept *organizational goals* as their own personal goals, and to justify their decisions to those below them. The development of management *ideology* justifying superior rewards and the right to give orders is part of this process. Bendix explains: "All economic enterprises have in common a basic social relation between the employers who exercise authority and the workers who obey, and all ideologies of management have in common the effort to interpret the exercise of authority in a favourable light."[11]

KEY ISSUES IN ORGANIZATION THEORY

Criticisms of the Weberian model of bureaucracy have developed into alternative theories of organizations. Weber's thesis that a bureaucratic structure is most appropriate for any type of capitalist economic activity has been largely replaced by *contingency theory*. It proposes that organizational structures and processes are contingent upon the immediate problems posed by their environment. There is, then, no one best way to organize. The basic question influencing organizational research today is: What structures and strategies does a particular organization require to survive?[12]

The many possible answers to this question are typically based on an *organic model*, which views organizations as social systems adapting to internal and external changes. This conventional view of organizations as "adapting social systems" is founded on the general sociological theory of structural functionalism.[13] Hence there is an emphasis on goal attainment, functions, structural adaptations, and a value consensus among organizational members. Conventional organization theory has been severely criticized for being too concerned with structure per se, loosing sight of the larger socio-economic, political, and historical context of which organizations are a part, ignoring the attitudes and behaviours of employees, and glossing over the realities of workplace power and conflict.[14] Nonetheless, some useful insights about organizations can be found in this empirical literature.

For example, in the 1950s Burns and Stalker studied synthetic fibre, electronics, and engineering industries and proposed a continuum of organizational forms from the mechanistic (or highly bureaucratic) to the organic. More open and flexible organizational structures and management styles were required, they concluded, in industries with rapidly changing technologies and market conditions.[15] Joan Woodward's seminal studies revealed a direct relationship between production technology, on the one hand, and structural forms and management styles, on the other. She discovered that bureaucracy and tight management controls are more appropriate in industries with mass production technology. When the work flow is varied, and production processes are non-routine and complex — as in craft or continuous process technologies — more flexible, organic structures function best.[16]

Woodward's research attests to the importance of technology as a key variable in organizational analysis. The concept of a *socio-technical system*, introduced by researchers at London's Tavistock Institute of Human Relations, takes this idea one step further. In their study of the mechanization of British coal mining, Trist and Bamforth documented how social relations within teams of miners were dependent on the technology used.[17] When the traditional hand method of mining was replaced by mechanical conveyer belts, destroying the technical basis for the work teams, the negative social-psychological consequences for workers hampered the operations of the new system. Thus, the notion of optimizing the fit between social and technical aspects of production has become an important principle in work design.

There is a tendency in this literature to *reify* organizations, that is, to discuss them as if they had a life of their own, independent of the actions and decisions of their members. Hence, we should remember that organization theory is largely about decision making. Given the constraints of technology, markets, government regulations, labour negotiations, and so on, what are the most appropriate choices for managers to make? This issue is taken up by the *strategic choice* perspective on organizations.[18] In contrast to contingency theory's emphasis on environmental and other constraints imposed on decision making, the concept of strategic choice draws our attention to the ways in which dominant groups (*coalitions*) actually choose among various strategies for structuring an organization, manipulating its environment, and establishing work standards. So to fully comp. hend the nature of work organizations, we must examine the guiding theories, actual practices, and supporting ideologies of management.

MANAGEMENT AND THE QUEST FOR CONTROL

The development of cost accounting techniques for calculating how much each factor of production — including labour — contributes to profits was one way capitalists initially tackled the problems of running increasingly large and complex enterprises. Appointing trained managers, often factory engineers, was an equally important social innovation.[19] Managers became a prominent new social group in the early twentieth century, shaping the course of economic development. As business historian Alfred D. Chandler Jr. suggests, the visible hand of the corporate manager replaced the "invisible hand" of market forces.[20] The so-called *managerial revolution* stemmed from the separation of corporate ownership from daily control functions.[21] Thus the board of directors, representing the shareholders, delegated managers the authority to operate the business profitably. In striving to meet their broad mandate, managers have transformed the organization and content of work.

In considering the evolving role of managers, it is important to distinguish between *ideology, theory,* and *practice.*[22] Management ideologies, as noted above, are used to justify existing authority relations in organizations. Joseph Smucker's research shows how Canadian managerial ideology has undergone several shifts since 1900. The self-image of managers moved away from "autonomous achieving individuals" to "organizational team workers" while the image of workers was transformed from "recalcitrants to malleable organizational components to 'associates.'"[23] A succession of theories influenced by these world views have attempted to specify "how to manage." But these theories are merely prescriptions for action. We must, then, look closely at how they are actually applied, and at the results.

One of the most vexing problems confronting management is how to obtain employee obedience and prevent opposition to authority. In this respect, the workplace is a microcosm of the larger society: maintaining orderly and harmonious social relations among unequals has always been a problem for those in power.[24] Another pressing concern involves motivating workers to achieve the quantity and quality of output considered necessary by management. Employers do not have complete control over the amount of effort expended by employees.[25] Hence, conflict often erupts over different perceptions of the "right" amount of effort for given wages and work situations.

The overriding task facing management, then, is how to create highly motivated and cooperative employees. This, according to virtually all theories of management, is the basic precondition for meeting organizational goals. But the various management theories have advocated different methods for achieving these goals. During this century, several distinct "schools" of management have appeared. The two most influential ones have been *scientific management* and *human relations.*

SCIENTIFIC MANAGEMENT

Charlie Chaplin's classic movie *Modern Times* humorously depicts the impact of scientific management on working conditions. The little comedian with the distinctive black mustache plays a harried factory worker whose job has been analyzed and redesigned by stopwatch-wielding efficiency experts. Every few seconds, Chaplin tightens a nut as another identical piece of equipment zips past on the assembly line. Chaplin is little more than an automaton whose actions are programmed by the production system. Once out on the street, he continues repeating the motions on anything that fits his two wrenches.

"Scientific management" began in the United States as a set of production methods, tools, and organizational systems designed to increase the efficiency of factory production. The term itself was coined in 1911. But this new approach to factory management and organization, popularized by an engineer named Frederick W. Taylor, had been developed by the end of the previous century.[26] Taylor and other "efficiency experts" extolled the virtues of scientific management, which soon spread across North America and, to a lesser extent, Britain and Europe. Taylor's theories were at the cutting edge of what Bryan Palmer refers to as the broad "thrust for efficiency" which contributed to the rise of twentieth-century industrial capitalism.[27] These early management consultants advocated workplace reorganization, job redesign, and tighter administrative and employee controls — all in a quest for higher efficiency and profits.

Taylor advocated the following steps for rationalizing the labour process: (1) shift the decision-making responsibility for doing a job from workers to management; (2) use scientific methods to determine the most efficient way of executing a job and redesign it accordingly; (3) provide a detailed description of how to perform each step in a job; (4) select the "best" worker to perform the job; (5) train workers to execute the job efficiently; and (6) closely monitor their performance.[28] Taylor believed his management techniques benefited all parties involved; yet their overriding effect was to give management tighter control over workers' activities by making all major work decisions. Critics argue that Taylorism degraded labour, minutely fragmenting tasks, reducing skill requirements, and eliminating workers' input into how their jobs should be done.[29]

Taylor was convinced that *worker soldiering*, or deliberate laziness, was the scourge of industry. He believed that workers consciously restricted production by keeping bosses ignorant of how fast a job could be done. In Taylor's rather alarmist language, "there could be no greater crime against humanity than this restriction of output."[30] His solution was to "scientifically" determine the "one best way" of performing a job through time-and-motion studies of each step. A base rate of pay was then tied to a production quota. If workers exceeded the quota, they received a pay bonus; lazy workers unable to achieve the quota would be forced to quit because the base rate fell below subsistence level. Thus, scientific management was founded on the assumption that workers were motivated by economic gain alone. Taylor preached that the scientific basis of a "fair day's wage" and the productivity gains through more efficient work methods would bring about a new era of industrial cooperation and harmony.

Taylor's view of human nature was coloured by his preoccupation with technical efficiency. The ideal worker, in his mind, was more like a machine than a human being. Taylor thus was a leading ideologue for early twentieth-century management, articulating its deep concerns about the *labour problem*. Industrial cooperation would only replace class conflict, he predicted, once a "complete mental revolution" had overtaken both management and labour. As Taylor wrote in a prominent Canadian business magazine just before World War I:

> The new outlook that comes to both sides under scientific management is that both sides very soon realize that if they stop pulling apart and both push together as hard as possible in the same direction, they can make that surplus [i.e., profits] so large that there is no occasion for any quarrel over its division. Labour gets an immense increase in wages, and still leaves a large share for capital.[31]

Scientific management failed to provide a successful formula for labour–management cooperation. In fact, the rhetoric of scientific objectivity was little more than an ideological justification for greater management control over labour. But in practice, its principles of job design and work organization — like job descriptions, planned work flows, detailed unit accounting, time-and-motion studies — became standard features of contemporary management.[32] Taylor's package of managerial reforms was seldom adopted completely. Yet various aspects of scientific management were introduced in many shops and factories in Canada around the turn of the century. By the 1920s these innovations were being used to overhaul large corporate and government offices.[33]

Basic principles of scientific management can still be found today in many organizations, including some in the booming service sector. For instance, Burger King attempts to maximize food sales and minimize labour costs by emphasizing sos — "speed of service."[34] This requires highly standardized work procedures and strict management controls in all Burger King outlets. Time-and-motion studies dictate how long it takes to make the fries, burgers, and drinks, exactly how workers should do these tasks, and where they should be positioned depending on the design of the kitchen.

There are few visible signs of rebelliousness against this regimented type of labour process by fast-food workers. However, the historical record contains many examples of workers resisting scientific management. Skilled industrial workers beseiged by managerial rationalizations in the early twentieth century responded by striking.[35] Auto workers were one occupational group that experienced a barrage of scientific management, along with extensive mechanization. In fact, the combination of scientific management techniques with mass production assembly-line technology created among the most alienating and stressful working conditions in modern industrial society. In many ways, Taylorism represented the practical application of bureaucratic principles within a manufacturing setting.[36] When Henry Ford introduced the moving assembly line in 1914, he was simply pushing forward via technology the logic inherent in scientific management and bureaucracy. The resulting increased monotony and speed of production sparked a huge increase in employee turnover. Only by doubling wages was Ford able to induce workers to accept the new production methods. Worker opposition to *Fordism* is never far under the surface. When General Motors opened a Vega plant in the early 1970s at Lordstown, Ohio, the relentless pace (increased from 60 to 100 cars an hour) of the line, coupled with more restrictive management, led to massive labour unrest and sabotage.[37]

In short, major human costs often accompanied increased efficiency, productivity, and profits. Other schools of management have attempted to counteract the harsh realities of Taylorism and Fordism by developing more humane working conditions. As one organizational researcher aptly concludes, scientific management principles "make superb sense for organizing production when robots rather than human beings are the main productive force, when organizations can truly become machines."[38]

THE HUMAN RELATIONS MOVEMENT

Bureaucracy, scientific management, and mass production technologies transformed work in the twentieth century. Many jobs became routinized and monotonous, stripped of opportunities for workers to use their minds or develop their skills and abilities. Employee dissatisfaction, often in the form of high turnover and absenteeism rates, or unionization, threatened to undermine the machinelike efficiency of the new industrial system. Taylor, Ford, and a host of efficiency experts sought to redesign production systems so that control would be firmly in the hands of management. Technical efficiency was paramount. However, gaining the cooperation of workers within an increasingly bureaucratized, mechanized, and regimented labour process remained problematic. Some employers responded with programs, broadly known as *corporate welfare* or *industrial betterment,* that emphasized the need to treat workers as human beings.

Popular in leading North American firms by the 1920s, corporate welfare programs tried to reduce the alienating effects of bureaucracy and the dissatisfactions of routinized tasks. The goal was a loyal and productive work force; the means were a healthier work environment and improved job benefits. Recreation facilities, cafeterias, cleaner and more pleasant work environments, coherent personnel policies, medical care, and pensions are major examples of corporate welfare efforts. Taylor and other efficiency experts were quick to dismiss these schemes as a waste of money. Yet many firms committed to scientific management also used welfare measures to gain greater cooperation from staff.[39] More than anything, the corporate welfare movement shows that the principles of bureaucracy and scientific management failed to address the key ingredient in modern industry — human beings. Not until the *human relations school of management* began to systematically examine some of the same concerns in the 1930s did the scientific management model face a serious challenge.[40]

Control within organizations depends upon rank-and-file employees complying with management directives. Such compliance can be achieved in three different ways: *coercive* management techniques rely on penalties and harsh discipline; *utilitarian* methods assume that employees are motivated by economic self-interest; while *normative* approaches assume that workers equate their own interests with organizational goals, thus becoming self-motivated to work hard.[41] Scientific management combined coercive and utilitarian methods with mixed results at best. The normative approach — cultivating a community of interests throughout the organization — is typically more effective. Workers personally identify with management goals, pursuing them as their own. In short, a normative approach to employee relations sharply contrasts with scientific management in its assumptions regarding human nature and motivation. Theoretically, the big happy corporate family of the human relations school replaced the carrot of incentive wages and the stick of harsh discipline. In practice, however, scientific management and human relations often operate side by side.

The human relations school of management originated in a series of studies conducted by Harvard Business School researchers between 1927 and 1932 at Western Electric's Hawthorne Works on the outskirts of Chicago.[42] Western Electric management was initially concerned with the effects of fatigue and monotony on production levels — central concerns of industrial psychologists at the time. Various studies examining the impact of rest pauses, hours of work, and lighting levels on productivity led researchers to the unexpected finding that work group social relations and employee attitudes had a major influence on production. Worker needs and motivations thus became key management concerns. And the workplace came to be viewed as a social (as opposed to a purely technical) system.

In the Relay Assembly Test Room study, workers were placed in two separate rooms. Researchers then recorded production while varying light intensity for one group but not the other. To their surprise, productivity in both groups increased regardless of lighting level. Only when light intensity was reduced to that of bright moonlight did productivity decline. Several variations on this study came up with the same puzzling findings. Searching for possible explanations, the researchers speculated that a fundamental change had occurred in the workplace. Involving workers in the study had the unintended effect of raising their morale; they now felt management cared about them as individuals. Productivity, concluded the researchers, increased as a result. This is the famous *Hawthorne effect*.[43] Herein lies a basic axiom of human relations management: the humane treatment of employees and the creation of an esprit de corps improves their motivation to cooperate and be productive.

In a subsequent phase of the research, interviews with employees revealed that work groups were governed by informal behavioural codes. This early attempt at employee counselling also tried to detect grievances and potential trouble spots in the factory.[44] The Bank Wiring Observation Room study further probed work group behaviour. For seven months, fourteen employees were observed as they wired telephone switching banks. Researchers documented how informal group norms replaced formal directives from management. The work team set its own production quotas, making sure that no member worked too hard or too slowly. Infractions of the group's rules, such as reporting violations of company policy to management, were punished. Generally, strong pressures to conform to the group norms prevailed.[45] This exposed the hidden side of the workplace, where workers consciously engage in practices to oppose or subvert established authority.

A remarkable feature of the influential human relations school is that it rests on shaky foundations. The Hawthorne studies, according to Alex Carey, were poorly conceived and incompetently executed.

Furthermore, the evidence did not really support the conclusions. Economic incentives and coercive supervision, Carey argues, seem to be better explanations of the observed productivity changes than was management's attention to human relations.[46] Leaping to the defence of the Hawthorne studies, Sonnenfeld retorts that the critics "demonstrate how easily the gunsmoke of academic snipers can obscure the conceptual contribution of these pioneering efforts."[47] Sonnenfeld asserts that the Hawthorne research advanced organizational theory beyond Taylorism, presenting a more complex social systems approach to organizational life.

Human relations management theory emphasized how workers' attitudes, values, emotions, psychological needs, and interpersonal relationships shape their work behaviour. This approach to management seeks the best match between the worker, given her or his personal background and psychological makeup, and the job. Careful recruitment and effective training of employees, as well as good quality supervision and communications, are therefore essential. The human relations perspective also assumes that people naturally want to cooperate. This is an explicit rejection of the utilitarian assumption of scientific management. Yet Elton Mayo and other human relations theorists claimed that workers are unaware of their cooperative instincts, acting instead on the basis of irrational "sentiments" or beliefs. For Mayo, the survival of society depended upon cooperation, so he advocated a new industrial order run by an administrative elite. The leadership of this elite would encourage the development of work environments that would bring out the cooperative instincts and productive potential of employees.[48]

Mayo and other human relations advocates consider workers unable to act in their own best interests. Less authoritarian leadership, careful selection and training of personnel, an emphasis on human needs and job satisfaction — these are the central contributions of the human relations approach. Yet lurking behind these management tactics is a contradictory view of the workplace.[49] On the one hand, human relations theory assumes that industrial harmony is normal and healthy and, conversely, that conflict is destructive. The possibility of conflicting interests between management and workers is denied, thus leaving no place for unions. On the other hand, human relations theory argues that workers must be closely regulated by management in the greater interests of cooperation and harmony. These inconsistencies have led some critics to label human relations theory an elaborate justification for management's manipulation of workers.[50]

No doubt most personnel managers today are sincere in their intentions to treat workers as human beings. But underneath the rhetoric of human relations, problems of power and inequality in organizations persist. In Charles Perrow's words:

> One may treat slaves humanely, and even ask their opinions on matters
> with which they are more familiar than the master. But to transform
> their basic dependence and this presumption of their incompetence
> with regard to their own interests, there must be an institutional order
> or public process whereby the opportunity and capacity for legitimate
> self-assertion is guaranteed. Such a political process does not mean
> conflict and struggle as such but a setting for ordered controversy and
> accommodation.[51]

Human relations theory has strongly influenced work reform
schemes such as job enlargement, job enrichment, participative
management, socio-technical planning, quality circles, and various
quality of work life (QWL) programs (reviewed in Chapter 9). A
common ideological thread unites these approaches. Employees are
to be treated humanely and provided with good working conditions.
But beyond a few concessions in the realm of decision making, most
of the authority remains with management.

THE INFORMAL SIDE OF ORGANIZATIONS

So far we have emphasized the formal structure of organizations and
the role of managers. We have alluded, however, to the existence of
an *informal* side to organizations, where employees reinterpret, resist,
or adapt to work structures and management directives. As Blau and
Scott explain:

> In every formal organization there arises informal organization. The
> constituent groups of the organization, like all groups, develop their
> own practices, values, norms, and social relations as their members live
> and work together. The roots of these formal systems are embedded in
> the formal organization itself and nurtured by the very formality of its
> arrangements.[52]

Thus, to get a complete picture of a work organization, we must
examine it from the vantage point of the informal practices and social
relations among employees. The glossy organizational charts found
in annual corporate reports present top management's image of how
things *ought* to operate. But employees further down the hierarchy
often see things differently.

Since the Hawthorne studies, the informal work group has been
under the sociological microscope. Some of the resulting studies have
highlighted the dynamics of conflict and power within work organizations. Despite management's efforts to design regimented work
procedures, employees often respond in ways that do not fit manage-

ment plans. Total control of people by bureaucratic structures, management discipline, and technology is difficult to imagine. Furthermore, there is an underlying tension between the cooperation necessary for any organization to function and the internal competition among individuals and groups over the distribution of power, rewards, and other scarce resources.[53]

Research in this tradition has also focused on work group relations, which are frequently a function of how production is organized. For example, assembly-line workers have fewer opportunities to develop strong social ties than do miners or firefighters whose jobs demand close team work. Indeed, job features, especially production technology, shape patterns of communication and interaction among workers.[54] But close interpersonal networks create a more cohesive group, increasing the potential for unified action in modifying or undermining official work directives. Thus technology and organizational structure can influence work group dynamics, which, in turn, may allow members to exercise some control over their daily working lives.

Donald Roy's participant-observer study of a Chicago machine shop graphically portrays work group dynamics and countersystems of production.[55] During the 1940s, Roy worked as a machinist in a shop that ran on a piecework payment system. Productivity was regulated by management through bonus payments for output above established quotas. Machine operators constantly battled over the base wage with time-study men trained in scientific management. The machinists invented ingenious shortcuts to maximize their wages while minimizing effort. This required "conspiracies" with other groups who supplied tools, maintained the machines, or delivered raw materials to deliberately break company rules.

The workers' *informal system of production* mainly involved what in shop-floor jargon was called "goldbricking" on "stinker" jobs. That is, on difficult jobs where they could not possibly earn a bonus, workers relaxed and enjoyed some free time. On easy jobs, however, they could "make out" by exceeding the quota to receive a bonus. Any production beyond an unofficial quota was stored up in a "kitty" to be used to boost output figures on a slow day. Management rarely challenged the workers' system, mainly because production always fluctuated within an acceptable range. Ironically, the workers had designed a more predictable and efficient production process. Another study by Roy showed how work groups also cushion the drudgery of low-skill, monotonous jobs by engaging workers in games and horseplay.[56]

Roy's research addressed a crucial question for management: Why don't workers behave more cooperatively and productively? Thirty years later, Michael Burawoy returned to the same factory Roy had studied.[57] Addressing identical issues from a Marxist perspective,

asked why employees work as hard as they do; why do they
themselves for management? His answer was that workers'
consent and cooperation is *manufactured,* largely through their own
actions, at the point of production. The reason for workers' diligence
has much to do with their general orientation to their work. These
machine shop employees saw their jobs as an elaborate game in which
they had a good chance of winning bonuses for exceeding established
production quotas. Participation in the game of "making out," or
earning a bonus wage, was essentially an individualistic response or
adaptation to an otherwise boring job. The game became an end in
itself. As long as each worker had a fair chance of "winning" bonus
wages, he or she would not challenge the rules. We will examine such
orientations to work in more detail in Chapter 6. What is important
here is that most workers construct their own informal group culture;
this alternative source of satisfaction can make work a little more
tolerable and pleasant.

A revealing study of how things really get done in work organizations is Melville Dalton's *Men Who Manage.*[58] Dalton's case studies
illustrate how managers also bend rules and short-circuit bureaucracy
in order to achieve their objectives. Especially fascinating is his
analysis of how official and unofficial rewards often compliment each
other, giving management a wider repertoire of means to achieve a
particular goal. The organizations Dalton studied were formal bureaucracies, at least on paper. But in practice the unofficial systems
guided actions. For instance, obtaining a promotion depended less
on merit than it did on social characteristics, for example, being a
member of the Masonic Order or the local yacht club. Employees at
all organizational levels regularly engaged in what, to the outside
observer, was dishonest activity. To grease the wheels of the bureaucracy, acknowledge someone's special services to the firm, or solidify
social relationships in order to get a job done, the company's resources were dispensed as personal rewards. Workers "borrowed"
tools and equipment; managers had home improvements done at
company expense. According to Dalton, this sort of "free-wheeling"
occurs throughout organizations just beneath the thin veneer of
bureaucracy. On a more theoretical plane, Dalton's perspective is
consistent with the strategic choice model's focus on how dominant
coalitions within an organization manipulate situations to achieve
their particular interests.

ORGANIZATIONAL CULTURE

We have documented how workers construct their own culture in the
workplace, replacing official rules and norms with their own. This
highlights the potential for conflicts between the official goals of

management and the unofficial, more personal goals of workers and work groups. But workplace cultures may also influence employee conformity and integration. This apparent paradox between workplace culture as a vehicle for employee resistance, on the one hand, and as the basis for a value consensus, on the other, is rooted in the two divergent theoretical traditions we first identified in Chapter 1. The former, which derives from Marx's view of society, emphasizes the dynamics of conflict; the latter draws on the work of French sociologist Emile Durkheim and his concerns about achieving social stability.[59]

The concept of *organizational culture* has recently become a prominent theme in the management literature. Shaping the dominant culture of an organization — that is, encouraging employees to identify strongly with the goals of the corporation — becomes a major task of management.[60] Viewed from this perspective, the norms and values of employee work groups become *countercultures* challenging the dominant organizational values. Corporations with strong internal cultures (e.g., Procter and Gamble's obsession with product quality or Hewlett-Packard's culture of constant innovation) send a clear signal to all employees.[61] Bluntly stated, these corporate cultures are meant to be "so strong that you either buy into their norms or get out."[62] Thus attempts to develop strong organizational cultures can be seen as the latest management strategy aimed at achieving what Etzioni calls *normative control*. Critics argue that this management approach is used to enforce conformity and muzzle troublemakers. To the extent that the "corporate family" values consensus, the open debate often necessary to solve problems may be stifled.[63]

Many large corporations such as IBM or Hewlett-Packard work hard to create a strong "corporate consciousness," a dominant system of beliefs and behaviour to which all members of the organization ideally are committed. Corporate values are reinforced, for example, by mythology that reveres the founders of the organization, or by rituals such as annual awards dinners where employees' achievements are publicly acknowledged. William Ouchi's research on successful North American corporations that emulate the Japanese style emphasizes their clanlike internal cultures:

> More than anything, culture implies a company's values, such as aggressiveness, defensiveness, or nimbleness — values that set a pattern for activities, opinions, and actions. Managers instill that pattern in their employees by example and pass it down to succeeding generations of workers.[64]

But we also know that most organizations have a variety of cultures dominant and counter — depending on the degree to which particular groups within them share similar work experiences. The organization of work may create strong occupational allegiances or professional alliances with values and goals not necessarily congruent with those of management. Power struggles between management and such occupational groups can erupt. This sort of cultural fragmentation can result in organizations saying one thing in their "philosophy," while the day-to-day operations reflect something quite different.[65]

Social anthropological methods are useful in studying organizational culture. Viewed from the perspective of their members, organizations become mini-societies. The shared beliefs, customs, rituals, languages, and myths serve as a sort of social glue, bonding together the diverse elements of the organization. *Culture,* then, refers to a system of shared meanings about how organizational life ought to be conducted. It can express how things really get done at an informal level. The culture metaphor, used broadly, shifts our attention away from the structure of an organization toward the processes by which employees actually carry out and collectively interpret work activities.[66]

THE LABOUR PROCESS DEBATE

Interwoven throughout our discussion of work organizations are the themes of power and conflict or, phrased differently, managerial control and worker resistance. These issues had been considered in only some of the organizational research of the 1950s and 1960s, but the *labour process studies* appearing in the 1970s reintroduced them to industrial sociology. Following Marx, this perspective views the *labour process* as (a) the human activity of work and the social relationships this entails; (b) the product or service being created; and (c) the instruments used in the work.[67] Now that we are familiar with some of the traditional theories and research on organizational structure and management, we can better appreciate the insights of this critical perspective.

We have already introduced (see Chapter 3) the seminal book that sparked the labour process debate. Harry Braverman's *Labor and Monopoly Capital,* published in 1974, emphasized management efforts to tighten control over workers' activities. For Braverman, the essence of all modern management was to be found in Taylorism, which fragmented and routinized work. Work in capitalist society had been largely deskilled and degraded. Modern management was synonymous with workplace control. Braverman refocused our attention on the twentieth-century development of monopoly — or corporate — capitalism and its impact on the organization and content of work. But critics have identified serious flaws in his analysis, some of which we have already noted.[68] First, Braverman implied that workers passively accept management assaults on their skills and job autonomy (seldom in *Labor and Monopoly Capital* can one find mention of workers actively resisting management). Second, his analysis of evolving work structures under monopoly capitalism contains many historical inaccuracies. Third, he is overly deterministic, suggesting that capitalism "needed" ever greater managerial controls in order to survive. In other words, the hidden logic of monopoly capitalism compelled capitalists to devise the sorts of workplace structures and controls we now have today. And fourth, Braverman inaccurately asserted that the principles of Taylorism were widely and unproblematically applied.

Given these criticisms, why has Braverman's thesis attracted so much attention? The answer, simply, is that he challenged work researchers to ask new questions about the development of the labour process. The debate over his work has led to a better understanding of how, to what degree, and under what conditions jobs may have been degraded, deskilled, and subjected to various types of management control.

The two core issues in the labour process debate are task deskilling (discussed in Chapter 3) and managerial control over work decisions, which we will concern ourselves with here. As we have seen, control is also a major theme in conventional organizational and management theories. It is not surprising, then, that the critical labour process perspective would take this as a starting point. However, the diversity of workplace control mechanisms documented by labour process researchers has eluded easy classification.[69] If labour process research is to significantly advance our understanding of industrial relations and workplace behaviour, then it must convincingly explain how and why different control systems emerge, persist, or are changed over time, and what functions they serve.[70] Despite its flaws, this literature suggests a few generalizations which move us in this direction.

First, contrary to Braverman's opinion, there is no inevitable and universal control strategy within capitalist systems of production. Nor are managers simply responding to some hidden logic of capitalist development. A fine balance of cooperation and conflict is typically achieved within the workplace — otherwise the organization would simply break down. (This would not serve the interests of either side, although radicals might see it as an opportunity for workers to seize control of the means of production.) A patchwork of control strategies has emerged through the confrontations, compromises, and negotiations that regularly occur between managers and workers. These dynamics are, of course, tempered by the immediate historical, industrial, and social context. Consider, for example, the contrasting workplace control arrangements found in sawmills of colonial Upper Canada, an auto factory in South Korea today, and your local convenience store. In short, the balance of power and control in any given workplace can range from strictly coercive, with management holding all the cards, to situations in which workers essentially have responsibility for regulating their own work behaviour.

Friedman, for instance, describes a shifting *frontier of control*, which is influenced by ongoing conflict and accommodation between employers and employees.[71] At issue is who sets the pace of work, hours of work, and order of task execution, and what constitutes fair treatment and just rewards. Sometimes workers gain a say in these matters through union bargaining. Or management may initiate work reforms giving workers what Friedman calls *responsible autonomy*. This is a way of obtaining worker cooperation by granting them some scope for making task-related decisions. The opposite strategy is *direct control*, which involves strict supervision and little job autonomy. Responsible autonomy is found in participative management and quality of work life (QWL) schemes; direct control is the harsh discipline of nineteenth-century factories or the regimentation of twentieth-century Taylorism and Fordism. These two control systems are best viewed as opposite ends of a continuum of employer–employee relationships and work decision-making arrangements, with many possible combinations falling between.

Examples of both types of control are found in the Canadian nickel mining industry. Wallace Clement's study of the International Nickel Company describes the introduction of sophisticated "people technology" at the ultra-modern Copper Cliff Nickel refinery.[72] Inco's emphasis on a "one big happy family feeling," a flatter job hierarchy, and a new on-the-job training system looks rather progressive. However, the effect was to break down traditional job autonomy and erode the union bargaining power of refinery workers. This increased the level of direct control by management. In contrast, Inco's teams of underground miners possessed considerable "responsible autonomy." These small, closely knit groups decided among themselves how and when to do each phase of the mining operation.

Michael Burawoy's study of machine shop workers (discussed earlier in this chapter) advances the debate by documenting how workers' on-the-job behaviour creates unspoken agreement with company goals.[73] Burawoy distinguished between the *despotic organization of work* (based on coercion and found typically in smaller firms struggling to survive in a competitive product market) and the *hegemonic* organization of work. The latter is characteristic of large, successful organizations — big corporations and major public sector institutions — where employees consider their futures to be linked with the success of the organization. Management's values are thus dominant or hegemonic. The presence of internal labour markets helps to maintain management control. Individual workers are encouraged to get ahead, and attractive job conditions foster a long-term commitment to the organization. Another important feature of the machine shop studied by Burawoy, you will recall, is that workers adapted to the production system by treating wage bonuses as a "game." In short, coercion was unnecessary for integrating workers into the labour process.

Richard Edwards and his colleagues present a theory of labour market segmentation based on different systems of workplace control. As we saw in Chapter 3, working conditions and work rewards vary significantly across labour markets situated in the primary and secondary sectors of the economy. But these radical economists take the idea of segmentation considerably further, asserting that employers can also be classified according to the expectations and rules governing employees' behaviour. In short, methods of control differ across labour markets. In their historical analysis, they argue that employers in the United States have gained the upper hand over workers through an evolving and increasingly elaborate "divide and conquer" strategy. Changes in the productive process and periodic economic crises have forced capitalists to devise new methods for directing, monitoring, evaluating, and disciplining workers. These methods of control have been determined by the degree of stability and commitment from workers required by employers in the several different labour markets. This segmentation of labour markets has resulted in a socially fragmented and politically weak working class.[74]

Bureaucratic control, which can lead to considerable employee integration, has evolved in large corporations in the core sector of the economy. Good salaries, generous benefits, and pleasant work settings are the inducements provided, usually to middle- and upper-level white-collar employees and some groups of skilled manual workers. The internal labour market, and the chance of an interesting and rewarding career, are part of this employment package. With *simple control,* which is more common in the secondary labour markets, employers regulate the labour process with traditional coercive or paternalistic methods, or, if the work organization is large enough to warrant it, with the aid of a hierarchy of authority. *Technical control* is achieved through production machinery, which can replace the direct supervision of simple control methods (an assembly line that determines the pace of work for a group of factory workers is a typical example).

The three control techniques highlighted in this analysis are useful as models against which we can compare specific work organizations, although it is clear that control relationships in the world of work are often too complex to fit into a simple typology. However, this theory of labour process dynamics has some major weaknesses. Are capitalists really as driven by a need to dominate labour as this analysis of evolving control techniques would suggest? An explanation of the evolution of the modern workplace emphasizing only the aggressive quest by management for the ultimate solution to the "labour problem" is overly simplistic.[75] We must also consider other forces, both inside and outside the workplace, which may restrict or encourage the development of particular decision-making and regulatory schemes in an organization. And, as Stephen Marglin provocatively suggests, we must ask a broader question: Are bosses really necessary? Why can't workers run enterprises collectively, thereby dispensing with unnecessary authority hierarchies?[76]

Keeping these points in mind, we can conclude with a few comments on the variety of Canadian labour process case studies presented in the book *On the Job*. These studies make it very plain that there is no single capitalist "labour process" and no ultimate strategy for management to exert control over workers. Editors Heron and Storey conclude that "workers and their employers are simply too stubborn and too resourceful to conform to any overly tidy theory."[77] The studies nevertheless underscore the importance of many factors that might influence the nature of workplace power and control relationships. These include gender, ethnicity, the skill level of workers, and labour recruitment difficulties. The social context of region and community, the type of product made and technology used, market pressures, and legislation governing labour relations can also play a part. Equally important are managerial ideologies popular in a given era and the degree of worker organization and collective resistance to management initiatives. In different combinations, these are the essential ingredients in the labour process. Future research comparing labour processes in different organizations, industries, historical periods, and societies will, we hope, add to our understanding of work relations, experiences, and structures.

CONCLUSION

We have covered a vast scholarly terrain. Much has been omitted and we have not spent enough time on some major contributions. Yet there is a continuity, a set of unifying themes underlying the various approaches that attempt to explain what happens inside work organizations. Let us conclude by reiterating these dominant themes.

Viewed as structures, most work organizations in capitalist societies (1) are put together according to the principles of bureaucracy, (2) have a specialized and coordinated division of labour, and (3) are run by professional managers. Production technologies, the nature of markets, the type of product or service, management's strategic preferences, and constraints in the social and political environment are among the factors influencing the specific features of an organization's structure. But we must also look beyond these structural aspects of organizations. Informal relationships and workplace norms, value systems — either work group countercultures or the dominant corporate culture — and the actions and reactions of non-managerial employees must all be taken into account if we are to understand the dynamics of work organizations. There is no one best way to structure an organization; the same is true for how to manage one.

Human actors create organizations. Even huge, bureaucratic corporations consist essentially of social relationships among individuals and groups. Especially fascinating is how these employees, from the night janitor to the president, compete to varying degrees for control of the firm's scarce resources: rewards, opportunities, power, influence, and status. To draw a fixed battle line between management, on one side, and subordinate employees, on the other, would be to caricature the often subtle and complex give-and-take processes at work. Certainly, worker–management conflict is a prominent theme in organizational studies. Sometimes conflict erupts, but typically truces, negotiations, and trade-offs create a workable level of stability and cooperation. Furthermore, power relations can also lead to confrontations between professionals, technical experts, and even different sectors of management. In sum, the dynamics of conflict and consensus, rooted in unequal power relations, are integral parts of work organizations. But these relationships can assume a myriad of different forms.

Finally, the challenge of organizational reform is an important topic in its own right. How can work be reorganized and tasks redesigned in order to achieve a better balance between the goals of satisfying, socially useful, and rewarding work, on the one hand, and economic efficiency and profitability on the other? Or does this pose an impossible trade-off? Are bureaucratic, managerial hierarchies really essential for the smooth functioning of capitalism? Can the alienating effects of Taylorism and Fordism be eradicated? In fact, there are some alternative forms of work organization that might be capable of democratizing and humanizing work. We will discuss worker co-operatives, industrial democracy, and autonomous work teams in the final chapter.

NOTES

1. See Presthus (1978).
2. Weber (1964): 338. See also Weber's essay on bureaucracy (1946, chapter 8).
3. Morgan (1986): 24-25. This book gives an excellent discussion of the multiple "images" of organizations portrayed in the literature.

4. Daft (1986, chapter 5). A good sociological analysis of bureaucracy and its problems is provided by Perrow (1986), especially chapter 1.

5. Peters and Waterman (1982).

6. Albrow (1970): 66.

7. Merton (1952).

8. Blau (1963). See also Crozier (1964), whose case studies of French bureaucracies show workers regularly circumventing formal rules.

9. Gouldner (1954).

10. Johnson (1980) explores the theme of power in the workplace. See also Hall's (1986) chapter on "The Power Dimension."

11. Bendix (1974): 13.

12. Daft (1986): 22. This is a standard text in the area. Also consult Pugh, Hickson, and Hinings (1985) for sketches of the major writers on organizations, and Etzioni and Lehman (1980) for a collection of sociological essays on organization theory and research.

13. See Burrell and Morgan (1979:154-60) for a discussion of the influence of functionalism on organization theory.

14. Donaldson (1985) offers a clear overview and defence of conventional organization theory. See Zey-Ferrell and Aiken (1981) for a collection of critical essays; see also Perrow (1986).

15. Burns and Stalker (1961).

16. Woodward (1980).

17. Trist and Bamforth (1951). The work of Trist and the Tavistock Institute is summarized in Pugh, Hickson, and Hinings (1985): 84-91. This systems approach has been especially influential in the social psychology of organizations, as seen in the popular text by Katz and Kahn (1978).

18. The key source for strategic choice theory is Child (1972). See also Chandler (1962) for a historical discussion of the importance of managerial strategies in shaping modern business enterprises in the U.S.

19. Pollard (1968).

20. Chandler (1977).

21. See Burnham (1941) and Galbraith (1967) for the "managerial revolution" thesis.

22. See Kelly (1982, chapter 2) for an analysis of Taylorism using this typology.

23. Smucker (1980): 163.

24. See Craven (1980, chapter 1) on the "labour problem."

25. Baldamus (1961).

26. Merkle (1980): 1-2.

27. Palmer (1975). For discussions of the spread of scientific management internationally see Littler (1982), Bendix (1974), Merkle, (1980). See Haber (1964) on the "efficiency craze" that influenced American culture in the 1920s, and Nelson (1980) for a thorough treatment of Taylorism.

28. Based on Morgan (1986:29-33) and Littler (1982): 51-52.

29. See especially Braverman (1974).

30. *Industrial Canada* (March 1913): 1106. For overviews of Taylorism, see Taylor (1919; 1947).

31. *Industrial Canada* (April 1913): 1224-5. On scientific management as an ideology see Whitaker (1979).

32. Kelly (1982, chapter 2) distinguishes between the theory, ideology, and practice of Taylorism.

33. The application of scientific management in Canada is discussed in Lowe (1984; 1987, chapter 2); Palmer (1979: 216-22); and Craven (1980): 90-110.
34. Reiter (1986).
35. See Heron and Palmer (1977) and Kealey (1986).
36. See chapter 6 on the alienating effects of assembly-line work. See also Rinehart (1987): 47-53; and on the stressful effects of this technology, see Lowe and Northcott (1986). A classic study of auto assembly-line workers is Walker and Guest (1952). Beynon (1984) describes working conditions and industrial relations at Ford in Britain, while Linhart (1981) focuses on a French Citroen factory. Meyer (1981) offers a good account of Ford's introduction of the assembly line.
37. See Aronowitz (1973, chapter 2).
38. Morgan (1986): 33.
39. Rinehart (1986): 53; Craven (1980): 100-5; Jacoby (1985).
40. Bendix (1974: 308-13) compares the views of the leading spokesperson for human relations, Elton Mayo, with those held by Taylor.
41. Etzioni (1975).
42. The research is described in Whitehead (1936) and Roethlisberger and Dickson (1939).
43. The Hawthorne effect also refers to the problem of *reactivity* in research methodology. The fact that people are aware of being part of a study may itself confound the results.
44. See Wilensky and Wilensky (1951).
45. A good summary is found in Homans (1950, chapter 3).
46. Carey (1967); Acker and Van Houten (1974); Franke and Kaul (1978); Perrow (1986): 82-85.
47. Sonnenfeld (1985): 111.
48. See Mayo (1945).
49. See Burawoy (1979): 7.
50. Rinehart (1987): 172-79.
51. Perrow (l986): 114. Chapters 2 and 3 of this book summarize the origins of human relations and the various strands of organizational research to which it gave rise.
52. Blau and Scott (1963): 6.
53. This theme is developed in Hill (1981), Watson (1987), and Salaman (1979, chapter 11).
54. Meissner (1969:5) documents how systems of worker relations, based "on mutual obligations for recognition, help, and sociability," vary according to the extent and type of mechanization.
55. Roy (1952, 1954).
56. Roy (1959-60).
57. Burawoy (1979).
58. Dalton (1959). Another insightful investigation of workplace "fiddling," or cheating, is Mars (1982).
59. On the Durkheimian overtones of the corporate culture literature, see Ray (1986) and Ouchi (1981, chapter 8).
60. Pettigrew (1979).
61. Peters and Waterman (1982): 76.
62. *Ibid.*, 77. It is interesting that several prominent "excellent" companies discussed in Peters and Waterman's book ran into problems subsequently. See *Business Week* (5 November 1984).

63. Morgan (1986): 128; Ray (1986).
64. Ouchi (1981): 195.
65. The following provide a good overview of this literature: Morgan (1986): 120-28; Fine (1984); Alliere and Firsirotu (1984); Ouchi and Wilkins (1985); Ray (1986); Jelinek, Smircich, and Hirsch (1983, entire special issue); Pettigrew (1979); Trice and Beyer (1984).
66. See Morgan (1986, chapter 5); Ranson, Hinings, and Greenwood (1980) analyze how organizational structures are continually produced and recreated by all members.
67. Marx (1967): 178.
68. See the discussion in chapter 3, summarized from Littler (1982: 27-30). Thompson (1983) gives a good overview of the labour process literature. See also Wood (1982); Zimbalist (1979); Heron and Storey (1986a) for case studies from Britain, the U.S., and Canada respectively.
69. Storey (1985).
70. Similar points are made by Burawoy (1978:235) and Thompson (1983, chapter 5).
71. Friedman (1977): 82-85.
72. Clement (1981): 204.
73. Burawoy (1979). This model is expanded in Burawoy (1985).
74. See Edwards (1979) and Gordon, Edwards, and Reich (1982). For critiques see Penn (1982), Wilkinson (1982), and Nolan and Edwards (1984).
75. Littler (1982:3) calls this the "panacea fallacy," a tendency to view management as engaged in a continual search for a magic solution that will stabilize relations with employees.
76. Marglin (1976); see also Landes (1986) for a critical discussion of this argument.
77. Heron and Storey (1986b): 33.

5

Women's Employment

INTRODUCTION

The decade of the 1970s saw tumultuous changes in women's economic roles. Traditional barriers to female employment began to crumble. The women's movement challenged the conventional wisdom about women's capabilities. Rising educational levels and job expectations made more women career-minded, and the economic necessity to be self-supporting or to contribute to the family income left some women little choice but to find a paying job. By 1980, over half of all adult women in Canada worked outside the home for pay.

This chapter examines the changing economic roles of women in Canada. We will review the dramatic increases in female labour force participation rates during this century, showing how the labour market has become segmented into men's and women's jobs. Despite having made significant gains in overall participation, job opportunities, and incomes, women still confront major inequalities. Women's work historically has been undervalued and poorly rewarded. Today gender remains a key determinant of inequality in our society.

To better grasp the causes and consequences of the gender-based inequalities in the work world, we must address the following questions: What forces have either pushed or pulled women out of the home and into paid employment, especially since the end of the Second World War? Why are women concentrated in a limited range of jobs at the bottom of the occupational ladder? How have these jobs become labelled as *female,* and, correspondingly, how have the most interesting and rewarding jobs been defined as *male?* What barriers still prevent equality of opportunities and rewards for women in the labour market? And finally, but perhaps most important, how can greater equality for women be achieved in the workplace?

WOMEN'S ECONOMIC ROLE IN HISTORICAL CONTEXT

Although history largely has been written from the perspective of men, even a quick glance back into the past reveals that women have always performed a vital, if somewhat unacknowledged, economic role. Native women, for example, were indispensible to the fur trade, the major industry during much of Canada's colonial period. White male traders relied upon native women to act as interpreters, prepare food, clean pelts for market, and to teach them wilderness survival skills.[1] Little wonder that fur traders sought out native wives. When an agrarian economy began to develop in Upper Canada during the nineteenth century, pioneer women played a key part. The family was the basic production unit. Males worked the fields, while women looked after all domestic work associated with child rearing, tending the livestock and garden, making clothes, and preparing food. The death of a wife was a major setback for the subsistence farmer. Quick remarriage thus was an act of economic survival.[2]

The absence of a wage labour market and the necessity of contributing to the household economy meant that few women were employed outside the home prior to the rise of industrial capitalism. Even in late nineteenth-century Canada, only a fraction of women were engaged in paid employment. In 1891, for example, 11.4 percent of women over age 10 were employed, accounting for 12.6 percent of the entire labour force.[3] The growing importance of factories on the industrial landscape around the turn of the century contributed to a redefinition of women's economic role. Employers in some light industries, such as textiles, recruited women as cheap unskilled or semiskilled labourers who, according to prevailing stereotypes, would be less likely to unionize and more tolerant of boring tasks.

Focusing on paid employment, however, ignores the work performed by the vast majority of women during this era. The unpaid domestic labour of women — to raise the future generation of factory workers and to feed, clothe, and care for the present generation of workers so that they could keep the wheels of industry turning — were all essential functions within capitalism. Out of these competing pressures on women emerged a gender division of labour that still persists today.

Early twentieth-century attitudes about women's economic roles distinguished between single and married women. The rapid expansion of manufacturing and service industries demanded a huge army of blue- and white-collar workers. The employment of young, single women prior to marriage became tolerated in domestic, clerical, sales, and some factory jobs. Once married, women were expected to retreat into the matrimonial home. Of course, some wives wished to remain in the labour force and still others were forced to stay through economic necessity. In these cases, married women laboured at the margins of the economy in domestic and other menial jobs which largely had been abandoned by single women.[4]

The industrialization process in Canada accentuated age and

gender divisions within the economy. Examining the work patterns of working-class women in Montreal, Canada's first large industrial city, Bradbury documents how age and sex determined who was drawn into the booming wage labour market. Women comprised about 35 percent of the city's industrial work force during the 1870s. In certain industries, such as domestic work and the sewing and dressmaking trades, four out of five workers were female. The vast majority of these working women were single. Given the scarcity of wage employment for wives, they could make a greater contribution to the family economy by being *household managers.* In this role, wives stretched the wages of male family members and single daughters as far as possible, occasionally supplementing this by taking in boarders or turning to neighbours or charities for help.[5]

Powerful social values justified this division of labour. Especially influential in perpetuating women's subordinate role as unpaid family workers was the ideology of the *family wage.* Working-class men organized into unions to wrestle better wages and working conditions out of reluctant employers. One of organized labour's key arguments was that wages should be high enough to allow a male breadwinner to support a wife and children. Cheap female labour would thereby be excluded from the workplace. Middle-class reformers also lobbied for restrictions on female employment in industry due to its presumed harmful personal and social effects. Employers responded to these pressures by limiting their hiring to mainly single women, further supporting this ideology. Despite its sexist tone, the family wage ideology indirectly may have benefited women by raising the standard of living in working-class families. The price, of course, was the restriction of women's labour market opportunities to areas in which they would not compete directly with men — hence the enduring myth of the "male breadwinner."[6]

This brief historical sketch has identified a number of prominent themes in the transformation of women's economic roles. First, although their widespread participation in the paid labour force is a recent development, women have always made essential economic contributions. Second, women's entry into paid employment occurred in ways that reproduced their subordinate position in society relative to that of men. Third, the interconnections between work and family are crucial to understanding how women were incorporated into the capitalist labour market of the twentieth century. These themes will be explored further in this chapter.

RISING FEMALE LABOUR FORCE PARTICIPATION

Few changes in post-World War II Canadian society have had as far-reaching consequences as the emergence of new female employment patterns. Virtually all industrial nations have experienced rising *female labour force participation rates* since the end of the war. But this trend has been especially rapid in Canada.

Table 5.1 provides a comparison of participation rates for nine major industrial nations between 1960 and 1981. Note that in 1960, Canada had the lowest level of female employment. Yet the following three decades witnessed a tremendous expansion of white-collar service sector jobs which, coupled with rising educational levels and a plunging birth rate, drew millions of Canadian women into employment. By 1981, our female labour force participation rate had shot past all the advanced industrial nations with the exceptions of Sweden and the United States. Indeed, Canada crossed a historic watershed as it entered the 1980s: more than half of all adult women were working outside the home for pay.

Table 5.1
Female Participation Rates in Nine Industrialized Countries,
1960, 1970, and 1981

	1960	1970	1981
Canada	30.1	38.3	51.6
United States	37.7	43.3	52.1
Australia	—	40.4	45.5
Japan	52.7	49.3	46.7
France	41.6	40.1	43.1
West Germany	41.2	38.4	38.5*
United Kingdom	39.5	42.0	46.6*
Italy	33.8	26.8	29.9**
Sweden	—	50.0	60.5*

* Preliminary figures.
** Rate in 1980.
Source: Jac-Andre Boulet and Laval Lavallee, *The Changing Economic Status of Women* (Ottawa: Supply & Services Canada, 1984), p. 6.

What social and economic factors account for this remarkable increase in female labour force participation? Clearly there was no single cause. The huge post-war baby boom generation was completing its education and flooding into the job market by the late 1960s. The growth of feminism contributed to more liberal social values regarding female work roles. Young women were becoming much better educated, which raised female occupational aspirations and made women more competitive with men in the job market. Traditional stereotypes of women's work began crumbling. The massive expansion of white-collar service sector jobs, where many employers prefer women, was a major influence on the demand for female labour. Many of these jobs were part-time and therefore convenient for married women with family responsibilities. Shrinking family sizes allowed married women to more readily pursue employment plans; and rising separation and divorce rates forced a growing number of women to find their own source of income. For many wives, upward trends in inflation and living standards strained family budgets, making a second income essential. In sum, the interaction of a great many supply and demand factors underlay the dramatic expansion of the female labour force. [7]

Currently not all women have the same likelihood of participating in the labour force. We can identify important variations in participation rates according to region, age, educational level, marital status, and family circumstances. Regionally, women in Alberta have the highest participation rate (over 60 percent in 1981) largely due to its booming energy-based economy in the 1970s. The situation in Newfoundland stands in sharp contrast. Because of this province's chronically weak economy and high unemployment rate, only 42 percent of adult women work outside the home. In short, local and regional job opportunities have a direct bearing on female participation rates.

Personal characteristics also influence work patterns. Single women have higher participation rates than married, widowed, or divorced women. Younger women, and those with higher educational levels, are more active in the labour force. For example, 78 percent of women aged 20 to 24 work for pay, as do 80 percent of those with a postgraduate university degree.[8] Family situation also matters, especially whether or not there are pre-school children in the home. For example, a study we conducted in Edmonton found that the major factor preventing wives from taking a paid job was the number of children under age 6 in the home.[9] Feminist organizations muster evidence such as this to support their calls for more widely available child care facilities (preferably at work sites), so that women with young children have the option of going out to work should they choose.

Lastly, financial necessity is undoubtedly a major reason why many women seek employment. Wives in low-income families may be compelled to work to help meet basic expenses. Better-educated middle-class women married to professional and managerial males have greater opportunities and the luxury of choice with regard to employment. [10]

WORK AND FAMILY
Domestic responsibilities have limited women's availability for paid

work outside the home. In other words, the male-female division of labour is based on the close links between family and paid work. Many feminists argue that women's subordination results from the combination of two systems of domination: capitalism and patriarchy. Capitalism incorporated earlier patriarchal social arrangements. Essentially *patriarchy* refers to forms of family organization in which fathers (and husbands) hold total power. Remnants of patriarchy still reinforce stereotypes of women as cheap and docile workers. Furthermore, women's traditional family roles of wife and mother often limit their employment opportunities and, for those who are employed, create a "double day."

A survey of employed married women in eight Canadian cities in 1958 offers some insights into the situation of working wives in the immediate post-war period.[11] Working mothers with young children were torn between the need to bring home a paycheque and the feeling that they should be at home looking after their children. Wives performed the housework even when they were employed. Women in the 1950s saw the home as their major priority; they adapted to conflicting social pressures by working before having children, withdrawing into the home to raise them, then returning to work at middle age after the children had grown up.[12]

Because most wives in the 1950s and 1960s responded to the demands of child rearing by leaving the labour force, employers assumed that women must have a weaker attachment to paid work than men. A 1982 national study found that the major reason married women under age 40 left their employment was child-raising responsibilities.[13] The same family constraints on employment for women clearly still exist; but the important point is that far fewer women leave the labour force at all, and those who do leave for a shorter time. Despite this, employers continue to discriminate against young women in hiring and promotion decisions, assuming that, like their mothers, they cannot be relied upon to stick with a job as long as a man.

Certainly in the last decade we have seen greater equality in the division of household chores between partners, especially in younger age groups. However, changes in this area of domestic life have not kept pace with wives' rising employment rates. Studies of family time budgets document how much time husbands and wives spend on household activities, from watching TV to washing dishes. This research indicates that working wives frequently have a double day. After putting in seven or eight hours on the job, some wives return home to cook dinner, clean up the house, keep the family budget, shop, clean clothes — all the domestic chores their mothers and grandmothers did as full-time housewives. In one study, Martin Meissner and his colleagues found that taking a job outside the home meant a *decrease* of 13.5 hours weekly in leisure time for a sample of British Columbia wives. Yet their husbands experienced no loss of leisure time — simply because they didn't share the housework.[14] The researchers conclude that time pressures and added workloads are the "double burden" of many working wives today.

Wives' household work varies depending on their class position and their husbands' occupation. Working-class wives have a higher probability of facing the combined stresses of poverty and menial employment. In contrast, wives of managerial and professional men often are caught up in a *two-person career*. A common assumption in large corporations is that male managers climbing the career ladder will have the unpaid services of a wife. Success in the corporate world demands almost excessive dedication to one's career, often resulting in low family involvement. Wives are expected to put on dinner parties, accompany their husbands to company social functions, make travel arrangements, and plan household moves. They are what Rosabeth Moss Kanter calls unpaid servants of the corporation.[15] Such wives find it difficult to pursue their own careers. And women attempting to establish themselves in corporate management, where expectations about two-person careers prevail, are obviously at a disadvantage. Such constraints on female roles are a product of how jobs are organized. Similar structural conditions are evident in farm families, where wives are economic partners with their husbands, and in many small businesses that rely on unpaid family labour.

OCCUPATIONAL SEX SEGREGATION

At the heart of gender inequalities in the work world is the structuring of the labour market into male and female segments. *Occupational sex segregation* refers to the concentration of men and women in different occupations. A potent combination of gender-role socialization, education, and labour market mechanisms channel women into a limited number of occupations in which mainly other females are employed. These *job ghettos* typically offer little economic security and little opportunity for advancement; furthermore, the work is often unpleasant, boring, and perhaps physically taxing. Females in job ghettos lack ready access to the more challenging, rewarding, and lucrative occupations dominated by males. These male segments of the labour market operate as *shelters*, conferring advantages on workers within them through entrance restrictions.[16]

These concepts of *ghettos* and *shelters* emphasize the unequal rewards and opportunities built into the job market on the basis of a worker's sex. It is especially important to recognize that job opportunities determine an individual's living standard, future prospects, and overall quality of life — in Max Weber's words, her or his *life chances*.

A recent study by the Organization for Economic Cooperation and Development underlines the serious consequences of labour market segmentation for women:

> ... labour market bias against women persists and this, in combination with the recession, has resulted in greater economic insecurity for them, and those who depend wholly or partly on their earnings. Inequality in the education system, along with the domestic division of labour, have combined to perpetuate occupational segregation and women's greater vulnerability to poverty and dependence.[17]

One of the fundamental processes underlying segmentation is *sex labelling*. Employers do not always make hiring decisions on strictly rational grounds, despite what economics textbooks would have us believe. If all hiring decisions were totally rational, women would have been recruited much earlier in the industrialization process and in far greater numbers, given their cost advantage as cheap labour. Patriarchal traditions narrowly defined female roles around child rearing and homemaking. In addition, as already mentioned, males opposed the employment of women in their occupations for fear of having their wages undercut. Women therefore were relegated to the less rewarding jobs men did not want. These occupations became labelled as *female*, guaranteeing that in future employers would only hire women, and, regardless of the actual skills demanded by the job, that pay and status would remain low.

Dominant social values about femininity and masculinity were used to define job requirements. For instance, by the late nineteenth century teaching, social work, nursing, and domestic work were socially acceptable for women. Society could justify this on the ideological grounds that these occupations demanded essentially "female" traits — caring for the sick, the old and the unfortunate, transmitting culture to children, and performing domestic chores. Exclusive male rights to the better jobs and higher incomes thus were unchallenged; the role of women as homemaker and wife was preserved. Once a job was labelled "male" or "female" it was difficult for workers of the opposite sex to gain entry.[18]

TRENDS IN OCCUPATIONAL SEX SEGREGATION

In Chapter 3 we documented sex differences in the occupational distribution of the labour force, noting that clerical work is the largest source of employment for women (Table 3.2). Table 5.2 shows that 79 percent of all clerks are female. In short, clerical work is the leading female job ghetto. Women also are concentrated in service occupations, health care, and teaching; again, these are all job ghettos in the sense that the majority of employees are women, although the pay and security provided in some (particularly nursing and teaching) is relatively good today.

Table 5.2
Employment Concentration of Women, Canada, 1984

Occupation	Women as a percentage of the total labour force in each occupational category
Managerial and administrative	31.9
Natural sciences, engineering, and mathematics	16.9
Social sciences	55.1
Religion	20.6
Teaching	59.3
Medicine and health	78.1
Artistic and recreational occupations	39.2
Clerical	79.1
Sales	43.4
Service	55.8
Agriculture	24.8
Fishing, hunting, and trapping	—
Forestry and logging	5.5
Mining and quarrying	—
Processing	22.0
Machining	7.2
Product fabricating and assembling	23.6
Construction trades	1.8
Transport-equipment operation	7.0
Materials handling	20.4
Other crafts and equipment operating	21.7
Unclassified	63.3
All Occupations	42.2

Source: Labour Canada, *Women in the Labour Force, 1985-86 Edition* (Ottawa: Supply & Services Canada, 1986), p. 19.

Has sex segregation in the labour market changed over the course of this century? Table 5.3 documents that in 1901, 71.1 percent of all employed women were concentrated in five occupations. Of this small group of socially acceptable "women's jobs," domestic servants were the most numerous, accounting for close to 36 percent of all employed women. Next in importance were seamstresses and school teachers, each employing roughly 13 percent of the female labour force. These three occupations fit our description of a job ghetto, given that between 78 and 100 percent of all workers in them were female.

Table 5.3
The Five Leading Female Occupations, Canada, 1901 and 1981

Occupation	Number of Women Employed	% of Total Female Labour Force in Occupation	Females as % of Total Labour Force in Occupation
		1901	
1. Domestic servants	84,984	35.7%	87.4%
2. Seamstresses	32,145	13.5	100.0
3. School teachers	30,870	13.0	78.2
4. Office clerks	12,569	5.3	21.4
5. Farmers and stock raisers	8,495	3.6	1.9
	Total	71.1%	
		1981	
1. Secretaries and stenographers	368,025	7.4%	98.9%
2. Bookkeepers and accounting clerks	332,325	6.6	81.9
3. Tellers and cashiers	229,320	4.6	92.7
4. Waitresses, hostesses and stewards, food and beverage	200,710	4.0	85.7
5. Graduate nurses	167,710	3.4	95.4
	Total	26.0%	

Sources: Canada, Dominion Bureau of Statistics, *Occupational Trends in Canada, 1901-1931* (Ottawa 1939), Table 8; Statistics Canada, 1981 Census, *Labour Force — Occupation Trends* (# 92-920).

This was not the case, however, for the two other main female occupations. Clerical work at the turn of the century was still a man's job, although by the 1940s the gender balance had shifted toward women. Interestingly, clerical work was one of the few traditionally male jobs to undergo this *feminization* process. Behind this change was a rapid expansion of office work accompanied by a more fragmented and routinized division of labour. As a result, a layer of new positions emerged at the bottom of office hierarchies, opening office doors to women.[19] Finally, the fact that "farmers and stock raisers" appears as one of the five prominent female occupations may at first glance seem peculiar. But considering that Canada was still mainly an agricultural economy in 1901, it is understandable that women would form a small part of the paid agricultural work force. The twentieth-century march of industrialization saw a decline of some female jobs, such as domestic work and seamstressing, and the rise of new employment opportunities in the expanding service industries. By 1981, the three leading female occupations were all in the clerical area. Waitressing and nursing, both long-standing female economic roles, had become even more important sources of employment.

Yet job ghettos still exist, attesting to the deep roots of occupational sex segregation. However, women are now entering a broader range of occupations. For example, the five main female jobs in 1981 account for only 26 percent of the entire female labour force. This is a positive sign of occupational diversification, but the trend should not be overstated. Comparing men and women in this regard, we discover that the twenty-one leading male occupations (measured in terms of the numbers employed) in 1981 accounted for only 25 percent of the total male work force. In contrast, the eighteen leading female occupations accounted for fully half of all employed women.[20] In brief, women have roughly half as many occupational avenues open to them as men.

GENDER STRATIFICATION WITHIN OCCUPATIONS

Thus far we have discussed broad historical patterns of *horizontal* occupational sex segregation. Now we will examine the related problem of *vertical* segregation. This refers to how a sexual division of tasks, status, and responsibilities exists within specific occupations.

As a general rule, men tend to be in positions of greater authority in organizations; consequently, men usually receive better job rewards than women. Let us take the teaching profession as an example. Over half of the women in teaching are in elementary classrooms, while males are concentrated in the higher-status, better-paying jobs in universities, colleges, high schools, and administration. Similarly in sales work, two-thirds of the women are sales clerks, the bottom of the ladder in this occupation. In contrast, men are overrepresented in sales supervisory positions.[21] The situation is much the same in the professions. Women have made significant inroads recently, particularly in law and medicine. However, there is still a tendency for them to enter specialties, such as family law or general medical practice. This reinforces the assumptions made by the male establishments in the professions about female colleagues being best suited to tasks calling upon their "natural" instincts as wives and mothers.[22]

The 1981 census documented that since 1971 women had made major breakthroughs in the male domain of management and administration. It is an encouraging sign that women now comprise

32 percent of all employees in this major occupational group (see Table 5.2). This is considerably higher than in other advanced industrial countries, suggesting that labour market barriers to women may indeed be more resistant to change elsewhere.[23] However, a detailed analysis of the managerial/administrative category reveals that women are clustered in the least responsible and lowest-paying jobs. In addition, female managers and administrators are concentrated in established female areas, such as teaching, personnel, sales, and office work. The largest number of female managers is in financial administration, which often can be a glorified form of clerical work. Conversely, few women have entered management positions in natural sciences, engineering, purchasing and production, construction, transportation, and communications — all economic activities dominated by men. Moreover, in 1981 only 6.3 percent of general managers and senior executives in the private sector were female. This adds up to a mere 3,175 women who have entered the top echelons of corporate decision making, out of a total female work force of over 5 million. As of 1984, none of Canada's largest private sector corporations had a female president or chief executive officer.[24] The opportunities for women to attain top management positions in the public sector are only slightly better.[25]

Male labour market shelters are sometimes referred to as *non-traditional* areas of employment for women. But women's increasing share of managerial and professional jobs suggests that the barriers which historically have restricted their access are now weakening. In the 1970s, for instance, 44 percent of female labour force growth occurred in occupations where men had dominated at the beginning of the decade. But these barriers are slow to crumble. Even if every woman entering the labour force in the next twenty years chooses what today is defined as a "male" job (e.g., more than half of the employees in it being male), the overall representation of women in these areas would only reach 35 percent.[26] Moreover, recent increases in female employment have been greatest in conventional job ghettos. For instance, the fastest growing occupation for women between 1971 and 1981 was that of electronic data processing equipment operator, basically a new type of clerical work.[27]

In sum, although recent evidence of expanding employment opportunities for women provides grounds for optimism, progress toward full gender equality in the workplace is slow. To achieve this goal in today's labour market, women would have to be represented in each occupation in proportion to their overall share of the labour force (now at 42 percent). This immediately raises the question (to which we return shortly) of how such changes can be achieved. But would women *want* full access to all male jobs, given that a good number are dirty, dangerous, physically exhausting, insecure, and low paying? The implication, of course, is that unless all jobs at the bottom of the occupational spectrum are reformed and upgraded, gender equality as we have defined it would only be a partial advance for women.

THE WAGE GAP

One of the most obvious consequences of labour market segmentation is the *wage gap*. Recall from Chapter 3 that women who work full-time for the entire year earn an average of about 65 percent of what similarly employed men earn. Despite women entering some of the higher-paying managerial and professional jobs, the overall wage gap has narrowed by only 2 percent since 1971.[28] This partly reflects the way in which employment growth trends often counteract each other. During the 1970s, the number of women in the twenty highest-paying occupations grew by more than fourfold, compared with a twofold increase for men. But this trend was offset by an expansion of female employment at the lower end of the pay scale. For example, in 1981, 27 percent of all employed women were in the twenty lowest-paying occupations, compared to only 13 percent of males. Also, the big rise in the number of part-time jobs has reduced the earning potential of many women.

The lower earnings of women have a direct impact on their living standards and quality of life generally. For instance, there is a strong relationship between being female and being poor. Four in ten families headed by women were living below the poverty line in 1984, compared to only one in ten led by men. Mother-led families are not much better off now than they were in the 1960s: 43 percent were below the poverty line in 1984 compared to 47 percent in 1969.[29] Of any group in Canadian society, women over the age of 65 are the most vulnerable to poverty; in 1982, 60 percent of all elderly unattached women lived in poverty, mainly due to inadequate pensions.[30]

The fifteen highest-paying occupations for males in 1980 are displayed in Table 5.4. It includes only full-time, full-year employees — an accurate way to compare male-female earnings differences because part-time workers, who are disproportionately female, are not included. The first thing to note is the low numbers of women in these well-paying jobs. It is also interesting that the ratio of female to male earnings in this top range of jobs mirrors the overall labour force pattern. For example, female physicians and surgeons earn about 60 percent of the salary of their male colleagues. In some fields the gap is wider. The ratio is 39 percent in sales and security trading, and 54 percent among general managers and other senior officials. In contrast, women who do succeed in entering some of these rewarding occupations can expect to earn a higher proportion of the male

Table 5.4

Occupations with the Highest Male Average Employment Income ($30,000 or more)
for Full-time, Full-year (49-52 weeks) Male Workers and Number of Men and Women
and Average Employment Income in these Occupations, 1980

	Males		Females		Female
	Number	$ Average Income	Number	$ Average Income	Average Income as % of Male Average Income
1. Physicians and surgeons	18,995	$59,834	3,065	$36,115	60.4%
2. Dentists	3,875	58,128	295	40,510	70.0
3. Judges and magistrates	1,335	51,795	—	—	—
4. Salesmen and traders, securities	6,385	46,718	1,575	18,375	39.3
5. General managers and other senior officials	68,120	46,160	5,205	24,915	54.0
6. Optometrists	920	42,256	—	—	—
7. Lawyers and notaries	21,970	40,978	2,835	23,935	58.4
8. Other managers (mines and oil wells)	2,280	40,506	555	19,303	47.7
9. Managerial occupations in natural sciences and engineering	10,085	38,948	595	23,322	59.9
10. Osteopaths and chiropractors	1,385	38,869	—	—	—
11. Pilots, navigators, and flight engineers	5,325	37,125	—	—	—
12. Petroleum engineers	3,035	36,882	—	—	—
13. University teachers	22,340	35,944	4,905	26,585	74.0
14. Administrators in teaching and related fields	16,345	35,434	4,450	25,772	72.7
15. Administrators in medicine and health	4,620	34,339	4,310	23,832	69.4

— Indicates that either no women were in this category or that the estimated number of women was less than 250. Statistics Canada does not release data on earnings where the numbers in the occupations are less than 250.

Source: Canada, *Report of the Commission on Equality in Employment* (Ottawa: Supply & Services Canada, 1984), p. 74.

salary than women in most other jobs — although rarely is this equal to men. Female university teachers and teaching administrators, for example, earn about 73 percent of the male salary. The main conclusion, then, is that in even the most lucrative occupations, being a female increases the probability of receiving a lower salary. Canada's highest-paid employees are executives in large corporations. Not surprisingly, there were no women among the exclusive group of corporate executives who earned over \$300,000 in 1983.[31]

Two forms of *discrimination* affect female earnings. The first is wage discrimination, in which an employer pays a women less than a man for performing the same job. The second stems from the segregated structure of the labour market documented earlier. Occupational sex segregation results in lower female wages by channelling women into low-paying job ghettos which, in turn, provide few opportunities for mobility into more rewarding jobs.

To what extent does each form of discrimination contribute to the overall wage gap? To answer this question one must look at an employee's education, training, work experience, occupation, industry, and geographic location of employment. These factors may influence a worker's productivity and, through this, his or her earnings. Research by Morley Gunderson, a labour economist, shows that when these productivity factors are taken into account (or statistically controlled), the wage gap in Ontario is reduced from around 60 percent to between 75 and 85 percent.[32] Differences in work experience, combined with the segmented structure of the labour market, emerge as the main determinants of sex differences in earnings. Applying this analysis to males and females employed in the same jobs within a single establishment, the earnings ratio narrows even further to between 90 and 95 percent. In short, there is little direct pay discrimination by employers, at least in Ontario; rather, it is the sex-segregated structure of the labour market that creates pay inequalities.

Human capital theory emphasizes that education is the great equalizer in the job market. Ideally, people with identical educational credentials should have the same amount of *human capital* and therefore be equally competitive in terms of earning power. But as Chapter 3 emphasized, it was the inability of human capital theory to explain why some individuals with equivalent education reaped unequal economic rewards that gave rise to the alternative labour market segmentation perspective. Nonetheless, education does matter to an extent. In post-World War II Canada, obtaining a good education has been a route to upward mobility for a sizeable number of children from working-class families.

Does the same hold true for women? There is little doubt that women have been becoming better educated. Between 1971 and

1981, full-time female university enrolment rose from 39 to 47 percent of the total. This entailed an increase in female enrolments of 54 percent between 1972 and 1981, compared with only 7.5 percent for men.[33] Women also entered a wider range of programs during this period, and more of them continued into postgraduate studies. Dramatic gains were made in male-dominated professions, notably law and medicine, with women comprising about 40 percent of these student populations by the early 1980s.[34]

Yet the larger picture shows that women still are concentrated in predominantly "female" programs of study. Forty percent of female undergraduates are in education, a field that has experienced a significant drop in job openings recently as the number of school-age children declines. By comparison, occupations with bright futures often are difficult for women to enter. For example, in 1981-82 only 6.3 percent of female undergraduates were in biological and agricultural sciences and 1.8 percent in engineering. The latter program has the lowest proportion of female students (8.5 percent); some sociologists attribute this to the strength of the male culture, which has long characterized the engineering profession.[35]

With the increasing number of female university graduates, have women been able to find the types of jobs for which they have been educated? A national study of 1976 college and university graduates found that, next to teaching, clerical work was the most common occupational destination of females. Nor can a well-educated woman expect to earn as much as a comparably educated man. The same study found that when men and women with equivalent qualifications and job duties were compared two years after graduation, men were usually better paid. In short, human capital theory fails to explain the employment realities of Canadian female university graduates.

EXPLANATIONS OF WORK-RELATED GENDER INEQUALITIES

Our key question is how occupational sex segregation has become so deeply entrenched. Once we can answer this, we are better able to inform public policy discussions about strategies for achieving equality in the workplace. However, a comprehensive theoretical model capable of adequately explaining the origins, development, and perpetuation of work-related gender inequalities has yet to be formulated. This largely stems from the long-standing male bias found in sociological research on work, which only recently has begun to disappear. Feldberg and Glenn thus distinguish between *job* and *gender* models of the workplace. The job model views male work attitudes and behaviours as products of working conditions and organizational position. When women are studied, the type of work they perform is considered irrelevant; rather, a gender model is used to account for females' relationship to employment on the basis of their personal characteristics and family roles.[36]

Relevant theories tend to be narrowly focused, dealing selectively with gender-role socialization, the family division of labour, the operations of the labour market, employee attitudes and behaviour in organizations, and so on. But as Reagan and Blaxall remind us, the problem is deeply rooted:

> ... occupational segregation of the sexes results from the interaction of a well-entrenched and complex set of institutions that perpetuate the inferior position of women in the labour market, since all pressures within society, be they familial, legal, economic, cultural, or historical, tend to reinforce and support occupational segregation.[37]

The two main competing theories of how labour markets operate are human capital theory and labour market segmentation (or dual labour market) theory. We have already criticized the human capital model for its inability to explain the persistence of sex segregation.[38] While the human capital model is concerned with factors influencing the characteristics of workers — the supply side of the labour market — the segmentation model examines how job requirements within organizations create a demand for particular kinds of workers. Labour market segmentation theory distinguishes between secondary and primary labour markets. The former, characterized by poor working conditions, typically are located in marginal, uncompetitive industries, which must constantly struggle to keep wage costs down. In contrast, corporations and state bureaucracies in the primary sector can afford to provide employees with relatively high wages, decent benefits and job security, and pleasant working conditions. Furthermore, internal labour markets are found almost exclusively within the primary sector. Employers thus obtain a stable, committed work force by providing employees opportunities to develop careers within the organization.

For the segmentation model to accurately explain why men and women hold different kinds of jobs, women would have to be concentrated in the secondary segment of the labour market. This is true to an extent, since women are overrepresented in service industries, which form a large part of the secondary sector. However, critics point out that many women are also employed in job ghettos as typists, cleaners, or food servers within the primary sector. In short, the segmentation perspective has difficulty accounting for sex differences in employment within the same industry or establishment. Moreover, the model cannot explain how sex segregation developed in the first place.[39]

The segmentation approach requires modification to incorporate gender as a major source of inequality in the labour market. Some researchers, for instance, link women's labour market position to their traditional roles within the family. Women's family roles have centred around activities such as raising children and caring for dependants; cooking, cleaning, and other services essential for family members to hold down jobs; and contributing a secondary income to the family budget — roughly in that order. Many employed wives find their loyalties divided between their employers and their families. The latter often take priority. Employers thus view these women as lacking commitment to work. Barriers to interesting and better-paying jobs consequently persist.[40]

But how do employers' stereotypes, the job expectations of female workers, restricted employment opportunities, and women's domestic roles interact within the workplace? The central issue here is whether female work patterns can be best explained in terms of women's early socialization, family roles and "feminine" qualities, or as a response to their employment conditions. Clearly all of these factors are important. The socialization of girls and boys into traditional gender roles creates cultural norms and expectations they will carry into the workplace as adults. For example, a recent survey of children aged 6 to 14 in Ontario, Quebec, and Saskatchewan documents the persistence of gender-role stereotyping. While the girls recognized the expanding occupational horizons of women, at a personal level they still held very traditional aspirations. As the researchers conclude: "Many seem to be saying 'Yes, women can become doctors, but I expect to be a nurse . . . .' " [41] Further discussions with these girls revealed that in adult life most imagined themselves as mothers with small children, supported by a husband. But it is *how* these socialization patterns are strengthened and reproduced within the workplace that is crucial to an understanding of female work behaviour.

Rosabeth Moss Kanter's research leaves little doubt that the main sources of gender inequality must be located within work organizations. Simply stated, Kanter's argument is that "the job makes the person." [42] She elaborates:

> Findings about "typical" behaviour of women in organizations that have been used to reflect either biologically based psychological attributes or characteristics developed through a long socialization to the "female sex role" turn out to reflect very reasonable — and very universal — responses to current organizational situations.[43]

Men and women employed in similar jobs in an organization thus will react in similar ways to their job conditions.

A good example of this is Donald Roy's study of male machine operators.[44] These men escaped the drudgery and isolation of their work — "kept from 'going nuts,' " in Roy's words — by engaging in idle chatter, playing silly games, and fooling around. Female key punch operators, file clerks, or assembly-line workers seek similar *relative satisfactions* to cope with the numbing tedium of their work. In either case, management will use the coping behaviour as evidence that these workers are incapable of performing more demanding jobs. This creates a double bind for employees: the most effective personal means of surviving in jobs at the bottom of the organization sends clear signals to management that they deserve to be kept there.

Kanter does not ignore possible sex differences in socialization or non-work roles. Rather, she underlines the pervasive influence of an individual's job content and organizational position on his or her attitudes and behaviour. The same argument is what Pat and Hugh Armstrong, two Canadian sociologists, identify as the *materialist* model of the sexual division of labour.[45] They document the strong connection between women's self-perceptions and the kinds of work they perform. The historical fact that men and women have performed different tasks in the home and in the labour force creates sex differences in work orientations. For example, women may be aware of their subordinate economic role, but they either rationalize it as an outcome of their domestic responsibilities, or else feel powerless to change it. Research on female clerical workers, for example, amplifies how gender itself is a powerful controlling device within organizations. Male managers draw on social stereotypes of women — as more oriented toward pleasing others, more sensitive to their surroundings, more honest and less mercenary than men — to devise paternalistic and subtly coercive methods of supervision that would not be used on men.[46]

In her analysis of gender divisions in organizations, Kanter goes even further. She shows how management is a social process that relies heavily on trust and conformity. To reduce uncertainty in decision making — the essence of managerial activity — a premium is placed on recruiting individuals who are predictable. The best way to achieve this is to recruit only those people who have social characteristics identical to the existing group of managers. This social cloning therefore reproduces male dominance in management and, moreover, creates an enormous barrier to women.

In sharp contrast, the role of the secretary is built around female stereotypes. Kanter uses the term *office wife* to describe the subordinate, paternalistic, and almost feudal relationship secretaries usually have with their male employers. The job becomes a trap through the dependency of managers on their secretaries and the personal loyalties that result. Many competent secretaries are not promoted because their good performance makes them indispensable to the boss. And unlike other positions in modern bureaucracies, there are no safeguards on the exercise of managerial authority and the expectation that personal services, like fetching coffee, are part of the job. Because secretaries are stuck in this role, they develop work orientations — such as self-effacement or timidity — which undermine advancement prospects.

Men who have more opportunities take advantage of them, and develop behaviours, values, and work attitudes that help them to get ahead. Once young male management trainees are identified as "fast trackers," the resulting halo effect creates the impression that they can make no mistakes. Conversely, women in dead-end jobs quite rationally "give up," losing work commitment and motivation. This signals to supervisors that such individuals do not deserve promotions or raises.

On the other hand, women who do succeed in entering management face the problem of *tokenism*. Kanter argues that being part of a tiny but visible minority in a group results in close scrutiny. This "gold fish bowl" phenomenon leads women, or members of visible minorities, to work twice as hard to prove themselves which, in turn, reinforces the dominant group's impression that these individuals are "different" and therefore do not belong. Furthermore, tokens lack the support systems so essential for surviving in the middle and upper ranks of organizations. But the problem is not sex or race per se; rather, it is one of being part of a group disproportionately underrepresented in a particular environment. What Kanter is telling us is that the structure of opportunities in an organization — basically, who has access to which positions, resources, and rewards — tends to create self-fulfilling prophecies.

TOWARD WORKPLACE EQUALITY

We have documented in detail the inequalities women face in terms of work opportunities and rewards. There are positive signs that barriers to full and equal participation of women in the labour force are slowing being eroded. But the agenda of equality in employment can be achieved more effectively and sooner through bold public policy initiatives. This chapter will conclude by exploring such strategies.

The 1984 Royal Commission on Equality of Employment (the Abella Commission) defines employment equity as a strategy to eliminate the effects of discrimination and to fully open the competition for job opportunities to those who have been arbitrarily excluded. "For women," the Commission's report asserts,

> equality in employment means first a revised approach to the role women play in the workforce. It means taking them seriously as workers and not assuming that their primary interests lie away from the

workplace. At the same time, it means acknowledging the changing role of women in the care of the family by helping them and their male partners to function effectively both as labour force participants and as parents. And it means providing the education and training to permit women the chance to compete for the widest possible range of job options. In practice this means the active recruitment of women into the fullest range of employment opportunities, equal pay for work of equal value, fair consideration for promotions into more responsible positions, participation in corporate policy decision-making through corporate task forces and committees, accessible childcare of adequate quality, paid parental leaves for either parent, and pensions and benefits.[47]

Far from advocating a social revolution, the Abella Commission was expressing the growing belief that men and women should not be treated differently in the labour market. The Commission concludes that voluntary measures for achieving employment equity will not eliminate the deeply entrenched and pervasive discrimination women face in Canadian workplaces; hence the need for legislation requiring employers to institute equal pay for work of equal value and to bring women to a point where they can compete on the same footing with men. An independent monitoring agency would be established to enforce the legislation, and employers would have to file annual reports on the position of women and minorities in their organizations.

The wage gap is the most obvious outcome of gender inequality in the labour market. The most effective way to close the gap is through *comparable worth* legislation. Currently a topic of heated public debate, comparable worth recognizes that occupational segregation underlies the wage gap. Comparable worth uses a standardized evaluation system that assigns points to jobs on the basis of their skill level, effort, responsibility, and working conditions. The objective is to reward all employees on the basis of their contribution to the employer, not on the basis of their personal characteristics. This will establish *equal pay for work of equal value* (a more far-reaching concept than *equal pay for the same work*, which affects far fewer women). The job of a female secretary can be compared, for example, with that of a male maintenance technician employed in the same organization.

Currently, pay equity legislation is in place or being introduced in Ontario, Manitoba, Quebec, and nationally for federally regulated industries. These laws are explicit in their intent. As the Ontario government's Green Paper on pay equity states, the legislation implemented in 1987 is designed as "a positive remedy to address an historical imbalance — the correlation between being a female employee and receiving lower wages."[48] Critics claim that the economy cannot afford the resulting wage increases, or that some businesses may be driven into bankruptcy. But for millions of employed women, comparable worth may provide long overdue recognition of their essential role in the Canadian economy.

Another instrument for achieving gender equality in employment is section 15 of the Canadian Charter of Rights and Freedoms. This section of the Charter became law in April 1985. It establishes for the first time in our history a constitutional entitlement to full equality for women in law, as well as in the *effects* of law. This latter point is a crucial one, for regardless of the wording or intent of a law, if in practice it results in discrimination against women then the courts could rule it to be unconstitutional. This legal process may gradually bring improvements for women.

In summary, Canada is beginning to rectify some of the most glaring problems women confront in the work world. Clearly any successful strategy must recognize that workplace inequalities are imbedded in the very structure of our society and, indeed, have deep historical roots. All of the employment equity programs recommended by the Abella Commission are reform-oriented, aiming to modify existing employment institutions, processes, and social relationships. But how effective will workplace reforms be at changing women's traditional non-work roles — especially within the family — and the supporting socialization processes and ideologies? The limitations of such reforms prompt some radical feminists, for example, to call for an eradication of the patriarchal relations underpinning the exploitation of women. Similarly, Marxists argue that only a socialist revolution can achieve equality between the sexes. These sorts of revolutionary changes are very unlikely. More realistically, reforms that correct both the economic and social barriers faced by women have better prospects for success. This will only happen, though, if women lead the way.

NOTES

1. The role of women in the fur trade is documented by Van Kirk (1977).
2. Johnson (1974): 16-17. See also Susanna Moodie's (1962 [1852]) contemporary account of pioneer life in Upper Canada (now Ontario). Excellent sources for women's history in Canada, including useful bibliographies, are the two volumes edited by Trofimenkoff and Prentice (1977) and Prentice and Trofimenkoff (1985).
3. Lowe (1987): 47. The data are from the 1891 census, the first to break down occupations by sex.
4. For historical background on the transformation of women's work during the rise of industrial capitalism, see Tilly and Scott (1978), Tentler (1979), and Rowbotham (1973, chapter 1). See also Pahl's (1984, chapters 1-5) account of the changing patterns of work for men and women, both inside and outside the home,

in pre-industrial and industrial England.

5. See Bradbury (1984).

6. On the family wage, see Humphries (1977) and Land (1980).

7. These factors are discussed in Armstrong and Armstrong (1984, chapter 6), Ostry and Zaidi (1972): 31.

8. Boulet and Lavallee (1984): 7-8. Data are from the 1981 census.

9. Lowe and Krahn (1985).

10. See Lowe and Krahn (1985:4) and Armstrong and Armstrong (1984): 172-73. While some studies find a negative relationship between family income and wives' labour force participation, suggesting that poor wives are more likely to work due to economic necessity, the influence of family economic resources is actually quite complicated. Wives in high-income families are better able to compete for jobs, and, furthermore, despite their relative affluence, these families may have high expenditures that demand two incomes. So the women who most need to work — the poor — are often less likely to for these reasons.

11. Canada (1958).

12. This post-World War II pattern is described in Ostry (1968).

13. Boyd (1985).

14. Meissner et al. (1975). For recent U.S. evidence of working wives doing a disproportionate share of housework, see Blumstein and Schwartz (1983). This study also found that even in cohabitation, where more egalitarian standards often prevail, women assume the burden of housework. For case studies of the contemporary household division of labour, see Luxton (1980) and Pahl (1984).

15. Kanter (1977, chapter 5); see also Mortimer et al. (1978).

16. See Feuchtwang for a definition of a job ghetto (1982): 251. Freedman (1976) discusses the concepts of labour market segments and shelters.

17. OECD (1985): 11. This study offers a comparative, theoretical discussion of occupational segregation.

18. For a fuller discussion of sex labelling, see Lowe (1987) and Oppenheimer (1970).

19. For an overview of the feminization of clerical work, see Lowe (1987).

20. Canada (1984): 68-69.

21. For 1981, from Boulet and Lavallee (1984): 52-56.

22. See Adams and Baer (1984) on Ontario lawyers, and Fromm and Webb (1985) for an analysis of the work experiences of male and female graduates from the University of Alberta Law School.

23. For a more complete discussion of trends in managerial and professional occupations, see Boulet and Lavallee (1984): 18-21.

24. *Globe and Mail* (2 June 1984): B1.

25. The Royal Commission on Equality of Employment (Canada, 1984, chapter 3) examined the employment problems of women in public sector organizations.

26. Boulet and Lavallee (1984): 17.

27. Canada (1984): 69

28. Most of the data reported in this paragraph are from Boulet and Lavallee (1984). See also Labour Canada (1986, section II).

29. National Council of Welfare (1985): 16. According to Statistics Canada, any individual or family who spends 58.5 percent or more of their income on the necessities of life is poor. This *poverty line* works out to an annual 1986 income of $21,705 for a family of four living in a city with over a half million people (National Council of Welfare 1986).

30. National Council of Welfare (1984a): 4-5. In 1981, 91 percent of men and 63 percent of women, ages 20 to 64, contributed to the government-run Canada Pension Plan. Males with private pension plans, who are in the minority, can share these with their spouses. But most private plans do not provide survivor benefits so that wives, who often outlive their husbands, can continue to draw the pension.

31. Forcese (1986): 62.

32. Gunderson (1982).

33. Boulet and Lavallee (1984): 27.

34. *Ibid.*, 60.

35. Hacker (1981).

36. See Feldberg and Glenn (1979). See also Brown (1976) and Acker (1978) for general discussions of the male biases in the sociological study of work. Hearn and Parkin (1983) offer similar criticisms of the organizational research field. For an informative discussion of gender as a key variable in sociological analysis, see Morgan (1986).

37. Reagan and Blaxall (1976): 2.

38. For a thorough discussion of human capital explanations of sex differences in occupations and earnings, see Blau and Ferber (1986, chapter 7).

39. For an elaboration of these criticisms, see Phillips and Phillips (1983, chapter 4) and Dex (1985): 130-41.

40. See Garnsey et al. (1985) for this argument. For examples of the interplay of family and employment in this way, see Johnson and Johnson (1982) and McNally (1979).

41. Labour Canada (1986): 55.

42. Kanter (1977): 67.

43. *Ibid.*, 9.

44. Roy (1959-60).

45. Armstrong and Armstrong (1984, chapter 6). This book is a good basic source on women's work in Canada.

46. Glenn and Feldberg (1977): 59. For a discussion of how management applies different recruitment and control strategies to men and women, see Acker and Van Houten (1974).

47. Canada (1984): 4.

48. *Globe and Mail* (20 September 1986).

6

Subjective Experiences of Work

INTRODUCTION

Thus far we have presented a largely structural analysis of work in Canada. Our focus has been on changes in occupational and industrial structures, technology, management strategies, labour markets, and the ways in which work is organized. This chapter provides balance to our emphasis on social structure by examining the subjective experience of work, that is, how individual workers actually experience their jobs. We explore questions about how much satisfaction individuals obtain from their work, and about the specific features of work that provide the most (and least) satisfaction. We also compare jobs in different labour market segments with respect to their intrinsic and extrinsic rewards. As we will see, there is an enormous literature on job satisfaction.

However, an overview of job satisfaction theories and research presents an incomplete picture of people's feelings about work. Some jobs are clearly more stressful than others, leaving workers physically and mentally fatigued at the end of a work period. We will thus approach the subjective dimension of work from the perspective of stress research. Our discussion will also lead us to the topic of worker alienation. Here we will discover two rather distinct approaches. The narrower social-psychological approach parallels job satisfaction research; the broader structural approach, in contrast, goes well beyond the concerns of the job satisfaction literature.

The central theme in this chapter is that one's work can affect one's psychological state. In research design terms, we are identifying the job as the independent variable and subjective responses to work as the dependent variable. But it is also important to go back a little further in the causal chain to examine the preferences and motivations workers bring to their jobs. Just ask several of your friends or classmates what they want to get out of a job, or what satisfactions they obtain from their work, and note the variety of answers. Some of this could be due to their work experiences, but some of it could also be attributed to their different work orientations. While our emphasis is on the shaping influences of job conditions, we will begin our discussion by considering how work values and orientations might be involved in the process.

WORK VALUES AND WORK ORIENTATIONS

Values, as sociologists use the term, are "standards used by members of a society to judge behaviour and to choose among various possible goals."[1] We could talk about how personal attributes such as honesty and industriousness are valued in our society, about how we value freedom of speech, and about the value placed on getting a good education. And we might ask about how work is valued or, in other words, about the *meaning of work* in a particular society. In this chapter, we will examine Canadian work values, noting how they differ from the dominant work values in different times and places.

Having identified *work values* as broad societal standards, we can define *work orientations* more narrowly as the meaning attached to work by particular individuals within a society. Blackburn and Mann define an orientation as "a central organizing principle which under-lies people's attempts to make sense of their lives."[2] Thus, studying work orientations involves determining how work fits into people's conception of what is important in their lives. In other words, do we continue to work out of economic necessity, because income from the job allows us to enjoy life away from work, or because we receive enjoyment and personal fulfilment from our work?

Obviously, work values within a society influence personal work orientations. But there are several reasons for distinguishing between these two levels of analysis. First, we cannot assume that broader work values are necessarily shared by all members of a society. In fact, as our discussion of managerial ideologies and practises in Chapter 4 demonstrated, particular work values have often been promoted by groups in power to gain the cooperation of their subordinates.[3] Second, it is possible that an individual's work orientations are shaped not only by larger societal work values but also by specific experiences on the job. Indeed, a worker whose job is dissatisfying may adopt work values that challenge or contradict the dominant work ideology.

The Changing Meaning of Work

The meaning attached to work has changed over the centuries, largely as a reflection of social and economic developments. The ancient Greeks and Romans viewed most forms of work negatively, considering it brutalizing and uncivilized. In fact, the Greek word for work, *ponos,* came from the Latin root word for "sorrow." According to

Greek mythology, the gods had cursed the human race with the need to work. Given these dominant work values, the ruling classes turned their attention to politics, warfare, the arts, and philosophy, leaving physical work to be done by slaves. Slavery was somewhat difficult to reconcile with a philosophy that all people are born free and equal. But, as Anthony argues, in ancient Greece and virtually all other societies "ideologies of work" justifying the domination of one group by another have been developed.[4]

Early Hebrew religious and cultural values placed a different but no more positive emphasis on work. Hard work was seen as the necessary atonement for original sin. According to the Old Testament, God banished Eve and Adam from the Garden of Eden to a life of hard labour. This "original sin" perspective on work remained part of the early Christian world view, with some variations. For example, during the eleventh through fourteenth centuries, leaders of some religious sects in Europe adopted a "cold shower" approach: the exhaustion produced by hard work would ensure that the needs of one's soul would take precedence over physical pleasures.

A more positive view of work was promoted by St. Thomas Aquinas during the thirteenth century. In attempting to rank occupations according to their value to society, Aquinas rejected the notion that all work is a curse or a necessary evil. Instead, he argued that some forms of work were better than others. Priests were assigned the highest ranks, followed by those working in agriculture, and then craft workers. Because they produced food or products useful to society, these groups were ranked higher than merchants and shopkeepers.[5] A comparison of this scheme to the contemporary occupational status scales described in Chapter 3 reveals some interesting reversals. The status of those involved in commercial activity — bankers, corporate owners, and managers, for example — has increased while farmers and craft workers have experienced substantial declines in status.

Martin Luther's ideas marked a significant change in dominant work values. Luther put forward the doctrine that work is "the base and key to life."[6] Although he did not reject the traditional negative assessment of work for profit, Luther went beyond the belief that hard work was necessary as an atonement for original sin. When he wrote: "There is just one best way to serve God — to do most perfectly the work of one's profession,"[7] he was articulating the idea of a "calling"; that is, industriousness and hard work *within* one's station in life was how to fulfil God's will. Whether or not the rural peasantry or urban working class actually shared these values is difficult to determine. However, to the extent that the ruling classes could convince those beneath them that hard work was a moral obligation, existing patterns of power and privilege could be maintained.

The Protestant Work Ethic

The Industrial Revolution transformed the social and economic landscape of Europe. These developments were mirrored in a new set of work values. In his famous book, *The Protestant Ethic and the Spirit of Capitalism,* Max Weber discussed how Protestant values and beliefs — particularly those of the Calvinists, a group which had broken away from the mainstream Protestant churches — actually contributed to the spread of capitalism in Europe.[8] Weber noted how the Calvinists embraced hard work, rejected worldly pleasures, and extolled the virtues of frugality. Thus, while religious principles encouraged individuals to make and reinvest profits, the unintended economic consequence was a fuelling of capitalist development.

Weber emphasized the Calvinist belief in "predestination." This doctrine held that entry into heaven could not be influenced by good works on earth because it was already predetermined by God. Weber argued that the uncertainties generated by such beliefs ("Am I among the chosen?") encouraged these Protestants to work extremely hard for success. While hard work and economic success could not be considered a "ticket" to heaven, they could serve to alleviate one's anxieties about being chosen. After all, the elect had been placed on earth to glorify God through their work. Weber further suggested that employees convinced of the merits of these work values would be dependable and hardworking.[9]

Weber was not attempting to prove that Calvinist beliefs *caused* capitalism. Instead, he was arguing that Calvinist doctrines translated into work values that provided favourable conditions for the growth of capitalism. Debates have developed over whether the Calvinists and other Protestant reformers acted as they did solely on the basis of their religion, and whether other groups not sharing their beliefs might have been equally frugal and economically successful.[10] Such debates raise doubts about whether a particular Protestant sect actually shaped the course of modern economic history. Nonetheless, Weber illuminated the importance for the development of capitalism of work values emphasizing the virtue of industriousness and the respectability of making profits.

Freedom and equality are additional secular values that fit into the belief system of industrial capitalist democracies.[11] The ideas that workers are participants in a labour market where they can choose their jobs, and that nobody is forced to remain in an unrewarding job, are central components of this belief system. Hard work and diligence, consequently, must explain why some people become so much more powerful and wealthy than others. Hence, equality does not refer to the distribution of wealth and power, but to access to the same opportunities for upward mobility in a competitive labour market.

For many employees, however, the daily realities of limited choice and managerial authority contradict these values.

A Declining Work Ethic?

How often have you heard or read that the work ethic is disappearing, that people today are no longer willing to work hard? This concern about a declining work ethic in industrial capitalist societies appears to be widespread. A variation on this theme involves unfavourable comparisons of the work commitment of Canadian or U.S. workers to that of workers in other societies (usually Japan). Do these concerns have a basis in fact? Is Canadian society experiencing a significant deterioration in work values? Before addressing these questions, we should note that such fears focus on only part of what Weber defined as the "Protestant work ethic." Weber was analyzing a complex set of work values, not just the willingness to work hard, diligently, and obediently in whatever job was available. Nevertheless, such "moral panics" are not new: previous generations have also voiced unease about a weakening will to work.[12]

Such concerns about a faltering work ethic prompted the Canadian government to sponsor the national Work Ethic and Job Satisfaction surveys in 1973 and 1974, involving roughly 2,000 and 1,000 Canadian adults, respectively. The results provided little support for the declining work ethic thesis. For example, few respondents agreed that they would rather collect unemployment insurance than hold a job. And very large majorities of the sample members stated that, given the choice, they would prefer working to not having a job, and that work was a central aspect of their lives. Paradoxically, these same respondents doubted the work commitment of other Canadians. Four out of five agreed, "There is an atmosphere of welfare for anybody who wants it in this country." People seemed to be saying that they personally wanted to work, but that our social institutions make it easy for others to avoid working. In other words, they were repeating the widely held opinion that the work ethic is failing, while demonstrating with their own responses that the belief might be inaccurate. Thus, the summary report concluded that "Canadians are committed to work."[13]

What about the claims that Japanese workers have a much stronger work ethic? The popular media idealize Japanese employees because they willingly work long hours, frequently forego holidays, and are strongly committed to their employers. For example, a recent survey of over 7,000 young Japanese labour force participants showed 79 percent reporting that they would not mind cancelling a date if requested to work overtime.[14] Typically, explanations of this behaviour focus on cultural factors, suggesting that the Japanese have always exhibited very strong patterns of conformity and social integration. Today the corporation has assumed the once central role of the family and the immediate community in the lives of Japanese workers. As we saw in Chapter 4, Japanese firms are characterized as "clans" or families because of their paternalistic form of management and emphasis on worker loyalty. From the vantage point of North America, the hard work of Japanese employees appears to be a key ingredient in the Japanese "economic miracle" of recent decades.

Clearly, Japan's strong economic performance, compared to almost all western nations, is difficult to dispute. However, the image of the highly committed and loyal worker may not accurately describe all members of the Japanese labour force. In some ways, the Japanese economy and labour market is highly segmented, more so than in Canada. Only about one-quarter of Japanese workers are employed in the huge, profitable, high-tech corporations so admired by Western observers. Most people find work in the smaller businesses that subcontract to make parts or provide services for the giant firms. [15] The major advantages of this arrangement for the large corporations include the flexibility of being able to expand and contract their labour force without hiring permanent employees, and reduced inventory costs through "just in time" delivery of components from the subcontracting businesses.

Employees in the core sector firms still work more hours per week than most Canadians, but the gap is shrinking. However, it is in the small firms and family businesses that extremely long hours combine with low pay, few benefits, and little job security to create sweatshop conditions that few Canadians would tolerate. Thus, willingness to work long and hard is better seen as an economic necessity than as a cultural trait. In fact, the gap between pay levels in the major firms and in this secondary labour market has been widening.[16] Along with much higher wages, major Japanese firms offer lifetime employment guarantees, a variety of fringe benefits, and opportunities for upward advancement within the corporation. Loyalty and commitment to the firm are fundamental to Japanese corporate culture, but these extensive economic inducements also play a major role in maintaining the stability of the system. According to some accounts, employee commitment may not be as strong as many advocates of Japanese-style management suggest. Critics argue that loyalty to the company is built on fears of job loss, and that the economic benefits provided to workers simply make it easier for corporations to demand compliance and hard work.[17]

This interpretation of Japanese workplace behaviour contrasts sharply with a cultural explanation. Certainly religious and cultural values may complement the effects of industrial organization and employment contracts, but in the end the latter are determinant. A recent comparative study found that Japanese workers were more likely than U.S. workers to be employed in firms where benefits were extensive, where some employee participation in decision making was encouraged, and where mobility opportunities and job security were provided. However, given a similar organizational context, there were few differences in commitment to one's firm between the two countries.[18] Thus, for workers in both the core and periphery sectors of the Japanese economy, economic and organizational factors have a significant influence on workplace behaviours and work values.

Returning to the Canadian Work Ethic and Job Satisfaction studies of the 1970s, we note the conclusion that "to some extent, at least, most people who work do so out of economic necessity."[19] A strong desire for work could reflect internalized work values, but it might also be a recognition that without paid work it is virtually impossible to enjoy a reasonable standard of living. In contemporary capitalist society, almost all labour force participants have little choice but to exchange their labour for a wage. Choosing to live on social assistance would be opting for a life of poverty. In short, Canadians' commitment to work is based both on a well-developed work ethic and a sense of economic necessity.

This argument counters fears of a weakening work ethic with the suggestion that commitment to work should be increasing because of the greater possibility of unemployment.[20] Recent opinion polls show that worry about personal job loss is widespread, especially since the high unemployment rates of the early 1980s. These polls also show that work remains a central aspect of most Canadians' lives. On this basis, *Maclean's Magazine* recently concluded that "it is clear that the job — whether it is fear of losing it or the joy of doing it — remains the focal point in the lives of most Canadians."[21]

So is the work ethic in danger in Canada or not? If we are referring to Weber's Protestant work ethic, we would probably have to conclude that this particular package of work values is not widespread. But if we look at the importance of work in the lives of Canadians, the evidence suggests that, along with individuals' families and friends, work is central to most people's lives. Or perhaps, as some analysts argue, the Protestant work ethic is a useful myth, and the predominant ethic is one emphasizing wealth rather than work. Kelvin and Jarrett elaborate:

> The "ethic" which has truly been predominant and pervasive is not a work ethic but, for want of a better term, a *wealth ethic*. Wealth is (quite correctly) perceived as the basis of economic independence; that is the key issue, and has been so for centuries. The "ethic" is to make or to have sufficient wealth not to have to depend on others; work is only one means to that end, and certainly not the one universally most esteemed:

not in any class. Provided that one has enough money to be independent, there is no great moral obligation to work, certainly not in the sense of gainful, productive employment.[22]

There is no easy answer to the question of whether work's centrality reflects internalized work values or grows out of economic necessity. While dominant societal values encourage people to want to work, the reason why any individual returns to her or his job, day after day, depends a great deal on the characteristics of the job and the employment relationship, the work orientations that an individual brings to or develops on the job, and the availability of other options.

Finally, we must at least briefly address the question of why fears about a failing work ethic surface so regularly. Perhaps each older generation looks at the younger generation and, seeing some experimentation with jobs and lifestyles, forgets its own similar experiences and concludes that values are slipping. For example, a 1984 opinion poll revealed that 63 percent of Canadians agreed that "the next generation will probably not be as dedicated to hard work as were previous generations."[23] Alternatively, such fears may have ideological roots. Given the often opposing interests between workers and employers, we might expect ongoing concerns about the work commitment of employees. Over the course of this century, Canada has developed welfare and unemployment insurance schemes in order to provide some assistance to those out of work. We often hear complaints that these programs encourage laziness and reward those unwilling to work. In fact, such concerns originally prompted the government to sponsor the Work Ethic and Job Satisfaction studies.[24] Ironically, the stigma attached to receiving welfare assistance, and the low level of assistance provided, may actually reinforce the work ethic.

Work as Self-Fulfilment

While working hard and getting ahead remain dominant values, they are not the only perspective on work found in our society. Another set of values, sharing the basic assumption that hard work is virtuous in itself, emerged during the seventeenth and eighteenth centuries.[25] This "humanist" tradition grew out of Renaissance philosophies that distinguished humans from other species on the basis of our ability to consciously direct our labour. A view of human beings as "creators" led easily to the belief that work was a fulfilling and liberating activity that constituted the essence of humanity. Only through work, then, could an individual achieve his or her human potential.

Karl Marx fashioned these Renaissance ideas into a radical critique of capitalism and a formula for social revolution. He agreed that the essence of humanity lay in work, but argued that capitalist relations of production did not allow workers to develop their human potential. Because they had little control over their labour and its products, they were engaged in *alienating* work. For Marx, capitalist economic relations stifled human independence and creativity. Only when capitalism was replaced by socialism would work be able to liberate human potential.[26]

Marx's theory of alienation, which we return to later in this chapter, has had a major impact on the sociology of work. Interestingly, the same types of humanistic work values that influenced Marx are also espoused by some contemporary non-Marxist students of the workplace, as we will note in our discussion of "quality of work life" (QWL) programs in Chapter 9. But QWL proponents would not agree that capitalism is at fault. They would argue, instead, that better organizational systems and job designs will allow workers more opportunities for involvement and skill development. But we must be alert to the possibility that "many historical . . . and contemporary views about work which have been regarded as axiomatic are ideological in that they are intended to influence the behaviour of subordinates."[27] No doubt many of the advocates of work reform are sincerely committed to humanistic work values. Yet many corporations have adopted QWL programs primarily in the hope that they will improve productivity while simultaneously making their work force less difficult to control.

Orientations to Work

Having examined societal work values, we can now focus our discussion on people's job expectations or, phrased another way, the type of work orientations they bring to their jobs. Is their work a major source of self-fulfilment, or is it merely a means of obtaining money to buy other satisfactions? Perhaps the job serves primarily as a context in which one maintains contacts with friends? Obviously not everyone will share the same orientation to work, so we should try to identify some of the sources of variation, including how work orientations may be influenced by experiences on the job.

In an influential article, David Lockwood tried to explain some of the variations he observed in British working-class "images of society." Lockwood was interested in the issue of working-class consciousness or, in other words, how British workers perceived social inequalities. He identified three distinct world views originating in different community and workplace experiences. *Proletarian* workers, argued Lockwood, see the world in much the way Marx had predicted: they perceive themselves to be in an "us against them" conflict with their employers. This image of society is more pronounced in industries such as shipbuilding and mining. The social organization of these industries intensifies worker–employer differences, leading to a heightened class consciousness.[28] *Deferential* workers also recognize class differences. But this type of worker accepts the status quo, believing that inequalities in wealth and power are justified. Provided they are treated decently, deferential workers are unlikely to engage in militant actions against employers. Lockwood located this world view in the traditional service industries and in family firms where paternalistic employment relationships foster the belief that the existing stratification system is normal.

Both of these traditional orientations, Lockwood argued, are found primarily in declining industries. *Privatized* workers, the third basic type, are more typical of the contemporary working class. This group tends to see society separated not into two major classes, but into many finer levels on the basis of income and possessions. Rather than expressing antagonism or attachment to their employers, their dominant feeling is one of indifference. Similarly, they are unlikely to develop strong ties with other workers, and are unlikely to participate in union activities. According to Lockwood, the "cash nexus" is the primary employment relationship for such workers. Work is simply a means of obtaining a better standard of living.

Lockwood's major concern was with the question of class consciousness, an issue to which we return in Chapter 8.[29] However, his theory of "instrumental" work orientations as an emergent form of consciousness informed the subsequent Affluent Worker Study. This study examined the work orientations, political attitudes, and work and community behaviours of a group of auto workers in Luton, a manufacturing town north of London, England.[30] These "affluent workers" had chosen to move to this new industrial town because the available jobs there would provide them with the money and security needed to enjoy a middle-class standard of living. The fact that work in the Vauxhall automobile factory was not intrinsically rewarding was of little consequence. The Luton workers were clearly not about to become militant. Indeed, it was argued that their choice of community reflected their preferences for extrinsic work rewards. Thus the source of these instrumental work orientations lay outside the factory. Society's emphasis on the importance of making money and getting ahead — values central to the institutions of capitalism — had left its mark on these workers' views about society and their place in it.[31]

Critics have pointed out that Goldthorpe, Lockwood, and their co-researchers in the Affluent Worker project were probably overgeneralizing from males in a single community to all twentieth-century industrial workers. Others have suggested that contemporary workers appear to be instrumental only in comparison to an idealized proletarian worker of the past.[32] Moreover, the study's own data only partially supported the theory.[33] Nevertheless, the Affluent Worker project was highly influential, drawing our attention to the ways in which the orientations and preferences of individual workers can influence their behaviour. This "action" perspective improved on previous research, which had tended to ignore the role of individual actors in the larger drama of industrial relations.

But Blackburn and Mann criticized this overly individualistic approach in their study of the labour market for male workers in the British city of Peterborough.[34] They found that most workers reported a variety of work orientations. In addition, there was often little congruence between an individual's expressed orientations and the characteristics of his job. One possible interpretation of this might be that most workers are unsure of what they want from a job. But Blackburn and Mann turned this explanation on its head, arguing that the major flaw with an orientations model of the labour market is that most people have very few choices about available jobs. They take whatever work they can get.[35]

It is equally possible that some work orientations are generated on the job, rather than brought to the job, as a literal reading of the Affluent Worker study would suggest.[36] If a job offers few intrinsic rewards or little opportunity to develop a career, workers may readjust their values and priorities accordingly. Commenting on the low level of skill required of many workers, Blackburn and Mann noted that most employees in their study had to use "more mental effort and resourcefulness in getting to work than in doing their jobs."[37] In the face of these constraints, individual orientations and preferences matter little.

In a classic study of American automobile workers, Ely Chinoy discussed how men performing monotonous tasks on an assembly line redefined the meaning of success. They dreamed of the day when they could get a slightly better job in the plant or even own a home.[38] Success was defined within the context of what they could realistically achieve, given their limited choices. Sennett and Cobb returned to the same theme two decades later in their book *The Hidden Injuries of Class*.[39] Their discussions with a cross section of American blue-collar workers revealed a tendency to downplay intrinsic work rewards while emphasizing pay and job security. Workers interviewed by Sennett and Cobb also redefined the meaning of success to accommodate their personal lives, frequently talking about how hard they were working in order to provide *their children* with the chance to go to college.

A recent Canadian study attacks the instrumentalism thesis more directly. MacKinnon studied male automobile workers in Oshawa, Ontario, a research setting chosen because of its similarities to the Luton research site in England. He found instrumental work values least prevalent among more highly skilled workers and, in contrast, more pronounced among those working on the assembly line. Mac-Kinnon concluded that people in low-skill jobs, who are allowed little control over their working conditions, will adapt by viewing the job in primarily material terms.[40] This argument is echoed by Rinehart's discussion of the contradictions between work attitudes and behaviours:

> Instrumental orientations should be understood as rational adaptations to jobs that are characterized by extreme specialization, subordination, and inequalities of prestige and treatment. If jobs are selected on the basis of economic criteria, this only reveals the flatness of the world of blue-collar work and not an absence of (abstract) desires for gratifying jobs.[41]

Having contrasted the two sides of the work orientations debate, it appears that both have some merit. The argument that jobs with few intrinsic rewards can influence workers to think in instrumental terms is perhaps more convincing, given the evidence of less instrumentalism among highly skilled workers. On the other hand, given the emphasis on financial rewards and material success in our society, we should not be surprised to find that some employees are motivated by instrumental work orientations.

How widespread are instrumental work attitudes in Canada? In the 1974 Work Ethic study, 33 percent of the sample agreed with the statement: "If I could earn $7 an hour [a high wage in 1974], I would take any job." But only 16 percent agreed with the more precise statement: "To me, work is a way to make money and I don't expect to get any special satisfaction or enjoyment from doing it."[42] Results from the 1983 Edmonton Area Study also suggest that only a minority of the population express instrumental sentiments. The statement, "My main interest in my work is to get enough money to do the other things I want to do," elicited agreement from 38 percent of the employed members of the sample. However, a much smaller proportion (11 percent) agreed with the statement "I don't care what job I do as long as it pays well."[43]

The 1974 Work Ethic Study presented sample members with a list of thirty-four intrinsic and extrinsic job characteristics, such as "have enough authority"; "opportunity to develop abilities"; "pay is good"; "people are helpful"; "chances to get ahead"; and "job security is good." Asked to rank these characteristics in terms of how important they were to them personally, respondents identified "work is interesting" as their highest priority. Of all the extrinsic characteristics, "job security" was considered most important, but ranked twelfth overall. "Good pay" was number seventeen on the list.[44] Again, the 1983 Edmonton Area Study provides comparable data. In this study, respondents were asked to choose from a list of five job characteristics what they would look for and prefer in a job; only 14 percent chose "pays well" as their first preference.[45]

Why do only a minority of Canadian workers appear to hold instrumental work orientations? Surely the debate over instrumentalism suggests these attitudes would be more widespread. Part of the answer lies in how respondents were asked about their work orientations. The questions tapped work orientations *in general*. Based on the argument that specific work experiences are largely responsible for instrumental orientations, we would hypothesize that if the same individuals had been asked about their orientation to *their own jobs*, a larger proportion might have admitted that they were doing it mainly for the money.

In summary, instrumentalism is not the only reaction to work exhibited by Canadians. Some people have a more intrinsic orientation to work, as the Work Ethic study demonstrated. For such individuals, opportunities to be creative, to develop special skills and abilities, to make decisions affecting one's work, and to take pride in what one has produced are highly important. In fact, few people are motivated by a single reason for working. Instead, they are likely to express commitment (somewhat tenuously) to a number of interrelated work orientations.[46] We probably all know some people who work extremely hard, driven by the goal of "getting ahead." It is not the money, but success itself that is important. Other individuals have a strong preference for outside work.[47] For still others, the importance of work lies in the social relationships maintained in the workplace.[48] Finally, for many women, preferences for part-time work may reflect compromises required by their much greater share of domestic and child-rearing duties.[49] But, in general, instrumental and intrinsic work orientations may be seen as the archetypes. And to a large extent the work that people do, or the work opportunities available to them, influence their work orientations.

JOB SATISFACTION AND DISSATISFACTION

Work orientations are general preferences for certain types of work, or expectations of what a job should provide. In addition to shaping work behaviours, these orientations affect other attitudes, such as job satisfaction, which is a more specific subjective reaction to the particular set of rewards provided by one's present job.[50]

The causes and consequences of job satisfaction and dissatisfaction have been debated extensively from a diversity of perspectives.[51] Many researchers assume that productivity is a function of job satisfaction. Thus, their goal has been to discover how to organize work and manage employees in a way that leads to increased satisfaction, productivity, and profits. Other researchers, adopting the humanistic view that work is a central part of the human condition, view satisfying and self-fulfilling work for as many people as possible as a desirable societal goal.

The Prevalence of Job Dissatisfaction

The most commonly used measure of job satisfaction in survey research is some variation of "All in all, how satisfied are you with your job?" In response, most workers report some degree of satisfaction with their work. For example, this question has been included several times in the annual Edmonton Area Study. Usually, about 80 percent of the employed sample members state that they are satisfied with their jobs.[52] These and other similar results would suggest that job dissatisfaction is not a serious problem, since only a small minority of labour force participants appear to experience it.

What, then, prompted the widespread concern in the 1970s about declining levels of job satisfaction? Some observers argued that a new generation of better-educated workers was expressing dissatisfaction with low-skill, routinized work, which offered few intrinsic work rewards. Being more educated, and having been raised in an era that increasingly emphasized self-fulfilment, individuals were bringing higher expectations to the job. In short, compared to previous generations of American workers, they were less instrumentally oriented.[53] However, surveys relying on standard job satisfaction measures were not picking up this apparent attitude shift. The 1973 Canadian Job Satisfaction survey showed 89 percent of its subjects reporting that they were at least "somewhat satisfied" with their jobs, including 40 percent who answered "very satisfied." Eighty-five percent of the respondents in a comparable U.S. study reported satisfaction with their jobs.[54]

It would appear that job dissatisfaction is not, and has not been, a very serious problem. However, there are several reasons why we could question such a conclusion. Rinehart points out that the work behaviours of Canadians tell us another story. Strikes and walkouts, absenteeism, and high quit rates when unemployment rates are low, all indicate considerable dissatisfaction with working conditions. In addition, Rinehart proposes that answers to general questions about job satisfaction are "pragmatic judgements of one's position *vis-à-vis* the narrow range of available jobs." Most workers look at the few alternatives they have and conclude, from this frame of reference, that they are relatively satisfied with their work.[55]

Looking at it another way, responses to general job satisfaction questions may be similar to replies to the question, "How are you today?" Most of us would say "fine" in response to the latter question, whether or not this was the case. More specific and probing questions are needed to uncover feelings of dissatisfaction with work. We should also recognize that in a society with highly individualistic work values, people may be unwilling to express dissatisfaction with their jobs because it could reflect negatively on their own ability and efforts. General satisfaction measures may "strike too closely and too directly at the worker's self-esteem."[56]

Clearly, additional measures of job satisfaction are required. The subjects in the 1973 Job Satisfaction survey were asked if they would take the same job again, given the opportunity to start over. Only 61 percent agreed; 33 percent said they would have some second thoughts, and 6 percent said definitely not. Similar responses were obtained with a question about recommending their jobs to a friend.[57] These *behavioural intention* measures typically reveal a higher degree of job dissatisfaction. Despite having said they are satisfied, the same individuals are less prepared to admit that this particular job is really one that they would prefer. Or, as Stewart and Blackburn put it, "satisfaction is expressed within a framework of what is possible, liking is expressed within a framework of what is desirable."[58] After examining national survey data on job satisfaction in the United States, Kalleberg and Griffin reached a similar conclusion: "Workers, then, report that they are generally satisfied with their job on most national surveys . . . perhaps because they have learned, via a variety of mechanisms and in a variety of institutions, to 'devalue' what they know they cannot achieve."[59]

Job Satisfaction and Individual Characteristics

What factors influence job satisfaction? Studies of this subject can be divided into those focusing on the nature of the job, and those emphasizing characteristics of workers.[60] The latter type of research, with which we begin this discussion, introduces work orientations into the explanation, suggesting that people react differently to work depending on their expectations and preferences.

Research results typically show greater satisfaction among older labour force participants.[61] Perhaps this is because older workers have reduced their expectations, becoming more accepting of relatively unrewarding work. We might call this an *ageing effect*.[62] On the other hand, a *cohort effect* might explain lower expectations (and consequently higher satisfaction) on the part of older workers. This assumes that older workers grew up in an era when simply having a secure job was all one desired, and when little self-fulfilment at work was expected. Third, we might propose a *life cycle effect*, arguing that older workers are more likely to have family and community interests that might compensate for dissatisfying work. A final explanation emphasizes the nature of the work performed, suggesting that older people have had more opportunity to move up into better, satisfying jobs.

Which is the best explanation? No single answer emerges from the empirical evidence. One of the more comprehensive recent studies concludes that all of these factors may be involved![63] Regardless, we know that older workers are more likely to report satisfaction with their work, and that this is due, not to some biological phenomenon, but to their cumulative social experiences in the workplace and the larger society.[64]

There are several hypotheses that could link education and job satisfaction. One derives from human capital theory (reviewed in Chapter 3), which suggests that higher education should lead to a better job and, in turn, more job satisfaction. The alternative hypothesis has received more attention. Many observers claim that well-educated individuals will have high expectations of work, and that many jobs cannot fill these expectations: "What is clear from almost every study of job dissatisfaction is that the placing of intelligent and highly qualified workers in dull and unchallenging jobs is a prescription for pathology — for the worker, the employer, the society."[65] Hence, given the same relatively unrewarding job, the higher an individual's education, the lower his or her satisfaction.[66]

Despite its intuitive appeal, there is little evidence for this argument. While we know that younger workers (who are presumably more educated) are less satisfied, they differ little from older workers in their adherence to intrinsic work values. In addition, studies focusing explicitly on well-educated blue-collar workers have not detected significantly more dissatisfaction than among their less educated co-workers. Perhaps the more educated workers anticipate future upward mobility, and so are willing to tolerate less rewarding work for a time.[67] This is not to suggest that jobs lacking intrinsic rewards are as satisfying as jobs providing such rewards. Rather, the evidence seems to indicate that intrinsically unrewarding jobs will have the same negative effect on all workers, regardless of their education.

Are women or men typically more satisfied with their jobs? Given that women are overrepresented in lower-status jobs in the secondary labour market, we might predict less satisfaction on their part. Yet the research evidence is fairly emphatic that, despite clear differences in work rewards, there is little difference between men and women in self-reported job satisfaction.[68] Such findings encourage researchers to examine work orientations, on the assumption that women may bring lower expectations to the job. The effects of gender-role socialization at home, in the school, and via the media may encourage women to place less value on the intrinsic and extrinsic rewards of work and more on social relationships in the family, the community, and on the job. Hence, the argument goes, women are more likely to tolerate and even express satisfaction with dreary jobs.[69] The 1973 Canadian Job Satisfaction survey did, in fact, find that women were more likely than men to value good social relationships in the work setting, and were more likely to be satisfied with these features of work, compared to extrinsic rewards such as pay and promotion opportunities.[70]

But, as we have already argued, such differences may be a product of the workplace itself. If women and men inhabit very different labour markets, their divergent work orientations and preferences may be adaptations to the type of work they typically perform. A study of post office employees in Edmonton tested this hypothesis by comparing men and women performing identical jobs. If working conditions are indeed the major source of work orientations, then we would hypothesize no difference between these two groups doing the very same jobs. In fact, the researchers found very few gender differences in job satisfaction, in how workers described their jobs, or in the particular features of work most likely to affect job satisfaction.[71]

A recent American study found similar levels of job satisfaction, and similar work orientations for both men and women, across a range of occupations. But when those employed in managerial or professional jobs were compared to those in clerical, service, and other blue-collar jobs, some interesting differences appeared. In the upper-level jobs, women and men reported very similar work orientations, and gave roughly the same assessments of intrinsic and extrinsic job rewards. In the lower-level jobs, women were less positive than their male counterparts in evaluations of extrinsic and intrinsic job rewards. They were also more likely than men to say that good social relationships in the workplace were important to them (men at this occupational level placed more value on extrinsic job rewards). In other words, in the primary labour market, few gender differences in satisfaction or orientations were observed. In the secondary labour market, women received fewer work rewards and were also more likely to say that they valued other things (such as social relationships) about their work. If gender-role socialization was the major determinant of differing work orientations, we would expect women in both labour markets to exhibit similar work orientations. But these results suggest that "gender differences in work values found in lower-level occupations represent an accommodation on the part of women to an impoverished work situation."[72]

Job Satisfaction and Work Content

We have been arguing that the nature of work itself may be more important than work orientations in determining job satisfaction. When asked for details about why they are satisfied or dissatisfied with their jobs, people will most often reply with a comment about the work itself. Consider, for example, the following job descriptions:

> Every morning even now, I'm happy to come to work; I look forward to it. I think it's because this business is, well, you never know when you come in here in the morning what's going to be asked of you. It could be different every day; generally it is.[73]

This Alberta-based oil-field service company manager had a very different assessment of his job than did the Ontario automobile assembly-line worker who concluded that:

> The only good thing about working on the assembly line from the job point of view is that you do the same thing day after day. Therefore, you're so damned good at it you can do it with your eyes closed. You don't have to get up in the morning and say "well, am I going to have a bad day or a good day?" If you're up to doing the job physically, it's a snap — once you get into things. That's about the only *good* thing about working on the assembly line.[74]

Reading between the lines, it is possible to detect preferences for certain types of work. But it is also very clear that the variety and challenge which prove satisfying for the manager are largely absent from the job of the assembly-line worker.

Much of the job satisfaction research literature has attempted to identify characteristics of jobs and work organizations that workers are most likely to find satisfying. Our discussion of management theories in Chapter 4 highlighted how employers' assumptions about what satisfies and motivates workers have changed over the years. Taylorism proposed that workers were basically satisfied by material rewards; human relations emphasized the importance of social relationships and cooperation on the job. A popular theory developed several decades ago by Frederick Herzberg drew from both traditions, emphasizing the extrinsic and intrinsic rewards of work. *Hygiene* factors like pay, supervisory style, and physical surroundings in the workplace could reduce job dissatisfaction, Herzberg argued; but only *motivators* such as the opportunity to develop one's skills, and chances to make decisions about one's own work, could increase job satisfaction.[75]

Influenced by Herzberg's two-factor model, most job satisfaction researchers now utilize multidimensional approaches incorporating both intrinsic and extrinsic rewards of work. Much of the recent research has built on large national studies such as the Canadian Job Satisfaction Study and the U.S. Quality of Employment Study. In these surveys, respondents were given a list of thirty-four job characteristics and asked to assess, first, how important each was to them and, second, how their work rated on these characteristics.[76] Detailed statistical analyses of responses to these questions identified six major dimensions of work. The first, an intrinsic reward dimension, emphasized interesting, challenging, self-directed work that allows personal growth and development. The other five extrinsic factors could be labelled as convenience (the comfort and ease of work); financial rewards (pay, job security, and fringe benefits); relationships with co-workers; career opportunities; and resource adequacy (availability of information, tools, and materials necessary to do a job).[77] Other researchers have catalogued the important dimensions of work somewhat differently, but all share an approach in which intrinsic rewards are considered to be at least as important as the material rewards of work.[78]

Despite our emphasis on work characteristics, it is clear that work orientations or preferences must remain part of the equation. While they may frequently be shaped by work experiences, they can also influence the subjective experience of work. With this question in mind, the analysts of the 1973 Canadian Job Satisfaction Survey compared the "importance" assigned to thirty-four specific job characteristics with respondents' actual assessments of their jobs along these dimensions.[79] Having calculated average importance scores and average job assessments for the national sample of workers, they then computed discrepancy scores by subtracting the latter from the former. The largest discrepancies appeared in the areas of opportunities for promotions, and potential for challenge and personal growth. On average, when comparing reports of what was desirable in a job with assessments of what their jobs were providing, Canadian workers appeared to be least satisfied with career potential and opportunities for personal fulfilment.[80]

In his theory of job satisfaction, Arne Kalleberg argues that it is the specific match between work rewards (characteristics of the job) and work orientations that determines one's degree of job satisfaction.[81] This would apply, he suggests, to both extrinsic and intrinsic dimensions of work. Using data from the 1973 U.S. Quality of Employment Study, Kalleberg found support for this model of how job satisfaction is generated. Job rewards had positive effects on expressions of job satisfaction, but work preferences had negative effects. Controlling on other factors, the more one values some particular feature of work (the chance to make decisions, for example), the less likely it is that job satisfaction will result.[82] However, the data also showed that job rewards had substantially larger effects on satisfaction than did work preferences.[83] In addition, Kalleberg's analysis led him to the conclusion that intrinsic job rewards were more important determinants of job satisfaction than were extrinsic rewards.[84]

We can broaden our focus by identifying some features of work organizations that might influence reports of job satisfaction from workers within them. Many studies have hypothesized that work in large, impersonal, bureaucratic organizations can be dissatisfying. Along with organizational size, technology has been a key variable in a number of studies. Although he framed his discussion within the context of worker *alienation,* Robert Blauner questioned how different industrial technologies might influence job satisfaction.[85] Traditional forms of craft work, requiring high levels of skill and allowing considerable worker autonomy, would be most satisfying, he predicted, while assembly-line work would be least satisfying. Blauner went on to argue that highly automated technologies would restore worker satisfaction to the levels produced by craft work, because of the autonomy experienced by workers in such settings. Thus, although he classified industries according to technology, Blauner's thesis really addressed issues of work complexity and autonomy.

In a recent study, Randy Hodson showed that both plant and corporation size can affect job satisfaction.[86] The larger the plant (or workplace), the more likely that individual workers will feel isolated within the bureaucracy. And the larger the corporation itself, the less likely that employees will be involved in decision making. Hodson also demonstrated that workers employed in capital-intensive industries were more likely to be satisfied with their work. He attributed this to these workers being given responsibility for the operation and maintenance of very expensive capital investments. In turn, this heightened responsibility strengthens employees' bargaining power to obtain better working conditions and more job security. Exercising power is in itself satisfying. Hodson concluded that Blauner's emphasis on technology was probably inappropriate, and that his findings were better interpreted from a perspective emphasizing power relationships between workers and employers.

In short, Hodson has recast these job satisfaction research findings within a labour market segmentation model. Donald Nightingale's Canadian research on employee decision making and job satisfaction can also be understood from this perspective.[87] In this well-designed study, Nightingale compared the subjective responses to work of employees in a sample of ten traditional organizations and ten organizations in which rank-and-file employees had a formally defined right to participate in at least some aspects of company decision making. Taking into account differences in the actual job descriptions, and differences among individual workers, he observed higher job satisfaction in the organizations in which employees had a voice in decision making. We know that employee participation programs are more common within the primary labour markets of government bureaucracies and core sector firms. Thus, along with better pay and more job security which core sector organizations can provide, workers within them may also experience more job satisfaction.

Consequences of Job Satisfaction and Dissatisfaction

"If the job's so bad, why don't you quit?" Many of us may have been tempted to respond to a dissatisfying job in this manner, but fewer have actually done so, for fairly obvious reasons. There may be some features of the job, such as the pay or the hours, which make it palatable, despite the absence of other work rewards. In addition, unless other jobs are available, most employees simply cannot afford to quit. Thus, job dissatisfaction, even if it is extreme, will not necessarily translate into quitting behaviour. It might, on the other hand, encourage individuals to call in sick or come in late more frequently.[88] Recent studies have also shown a relationship between job dissatisfaction and overt acts of employee deviance such as theft of company property, or the use of drugs and alcohol on the job.[89] Dissatisfaction with work is also correlated with the number of complaints and grievances filed in unionized work settings.[90] As for non-unionized workers, surveys have shown that those dissatisfied with their work are more likely to view unions positively, and more likely to join a union, if given a chance.[91]

From an employer's perspective, however, the critical issue is whether increases in job satisfaction will boost productivity. If dissatisfaction leads to tardiness, absenteeism, deviance, or quitting, will improvements in the quality of work life lead to a happier and more productive work force? Although one can find examples of research showing such a relationship, the safest answer to the question would be "don't count on it."[92] Recent attempts to summarize the many studies addressing this question conclude that, at best, the relationship between satisfaction and productivity is very weak, or is only present in some work settings.[93]

There are several possible explanations of this non-relationship. First, productivity is more often a function of technology and workers' skills than of their attitudes. Thus, even if high levels of satisfaction are evident, low skill levels, inadequate on-the-job training, or obsolete machinery will limit opportunities for productivity increases.[94] Second, work group norms and expectations must be taken into consideration. Managers and consultants who have introduced "job enrichment" programs, and perhaps even found higher levels of satisfaction as a consequence, have frequently been disappointed to discover that productivity increases did not follow. They failed to realize that workers might view an improved quality of work life as their just reward, or that informal work norms and long-standing patterns of production behaviour are difficult to alter.[95]

Finally, it may be that productivity can be influenced by job satisfaction, but only under certain conditions.[96] Our earlier discussion suggested that workers in menial jobs might report job satisfaction because they were assessing their work within a limited set of alternatives. Workers in higher-status jobs might, on the other hand, report satisfaction because of tangible work rewards. If so, perhaps productivity increases due to job satisfaction might only be expected within the latter group. One of the recent overviews of this relationship supports this hypothesis, demonstrating that the productivity-satisfaction link is strongest among professional, managerial, and supervisory workers.[97]

WORK AND STRESS

Defining work-related *stress* independent of *job dissatisfaction* is not an easy task. In fact, many researchers studying stress and its consequences rely on measures that might, in a different context, be considered indicators of job dissatisfaction. However, we do realize that it is possible to feel dissatisfied with work without experiencing a great deal of stress. It is useful, then, to conceive of stress as a multidimensional problem — with job dissatisfaction as one component — that can lead to serious mental and physical health disorders.

It is also helpful to distinguish *stressors* (or strains) from an individual worker's reactions to them. Stressors are objective situations (noisy work environments, competing job demands, or inadequate equipment, for example) or events (a dispute with a supervisor, or news of a possible plant shutdown) that have the *potential* to produce a negative subjective response. Thus, work-related stress is an individually experienced negative reaction to a job or work environment.[98] Obviously the absence of stress does not imply the presence of job satisfaction. But what distinguishes stress reactions are the wide range of ill-health symptoms. Research in many different settings has shown that physical reactions can include fatigue, insomnia, muscular aches and pains, ulcers, high blood pressure, and even heart disease. Depression, anxiety, irritation, low self-esteem, and other mental health problems are among the documented psychological reactions to stressful work. The research literature has also shown that the effects of work-based stressors can be conditioned by individuals' psychological coping mechanisms and by the amount of social support they receive from family, friends, and co-workers.[99]

Many jobs in the secondary labour market may generate stress because of their low pay and limited job security. Obviously constant worry about paying bills or about potential job loss can be considered a form of work-related stress. But most research on this subject has concentrated on stressors in the work environment.[100] Continual

exposure to health and safety hazards, the necessity of wor
unpleasant setting, shift work, or long hours can all be
Similarly, fast-paced work (especially when the pace i
machine) and inadequate resources to complete a task ar
stressors. Equally important, working at tasks that underutilize one's
skills and abilities, or which allow little latitude for decision making,
are stressful for many workers. Finally, many of us have personally
encountered the stress an unreasonable and overly demanding supervisor can create.

All of these stressors have one thing in common. As described, they
are factors over which individual workers have little control. If we
redefine stressors as "job demands," we can see that stress is more
likely to be created if demands are high, but an individual worker's
choice of responses is limited.[101] To take a specific example, reports
of "burnout" among social workers, teachers, and nurses largely
reflect constant interaction with clients, in combination with limited
resources to actually help many of these people.

Researchers have repeatedly found highly routinized, machine-
paced work to be extremely stress-provoking. Assembly-line jobs are
often considered to be among the most stressful.[102] Some people
adapt to assembly-line work by daydreaming or "tuning out" the
boredom. But psychological and physical health problems can also
arise. Linhart graphically describes an extreme reaction to the line in
a French autombile factory:

> He was fixing parts of a dashboard into place with a screwdriver. Five
> screws to fix on each car. That Friday afternoon he must have been on
> his five hundredth screw of the day. All at once he began to yell and
> rushed at the fenders of the cars brandishing his screwdriver like a
> dagger. He lacerated a good ten or so car bodies before a troop of white
> and blue coats rushed up and overcame him, dragging him, panting
> and gesticulating, to the sick bay.[103]

WORK AND ALIENATION

Alienation is another term frequently associated with negative subjective reactions to work. However, there is not a consensus on its
meaning.[104] Frequently we find references to the causes and consequences of "job satisfaction and alienation" with little attempt to
distinguish between the two concepts. Among most sociologists,
though, alienation is considered to be a much broader philosophical
concept. The verb "alienate" refers to an act of separation, or to the
transferral of something to a new owner. Marx used the term in this
sense when he discussed the "alienating" effects of capitalist production relations on the working class. Used as a noun, "alienation" refers

to the overall experience of work under these conditions.

Marx identified the following sources of alienation under capitalism. Products produced did not belong to those who made them. Ownership remained with those who owned the enterprise and who purchased the labour of workers employed within it. Decisions about what to produce and about the sale of the finished products were not made by the workers themselves, and profits generated in the exchange remained with the owners of the enterprise. In fact, given an extensive division of labour, many of the workers involved in the productive process might never see the finished product itself. Thus, workers were alienated from the product of their own work. Marx also emphasized alienation from the activity of work. Transfer of control over the labour process from individual workers to capitalists or their representatives meant that individual workers had lost the chance to make decisions about how the work should be done. In addition, extensive fragmentation of the work process had taken away most of the intrinsic rewards of productive work.

Alienation also involved separation of individual workers from others around them. Obviously, bureaucratic hierarchies could have this effect. But more importantly, because the essence of capitalist employment relationships is the exchange of labour for a wage, work was transformed from a creative and collective activity to an individualistic, monetary activity. Work itself had become a commodity. As a consequence, Marx argued, workers were alienated from themselves. Capitalist relations of production had reduced work from its role as a means of human self-fulfilment to a market transaction.[105]

This structural perspective on alienation from work is built around several central assumptions. First of all, alienation occurs because workers have little or no control over the conditions of their work, and few chances to develop to their fullest potential as creative human beings. Second, the source of alienation can be traced to the organization of work under capitalism. Third, given that alienation is characteristic of capitalist work relations, it exists even if workers themselves do not consciously recognize it. Alienation, then, is a "condition of objective powerlessness."[106] Whether or not individual workers become aware of the cause of their discontent with work depends on a variety of other factors. In the absence of a well-defined alternative to the current economic system, we would not expect most workers to be able to clearly articulate their alienation, or to act on it.[107] Apathy, or an attempt to forget about work as soon as one leaves it behind, are common responses of many workers to a situation to which they see no viable alternatives. But discontent does exist, as demonstrated by the frequency of strikes, walkouts, and other behaviours showing frustration and unhappiness with the conditions of work.[108] We will address this issue more fully in Chapter 8.

The (social-psychological) perspective on alienation shares with the *structural* perspective an emphasis on powerlessness of workers, and the conclusion that many jobs offer limited opportunities for (personal growth and self-fulfilment. While the Marxist analysis emphasizes separation from the product and the activity of work, from co-workers and from oneself, the social-psychological approach attempts to measure feelings of "powerlessness," "meaninglessness," "social isolation," "self-estrangement," and "normlessness."[109] Despite obvious overlaps in the two sets of ideas, closer examination of the social-psychological research reveals that its focus is mainly on the absence of intrinsic job rewards.[110]

Social-psychological studies of alienation, moreover, are unlikely to lay all or much of the blame on capitalism itself. Instead, technologies that allow workers few opportunities for self-direction, bureaucratic work organizations, and modern mass society in general are identified as the sources of alienation. This perspective also differs from the the structural approach in its emphasis on *feelings of alienation* or, in other words, on the subjective experience of alienating work conditions. Researchers within this approach have relied primarily on the self-reports of workers, in contrast to the Marxist focus on the organization and content of work.[111]

Alienation from work, from this perspective, resembles job dissatisfaction, although explanations of the sources of alienation have pointed more explicitly at the negative consequences of work fragmentation and powerlessness. The job satisfaction literature examines a broader array of causal variables. Job satisfaction researchers have also attempted to incorporate work orientations into their models. For example, a common argument in the job satisfaction literature is that workers with instrumental attitudes will more easily tolerate work with few intrinsic rewards. However, we have already argued that instrumental attitudes may be developed *because of* participation in such work. Since some social-psychological studies of "alienation" actually define the phenomenon as an "extrinsic orientation to work,"[112] there is really more congruence between the two research traditions than first impressions would suggest. Hence it is not surprising to find studies that examine alienation and job dissatisfaction simultaneously, or writers who use the two terms interchangeably.[113]

A key social-psychological study of alienation is Robert Blauner's *Alienation and Freedom.*[114] Blauner defined "alienation" in standard terms of powerlessness, meaninglessness, isolation (or social alienation), and self-estrangement. The centrality of powerlessness in Blauner's theory of alienation is clear from his use of "freedom" to refer to the ability to choose how one does one's work. Blauner compared work in four different industries to test his thesis that

Technology = decides degree of alienation

technology (and the attendant division of labour) is a major determinant of the degree of alienation experienced at work. He argued that
the traditional printing industry, which at the time still operated
largely in a craft-work mode, produced low levels of alienation
because of the considerable autonomy of workers and the high levels
of skill required. The textile manufacturing industry was an interme-
diate step in the process of technological development culminating
in the assembly lines of the automobile industry. Here, alienation was
most acute because of low-skill, repetitive tasks that deprived workers
of control over their actions.

Blauner argued that new automated technologies would reverse
this trend. In work settings such as oil refineries, skill levels were
higher, tasks were varied, and individuals could make a wide variety
of decisions about how they would do their work. And since this
industry was providing us with a glimpse of the future of industrialized
societies, the prospects for individual "freedom" were good. Blauner
predicted that alienation would decline as fewer workers were employed in mass production settings.[115]

Alienation and Freedom has been both influential and controversial.
Two decades later, it is obvious that Blauner misjudged industrial
trends, given the degree to which deskilling of work has continued.
Some of Blauner's critics focus on his conceptualization of alienation,
arguing that his social-psychological approach was not addressing
alienation in the way Marx defined it. Other criticisms are methodological, or challenge Blauner's interpretation of his own data.[116]
Duncan Gallie's comparative study of refinery workers in France and
England has highlighted cross-cultural differences in workers' responses to technology, an important point Blauner overlooked.[117]

Perhaps the most damaging criticism is that Blauner was engaging
in *technological determinism* by not stopping to ask why different technologies are designed or chosen by those who control an enterprise.
Blauner was undoubtedly correct about the negative consequences of
continued exposure to low-skill, routinized work. But he failed to
address the fact that assembly lines and hierarchical work organizations were developed, not only in the hope that efficiency would be
increased, but also to maintain control over workers.

"THE LONG ARM OF THE JOB"

Let us return to a question we raised at the beginning of this chapter:
Should feelings about work be treated as causes or as effects in an
analysis of the subjective experience of work? Our brief historical
discussion of changing work values highlighted the apparent prevalence of instrumental orientations in industrial capitalist societies. At
the same time, an alternative set of values idealizing the intrinsic

rewards of work has also emerged. Individuals today are exposed to (at least) two competing value systems: the first suggesting that the monetary rewards of work are paramount; the second emphasizing how human beings should achieve self-fulfilment through their work. From here, it is only a short step to the argument that because of different socialization experiences and different personalities, some workers would be primarily instrumentally oriented while others would be more motivated by the intrinsic rewards of a job. In short, it could be argued, work orientations or preferences are brought to the job, and will influence feelings of satisfaction with or alienation at work. They might also lead a person to choose one line of work over another.

But most research findings tend to support the alternative hypothesis. Participation in low-skill or highly routinized work, which offers little self-direction and few intrinsic rewards, can produce instrumental work attitudes. For many workers, adherence to such values may be a means of adapting to employment that has little but a paycheque to offer. Despite such adaptations, there is still evidence that work largely devoid of intrinsic rewards produces dissatisfaction. Although there are differences in definition and in focus, studies of job satisfaction and of social-psychological alienation highlight the negative consequences of participation in work that is repetitive and routine, offering few chances for individual decision making and for the development of personal skills and abilities. In addition, studies of workplace stress have highlighted some of the same features of work as potential stressors. In short, we would allow that work orientations brought to the job may affect how an individual feels about the work. Yet the nature of the work itself is likely to have a larger impact on both an individual's feelings of satisfaction, alienation, and stress, as well as on her or his work orientations.

We have suggested that work-related stress does not get left behind at the end of the workday. Chronic work pressures can have severe consequences on an individual's overall quality of life. On the other hand, researchers have observed that those who report satisfaction with their work are also more likely to feel satisfied with life in general.[118] But are there any other effects a job can have on an individual away from work? William Faulkner appeared to think so when he wrote, "You can't eat for eight hours a day nor drink for eight hours a day nor make love for eight hours a day — all you can do for eight hours is work. Which is the reason why man makes himself and everybody else so miserable and unhappy."[119] Social scientists have been unable to demonstrate outcomes as universal as this, but there is accumulating evidence that continued exposure to some kinds of work can have long-lasting (if not permanent) effects on non-work behaviours and even on one's personality.

Martin Meissner has argued that the "long arm of the job" has an impact on one's life away from work. In his study of male British Columbia sawmill workers, he tested two rival hypotheses about how the nature of work might affect after-work behaviours. The _compensatory leisure_ hypothesis proposes that people will look for activities away from work that will compensate for what is absent in their jobs. Thus, workers who have little opportunity to develop their skills and abilities on the job might look for such opportunities away from work. The _spillover_ hypothesis suggests that the effects of work will spill over into after-work activities. Meissner concludes that there is a "spillover" effect. Workers who had little chance to make decisions about how their work should be done were considerably less likely to engage in free-time activities that required or allowed this kind of individual discretion. Similarly, those who had few opportunities for social interactions at work were more inclined toward solitary leisure-time activities. In brief, "the design of industrial work creates or prevents opportunities for the development or maintenance of discretionary and social skills."[120]

One could always argue that the subjects in Meissner's study had chosen their jobs in order to satisfy their own personal preferences. Such an emphasis on work orientations would explain, for example, that individuals with a preference for solitary activities would choose both their jobs and their leisure activities with this in mind. While plausible, this explanation is not that convincing for several reasons. First, it suggests that labour force participants have considerably more choice among jobs with widely differing characteristics than is typically the case. Second, subsequent studies comparing these two hypotheses have generally come to the same conclusion.[121] Third, there is research demonstrating even more conclusively that work with limited scope has a negative effect on personality.

Melvin Kohn and his associates have been examining this relationship for many years with a primary emphasis on the concept of "occupational self-direction." Kohn argues that work which is free from close supervision, which involves considerable complexity and independent judgement, and which is non-routine in nature will have a lasting positive effect on one's personality and psychological functioning. Specifically, individuals whose work allows self-direction are more likely to develop a personality that values such opportunities and a more self-confident, less fatalistic, less conformist approach to life. They will exhibit greater flexibility in dealing with ideas. Alternatively, jobs allowing little self-direction are more likely to lead to psychological distress, a finding we have already documented in our discussion of work-related stress.

Kohn can argue his case with confidence because of his use of longitudinal data. By comparing the jobs and personalities of his

sample of male labour force participants at two points i
years apart), he can clearly demonstrate the personality
those who have or have not had the opportunity to w
allowing self-direction. Hence, he has also been able to d
that "[b]oth ideational flexibility and a self-directed orien   ___,
in time, to more responsible jobs that allow greater latitude for occupational self-direction."[122] Similar studies of female labour force
participants,[123] and of young, middle-aged, and older men in both the
United States and Poland have shown that these reciprocal effects of
work on personality are not just restricted to middle-aged males in the
United States.[124] The overall conclusion left by this extensive body of
research is that intrinsically rewarding work, particularly work that
allows self-direction, can have important consequences for the personalities and careers of those fortunate enough to participate in it.

work with Intrinsic reward ⟶ personalities & careers
+ self-direction

NOTES

1. Spencer (1985): 616.
2. Blackburn and Mann (1979): 141.
3. See Anthony (1977) for an interesting and provocative analysis of the "ideology
   of work."
4. Anthony (1977, chapter 1). See Burstein et al. (1975:10-11), Smucker (1980:280-
   81), Peitchinis (1983:160-62), Kumar (1984), and Rose (1985:27-30) for additional discussions of the changing meaning of work.
5. Rose (1985): 28.
6. Mills (1956): 216.
7. Burstein et al. (1975): 10.
8. Weber (1958).
9. *Ibid.*, 177. Anthony (1977:43) comments wryly: "The engagement of God as the
   supreme supervisor was a most convenient device; a great part of the efforts of
   modern management has been aimed at finding a secular but equally omnipotent
   equivalent in the worker's own psyche."
10. See Marshall (1982) for an interesting discussion of these debates. Anthony (1977,
    chapter 2) and Smucker (1980, chapter 2) provide useful overviews of Weber's
    arguments. Furnham and Lewis (1986, chapter 8) summarize the social-psycho-
    logical literature on the Protestant work ethic.
11. See Smucker (1980): 49-52
12. See Burstein et al. (1975:12) for a series of historical examples.
13. *Ibid.*, 12, 22, 60; see also Economic Council of Canada (1976, chapter 9). Hamilton
    and Wright's (1986) review of U.S. survey data leads them to conclude that there
    is little evidence of a decline in commitment to the work ethic (p. 288).
14. Horvat (1983).
15. Rose (1985): 37.
16. Stokes (1982); see also Martin (1984).
17. See, especially, Kamata's (1983) personal account of life in a Toyota factory.
    Glabermann (1983), Rose (1985:38), and Gill (1985:32) also comment on
    discrepancies between the stereotype of Japanese work organizations and the
    reality. Lincoln and Kalleberg (1985:739) note the similarity to arguments of

labour market segmentations theorists such as Richard Edwards (1979).

18. Lincoln and Kalleberg (1985).

19. Burstein et al. (1975): 19.

20. See Williams (1983), who explicitly links concerns about unemployment to expressions of commitment to work among Australian workers. She concludes that shrinking possibilities for paid work lead to greater, rather than less, commitment to work.

21. *Maclean's Magazine* (7 January 1985) p. 34. See Johnston (1986:133) for a summary and discussion of recent polls dealing with the issue of unemployment in Canada.

22. Kelvin and Jarrett (1985): 104.

23. *Maclean's Magazine* (7 January 1985).

24. Burstein et al. (1975): 12.

25. See Anthony (1977:45-51) for an interesting discussion of the common roots of these two rather different ideologies of work.

26. Grabb (1984:20-26) provides a useful summary of Marx's views on work in capitalist society.

27. Anthony (1977): 2.

28. Lockwood (1966) emphasizes highly evident differences in wealth and power, few chances for upward mobility, and tightly knit occupational communities (of miners, for example) as important determinants of proletarian attitudes in such communities; this argument is quite similar to Kerr and Siegel's theory of the inter-industry propensity to strike, mentioned in chapter 8.

29. See Bulmer (1975) for a variety of assessments of Lockwood's typology and empirical studies based on it.

30. See Goldthorpe et al. (1969), one of the several books based on this study.

31. See MacKinnon (1981:256), who summarizes what he calls "instrumental theory."

32. See the research articles in Bulmer (1985).

33. MacKinnon (1981): 259.

34. Blackburn and Mann (1979, chapter 6).

35. *Ibid.*, 155.

36. Beynon and Blackburn (1972): 158; Rinehart (1978).

37. Blackburn and Mann (1979): 280.

38. Chinoy (1955).

39. Sennett and Cobb (1972).

40. MacKinnon (1981): 269.

41. Rinehart (1978): 7.

42. Burstein et al. (1975): 23, 19.

43. Unpublished results from the 1983 Edmonton Area Study, a random sample in-person survey of 420 Edmonton adults. This was the seventh in an annual series of surveys conducted by the Population Research Laboratory, Department of Sociology, University of Alberta.

44. Burstein et al. (1975): 31.

45. Unpublished survey results; the other possibilities were decision-making potential, feelings of accomplishment, pleasant and helpful co-workers, and job security.

46. Blackburn and Mann (1979): 145, 162.

47. *Ibid.*, 148.

48. Beynon and Blackburn (1972:84) describe part-time factory workers who valued their contacts with friends at work as much as the job itself.

49. See McNally (1979) on the work attitudes and behaviours of female temporary office workers.

50. Blackburn and Mann (1979): 167.

51. More than a decade ago, Locke (1976:1297) stated that there were over 3,000 relevant publications, while Burstein et al. (1975:15) placed the total at over 4,000. See Hamilton and Wright (1986, chapter 6) for a recent overview of survey research on job satisfaction in the U.S., which is highly critical of much of the literature in this area.

52. Unpublished survey results. The question is asked using a 7-point (strongly disagree to strongly agree) response scale. In 1981, 82 percent agreed with the statement (scores of 5, 6 or 7 on this scale). In 1982 and 1983, 79 percent and 85 percent agreed, respectively. The 1986 survey revealed a lower level of satisfaction (73 percent in agreement). However, until subsequent surveys replicate this lower value, it is premature to comment on a possible drop in the prevalence of job satisfaction in this city.

53. See, for example, O'Toole (1974), Sheppard and Herrick (1972), and Aronowitz (1973).

54. Burstein et al. (1975): 28; Chelte et al. (1982) examined a series of job satisfaction surveys during the 1970s, and found only one which did not reflect the long-term, stable pattern of high levels of reported job satisfaction; Hamilton and Wright (1986:231) reach the same conclusion; see also Hall (1986): 92.

55. Rinehart (1978): 7.

56. Burstein et al. (1975): 28; see also Hall (1986): 92.

57. Burstein et al. (1975): 29.

58. Stewart and Blackburn (1975): 503.

59. Kalleberg and Griffin (1978): 390.

60. Hall (1986:94) makes a similar distinction between "internal" and "external" determinants of job satisfaction.

61. See Burstein et al. (1975:43) for Canadian evidence.

62. Rinehart (1978:8) makes this argument, which parallels his thesis that routine work can generate instrumental work orientations.

63. Kalleberg and Loscocco (1983); Hamilton and Wright (1986:288) conclude that the explanation lies primarily in the better jobs held by older workers.

64. Beynon and Blackburn (1972): 153.

65. O'Toole (1977): 60.

66. Zeitz (1983): 1091.

67. Burstein et al. (1975:45) provide Canadian data on differences in intrinsic work attitudes by age. Glenn and Weaver (1982) discuss the inconclusive findings in studies linking education and job satisfaction. Wright and Hamilton (1979) suggest the "future upward mobility" explanation.

68. See Northcott and Lowe (1987) and Mottaz (1986) for two recent overviews of research on this topic.

69. Murray and Atkinson (1981), who are among those who find women reporting higher job satisfaction than men, argue this "lower expectations" thesis, as do Glenn and Weaver (1982): 53.

70. Burstein et al. (1975): 57.

71. Northcott and Lowe (1987).

72. Mottaz (1986): 372. It remains possible that women least influenced by gender-role socialization are those most likely to end up in the primary labour market.

However, on the basis of analyses of longitudinal data, Miller (1980:361) concludes that "job conditions are more strongly related to job satisfaction than are the social characteristics of the workers or the predispositions they bring to the job."

73. House (1980): 101.
74. Wells (1986b): 335.
75. Herzberg (1966, 1968).
76. See Burstein et al. (1975) for a report on the Canadian study and Quinn and Shepard (1974) on the American survey.
77. Kalleberg (1977): 128; Burstein et al. (1975:80) subdivided these 34 items somewhat further.
78. Nightingale (1982:129-33), for example, identifies ten dimensions of work (variety, autonomy, skill level, novelty, intellectual demands, required interaction with other people, conflicting demands, physical conditions of work, amount of feedback, and the ability to complete tasks) independent of extrinsic rewards, which he sees as capable of influencing job satisfaction.
79. Burstein et al. (1975:31-34) label these self-reported job descriptions as "satisfaction" scores, but they are really only job descriptions. While workers may agree that, in their jobs, "The chances for promotion are good"; or "I have an opportunity to develop my own special abilities"; or "The pay is good," it does not necessarily follow that they feel satisfied by this. They may, depending on their own preferences, merely be indifferent.
80. See Hodson (1985) for a recent study showing how upward mobility, the belief that further career development is possible, and favourable comparisons with others' careers all influence job satisfaction.
81. Kalleberg (1977) uses the term "work values" for what we have been calling "work orientations" or "work preferences." He also builds "degree of job control" into his model to account for the fact that some people have greater access to better jobs which, in turn, provide more job rewards. See Kalleberg and Griffin (1978), who examine this last issue in more detail.
82. The implication of this finding and interpretation is that a job allowing considerable decision making might be more satisfying to someone with low expectations in this regard than to someone with high expectations. See Loher et al. (1985) for an overview of job satisfaction studies that reaches a different conclusion. They argue that "the more complex and enriched a job is, the more likely the ... person who possesses a high need for personal growth and development is to be satisfied with that job" (p. 287).
83. Blackburn and Mann (1979:167) also note that their British data show only minor effects of work orientations on job satisfaction.
84. Hall's (1986:95-99) overview of the recent research literature on the topic reaches the same conclusions: work preferences are less significant than job characteristics — and may be shaped by work experiences — and intrinsic rewards are generally of more importance than extrinsic rewards in determining job satisfaction.
85. Blauner (1964).
86. Hodson (1984).
87. Nightingale (1982).
88. Hall (1986): 93.
89. Hollinger and Clark (1982); Hall (1986): 110. In an insightful analysis of the

varieties of workplace crime, Gerald Mars (1982) makes the case that much of this deviant behaviour is an attempt by workers "to control their jobs rather than be controlled by them" (p. 206).

90. Locke (1976): 1332.

91. Kochan (1979): 25; see Berger et al. (1983) who reverse the question in their analysis of the effects of union membership on job satisfaction.

92. Locke (1976): 1333; Macarov (1982); Hall (1986): 92.

93. Petty et al. (1984), who examined over 40 studies on the topic, and Iaffaldano and Muchinsky (1985), who considered 74 different pieces of research, were conducting meta-analyses — statistical analyses summarizing the results of a series of studies that all tested the same hypothesis.

94. The high levels of productivity in Japanese industry, despite relatively low levels of job satisfaction among Japanese workers (see Lincoln and Kalleberg 1985:738) suggest that productivity is determined primarily by other factors.

95. Macarov (1982:71) comments on how "quality of work life" programs are often introduced on the assumption that satisfaction alone will stimulate productivity, or that workers will feel a moral obligation to repay the favour to their employers. He suggests that productivity increases might only be obtained if management and workers had an explicit agreement to this effect prior to introduction of the program. Tausky (1978:106-7) also discusses job redesign efforts and notes that productivity increases cannot be expected to follow. However, he suggests that higher training and other costs that will accompany serious efforts at job redesign may be partially responsible for the failure to realize productivity increases.

96. Locke (1976): 1333.

97. Petty et al. (1984).

98. Fraser (1983); Kessler (1983).

99. House (1981).

100. See Selye (1976), Kasl (1978), McLean (1979), Fraser (1983), and Lowe and Northcott (1986, chapter 1) for overviews of stress research.

101. Karasek (1979) conceptualizes stress and stressors in this manner and distinguishes between active jobs where individual decision-making potential is high and passive jobs where it is largely absent. Stress is more likely to be problematic, he reasons, in passive jobs.

102. Caplan et al. (1980) compared workers in 23 different occupations and concluded that assembly-line work was the most stressful; Hamilton and Wright (1986:266) conclude that U.S. survey research shows assembly-line jobs in the automobile industry to be "among the most objectionable jobs." See Lowe and Northcott (1986) for a study of stress among Canadian postal workers employed in a machine-paced work setting, and MacFarlane (1984) for a description of work in the automated post office. Wells (1986b) discusses assembly-line work in a Canadian automobile plant, and Johnson (1983) provides a number of accounts of assembly-line work in factories.

103. Linhart (1981): 57.

104. Grabb (1984): 24; Rinehart (1987): 17.

105. See Archibald (1978:35-43), Hill (1981:100-101), Grabb (1984:24-26), and Rinehart (1987:13-17) for more detailed discussions of Marx's writings on alienation.

106. Rinehart (1987): 17-18.

107. On the absence of widespread social unrest, see Mann's (1970) classic analysis of

"the social cohesion of liberal democracy." Abercrombie et al. (1980) continue the discussion of the "dominant ideology" and how it might affect the attitudes and behaviour of the working class. See also Prandy (1979).

108. Rinehart (1987): 18. See Howard (1985:90) for comments on how high job stress can lead to spontaneous protest, but more often to apathy and depression, given the difficulty of reacting against a large, powerful, and impersonal work organization.

109. Seeman (1959, 1967, 1975) has been most influential in developing this conceptual framework.

110. Seeman (1967:273), for example, defines "alienation" as "work which is not intrinsically satisfying." Seeman's (1975) overview of alienation studies demonstrates that this type of social-psychological research is not restricted to studies of work per se. Inspection of some of these more general studies of alienation in modern Western society reveals how the emphasis on "social isolation" and "normlessness," in particular, draws much more on Durkheim's analysis of "anomie" than on Marx and his assessment of "alienation" (Hill, 1981:91). See Archibald (1976) for additional critical discussions of the measures used in, and assumptions underlying, this research tradition.

111. See Hall (1986:105-9) for a useful overview of these two approaches; Seeman (1975:92) also notes the distinction based on self-awareness of alienating work.

112. Seeman (1967): 273. See also MacKinnon (1981:264), who argues that the "material conditions of labour . . . determine alienation, self-estrangement and instrumentality."

113. Nightingale's (1982) study of employee participation in decision making within Canadian workplaces considers both job satisfaction and alienation, conceptualized in this subjective sense, as potential outcomes of workplace organization; see also Nightingale and Toulouse (1978).

114. Blauner (1964). See Hall (1986:105-8) for a brief overview of Blauner's book and some recent research attempting to replicate his findings.

115. Blauner (1964): 182.

116. Hill (1981:90-102) presents a useful review of these criticisms; see also Eldridge (1971) and Archibald (1978): 124-30. The debate generated by Blauner is continued in recent articles by Hull, Friedman, and Rogers (1982), and Vallas and Yarrow (1987).

117. Gallie (1978).

118. White (1981) reports such a correlation, but notes that it is relatively weak.

119. Quoted in *Working* by Studs Terkel (1972): *xi*.

120. Meissner (1971): 260.

121. Staines (1980) reviews the research literature on this topic and concludes that there is more support for the spillover than for the compensation hypothesis. But the compensatory leisure hypothesis does explain, as we might expect, why individuals who have to work hard physically are more likely to choose less strenuous leisure activities.

122. Kohn and Schooler (1983): 152; see also Kohn (1976) on the effects of work conditions on feelings of alienation. Kohn and Schooler (1983) present a collection of research papers encompassing much of the research they and others have done in this area over the years.

123. Miller et al. (1979).

124. Miller et al. (1985).

7

Unions and Industrial Relations

INTRODUCTION

Early in December, 1986, unionized workers at the Gainers meatpacking plant in Edmonton voted to return to work after six and one-half months on the picket line. Thus ended one of the country's most bitter labour disputes in recent times. Violent clashes erupted between strikers and police when the company started bussing strikebreakers across the picket line to keep the plant operating. These ugly scenes drew national attention. Many members of the public supported the union's campaign to boycott Gainers products, a tactic aimed at forcing Peter Pocklington, the outspoken owner of the firm, to bargain in good faith. Pocklington had guaranteed the strikebreakers jobs in the plant. This manoeuvre would have destroyed the union; as it was, union members ended up negotiating to get their jobs back. The settlement of the strike came only after the personal intervention of the Premier of Alberta. It was certainly no Christmas present for the union members — they would probably never make up their lost wages. They did, however, retain their jobs and their union. But the wage concessions Pocklington had demanded as his price for keeping the firm open meant that Gainers' employees would still earn well below the industry average.

The Gainers strike was in some ways unique. Most Canadian employers are not as motivated as Peter Pocklington is by a right-wing, free-enterprise ideology; picket-line violence is a rare phenomenon; consumer boycotts of a striking firm's products are one of the least used, and least effective, weapons in labour's arsenal; and seldom does a provincial premier intervene to force a settlement. But viewed from a distance, the strike raises some questions that go to the very heart of union–management relations in advanced capitalist societies.

The confrontation pitted the free-market principles of capitalism against the rights of workers to collective bargaining, job security, and a living wage. The firm's owner threatened to close the plant. What rights do employees have that can counterbalance this exercise of raw economic power? Is conflict inherent in capitalist employment relations? Or conversely, to what degree are there shared interests between workers and employers? Are there circumstances under which labour and management can cooperate to mutual benefit? What is the role of government in regulating the relations between labour and capital? Even more basic, why do workers join a union in the first place? Finally, what improvements in wages and working conditions have unions achieved through collective bargaining?

These are the sorts of industrial relations issues to be examined in this chapter. From a sociological perspective, we shall focus on power, conflicts and compromises over the distribution of resources in the workplace, and on employee collective action. These themes are highlighted in the study of unions, the major organizations representing the interests and aspirations of employees in capitalist society. We therefore will explore the nature and development of the labour movement in Canada, as well as how union–management relations are regulated through a complex legalistic framework. The causes and implications of industrial conflict, an equally important question, are the subject of the next chapter.

THEORETICAL PERSPECTIVES ON THE LABOUR MOVEMENT

We can begin to understand why unions developed in the first place by reviewing some of the early theories of the labour movement. In a classic work on British trade unionism, Sidney and Beatrice Webb suggested that workers' pursuit of higher wages expressed a more basic desire to reduce employer domination.[1] Collective action could improve working conditions and reduce the competition for jobs that drives wages down. Furthermore, the Webbs argued, it could curb an employer's authority by instituting common rules governing the employment relationship. Selig Perlman stressed the role of unions in controlling jobs.[2] After studying the International Typographical Union, the oldest union in America, Perlman concluded that workers develop an awareness that jobs are scarce and must therefore be protected through unionization.

Michael Poole sheds additional light on the emergence of the labour movement in his discussion of the various goals it pursued.[3] Unions can be seen as moral institutions, fighting against the injustices and inequalities of capitalist industrialization; revolutionary organizations intent on overthowing capitalism; psychological or defensive reactions against the threat early capitalism posed to workers' jobs; responses to economic realities, aimed at achieving better wages and working conditions; and political organizations extending workers' rights into the industrial arena.

Generally speaking, it was the often harsh working conditions endured by industrial workers in the late nineteenth century that sparked the first major surge of unionization. Yet the basic idea that workers are motivated to unionize by the desire to gain greater control over their jobs, as well as fair treatment and just rewards, remains a dominant theme in industrial relations. Mainstream industrial relations theory views job regulation as the core of worker–management relations.[4] In other words, the rules and regulations that form the basis of collective agreements are assumed to inject stability into employment relations by tilting the balance of power slightly away from management toward workers.

However, this perspective overplays the importance of predictable and harmonious industrial relations, and downplays the importance of conflict. That is, by focusing on the system of rules, regulations, and institutions governing industrial relations, the mainstream perspective does not question the existing distribution of power between workers and management. It also presents an incomplete picture of industrial relations, due to a narrow focus on the *formal* aspects of the system, such as legislation and collective bargaining. There is an equally important *informal* side involving daily interactions between workers and employers, as "the rules of the game" on the job constantly are renegotiated. It is therefore helpful to acknowledge that work is a power relationship in which conflict is always a possibility.[5] As Richard Hyman explains: ". . . in every workplace there exists an invisible frontier of control, reducing some of the formal powers of the employer: a frontier which is defined and redefined in a continuous process of pressure and counter-pressure, conflict and accommodation, overt and tacit struggle."[6] Hyman proposes a more critical perspective on industrial relations, defining it as the process of control over work relations, especially involving unions.

POWER, CONFLICT, AND COOPERATION

It is important to understand the role of conflict in union–management relations. Collective agreements negotiated and administered under provincial and national labour laws seek to avoid open conflict. Indeed, the thrust of modern industrial relations practice is the avoidance of conflict. Thus, for the system to operate with some degree of fairness and equity for workers, who on the whole are in the weaker bargaining position, there must be the threat of conflict that could disrupt the employer's business. A stock criticism of the Canadian industrial relations scene concerns its adversarial nature. The Federal Task Force on Labour Relations, responding to these concerns, explained the underlying conflict in these words:

> Paradoxical as it may appear, collective bargaining is designed to resolve conflict through conflict, or at least through the threat of conflict. It is an adversary system in which two basic issues must be

resolved: how available revenue is to be divided, and how the clash between management's drive for productive efficiency and the workers' quest for job, income and psychic security are to be reconciled.[7]

We must also view industrial relations as a continuous process. New problems regularly confront the parties in collective bargaining. Solutions for one side may create difficulties for the other, as in cases of wage rollbacks. Or an agreement may be based on compromises both sides have trouble living with (for example, when a third-party arbitrator imposes a "solution"). Part of the difficulty is that workers and management have different definitions of social justice and economic reality.[8] Peter Pocklington considered low pork prices, strong competition, and a high local unemployment rate good enough reasons to maintain a two-year-old wage cut. His employees, though, considered it grossly unfair that they were being paid several dollars an hour less than other meatpackers across Canada for the same work, especially after Gainers recently had made a profit. We are thus wise to remember Tom Keenoy's comment that: ". . . at best, most solutions in industrial relations should be seen as no more than temporary arrangements between employer and employee. Indeed, this relationship is best thought of as one in which there is a *permanent* potential for differences of opinion and conflict. . . ."[9]

There is another paradox here. Work organizations typically have a division of labour that requires collective interdependence. Management therefore must balance the need to control employees with the necessity of achieving a workable level of cooperation and commitment from them. Stephen Hill's book, *Competition and Control at Work*, explores this basic tension.[10] More specifically, workers and managers must cooperate to provide goods or services. Yet in doing so, each side also strives to maximize its particular interests. Workers aim for more wages, better working conditions, and more autonomy in their jobs. Employers pursue higher profits, lower costs, and increased productivity. The chronic tension between these opposing interests forces trade-offs on both sides; it may also generate open conflict. Of course, we must recognize that not all union–management negotiations are a *zero-sum game*. That is, the only way one side can gain something is for the other to give something up. Indeed, in regard to some issues, such as improved health and safety conditions, negotiations can produce a *win-win* situation in which both workers and management benefit.[11]

There is a general consensus among scholars that the industrial relations systems in modern capitalist societies "keep the lid on" conflict. Having observed the oppressive conditions under which mid-nineteenth-century factory workers toiled, Marx was driven to the conclusion that eventually their misery and poverty would ignite a revolution. But as Stephen Hill notes, even Marxists, committed to the belief that capitalism pits the workers and bosses against each other in constant struggle, acknowledge that collective bargaining integrates workers into the existing economic system.[12] For many Marxists, unionism itself embodies a basic contradiction by striving to solve workers' problems within the parameters of capitalism. This is why Lenin, father of the Russian Revolution, dismissed trade unions as only capable of reforms, not revolution. But to lay all the blame on capitalism is to ignore the basic dilemma of the *distribution of scarce resources*, which all societies must face.[13]

Thus, in some respects, unions function as *managers of discontent*.[14] In other words, unions in Canada and other advanced capitalist societies channel the frustrations and complaints of workers into a carefully regulated dispute resolution system. Unions help their members to articulate specific work problems, needs, or dissatisfactions. Solutions then are sought through collective bargaining, or through the grievance procedure. In Canada, for example, labour legislation prohibiting strikes during the term of a collective agreement puts pressure on union leaders to contain any actions by rank-and-file members that could disrupt the truce with management. This may seem ironic, considering that unions developed in response to the deprivations of early industrial capitalism. But unions today operate in ways that contribute to the maintenance of capitalism, seeking reforms that smooth its rough edges.

A final consideration in our discussion of conflict and cooperation is internal union democracy. Generally speaking, unions are democratic organizations whose constitutions allow members to regularly elect leaders. Theoretically, this should make leaders responsive and accountable to rank-and-file members, translating their wishes into tangible collective bargaining goals. But despite this, there has been a long sociological debate about the pitfalls on the road to union democracy.

Robert Michels was the first to investigate the problems of union bureaucracy and democracy.[15] His study of German trade unions and the Social Democratic Party prior to the First World War concluded that leaders in working-class organizations always dominate members. Michels explains his famous *iron law of oligarchy* in technical, organizational, and psychological terms: leaders develop expert knowledge, which gives them power; once in office, leaders can control the organization to maintain their power; the masses tend to identify with leaders, and expect them to exercise power on their behalf. But in Canada and elsewhere we have recently witnessed the emergence of strong rank-and-file movements challenging entrenched union leadership cliques and, in effect, opposing oligarchic rule. What Michels discovered was not a universal trait of unions, but a potential problem faced by all large bureaucratic organizations.

WHAT DO UNIONS DO?

How do unions set goals and devise strategies to attain them? Of great interest to sociologists is why unions, rather than espousing revolutionary aims, have engaged in largely conservative and defensive actions. Typically, the daily activities of unions revolve around two types of goals: control over work, and the rewards of work.[16] It is not inconceivable that demands for control over the work process could, if they escalated, spark radical challenges to the capitalist system of business ownership. Yet historically such demands often involved skilled craftsmen fighting to defend their relatively privileged position in the labour market against the onslaught of modern production methods. Their goal, in short, was to preserve the status quo.

There are frequent compromises between control and economic rewards. Workers may be forced by their immediate economic needs to pursue the latter to the exclusion of the former. In addition, employers are sometimes willing to give up more of their profits rather than concede to workers greater decision-making authority. The emphasis on material gains rather than job controls has become a hallmark of the North American labour movement, and is known as *business unionism.*

How does the public view the activities of unions? Since the 1950s, Canadian public opinion has grown less favourable toward the role of unions in our society. Gallup polls routinely ask respondents if they think unions are good or bad for the country. In polls taken between 1950 and 1958, 12 to 20 percent of respondents said unions were bad while 60 to 69 percent said they were good. However, responses to the same questions in 1976-1982 polls show a decisive shift in public opinion, with "bad" responses increasing to between 30 and 42 percent.[17]

Public attitudes toward unions are, however, usually more ambiguous than suggested by Gallup polls. For example, the authors' study of Winnipeg and Edmonton residents found that individuals hold both positive and negative images of unions, depending on the specific issues at stake. Many respondents believed that unions contributed to inflation, while also recognizing that they had achieved material gains for members. At a general level, this study identified two different images of unionism: a *big labour* image, which sees unions as too powerful, inflicting harm on society and therefore requiring greater government regulation; and a *business unionism* image, which focuses on the positive gains in wages and working conditions unions have made through collective bargaining.[18] Both images are reinforced by the media, which frequently portrays unions in a negative light.[19]

Does the conventional wisdom that unions further their members' interests at public expense have a basis in fact? The most thorough analysis of what trade unions actually do is a study by two Harvard University economists, Richard Freeman and James Medoff, who make a useful distinction between the two "faces" of unionism.[20] The *monopoly face* deals with unions' power to raise members' wages at the expense of employers and other workers. The *collective voice face* shifts attention to how unions democratize authoritarian workplaces, giving workers a collective voice in dealing with management. Their evidence supports the collective voice perspective.

Freeman and Medoff admit that unions do impose some social and economic costs. But these are far outweighed by their positive contributions. Unions significantly advance workers' economic and political rights and freedoms. And, to the chagrin of their opponents, unions also boost productivity. As Freeman and Medoff explain, unions improve productivity through lower employee turnover, better management performance, reduced hiring and training costs, and greater labour–management communication and cooperation.[21] But because of higher wage costs, productivity gains do not make unionized firms more profitable.

Even though they are examining American unions, Freeman and Medoff's conclusions deserve careful attention. They show that in addition to raising members' wages relative to non-members, unions

> . . . alter nearly every other measurable aspect of the operation of workplaces, from turnover to productivity to profitability to the composition of pay packages. The behaviour of workers and firms and the outcomes of their interactions differ substantially between the organized and unorganized sectors. On balance, unionization appears to improve rather than to harm the social and economic system.[22]

THE EMERGENCE OF THE CANADIAN LABOUR MOVEMENT

The Canadian labour movement has evolved into a major force in the economic life of the nation. Its history is tied to the development of capitalism. But as workers in the late nineteenth and early twentieth centuries reacted to the inequalities and deprivations of their employment by organizing unions, they had to fight to gain this right. The story of unions is a human drama in which groups of workers often struggled against strong-willed employers, and a reluctant state, to gain higher wages, better working conditions, and some control over their daily working lives.

Skilled craft workers were the first to unionize. The earliest union was organized by printers in York (now Toronto). Carpenters, bricklayers, masons, cabinetmakers, blacksmiths, shoemakers, tailors — these were the pioneers of the union movement before the days of modern industry. A strike by Toronto printers in 1872 resulted in the Trade Union Act, which no longer made it an illegal conspiracy in restraint of trade for workers to unionize. Other significant events that laid the foundations for trade unionism in Canada were the Nine-Hour Movement in the 1870s, involving working-class agitation for shorter working hours, and the creation of the Trades and Labour Congress (TLC) in 1883 as the first central labour body.[23]

Craft pride based on the special skills acquired through a long apprenticeship, solidarity with fellow artisans, and a close integration of work and community were the hallmarks of these early unions. Craftsmen (there were no women among them) were the "aristocrats" of the working class. Printers, for example, reinforced their status by referring to themselves as a "profession." And like other crafts, shoemakers drew on a long heritage to bolster craft pride. "From medieval craft lore, the shoemakers brought forth St. Crispin as a symbol of their historic rights and their importance to the community," reports historian Greg Kealey.[24] *Craft unions,* organized according to specialized craft skills, served their members in several important ways. They were "benevolent societies," providing members with a form of social insurance years before the rise of the welfare state. They also protected members' position in the labour market by regulating access to the craft, thus monopolizing its unique skills. And as small local enterprises of the nineteenth century gave way to the factories and large corporations of the twentieth, unions provided craftsmen with a defence against the erosion of their way of life. Artisans opposed scientific management, the mechanization and reorganization of craft production into factories, and other attempts by employers to undermine the skills and responsibilities on which their craft traditions were based. Moreover, the tightly knit social relations of working-class artisanal communities — reinforced by educational institutes, parades, picnics, and other neighbourhood events — bolstered these reactions to the march of modern industry.[25]

Craft unions dominated the young Canadian labour movement well into the twentieth century. These *international* unions were American-based and affiliated with the conservative American Federation of Labour. The iron molders' union was the first international to set down permanent Canadian roots, in 1859. This was a time when the labour market for many skilled trades spanned both sides of the Canada–U.S. border. The internationals quickly came to control the Canadian labour scene. At the 1902 convention of the TLC, the AFL unions purged their Canadian-based rivals (any organization duplicating one in the AFL was banned) and stole power from more radical Canadian labour leaders.[26]

The craft principle underlying the early AFL unions contrasts with *industrial unionism,* where all workers in an industry are represented by the same union, regardless of their occupational skills. The Knights of Labour, the earliest industrial union in Canada, organized its first local assembly in Hamilton in 1875. For a brief period in the 1880s, they challenged the dominance of the AFL craft unions. Driven by an idealistic radicalism, the Knights' immediate goal was to organize all workers into a single organization, regardless of their sex, skill level, craft, or industry of employment. They saw their efforts ultimately leading to the abolition of the capitalist wage system and the creation of a new society. Their membership peaked in 1887, with more than 200 local assemblies representing workers in 75 occupations. A combination of factors led to the Knights' demise: rapid membership growth that made it difficult to maintain idealistic philosophy, regular defeats at the hands of employers, internal political rivalries and, perhaps most important, growing hostilities with the AFL unions and a recognition among craft workers that uniting with unskilled workers in industrial unions would jeopardize their interests. The Knights survived longer in Canada than south of the border, although by the early years of the twentieth century they had all but disappeared.[27]

Only a handful of industrial unions surfaced in the early twentieth century. Several were part of the rising tide of labour radicalism, which reached a crest with the 1919 Winnipeg General Strike. There was a distinctive regional flavour to these working-class protests, as most took root in western Canada. The Western Federation of Miners, an international union but arch-rival of the AFL, gained a foothold in B.C. mines. The radical ideology of the Chicago-based Industrial Workers of the World (the "Wobblies") attracted unskilled migrants employed in lumbering, mining, agriculture, and railways in the West prior to the First World War. The Wobblies advocated a form of *syndicalism,* a belief that international industrial unions and general strikes are the main vehicles for working-class emancipation.

Our discussion would be incomplete without mention of the One Big Union. This revolutionary industrial union received widespread support in the western provinces, particularly among miners, loggers, and transportation workers, around the time of the Winnipeg General Strike. The OBU called for secession from the conservative AFL and its Canadian arm, the TLC. But its support for the Russian Revolution brought counterattacks from employers, governments and craft unions, and eventual defeat in the 1920s.[28]

Not until the 1940s did industrial unionism become firmly established in Canada. The opening round was the United Auto Workers Union's (UAW) milestone victory in 1937 against General Motors in Oshawa, Ontario. The UAW sprang up under the banner of the left-leaning Congress of Industrial Organizations (CIO) in the 1930s to

organize unskilled and semiskilled workers in mass production industries. Many of the the initial forays into the auto, electrical, rubber,
and chemical factories of corporate North America were led by
communist organizers. Craft union leaders opposed the CIO largely
on political grounds, despite the fact that Canadian workers embraced the CIO form of industrial unionism.[29]

In 1956, Canadian craft and industrial unions buried their differences, uniting skilled and unskilled workers within a single central
labour body. This marked the merger of the craft-based TLC and the
industrial unions of the Canadian Congress of Labour, resulting in
the creation of the Canadian Labour Congress (CLC). A similar
merger of the AFL and the CIO had occurred one year earlier in the
United States. The CLC remains Canada's "house of labour," and its
affiliated unions represent 58 percent of organized workers in the
country.[30] The CLC promotes the economic, political, and organizational interests of affiliates by providing research, education, organizational and collective bargaining services, as well as by eliminating
jurisdictional conflicts and organizational duplication.

THE ROLE OF THE CANADIAN STATE IN INDUSTRIAL RELATIONS

Canada's contribution to the quest for industrial peace has been the
development of a legislative and administrative framework that casts
the state into the role of "impartial umpire," mediating between
labour and capital.[31] The architect of this system was William Lyon
MacKenzie King, the first federal Minister of Labour and later a
Liberal prime minister. King's 1907 Industrial Disputes Investigation
Act (IDIA) became the cornerstone of Canada's modern industrial
relations policy. The act provided for compulsory conciliation (fact-
finding) in disputes during a "cooling off" period, a tripartite board
of arbitration, and special treatment of public interest disputes
involving public services. At first, the act was applied to disputes in
coal mines and railways. Its scope was extended during the First World
War, and in the 1950s its principles were incorporated into provincial
legislation. In some instances, the state used the powers of the act to
legislate an end to strikes. There is little question that this sort of
intervention has shaped the pattern of industrial conflict in Canada
(some would argue in the interests of employers).[32]

State intervention in industrial conflict is not a twentieth-century
invention, however. Pentland, for example, documents the role of
the British army in suppressing unrest among colonial labourers
building the the Rideau Canal in 1827. He concludes: "Intervention
by the Canadian state on behalf of employers in more recent years
should not be regarded as novelties, but as fruits of what employers

and officials learned about 'labour problems' in the middle of the nineteenth century."[33] Yet it was the 1907 IDIA that marked the first major step toward the *institutionalization* of industrial conflict through the control of law.[34]

We can identify four major phases in the development of the legal framework for industrial relations in Canada.[35] In the first, or pre-Confederation phase, common law prohibited collective bargaining. The second phase was entered with the 1872 Trade Union Act, passed by the Conservative government of Sir John A. MacDonald. This neutralized the legal restrictions to unionism, but did not grant workers positive legal rights or protections that facilitated collective bargaining. The National War Labour Order (P.C. 1003) launched the third, or modern, phase in 1944. Modelled on the 1935 U.S. National Labour Relations Act (Wagner Act), P.C. 1003 granted employees in the private sector collective bargaining rights, set down union certification procedures, spelled out a code of unfair labour practices, and established a labour relations board to administer the law. These measures paved the way for a post-war labour–management pact designed to maintain industrial peace. This truce was enshrined in the federal 1948 Industrial Relations and Disputes Act and in subsequent provincial legislation. The fourth phase involved the rise of public sector unions. The movement toward full-fledged public sector unionism began in Saskatchewan in 1944. But the real push started when Quebec public employees were granted collective bargaining in 1964. Another major breakthrough was the 1967 Public Service Staff Relations Act, which opened the door to unions in the federal civil service.

The intent of all these legislative changes was to establish industrial peace. It is obvious that one of their unintended effects was to spur the growth of unions. But the goal of conflict reduction should not be underestimated. The centrepiece of the 1907 IDIA was the regulation of work stoppages through compulsory postponement of strikes and lockouts, mediation or conciliation, no strikes or lockouts during the term of a collective agreement, and alternative means of disputes resolution. The act also made strikes or lockouts illegal in key industries (transportation, communications, mines, and public utilities) until a board of inquiry had studied the problem and its conciliation report had been made public. These methods of institutionalizing conflict have been fine-tuned over the years; but work stoppages are still illegal during the term of a collective agreement (although they do occur) and the state has removed the right to strike altogether from certain public employees who perform "essential services."

UNION MEMBERSHIP GROWTH TRENDS

Table 7.1 traces union membership growth in Canada since 1911.

There are now over 3.7 million union members, representing 37.7 percent of the entire labour force. Considering that only 4.9 percent of all non-agricultural employees belonged to unions in 1911, this is an impressive record of expansion. Scanning the table, we can identify three major spurts in membership growth. The first two coincided with the two world wars. This is not surprising, because national mobilization for these wars resulted in economic growth, labour shortages, and a need for a high level of cooperation between employers and employees — all of which are key ingredients for successful union recruitment. It was in the years during and immediately following World War II that Canada's contemporary industrial relations system took shape. Massive changes in the size, composition, legal rights, and goals of the union movement have occurred since the 1940s. The third growth period was the 1970s. The rise of public sector unions, largely facilitated by supportive legislation, brought many civil servants, teachers, nurses, and other public employees into labour's fold.

The 1981-82 recession, employer pressures for wage rollbacks and other concessions, and government's whittling away of collective bargaining rights have all created a more hostile climate for labour relations. Despite these adversities, Canadian unions have managed to keep growing. Union membership (*density*) has remained constant for the past decade only because the labour force has expanded more rapidly. The proportion of workers covered by collective agreements (even though some may not be union members) is a broader measure of the extent of collective bargaining. This figure has risen from 33 percent in 1943 to 58 percent in 1983 for all workers. It is even higher among blue-collar workers (73 percent) and government employees (90 percent). For the first time in four decades, total union membership declined between 1982 and 1983 by over 50,000. However, union density peaked in 1983 at 40 percent of the non-agricultural labour force, largely because of rising unemployment and contraction of the labour force.[36] This slipped to just under 38 percent by 1986.

The labour movement has undergone organizational changes as well. Most notable is the trend toward consolidation, a result of mergers and membership growth since the 1960s. Between 1963 and 1982, average membership in each union increased from 8,587 to 15,320, while the number of unions only increased from 161 to 220. But these 220 unions chartered 14,000 locals, the basic self-governing unit of the labour movement and the legal entity for collective bargaining. Membership in locals ranges from 10 to 25,000, with an average size in 1981 of 235. In short, despite these consolidations, Canadian labour remains fragmented and, consequently, collective bargaining is very decentralized. Unlike some European nations, where industry-wide national bargaining is the norm, the Canadian pattern of single-establishment, single-union bargaining results in over 22,000 collective agreements.[37]

Table 7.1
Union Membership Growth in Canada, 1911-1986

Year	Union Membership (Thousands)	Union Membership as a Percentage of all Non-Agricultural Paid Workers
1911	133	4.9
1916	160	*
1921	313	16.0
1926	275	12.0
1931	311	15.3
1936	323	16.2
1941	462	18.0
1946	832	27.9
1951	1,029	28.4
1956	1,352	33.3
1961	1,447	31.6
1966	1,736	30.7
1971	2,231	33.6
1976	3,042	37.3
1981	3,487	37.4
1986	3,730	37.7

* Data unavailable.
Source: Gary N. Chaison, "Unions: Growth, Structure, and Internal Dynamics." In John Anderson and Morley Gunderson, eds., *Union Management Relations in Canada* (Don Mills: Addison-Wesley, 1982), p. 149, for 1911 to 1976; for 1981 and 1986, *Directory of Labour Organizations in Canada, 1986* (Ottawa: Supply & Services Canada, 1986), p. 18.

Viewed from an international perspective, in 1961 Canada had the lowest level of union membership among seven major industrial nations (Table 7.2). However, it experienced the highest rate of union membership growth over the next twenty years. Canada's union density has surpassed that of the United States and Japan, but it still falls well below the high levels found in Sweden, the most unionized capitalist society, or Australia and the United Kingdom. This dramatic growth rate of Canadian unions relative to those in other countries, especially the United States, is a significant development. Canadian unions appear to have weathered the economic storms of the 1970s and 1980s quite successfully. In contrast, unions in most western capitalist countries have lost membership.[38]

Table 7.2
Union Membership Density and Growth in Selected Industrial Countries,
1961-1981

Countries	Membership as a Percentage of Wage and Salary Earners		Average Annual Change, 1961-81 (Percent)
	1961	1981	
Sweden	62.5	88.8	3.1
United Kingdom	43.4	57.5	1.1
Australia	59.0	55.8	2.4
West Germany	30.9	41.9	2.0
Canada	29.5	35.3	4.6
Japan	34.3	30.6	2.2
United States	30.2	24.7*	1.7

*Estimate for 1980.
Source: Pradeep Kumar, "Union Growth in Canada: Retrospect and Prospect." In W. Craig Riddell, ed., *Canadian Labour Relations* (Toronto: University of Toronto Press, 1986), p. 127.

Unions in the United States, for example, are engaged in a struggle for survival. Membership has plunged from one-third of the work force in the mid-1950s to about 19 percent today. Observers attribute this decline to a number of factors, in particular to fierce anti-union campaigns launched by employers, and facilitated in part by labour laws that allow these coercive tactics. Also significant is the shift of employment away from the union strongholds of the northeastern industrial regions to the Sun Belt states, where "right to work" laws undermine the incentive for workers to join unions. Several distinctive features of Canadian unions, as well as their broader social environment, help to explain why they have not suffered the same fate. Most important are their more militant character, widespread public sector collective bargaining facilitated through legislation, and nationalist demands for greater local control of union affairs. The U.S. experience clearly shows the decisive role legislation can play in encouraging or inhibiting free collective bargaining.[39]

THE CURRENT STATE OF UNIONS IN CANADA

The likelihood of a Canadian worker being a union member, or joining one in the future, varies according to sex, industry of employment, occupation, and province of residence. Table 7.3 shows that as of December 1984, 41.5 percent of the males and 31.9 percent of the females in the labour force were unionized. The industries with the highest levels of union membership are public administration and transportation, communication and other utilities (66.6 and 60.1 percent respectively). The least organized industries are finance, insurance and real estate, and trade (9.2 and 12.5 percent respectively). Note that these differences in overall unionization rates are reflected in female membership trends. Thus a worker's sex is less important than industry of employment in explaining whether or not he or she will be a union member.

Another way of examining union membership is by occupation. In Table 7.4 we find that sales, and managerial and administrative employees are least likely to be union members. Conversely, the most highly unionized jobs are in teaching and medicine (74.0 and 63.9 percent respectively; the latter occupational category includes nurses and other health care workers, but not doctors). The recent unionization of white-collar workers such as these has given a whole new complexion to the labour movement. The traditional, blue-collar union strongholds in craft jobs, processing, fabricating, transportation, materials handling, and construction now have union densities ranging from 45 to 58.1 percent.

In short, the composition of the labour movement has been dramatically transformed since the 1960s. The typical unionist in the 1980s is a white-collar worker employed in the service sector, and is increasingly likely to be a woman. Between 1971 and 1983, for example, the growth of union membership in manufacturing stagnated. The two major unions in manufacturing, the United Steel Workers and the United Auto Workers, suffered the greatest membership losses of any labour organizations in Canada during the 1981-82 recession.[40] In contrast, membership in those industries providing personal and business services expanded by 144 percent over the same period.[41]

Regional differences in economic performance and industrial mix, as well as provincial variations in labour legislation, also influence union membership. The level of union density ranges from a low of 28.4 percent in Alberta to a high of about 43 percent in British Columbia and Newfoundland.[42] In economic terms, these inter-provincial differences reflect the concentration of traditionally well-organized industries in B.C., especially mining, forestry products, and construction. They also mirror the individualistic, free-enterprise philosophy of the Alberta government and the energy and service firms that dominate the provincial economy. Newfoundland's situation is due to the disproportionately large size of the unionized public sector in an otherwise depressed economy and the strength of unions in the fishing industry. This brief sketch hardly does justice to the multitude of complex factors shaping union growth trends across Canada, but it does underline the impact of industrial structure, class composition, political culture, and labour legislation on regional membership trends.

Table 7.3
Union Membership and Unionization Rates by Industry and Sex,
Canada, December 1984

Industry	Union Membership				Unionization Rate		
	Women (000s)	Men (000s)	Total (000s)	Women as a percentage of total (%)	Women (%)	Men (%)	Total (%)
Goods-producing industries	179	909	1,087	16.5	28.5	45.7	41.6
Agriculture	*	*	*	*	*	*	*
Forestry, fishing, and trapping	*	23	25	*	*	38.3	39.7
Mines, quarries, and oil wells	*	57	60	*	*	36.3	32.8
Manufacturing	173	683	856	20.2	32.9	49.6	45.0
Construction	*	144	145	*	*	42.7	38.7
Service-producing industries	1,158	1,230	2,386	48.5	32.5	38.9	35.5
Transportation, communication, and other utilities	103	360	463	22.2	55.4	61.5	60.1
Trade	70	132	201	34.8	8.9	15.9	12.5
Finance, insurance, and real estate	28	20	48	58.3	8.3	11.0	9.2
Community, business, and personal service	756	404	1,159	65.2	38.9	36.7	38.1
Public administration	201	314	515	39.0	64.8	67.7	66.6
All industries	1,336	2,138	3,474	38.5	31.9	41.5	37.2

* Sample inadequate for reliable estimate.
Source: *Women in the Labour Force, 1985-86 Edition* (Labour Canada, Women's Bureau, 1986), p. 98.

The present character of the labour movement is expressed by its largest organizations. Table 7.5 lists the ten largest unions in 1986. The top three all represent government and other public sector employees. CUPE members are from a diverse range of jobs in municipalities, electrical utilities, social services, child care centres, schools,

Table 7.4
Union Membership and Unionization Rates by Occupation and Sex, Canada, December 1984

| | Union Membership | | Unionization Rate | | |
| | Total union membership (000s) | Women as a percentage of total (%) | | | |
Occupation			Women (%)	Men (%)	Total (%)
Managerial and administrative	189	30.2	16.7	19.6	18.7
Natural sciences	117	18.8	35.5	31.7	32.3
Social sciences	68	69.1	54.0	33.9	45.9
Religion	*	*	*	*	*
Teaching	367	55.6	73.6	74.4	74.0
Medicine	334	84.4	64.4	61.2	63.9
Artistic	30	30.0	15.5	26.3	21.7
Clerical	545	68.3	26.1	45.5	30.2
Sales	65	33.8	5.7	12.9	9.0
Service	365	41.1	22.0	36.0	28.5
Farming	9	*	*	12.9	10.6
Fishing	*	*	*	*	*
Forestry	21	*	*	40.8	42.9
Mining	25	*	*	40.7	41.7
Processing	215	15.8	48.6	60.3	58.1
Machining	124	7.3	50.0	56.4	55.9
Fabricating	399	20.3	40.7	47.5	46.1
Construction	254	*	*	56.9	57.0
Transportation	154	4.5	25.0	47.0	45.2
Materials handling	117	22.2	49.1	49.2	49.2
Other crafts	72	11.1	33.3	57.1	52.9
All Occupations	3,474	38.5	31.9	41.5	37.2

*Sample inadequate for reliable estimate.
Source: *Women in the Labour Force, 1985-86 Edition* (Labour Canada, Women's Bureau, 1986), p. 99.

libraries, colleges and universities, hospitals, nursing homes, and many other public institutions. NUPGE is the umbrella organization for the various provincial government employee unions, and PSAC represents federal government workers. These unions are at the crest of the wave of public sector unionism, signalling as well a new brand of worker militancy. Nurses, teachers, librarians, social workers, clerks, university professors, and other white-collar employees have taken to the picket lines to pressure their employers (ultimately the government) into improving wages and working conditions and maintaining the quality of public services.

Table 7.5
Ten Largest Unions, Canada, 1986

Union	Membership, 1986
1. Canadian Union of Public Employees	304,300
2. National Union of Provincial Government Employees	254,300
3. Public Service Alliance of Canada	182,000
4. United Steel Workers of America	160,000
5. United Food and Commercial Workers International Union	156,000
6. International Union, United Automobile, Aerospace and Agricultural Implement Workers of America*	140,000
7. Social Affairs Federation Inc.	93,000
8. International Brotherhood of Teamsters, Chauffeurs, Warehousemen and Helpers of America	91,500
9. School Board Teachers' Commission**	75,000
10. Service Employees International Union	70,000

* This union became autonomous from its U.S. parent in 1986, creating The Canadian Auto Workers Union.
** Previously part of the Quebec Teaching Congress.
Source: *Directory of Labour Organizations in Canada, 1986* (Ottawa: Supply and Services, 1986), p. 15.

A watershed in the Canadian labour movement was reached in 1967 when the federal government passed the Public Service Staff Relations Act. This opened the door to collective bargaining for federal civil servants. Provincial government employees were already moving in this direction, with the granting of collective bargaining rights to Quebec public employees in 1965. Unionism soon spread into municipal governments, hospitals, schools, prisons, social services, and other expanding public institutions.[43] Consequently, the international unions representing mainly male craft and industrial workers have lost their once dominant position in the Canadian labour movement.

The rise of public sector unions has also helped to Canadianize the labour movement. At the turn of the century, U.S.-based international unions represented about 95 percent of all unionized workers in Canada. By 1969, this had dropped to 65 percent and, with the ground swell of nationalism since the 1970s, has continued to decline to 39.1 percent in 1986.[44] Not surprisingly, the recent upsurge in union growth is largely through the efforts of national public sector unions. Equally important in explaining the Canadianization trend is the push for greater autonomy, or outright independence, within Canadian sections of international unions.

The vulnerability of Canada's branch-plant economy taught growing numbers of workers the need for greater local control of union activities. A strong argument in support of international unions is that they are labour's best defence against the global strategies of multinational corporations. Yet the internationals have not always been effective in dealing with the sorts of problems multinational corporations created for Canadian employees. For example, officials at the U.S. headquarters of these unions sometimes equated layoffs or plant closures in Canada — associated with multinational firms shifting production to their U.S. facilities — with more jobs for their much larger American memberships. Different bargaining agendas also tended to arise in the two countries, reflecting their distinctive industrial relations environments. Canadian auto workers, for instance, roundly rejected the concessions made to employers by the U.S. wing of their union. Furthermore, some Canadian members of international unions felt that their dues were flowing into the American headquarters, with few services or benefits flowing back. These and other factors have prompted a growing number of separations. The Communications Workers of Canada, the Energy and Chemical Workers, the Canadian Paperworkers Union, and the Canadian Auto Workers Union were all created in this way. Usually good "fraternal" relations are maintained, however, with their former parents to the South.

WOMEN AND UNIONS

Why is the level of unionization about ten percentage points lower among female workers compared to male workers (see Table 7.3)? Traditionally, it has been assumed that women, given their family responsibilities, naturally would be less interested in unions. As a result of their domestic roles, so the argument goes, women's ties to the labour force were weak. Hence, work problems that might prompt unionization were of little concern. Old myths die hard, but close scrutiny of recent membership trends totally shatters this one. Women made up only 16.4 percent of all union members in 1962, yet by the end of 1984 this figure had jumped to 38.5 percent. In fact, women have been joining unions at a much faster rate than men. Between 1970 and 1980, female union membership increased by 81.8 percent, compared to a 25.4 percent increase for men. These membership patterns strongly parallel the remarkable jump in female labour force participation, especially in the service sector, and the rapid growth of public sector unions since 1970. It seems obvious that women are not apathetic, passive, or basically disinterested in collective action — if, in fact, they ever were.[45]

Indeed, women are often more pro-union than men because of their inferior position in the firm.[46] Kate Purcell rejects the "passive woman worker" argument on the grounds that industrial patterns of unionism are decisive in who joins. Men and women alike join unions and engage in militant action according to the established patterns of their industries or occupations.[47] Miners and forestry workers, for example, are highly unionized and often quite militant. But because these are *non-traditional* areas of women's employment, we would not expect to find many female unionists in these industries.

Thus, the sex segregation of the labour market (discussed in Chapter 5) is the key factor in female unionization patterns. We have seen how historically women's employment has been restricted to a few predominantly female job ghettos. The oppressive and unrewarding character of this type of work — not the fact of being female — underlies the lower rate of female unionization. Conditions in job ghettos undermine collective action as a way of solving job-related problems. Workers, be they male or female, are far more likely to quit than to stay and fight for changes. The centres of union strength in the past were in skilled trades, manufacturing, resource, and transportation industries, all areas employing very few women.

What has been the role of male-dominated unions in keeping women out of certain jobs and, therefore, out of unions? There are numerous examples of craft and industrial unionists adopting policies that restricted female access to their jobs, mainly due to fears about having their wages undercut. Early this century, craft unions lobbied with middle-class reformers to keep women out of the industrial labour force (allegedly to protect them). Such efforts discouraged union initiatives by women, thereby defining the union movement as a male institution. In Canada, for example, the failure of the 1907 strike by female Bell Telephone operators in Toronto was partly due to the lack of support their unionization campaign received from the International Brotherhood of Electrical Workers, an exclusively male craft union.[48]

For many women, therefore, the option of joining a union did not exist. Only in the last decade, for example, were major organizing efforts launched in the largely female trade and financial industries. Massive counterattacks were mounted by management in banks and in the retail stores. Despite a huge investment of organizing resources since the late 1970s, the CLC has achieved only limited success in unionizing banks. More recent breakthroughs in achieving union certification in big department stores, such as Eaton's and Simpsons, initially augured well for union expansion in the retail sector. Yet the 1987 decertification of unions by employees in five Ontario Eaton's stores represents a major setback.[49]

Women's demands for equality of opportunities and rewards in the workplace already have had a major impact on Canadian unions. The CLC now has its first female president, and women are comprising a growing share of elected union officers and paid staff, especially in public sector unions. Women's issues, such as employment equity, child care, and parental leave have become important collective bargaining objectives for a growing number of unions today.[50]

MANAGEMENT OPPOSITION TO UNIONS

Despite laws giving each employee the right to join a union and to participate in free collective bargaining, employer opposition to unionism frequently has been a major obstacle to putting these rights into practice. Workers who encounter strong management opposition to their union organizing activities may legitimately fear for their jobs, which will have a chilling effect on the union campaign. Moreover, if an employer should choose not to recognize a union after it has been legally certified in the workplace, it is very difficult for members of that union to exercise their legal rights. Prior to the introduction of a legal framework for union certification and collective bargaining procedures during World War II, many industrial disputes were over the employer's refusal to recognize its workers' union. Surveying the historical record, Pentland observes: "It is sad but true that Canadian employers as a group — and Canadian governments — have never taken a forward step in industrial relations by intelligent choice, but have had to be battered into it."[51]

White-collar workers in the private sector are the largest unorganized group remaining in the labour force. Strenuous efforts by employers to remain "union free," coupled with feeble government action to promote private sector union recognition, has created an inhospitable climate for unionism. There are several reasons for this.[52] White-collar employees often have direct contact with management and therefore may identify more closely with the company ideology than do blue-collar workers. The fact that management openly disapproves of unions can make white-collar workers reluctant to join one. Workers join unions for the benefits, such as better working conditions, higher wages, job security, or access to a grievance procedure. Concrete proof that unions can deliver "the goods" obviously is lacking in industries that have never had high levels of unionization. The difficulties of overcoming these obstacles discourages unions from launching recruitment drives. Consequently, the option of joining a union has not been available to many private sector white-collar workers.

The form of employee relations usually preferred by management is to deal with each worker individually. This creates a David and Goliath situation, pitting individual employees against the power of a corporation. However, the once virulent anti-unionism of Canadian business has softened somewhat into a grudging acceptance. Joseph Smucker's analysis of changing managerial ideologies from 1901 to

1970 indicates that collective bargaining has come to be accepted as a "necessary evil."[53] Instead of fighting unions head-on, managers now criticize them as being unrepresentative organizations under misguided leadership. An underlying concern is over the issue of what constitutes *management's rights*. There are still some employers today, like Peter Pocklington, who zealously believe that the owners of a business should unilaterally define the employment relationship; in such cases, the right to manage takes priority.

Some leading corporations have adopted a velvet-gloved strategy. This *positive labour relations* approach is based on maintaining high-quality personnel policies and good working conditions. In some cases, a company union is set up to create the facade of democratic employee representation. The basic assumption behind this approach is that if management treats employees well and listens to their concerns, a union will be unnecessary. IBM is a prime example of positive industrial relations in action. In Britain, recently, the corporation's 13,000 employees were balloted at the request of the government's industrial relations board to find out if they desired union recognition. Only about 4 percent of the staff were in favour of unionization. This vote was not the result of corporate coercion or intimidation, as is becoming increasingly common in the United States (although not in IBM). Rather, it reflects the great deal of attention and resources the company devotes to personnel matters.

IBM can afford to do this, given its size and profitability. Here are some key company policies: no layoffs; the same fringe benefits package for all staff (an attempt to eliminate major status differences); merit pay and a sophisticated job evaluation system (the firm is the industry leader in salaries); open communication channels between management and employees; a form of internal grievance system, which acts as a safety valve for discontent; and developing "people" skills among managers so that discontent can be pre-empted. These policies engender a corporate culture based on strong employee loyalty and identification with management's goals.[54] Wherever corporations such as IBM, Xerox, or Hewlett-Packard operate, they implement this approach. Some Canadian firms, most notably the Hamilton steel producer Dofasco, have developed their own unique brand of corporate welfarism to obtain the cooperation of employees.[55]

THE FUTURE OF UNION–MANAGEMENT RELATIONS

Crystal ball gazing is not a very scholarly activity, but we should at least contemplate likely future scenarios in Canadian industrial relations. The collective bargaining agenda is being transformed. Declining productivity growth since the mid-1960s, coupled with the severe

1981-82 recession and slow recovery, have forced unions to rethink their negotiating priorities. Unfortunately for organized labour, the challenge of the 1980s and beyond will be to protect members' jobs.[56] In this respect, the Gainers dispute may indeed be characteristic of tough fights ahead over the issue of job security. Unions also face employer demands for wage and benefit concessions. *Concession bargaining*, as it is called, began seriously in 1983, and as a result wage settlements have dropped sharply.

This realignment in collective bargaining reflects underlying economic trends. Rising international competition, pressures to accelerate the pace of technological innovations, government deregulation of industry, the growing need to maintain greater flexibility in staffing and production systems, and rising deficits in the public sector — these are the factors motivating employers to slash labour costs, boost employee productivity, and intensify the work process.

The 1985 strike by 3,000 Air Canada ticket agents brought together for the first time issues that may become more prominent in the future. These included the use of part-time employees, technological change, the rights of women workers, and the effects of industry deregulation. Deregulation in 1984 forced airlines to reduce labour costs because of mounting competition. The union was concerned that management wanted to make the job of ticket agent a part-time one, using machines to issue tickets and check in passengers. At stake were full-time incomes for female employees. The big issue raised by this dispute is the necessity of directly involving workers in the process of workplace change.

This suggests that unions and management must strive for greater cooperation in the future. While in principle this sounds laudable, there are (as with everything in industrial relations) two competing perspectives on what cooperation may entail. Many people, especially in business and government circles, believe that labour–management relations in Canada are too adversarial. Craig Riddell articulates the case in favour of less conflict and more cooperation:

> Labour–management cooperation is advocated not for its own sake but because it may yield tangible returns, both to those involved in labour relations and to society more generally. Increased cooperation, employee involvement in planning and decision making, and consultation, although not without some costs, can yield higher levels of job satisfaction and a more enjoyable work environment for employees. Greater employee involvement in planning and decision making may also result in improved productivity, better product quality and more competitiveness. Each of these improvements can benefit both employers and employees by producing both higher profits *and* job satisfaction and wages, as well as more employment opportunities. In addition, the need for flexibility and adaptability in our economy is more likely to be

met in an open labour relations environment. Finally, reductions in labour–management conflict, expressed through strikes, lockouts, grievances, absenteeism and so on, could also occur.[57]

Unions have a very different perspective on labour–management cooperation. In organized labour's experience, management wants workers to cooperate on *its* terms, and often substitutes this for tangible improvements in working conditions. Only in bad times do employers want cooperation, just as they want concessions. Cooperation is therefore defined by management as a problem of improving competitiveness and efficiency and lowering costs, rather than as a problem of balancing legitimate worker concerns with society's objective of improving production.[58] It is not that unions dismiss the importance of productivity, competitiveness, and organizational flexibility. They simply want cooperation and consultation on these issues to be fully open and democratic. This may well produce significant benefits for labour, management, and society as a whole.

NOTES

1. Sidney and Beatrice Webb (1894, 1911). See Poole (1981, chapter 1) for an overview of early theories of the labour movement.
2. Perlman (1928).
3. Poole (1981, chapter 1). This classification is based on Perlman (1958).
4. Bain and Clegg (1974). The systems model of industrial relations was pioneered by John Dunlop (1971). For critical assessments, see Poole (1981, chapter 2); Crouch (1982, chapter 1); and Hyman (1975, chapter 1). The systems approach is applied to Canada by Anderson and Gunderson (1982a).
5. For a discussion of work as a power relationship between employees and employers, see T. Johnson (1980).
6. Hyman (1975): 26.
7. Canada (1969): 119. On the same theme, see also Barbash (1979).
8. See Poole (1981, chapter 8) for a discussion of the importance of workers' values and perceptions in the study of industrial relations, given that these are the basis of their actions. See also Hyman and Brough (1975) on value systems in industrial relations. Keenoy (1985:15-20) elaborates the point that workers and managers hold different definitions of reality.
9. Keenoy (1985): 12.
10. See Hill (1981), especially chapter 7 on unions.
11. For a discussion of *zero-sum* versus *win-win* bargaining models, see Downie (1982).
12. Hill (1981, chapter 7).
13. Crouch (1982): 37-38. This paragraph draws on Crouch's distinction between "radical" and Marxist approaches to trade unionism.
14. The phrase *managers of discontent* was coined by C. W. Mills (1948) in his famous book on trade union officials. An especially interesting discussion of the mobilization and management of discontent is provided by Batstone et al. (1978, chapter 16). They identify contradictory pressures on union leaders, who must create

"righteous indignation" only to have to cool it later. See also Keenoy (1985:75-76) on this concept.

15. Michels (1959). For a useful discussion, see Crouch (1982): 163-74. An important contribution to the debate is Lipset, Trow, and Coleman (1956). See also Freeman's (1982) Canadian study of local 1005 of the steelworkers' union.

16. Crouch (1982) elaborates on these points in chapter 4.

17. Riddell (1986a): 5.

18. Krahn and Lowe (1984).

19. See Hackett (1982) for an insightful analysis of pro-management biases in how Canadian television reports labour relations.

20. Freeman and Medoff (1984): 5-11.

21. See Freeman and Medoff (1984, chapter 11) on the impact unions have on productivity.

22. Freeman and Medoff (1984): 19. There is no comparable Canadian study. However, Gunderson (1982) offers a summary of the empirical research on how unions affect wages, fringe benefits, and productivity in Canada. A December 1984 hourly wage survey in Canada found that unionized workers earn 30 percent more on average than non-union workers (Labour Canada 1986): 100.

23. Basic sources for historical accounts of the rise of the Canadian labour movement include Lipton (1968), Forsey (1982, 1985), Palmer (1983), Smucker (1980, chapters 7 and 8), Morton (1982), Laxer (1976), and Logan (1948). The Canadian labour history journal, *Labour/Le Travail,* is also an excellent source, as occasionally is the industrial relations journal, *Relations industrielles/Industrial Relations.*

24. Kealey (1980): 292.

25. The work of Palmer (1979), Kealey (1980), Heron (1980), and various contributors to the journal *Labour/Le Travail* best represent this field. Compare Kealey's (1981a) and Bercuson's (1981) assessments of the contributions of the new labour history.

26. See Babcock (1974) on the influence exerted by the AFL and its leader, Samuel Gompers, on the Canadian union movement.

27. Kealey (1981b).

28. On labour radicalism during the early twentieth century, see Robin (1968) and McCormack (1978), who focuses specifically on the West. See also Bercuson (1978) for a study of the OBU.

29. Two key CIO organizing drives are described in Abella (1974) and Moulton (1974).

30. Kumar (1986): 102-3. He also describes the four smaller union centrals in Canada, two of which are based in Quebec .

31. The definitive work on this topic is Craven (1980). See also Pentland (1979).

32. Huxley (1979).

33. Pentland (1981): 196; see also pp.187-96 on this topic. Craven (1980:158), while emphasizing the pivotal role of King, notes that state intervention had become established practice long before Confederation .

34. The institutionalization of conflict thesis was put forward by sociologists to explain the relative peacefulness of union–management relations in the immediate post-war period. Some U.S. academics went as far as to suggest that the decline in industrial disputes signalled a lessening of class distinctions and class conflict. See Crouch (1982:106-9), Hill (1981:124-27), and Ingham (1974) for evaluations of this thesis.

35. This account is from Riddell (1986a).

36. Kumar (1986): 95-96. For overviews of union growth trends in Canada, see Kumar (1986:106-33) and Chaison (1982).

37. Kumar (1986): 121-22; also pp. 96-97.

38. *Monthly Labor Review* 108 (September 1985): 20. International comparisons of union membership data must be approached with caution, given different methods of data collection.

39. For discussions of the decline in U.S. union membership, with comparisons to the Canadian scene, see: Freeman and Medoff (1984): 228-43; Rose and Chaison (1985); Riddell, (1986a): 8-10; Lipset, (1987); and Kumar (1986): 126-33. Milton (1986) examines the waning power of U.S. unions, arguing that a new system of industrial relations is emerging which holds out few prospects for greater democracy in the workplace.

40. Kumar (1986): 140.

41. Membership in manufacturing increased from 775,448 to 782,809 and in services from 418,453 to 1,022,593 between 1971 and 1983. Based on data from the *Corporations and Labour Unions Returns Act* (Statistics Canada 1974): 71; (1986): 70.

42. Labour Canada (1986): 97.

43. Government employee unions emerged from traditional and rather docile staff associations. CUPE was well established in the 1960s, with 97,000 members at the start of 1967 (*Financial Post*, 3 February 1979). Its more than threefold growth in less than twenty years makes it the first union in the country to break the 300,000 membership mark — representing over 8 percent of all trade unionists in 1986.

44. See Morton (1982:110-11), Laxer (1976), Abella (1974), Crispo (1967), and Chaison and Rose (1981) for discussions of national unions and the role of nationalism. The *Directory of Labour Organizations,* published annually, contains complete data on membership according to type of union.

45. Data on female union membership are from CALURA (Statistics Canada, 1973): 13; (1979): 48. White (1980) is a useful source on women in unions in Canada, as is the collection of essays by Briskin and Yanz (1983).

46. Based on a major U.S. study of employee voting in union representation elections. See Farber and Saks (1980), Antos, Chandler, and Mellow (1980); see also Marchak (1974) for an interesting study of white-collar unionism in Canada.

47. Purcell (1979): 122-23.

48. On the Bell strike, see Sangster (1978). A general sociological discussion of women in Canadian unions is provided by Baker and Robeson (1986). For interesting research and analysis of women in the U.S. labour movement, see Gabin (1979-80), Milkman (1985), and Kessler-Harris (1975).

49. On the bank organizing drive, see Lowe (1981), Ponak and Moore (1981), and Beckett (1984). For an account of the unsuccessful 1948-52 Eaton's organizing drive, see Suffrin (1982). The monthly CLC publication, *Canadian Labour,* covers recent developments in banking and retail unionism.

50. The CUPE monthly publication, *The Facts,* covers these issues very well. See also Attenborough (1982) and Chaison and Andiappan (1982).

51. Pentland (1979): 19. Jamieson (1971:51-52) echoes this point, claiming that management opposition to collective bargaining has been a dominant theme in Canadian labour history. See Bendix (1974) for a detailed analysis of U.S. employers' anti-union tactics during the early twentieth century.

52. See Bain (1978): 23.

53. Smucker (1980, chapter 7).

54. This account of IBM is from Keenoy (1985): 98-102. For discussions of corporate culture, see chapter 8 below.

55. See Storey (1983) on the "Dofasco Way" of employee relations.

56. *Globe and Mail* (10 January 1987): A8.

57. Riddell (1986b): 2.

58. United Auto Workers (1985): 151-52.

8

Industrial Conflict

INTRODUCTION

Mention unions to most Canadians and they will start talking about strikes. According to conventional wisdom, unions in this country are strike-happy and our entire industrial relations system is far too adversarial. But do the facts support these opinions?

This chapter investigates the basis of industrial conflict. Before addressing why workers go on strike, we will take up the prior question of why they organize collectively. This is the obvious prerequisite to any strike. Comparisons with patterns of trade unionism and industrial conflict in other countries will help us to evaluate the popular complaint that Canadian workers are too strike-prone. Finally, strikes will be considered within the context of the larger political arena. Are strikes a sign of worker militancy? Does industrial conflict have any connection with working-class politics? After all, many of the grievances fuelling strikes could be blamed generally on the capitalist system itself. But do union members and non-union workers themselves make such connections?

FROM INDIVIDUAL TO COLLECTIVE ACTION

Despite a huge literature on unions and industrial relations, we still lack a thorough understanding of why workers come to act collectively.[1] The very idea of collective action seems contrary to the individualistic norms of capitalist employment relations. The industrial relations literature contains two approaches to union formation. The first traces union growth at the aggregate level, concentrating on how the larger social and economic environment influences union membership. The other focuses directly on why individuals decide to vote for or against union representation in workplace elections. Characteristic of this approach is the assumption that workers are "rational economic actors," who calculate the costs and benefits of joining a union in order to maximize their economic self-interest.[2] The decision to strike is treated in the same manner. While both of these perspectives are informative, their emphasis on either macro- or micro-economic issues limits their explanatory power.

Sociological approaches draw insights from the above industrial relations literature, but go beyond it by conceptualizing unions as social movements that unite members into actively seeking shared goals. But as bureaucratic organizations, unions also require rules and sanctions that will regulate the behaviour of members. As Alan Flanders writes, "trade unions need organization for their power and movement for their vitality."[3] Both qualities are essential for unions to achieve their social and economic objectives. This broader perspective focuses, at the individual level, on why employees would organize into unions to collectively pursue common goals. In addition, it incorporates an analysis of the economic and social conditions that encourage or inhibit unionism and, moreover, raises questions about the internal dynamics of unions.

Economists have posed two dilemmas that a worker must resolve if he or she is to seriously consider joining a union or, if already a member, becoming an activist. The first is the *free-rider* problem. Mancur Olson asserts that individuals will not naturally organize to further their collective interest. "The rational worker," explains Olson, "will not voluntarily contribute to a union providing a collective benefit since [s]he alone would not perceptibly strengthen the union, and since [s]he would get the benefits of any union achievements whether or not [s]he supported the union."[4] Just like social movements concerned with environmental, peace, or feminist issues, unions provide *collective goods.* In other words, all potential members have access to the organization's achievements — cleaner air and water, a world with fewer nuclear weapons, employment equity programs, or a grievance procedure and negotiated regular wage increases — whether or not they have assisted in achieving these objectives.

The second dilemma, also relevant to a sociological perspective on collective action, is Albert Hirschman's *exit* and *voice* methods of expressing discontent.[5] According to Hirschman, a dissatisfied employee can either leave his or her employer or stay and push for changes. The presence of a union increases the chances of the latter strategy. But in non-union workplaces, the poor employment conditions that could spark an organizing drive also increase the chances of an individual opting to quit. This is a major obstacle to unionization in low-wage job ghettos in the service industries today.

However, we have already noted that many people do not have other employment options. Unemployment may be high in their community, or their particular skills may not be in demand. Consequently, they adapt to their limited opportunities, perhaps becoming increasingly apathetic and alienated on the job. But while it is true that apathy and alienation stifle collective action, it would be wrong to assume that these conditions cannot be overcome. Instead, we should ask why some groups of employees mobilize while others do not.

The process of mobilizing initial support for a union requires obtaining signed union cards from the majority of employees in the workplace. It also requires the financial assistance and organizational expertise of an established union. Once organized, a union faces the problem of rallying members in support of collective bargaining goals. Ultimately, this could involve strike action. According to Charles Tilly's research on the causes of social protest, essential here is a sense of shared identity within the group.[6] Collective action in the workplace will be easier when the work group is an important part of each employee's life. Strong social ties inside and outside the workplace integrate employees into the group. Individual interests become synonymous with group interests, acting as a springboard to collective action. Good examples of groups possessing this *solidarity* are printers, miners, fishers, and other occupations in which the occupational culture encompasses all of a worker's life.[7] As we will shortly see, the level of unionization and industrial militancy tends to be high under these conditions.

Assuming the existence of a cohesive group, what pushes its members into common action? The role of the group leader is obviously a central one. Especially important are *organic leaders* who, by virtue of being part of the group, are best able to tap its potential for collective action. This is because they understand the experiences of group members and can gain their trust better than an outsider could. In short, a leader can build up group solidarity, create an awareness of common interests, help to map out a realistic program of action, and seize opportunities to launch the plan.

But we are not suggesting that all union activity can be reduced to the characteristics of a particular group, its members and leaders. Also important is the environmental context, which might involve a supportive community, a hostile employer, or fair labour legislation — all factors that can either encourage or dampen union activity. Even if such conditions are favourable, employees ripe for unionization still may not act. Similarly, unionized workers facing a deadlock in negotiations with management over a new collective agreement may not strike. Often missing is one or more precipitating factors — an arbitrary change in work practices, the denial of a long-awaited salary increase, the dismissal of co-workers, or a pent-up sense of being treated unfairly by management. Such perceived injustices could serve as the catalysts for mobilization.

In summary, a solid organizational base, strong leadership, shared understandings of who is responsible for employees' grievances, support from other groups in the community, and an ability to overcome management opposition to unionization are all key ingredients for collective action.[8]

WHAT ARE STRIKES?

Strikes can be high drama on the stage of industrial relations. The public views strikes as an inconvenience or even as a major social problem; many politicians and business leaders argue that strikes harm the economy. The participants seldom want strikes, least of all the union members who will never recoup lost wages should the dispute drag on. If conflict has been largely institutionalized, as described in Chapter 7, why do strikes occur at all? What motivates workers to strike, and what are the larger social and economic implications of their actions?

Let us begin with a widely accepted definition of a *strike* or *lockout:* "A temporary stoppage of work willfully effected by a group of workers, or by one or more employers, with a view to enforcing a demand."[9] During the period from 1966 to 1983, about 12 percent of negotiations ended in a strike.[10] In other words, strikes may be described accurately as infrequent events. Contrary to public opinion, settlement of union–management disputes without recourse to work stoppages is clearly the norm in Canada. There evidently is some truth to the institutionalization of conflict argument.

Strikes are, nonetheless, central to the wage–labour relationship. If workers are selling their labour power to an employer in return for wages, their ultimate bargaining lever is to withdraw that labour. Even before the emergence of industrial capitalism in Canada, strikes erupted as workers protested against harsh treatment. For example, carpenters imported to build ships in colonial New France staged a slowdown to win living expenses above basic wages.[11] We have already mentioned that the struggling nineteenth-century labour movement mounted several landmark strikes, most notably the 1872 Toronto printer's strike and the Nine Hour Movement agitations around the same time.

But strikes are only one possible manifestation of workplace conflict. Richard Hyman distinguishes between *unorganized* and *organized conflict.*[12] The former is not a calculated strategy, and typically involves workers responding to oppressive situations by individual absenteeism, quitting, or sabotage. The latter is a planned collective strategy to change the source of discontent. Recall from Chapter 7 that strikes in Canada are only legal after the collective agreement has expired and specific conditions, such as a strike vote, have been met. Unauthorized strikes during the term of an agreement, often spontaneous responses by rank-and-file workers to an immediate problem in the workplace, are known as *wildcat strikes.*[13]

Not all strikes are over economic issues, nor do they exclusively involve working-class unionists. They can be political, as in the case of the CLC's 1976 national day of protest when over one million employees took to the streets to voice their opposition to the Trudeau government's imposition of wage and price controls; or the British Columbia Federation of Labour's concerted opposition in the spring of 1987 to new legislation that would seriously weaken unions. Strikes can involve work stoppages by high-status professionals, the 1986 Ontario doctors' strike over the right to extra-bill patients being a prominent example. Finally, strikes do not necessarily entail all members of the union leaving the work site as a group. Under certain situations, rotating, hit-and-run, work-to-rule, or sit-down forms of strike activity effectively communicate workers' demands to management.

Our emphasis on strike activity may leave the impression that workers are the disruptive factor in what otherwise would be harmonious labour relations. The key word here is "relations," for there are two parties (three if the government intervenes) in every strike. Seldom is the employment relationship a balanced one, for employers inevitably wield greater power. After all, management holds the final bargaining chip — the keys to the factory gate or office door, and therefore to the workers' jobs. Nonetheless, in the public mind unions are the "cause" of conflicts.

The United Auto Workers attempted to set the record straight in their brief before the Royal Commission on the Economic Union and Development Prospects for Canada: "No matter how legitimate our demands are, it is the *unions* who have to initiate strike action. This reinforces the public bias of blaming workers for management–labour conflict."[14] The brief debunks the myth that unions are too powerful and strike-happy by outlining the underlying causes of three of the union's recent disputes. These included the unwillingness of an employer to recognize a legitimately organized union local, employer attempts to force wage and benefit rollbacks, and concerns about plant closures. These are not isolated instances. Rather they are typical of how employers are able to muscle unions into a tight economic corner from which strike action is often the only rational escape.

CANADIAN STRIKE TRENDS

Figure 8.1 identifies four stormy periods of industrial conflict in Canada during the twentieth century. It traces the contours of strike activity by the percentage of total working time it accounts for each year. This is a standardized measure, helping us to trace out strike patterns over time. As a note of caution, however, we should mention that this way of measuring strikes conceals important fluctuations in their size, duration, and frequency. Nonetheless, work stoppages rarely account for more than 0.5 percent of all working time in

Canada. This again suggests that the seriousness of the strike "problem" often gets blown out of proportion.

Figure 8.1
Strikes and Lockouts in Canada as a Percentage of Total Working Time:
1919-1983

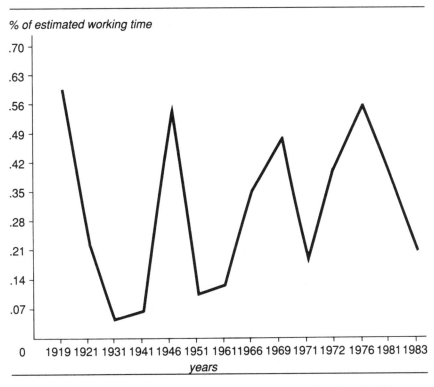

Source: Gérard Hébert, "Strikes and Lockouts," *The Canadian Encyclopedia* (Edmonton: Hurtig, 1985), p. 1765.

Prior to union recognition and compulsory collective bargaining becoming encoded in law during World War II, most strikes were precipitated by an employer's refusal to recognize the existence of a union, much less bargain with it. The historic peak in labour militancy occurred at the end of World War I. Workers across the country were agitating against oppressive working conditions, low wages, and declining living standards due to soaring wartime inflation. Most of all, they wanted recognition of their unions. Western Canadian unions were far more militant and inclined toward radical politics than those in the East. Thus, in 1919, when Winnipeg building and metal trades employers refused to recognize and negotiate with unions over wage increases, the Winnipeg Trades and Labour Council called a general strike.

A massive display of working-class solidarity erupted, bringing the local economy to a halt. Sympathy strikes spread to other cities across Canada, and even into the United States. The battle lines of open class warfare (one of the few instances of this in Canadian history) were drawn when, fearing a revolution, Winnipeg's upper class fought back with the help of the state. For several days, strikers squared off against police and employer-sponsored armed vigilantes. The confrontation ended in violence after the Royal Northwest Mounted Police, sent in by the federal government, charged a crowd of demonstrators. Strike leaders were arrested and jailed, the workers' demands still unmet.[15]

Other issues were also at stake in early twentieth-century strikes. Skilled artisans in the nineteenth century were able to retain much of their craft status, pride, and economic security through their control of the production process. This was eroded by industrialization after 1900, as advancing technology and scientific management techniques undermined craft workers' autonomy. These skilled workers reacted angrily. Thus, many of the 421 strikes and lockouts that occurred between 1901 and 1914 in southwestern Ontario manufacturing cities were sparked by craft workers resisting rationalizations of the work process.[16]

Returning to Figure 8.1, it is clear that strike activity declined with rising unemployment during the depression of the 1930s. As a rule, unions are less likely to strike in tough economic times. Conversely, when industry is booming and there is a relative shortage of labour reflected in low unemployment rates, a strike becomes a more potent bargaining lever. The World War II era marked the rise of industrial unionism in manufacturing industries. These organizing drives accelerated as military production demands helped to restore the ailing economy. Again, union recognition was a dominant issue driving workers in automobile factories, steel plants, and mines onto the picket lines.

An important outcome of the 1945 Windsor, Ontario, Ford Motor Company strike by the United Auto Workers was a Supreme Court ruling guaranteeing union security. On the assumption that a union must act on behalf of all employees in a workplace, financial support for these activities was provided through automatic deduction of union dues from everyone — union members or not — in a bargaining unit. The *Rand Formula* for a *union shop* and *union dues check-off* became a standard feature of post-World War II collective agreements.

Canada experienced a series of strikes in the mid-1960s. The fact that about one-third of these work stoppages involved wildcat strikes (mainly over wages) led the government to perceive a serious crisis in industrial relations. A task force, chaired by Professor H. D. Woods of McGill University, was set up to investigate the causes of industrial unrest and to recommend ways of achieving labour peace. Yet rampant inflation during the 1970s, and an increasingly militant mood among public sector workers, escalated labour–management confrontations.

The most recent strike wave reached its apex in 1976. The Trudeau government's imposition of wage and price controls between 1975 and 1978, as part of its anti-inflation program, made strikes over higher wages a futile exercise.[17] The recession of 1981-82 has further dampened strike activity, as is evident from the chart. Ironically, the fact that Canada's lost working time due to strikes and lockouts is at a twenty-year low is now being used by the federal government to attract foreign investors looking for stable industrial relations.[18]

How does Canada's strike record compare with that of other industrial nations? Recognizing the difficulties involved in making international comparisons of strike activity (due to differences in how strikes are defined and measured) we nonetheless can get a rough idea of where Canada stands in this regard from the data in Table 8.1. [19] Based on the annual average of working days lost for every 1,000 employees between 1975 and 1984, Canada had the second highest rate next to Italy. We must be wary, however, of taking these trends at face value without examining what lies behind them.

Table 8.1
Strikes and Lockouts in Selected Industrial Countries, 1975-1984

Country	Working Days Lost Per Thousand Employees, 1975-1984 Annual Average
Italy	1,230
Canada	790
Australia	530
United Kingdom	500
United States	210
France	150
Sweden	140
Japan	50
West Germany	50

Note: Countries are rank-ordered by the volume of industrial disputes.
Source: "International comparisons of industrial stoppages for 1984," *Employment Gazette* 94 (July 1986), p. 267.

EXPLAINING STRIKES

Are Canadian workers really more strike-prone than their counterparts in other countries, or do other factors underlie the ranking in Table 8.1? This is a very complex question, but it is fairly clear that a major reason for Canada's record is the length of strikes in this country. For example, the average duration of work stoppages between 1977 and 1981 was twenty days in Canada, seven in the U.K., five in Germany and Sweden, and fewer than four in France, Italy, and Japan.[20] Italy has such a high strike rate because disputes, while short, are very frequent and involve many workers. By contrast, the Swedish system of centralized bargaining and powerful unions with huge strike funds means that a work stoppage could quickly cripple the economy. This imposes considerable pressure to peacefully resolve potential disputes. In Japan, unions are closely integrated into corporations in what really amounts to a type of company unionism. Strikes are infrequent; workers voice their grievances by wearing black armbands or by making other symbolic gestures calculated to embarrass management. West German union–management collective bargaining is quite centralized, but at the individual workplace specific employment conditions are frequently negotiated by employee-elected works councils. West German laws require these participatory councils; they also make it very difficult to strike.

The legislation governing collective bargaining is equally important. The North American system of bargaining is highly decentralized and fragmented, involving thousands of separate negotiations between a local union and a single employer, each of which could result in a strike. Low-strike nations such as West Germany and Sweden avoid these problems by having national or industry-wide agreements, and by legislating many of the quality-of-working-life issues Canadian unions must negotiate with employers on a piecemeal basis. In addition, laws in these countries give employees greater participation in enterprise-level decision making. This provides unions with more information about the firm's operations and opens up communication channels with management.

There are also major industrial and regional variations in strikes, which may result from how industries are organized. The least strike-prone Canadian industries are finance, trade, and services, which makes sense given their low unionization levels. Of the highly unionized industries, mining has historically been the most strife-ridden. Similarly, B.C. and Quebec have higher than average strike rates because of their high concentration of mining and other strike-prone industries.[21] One prominent but widely challenged interpretation of inter-industry differences in strike behaviour is Kerr and Siegel's *isolation hypothesis*. They propose that isolated industries have higher strike rates than those where workers are integrated into the larger society. Isolated workers ". . . live in their own separate communities: the coal patch, the ship, the waterfront district, the logging camp, the textile town. These communities have their own codes, myths, heroes, and social standards."[22] Canada has always had large numbers of remote, resource-based, single-employer towns where a combination of social isolation and unpleasant work moulds workers into a cohesive group in opposition to management.

Research by Eric Batstone and his colleagues in a British auto plant adds to our understanding of strikes by highlighting the day-to-day processes that may culminate in a strike.[23] Strikes, argue these researchers, don't just happen. Rather, they are a form of collective action requiring a high degree of mobilization. How production is organized, the type of technology used, and the formal institutions regulating union–management relations shape the context for this mobilization. But a crucial (yet largely ignored) ingredient of mobilization is how the social relations within the union allow certain individuals and groups to shape the course of events leading up to a strike. This mainly occurs through the identification of potential strike issues and through the use of rhetoric, which justifies the escalation of collective action.

At the time of the Batstone study, most British strikes were unofficial stoppages initiated on the shop floor, not by top union leaders or by a democratic vote by all members. Canadian strikes are more strictly regulated by law, although new British legislation has moved in this direction. But the Batstone study offers some important insights about strikes in general. Workers usually do not want to strike, so they must develop a vocabulary to justify such action. This requires the translation of specific grievances into the language of broad principles and rights. Furthermore, disputes over wages also typically involve *effort bargaining.* That is, even if management refuses to grant wage increases, workers can informally shift their bargaining tactics to the other side of the wage-effort equation through slowdowns, refusal of overtime, and unauthorized work breaks. Finally, the study refutes the common view that the most powerful unions throw their weight around by striking. A basic contradiction of trade unionism, especially when examined at the shop-floor level, is that ". . . the groups of workers most able to strike (in terms of bargaining awareness and collective strength) may rarely have to resort to strike action."[24]

WORKER MILITANCY AND CLASS POLITICS

Social scientists often use strikes as a measure of worker militancy. Are strikes actually deeply rooted in class antagonisms, reflecting basic working-class discontent? Or do unionized workers act instrumentally, simply out of economic self-interest? General strikes have temporarily disrupted the economies of several advanced capitalist societies in recent years, and there is heated debate over how to interpret these events. Are they signs of heightened class consciousness, or are they merely pressure tactics to force changes in specific government or employer policies? Economists have calculated that strikes only have a modest impact on the economy.[25] As sociologists, we are interested in the broader implications of strikes for class consciousness, and for working-class political action.

Michael Mann's comparative study of industrial conflict addresses this question.[26] Workers in France and Italy, he found, were more politically radical than those in Britain or the United States, who identified more closely with management. But the political potential of the French and Italian working classes was frequently limited by their failure to articulate an alternative social system and to chart a course toward it. Mann argues that strikes can be *explosions of consciousness*. But the working-class solidarity they generate rarely gathers momentum beyond the immediate event. Ultimately, then, strikes by even the most politically radical workers are transformed into tactical manoeuvres to obtain concessions from employers.

Most workers, according to Mann, possess a *dual consciousness*. Instead of having a unified understanding of how their work dissatisfactions are organically linked to the operations of capitalism — real class consciousness in the Marxian sense — workers tend to compartmentalize their work experiences from the rest of their lives. They develop a "pragmatic acceptance" of the alienation and subordinate status they endure at work. Satisfactions in life are found in the basic pleasures of family, friends, and community — not in the quest for a new society.

Several more recent comparative studies have carried this discussion further, trying to identify which factors may transform varying degrees of working-class consciousness into collective action.[27] Duncan Gallie has investigated the nature and determinants of workers' attitudes to class inequalities in France and Britain.[28] These two countries have similar levels of socio-economic development, but the French working class is radical, while its British counterpart is moderate. Indeed, Gallie points out that the May 1968 general strike in France was "arguably the most powerful strike movement unleashed in the history of capitalist society," challenging its very foundations.[29] Why is it, asks Gallie, that major social inequalities are accepted by British workers as inevitable, while for the French they become a source of resentment and a catalyst for industrial militancy and political radicalism?

Gallie's evidence shows that workers in both France and Britain recognize class-based inequalities in opportunity, wealth, and privilege. They differ, however, in their attitudes toward these inequalities. For French workers, class position is an important part of personal identity. They identify with the larger working class, resent the system that puts them at the bottom, and believe that political action can improve their situation. British workers, in contrast, are more concerned about changing things in the workplace rather than in the larger society. Gallie's explanation of these differences hinges on the role of left-wing political parties in translating workplace experiences into a radical critique of society. French employers exercise greater unilateral power than do their British counterparts, and workplace industrial relations in France are not governed by mutually agreed upon rules; social inequalities are more pronounced there than in Britain. Furthermore, France has a revolutionary political tradition going back to the early nineteenth century. Hence workers' grievances with their employers are more intense and more readily carried outside the workplace, where they are moulded into a broad counter-ideology by exposure to trade unions and radical politics (especially the Communist Party).

Scott Lash provides another insightful perspective on the determinants of worker militancy, with conclusions echoing those of Duncan Gallie. He compares the radical French and the conservative American working classes.[30] Data collected at industrial sites in both countries show that differences in objective employment conditions cannot account for variations in militancy. Lash's alternative explanation focuses on how ideological and cultural factors shape militancy. Trade unions and political parties in a society or region are vehicles for socialization, transmitting to workers ideologies of natural rights in the workplace and in the political arena. Exposure to left-wing political parties determines *societal radicalism*. Socialization by trade unions — "industry's alternative rule-makers" — is the most important cause of *industrial radicalism*.[31] Both kinds of radicalism aim to achieve broader legal rights that would confer power to individual workers. Militant workers do not, therefore, necessarily try to overthrow existing institutions, but rather use them to their collective advantage.

What about the Canadian situation? Gallie and Lash conclude that unions and political parties are the main vehicles for channelling general working-class discontent into collective action. Have Canadian unions, which are basically reformist in orientation, had the same role?[32] The Canadian Labour Congress did help to found the New Democratic Party in 1961, and remains closely affiliated with it. However, if all union members voted for the NDP , it should have formed the government by now. In short, for Canadian workers, union membership does not necessarily mean support for left-wing politics.

But perhaps involvement in strikes has a radicalizing effect on worker consciousness? It would appear that this seldom is the case. Because strikes involve the organized and better-off members of the working class, resulting improvements in wages and working conditions may further divide the working class. Michael Smith claims that if strikes bring gains for the unionized workers involved, the more disadvantaged unorganized workers may see this as proof of the unfairness of the system.[33] Cynicism, political alienation, and anti-union feelings may result. So even though strikes may briefly kindle the flames of class consciousness among strikers, their overall political impact within the Canadian working class may be regressive.

One of the few Canadian studies to probe these theoretical issues examined the ideologies of male manual workers in an aircraft repair plant, where skill levels were high, and a home insulation factory employing low-skilled labourers. There was no significant difference in political attitudes or class ideology according to the skill levels of the workers.[34] Further analysis revealed that commitment to left- or right-wing political ideologies was unrelated to a wide range of other work and non-work factors.[35] The researchers concluded that — at least among the male blue-collar workers they studied — a coherent and integrated set of political views was absent. Worker consciousness regarding class and politics tended to be fragmented and often contradictory. For example, some of the same individuals who believed that corporate profits should be more equally distributed — a left-wing position — also agreed that trade unions are too powerful — a right-wing stance. But this does not demonstrate an acceptance of the capitalist status quo or, alternatively, a rejection of socialism. Rather, it suggests that workers' limited encounters with alternative ideologies lead them to question the system only on certain issues.

Other attitude surveys reinforce this assessment of class consciousness among Canadian workers. For instance, Johnston and Ornstein used 1977 national survey data to examine the political ideologies of employed males and females.[36] They found class differences in support for social welfare programs and the redistribution of income, with the working class being more egalitarian. But class position was unrelated to feelings of being able to influence the political process, as well as to political involvement. Thus, while the working class is slightly to the left politically, it does not possess a well-developed class consciousness. "Left-wing political organizations and trade unions," conclude Johnston and Ornstein, "have evidently failed to transform class differences in attitudes to social policy into coherent and durable perceptions of class structure and the political system."[37] Even the economic crisis of the late 1970s and early 1980s, marked by high inflation and rising unemployment, did not further polarize class ideologies along the left-right political spectrum.[38]

THE FUTURE OF WORKER MILITANCY

Despite the absence of a solid working-class radical ideology and, moreover, a decline in strike activity in Canada, there have been several recent outbursts of worker militancy that deserve careful scrutiny. Can we expect to see an upswing in industrial conflict in the future, coupled perhaps with a leftward shift in working-class politics? Some observers believe that future working-class mobilization could be provoked by employer and government demands for greater productivity, economic concessions, and more management rights.

A graphic illustration of this is the British Columbia Solidarity Movement, which sprang up in opposition to the Social Credit government's 1983 public sector restraint program. Proposed legislation would have limited the scope of public sector bargaining, allowed the firing of employees at will, cut back on social services, ended rent controls, and abolished the Human Rights Commission. The launching of Operation Solidarity by the B.C. Federation of Labour was a delayed reaction, following the more militant responses by the grass-roots Lower Mainland Budget Coalition.

Bryan Palmer's analysis of the Solidarity Movement raises some provocative questions.[39] Class relations in Canada have begun to realign, argues Palmer, and the 1983 events in British Columbia signal that class conflict may be on the rise. Palmer goes so far as to call the protest marches, public rallies, picket-lines, and community-based resistance during the summer of 1983 "class warfare." These actions reflected mass opposition to the proposed legislation, rather than merely a response from union leaders. In fact, the moderate leadership of Operation Solidarity rejected calls for a general strike that would have deepened the conflict. Negotiations between the government and mainstream union leaders eventually resulted in minor revisions to the legislation.

Not everyone would agree with Palmer's Marxist interpretation of the events in British Columbia. It may be premature to draw conclusions about realignments in class relations on the basis of the B.C. case alone. (We can only speculate about other possible outcomes of this confrontation had organized labour not become involved.) What seems clear, though, is that major offensives against employee rights and social institutions may provoke a show of force from the usually docile labour movement. Yet such reactions are frequently defensive, with unions scrambling to preserve past gains rather than launching mass protests intended to bring the capitalist system to its knees.

The environment of labour relations became even more restrictive during the recession of the early 1980s. Canadian employers are resorting to lockouts more than ever before. Lockouts resulted in fewer than 10 percent of work stoppages from 1977 to 1981, but the period from 1982 to 1984 saw this jump to 22 percent.[40] Several provincial governments have recently introduced public sector restraint legislation, and the use of court injunctions and legislation to end strikes is growing. Major strikes, such as the 1986 Gainers dispute in Edmonton and the 1987 letter carriers' strike have witnessed the increased use of police to escort strikebreakers across picket lines. On the other hand, there have been positive breakthroughs for labour, such as Quebec's anti-strikebreaking legislation. But these are exceptions, and the new developments may undercut the post-World War II labour–management accord by placing severe restrictions on free collective bargaining, especially by public employees.[41]

These backward steps violate international labour conventions. Usually International Labour Organization (ILO) investigations focus on repressive states such as Chile, Poland, South Africa, and Argentina. But three provincial governments have been recently investigated by the ILO because of their restraints on public employee unions. The ILO was concerned with two Alberta laws, one restricting the right of public servants to strike, and the other making unions liable for up to six months in forfeited union dues in the event of illegal walkouts. It has also investigated the Ontario government's Inflation Restraint Act of 1982, which suspended collective bargaining rights for half a million provincial employees for two years, and a 1983 Newfoundland law banning rotating public sector strikes and preventing certain public employees from joining unions.[42]

Organized labour took these cases to the Supreme Court, hoping that Canada's new Charter of Rights and Freedoms would disallow these laws restricting workers' rights. But in the spring of 1987, the Supreme Court ruled that the Charter guarantees neither the right to strike nor the right to bargain collectively. Clearly, this particular interpretation of the Charter's guarantee of "freedom of association" will have profound implications for organized labour.[43] In short, there is evidence that basic trade union rights are fundamentally threatened in Canada. What remains to be seen is whether these assaults on workers and their unions will heighten class consciousness and spark greater political action.

NOTES

1. Almost 40 years ago John Dunlop (1948) observed that a key issue raised by classical theories of the labour movement remained unanswered: How is one to account for the origins and emergence of labour organizations, what background conditions and specific circumstances stimulate this development, and why have some workers organized while others have not?

2. A good example of an aggregate union membership growth model is Bain (1970). Canadian research is summarized in Chaison (1982) and Kumar (1986). Also important are studies of voting behaviour in U.S. National Labour Relations

Board representative elections, similar to certification votes in Canada. See Getman et al. (1976) and Farber and Saks (1980). There are no comparable Canadian studies, although Lowe (1981) discusses the initial union organizing activity in several bank branches.

3. Flanders (1970): 44.

4. Olson (1965): 88. See Crouch (1982:51-67) for a discussion of Olson's ideas, and Fireman and Gamson (1979) for a critique of Olson's utilitarian logic.

5. Hirschman (1970).

6. Tilly (1978).

7. Tilly's (1978:64) example is Lipset, Trow, and Coleman's (1956) study of union democracy, which found that printers' union locals "have both distinct, compelling identities and extensive, absorbing interpersonal networks," and incorporate much of the members' lives. Clement's studies of miners (1981) and fishery workers (1986) provide good Canadian examples. See also Fireman and Gamson (1979:22), who argue that a *solidary group,* defined in terms of a high level of member integration, is more likely to engage in collective action than groups lacking this quality.

8. Crouch's (1982) rational choice model of trade unionism focuses even more directly on the attitudes and beliefs of individual employees, as well as on the larger contextual constraints on their actions. For Crouch, the most pressing question in studying unionism concerns why it is rational for workers to combine together into unions at all (p. 45). He answers that union membership is a function of the degree to which a worker perceives a union as useful, has no other viable means for advancing his or her economic interests, and has ready access to the union's resources (p. 67).

9. Lacroix (1986): 172. This definition is used by the International Labour Organization.

10. Riddell (1986a): 32.

11. Pentland (1981): 27.

12. See Hyman (1978, chapter 3) on the sociology of industrial conflict.

13. Gouldner (1955) is the classic study of a wildcat strike. Jamieson (1971, chapter 7) discusses the wildcat strikes that characterized the turbulent industrial relations climate in Canada during the 1960s. See also Fisher's (1982) analysis of wildcat strikes in B.C. between 1945-75 and Rinehart (1987:145-47) for a general discussion of the radical overtones of wildcats in Canada.

14. United Auto Workers (1985): 153. See Finn (1984) and Hackett (1982) on the role of the media in shaping public perceptions of unions.

15. On the Winnipeg general strike and its context, see Bercuson (1974), Jamieson (1971, chapter 3), Kealey (1984), and Penner (1973).

16. Heron and Palmer (1977).

17. On the impact of wage and price controls, see Reid (1982).

18. *Globe and Mail* (4 April 1987): A3.

19. See Lacroix (1986:172-74) for discussion of these methodological problems.

20. Riddell (1986a): 40. Adams (1982:469-72) examines these international differences, including how industrial dispute patterns have varied within nations over time.

21. See Anderson and Gunderson (1982b) for a discussion of these trends. See Craven (1980, chapter 8) for early conflicts in mining; see also Frank's (1986) study of militancy among Cape Breton coal miners and Seager's (1985) analysis of radical

politics among western coal miners.

22. Kerr and Siegel (1954): 191. For critiques, see Shorter and Tilly (1974:287-305) and Stern (1976). Fisher (1982) and Anderson and Gunderson (1982b:226-27) find empirical support in Canada for the Kerr and Siegel thesis.

23. Batstone et al. (1978). See especially chapter 1 for a critical discussion of the literature on theories of strikes.

24. *Ibid.*, 223.

25. For an analysis of the economic costs of strikes, see Anderson and Gunderson (1982b), and Freeman and Medoff (1984): 218-20.

26. Mann (1970).

27. According to Form (1983:175), this question is the weakest link in Marxist theories of class.

28. Gallie (1983).

29. *Ibid.*, 8.

30. Lash (1984).

31. *Ibid.*, 60.

32. Smucker (1980, chapter 11) examines historically the ideologies of the Canadian labour movement in the context of his broader discussion of working class consciousness.

33. Smith (1978). See also Form's (1985) discussion of the political consequences of divisions within the American working class.

34. Tanner (1984). See also Keddie (1980).

35. Tanner and Cockerill (1986).

36. Johnston and Ornstein (1985).

37. *Ibid.*, 385.

38. Baer, Grabb, and Johnston (1987).

39. Palmer (1986).

40. For recent strike data, see the annual Labour Canada publication, *Strikes and Lockouts in Canada.*

41. This is persuasively argued by Panitch and Swartz (1985).

42. *Globe and Mail* (3 April 1985): A4.

43. For a discussion of the Supreme Court's ruling and its possible implications, see *Globe and Mail* (16 April 1987): A7.

9

Work in Transition

INTRODUCTION

We have covered much ground in trying to achieve a better understanding of present work arrangements. In doing so, we moved back and forth between two different levels of analysis. We have focused on the structures of work, ranging from bureaucracy, technology, and Taylorism to industrial relations systems and labour markets. This *macro* approach has been juxtaposed with a more *micro* emphasis on individual employees and managers and their work groups. Here, behaviours on the job, subjective experiences of work, and reciprocal relationships between people's jobs and other aspects of their lives have been important issues.

In this final chapter, we will examine the interplay between structural forces of change, on the one hand, and the needs and aspirations of individual employees, on the other. Tensions between employees' concerns about the quantity and quality of work, and employers' emphasis on competitiveness and productivity, frame the agenda for debates about the future of work. Thus we will be discussing what might be defined as workplace problems, but from a variety of different perspectives. From the vantage point of employees, unions, and some community organizations, solutions include attempts to improve the quality of work experiences through job redesign, via employee participation in decision making, and through increased attention to workplace health and safety. But these initiatives also need to be considered against the backdrop of new economic realities confronting employers. This chapter, therefore, explores the micro-electronics revolution and current debates about industrial restructuring, two powerful forces that are having a substantial impact on western industrial economies, and that are presenting a host of new challenges, opportunities, and potential problems for the future.

WORK HUMANIZATION THROUGH JOB REDESIGN

We have amply documented the problems of bureaucratic hierarchies, assembly-line technology, and fragmented tasks with minimal content. The costs to workers, management, and society can be great:

job dissatisfaction, stress, alienation, low productivity, and failure to meet the challenges of today's changing economic environment. What are the alternatives to the legacy of Taylorism, Fordism, and bureaucracy? The search for democratic forms of work organizations and innovative job designs has accelerated in recent years. But do these reforms significantly redistribute power and enhance the quality of working life? Who really benefits from them?

"QWL." — short for *quality of working life* — became a buzzword among managers, public policy makers, academics, and consultants during the 1970s. QWL is an umbrella term covering many different strategies for humanizing work, improving employee–employer cooperation, redesigning jobs, and giving employees greater participation in management. In North America, management has usually initiated these programs. The underlying goal has been to improve employee satisfaction, motivation, and commitment, on the expectation of payoffs in terms of higher productivity, quality, and profits. Its proponents have stressed that, ideally, employers and employees will all benefit: "With QWL there are no losers — everyone wins."[1]

The spread of the work reform movement is due to a convergence of factors. Managers are struggling to adapt to growing international competition, shifting product markets, and automation — challenges that open the door for more creative and flexible means of organizing work. At the same time, there are rising demands from workers and unions for more satisfying, healthier, and less authoritarian workplaces. Theoretically, QWL claims to combine both humanistic and economic objectives: challenging, involving, and rewarding work experiences for employees and, for the employer, more productive utilization of the firm's human resources. Yet the lofty rhetoric of QWL advocates often fails to translate into successful applications.

QWL has diverse intellectual roots. Its core ideas came from the Tavistock Institute's socio-technical systems approach to job design; Norwegian E. Thorsrud's experiments on self-managing groups; Swedish studies on work reform and employee well-being; and Frederick Herzberg's theory that work is satisfying only if it meets employees' psychological growth needs.[2] In addition, the emphasis in human relations management theories — that worker participation in decision making is a means of creating cooperative work relations — is congruent with QWL themes. Human resources management, an influential revision of human relations theory, assumes that employee satisfaction and morale are nurtured in a climate of participative management.[3] The political left has also taken up the banner, with Marxists and socialists asserting that workers have a basic human right to control the productive process. Solutions along this line range from worker-owned-and-operated firms (cooperatives) within capitalism to revolutionary socialism.[4]

A quick overview of some of the major QWL techniques would be useful. *Job enlargement* is meant to expand a job horizontally, adding related tasks to put more variety into the work done by an individual worker. *Job enrichment* goes further, combining operations before and after a task into a more complex and unified job. For example, in the case of a machine operator in a clothing factory, job enrichment might mean that the operator would now be responsible for obtaining necessary materials, doing the administrative paperwork associated with different production runs, and maintaining the machines. This might not be an enormous change, but it would lead to a more varied, demanding, and responsible job. *Job rotation* refers to workers moving through a series of work stations, usually at levels of skill and responsibility similar to their original task. This tactic is frequently used to inject some variety into highly repetitive, monotonous tasks. When job rotation is combined with more fundamental redesign strategies (especially the use of work teams), an employee can develop a considerable range of new skills.

An *autonomous work team* consists of roughly a dozen employees who are delegated collective authority to decide on work methods, scheduling, and quality control. They might also perform what would have previously been supervisory tasks, such as administration, discipline, and hiring. *Quality control circles,* which do not go as far in the delegation of authority to workers, were originally developed in Toyota and other Japanese corporations, and have recently become popular among North American firms threatened by foreign competitors. QC circles place responsibility for monitoring quality and troubleshooting problems on production workers.[5]

The smorgasbord of QWL programs implemented by Canadian employers has resulted in both successes and failures. Attempts at work reform have generated heated debate between advocates — usually managers and QWL "experts" — and critics, generally trade unionists. What does the evidence tell us about the costs and benefits of QWL, and how serious are the critics' objections?

Donald Nightingale's research, already mentioned in Chapter 6, examines the benefits of QWL for Canadian workers. He compared ten firms with varying degrees of participative management with a matched sample of ten traditionally managed firms. The essence of workplace democracy, Nightingale asserts, is "that labour as a legitimate stakeholder in the enterprise has a moral right to play a role in the management of the enterprise."[6] A further assumption is that an individual's potential can be developed best in non-authoritarian work structures with meaningful and interesting tasks. Equally important is the premise that bureaucratic organizations and Taylorist work design principles stifle personal development.

Nightingale compared traditional and democratic firms along

several dimensions. The value systems in democratic firms reflected a human relations approach. However, the quality-of-working-life benefits of participative management were modest at best. For instance, there were no significant differences between the two types of organizations in employee stress symptoms. Workers in democratic organizations, especially the rank and file, experienced slightly higher job satisfaction. They also expected more from their jobs, especially in the realm of decision making. In addition, their mental health was slightly better than was that of the comparison group in traditional firms. Interestingly, Nightingale did not examine productivity differences, on the grounds that this could not be accurately measured across twenty firms.

Other evaluations of Canadian QWL initiatives document positive effects, ranging from higher employee satisfaction, morale, commitment, and concern with economic performance to better earnings, improved supervision and labour relations, and productivity gains. On the negative side, QWL experiments have also resulted in declining work performance, heightened union–management tensions, employee dissatisfaction, and a breakdown in communications.[7] One electronics firm that introduced an employee stock ownership plan, employee representation on the board of directors, and an elected employee council found the overall impact on non-managerial employees to be negative.[8] A study of quality control circles at a General Motors plant concluded that the scheme was intended to raise productivity and trim costs by co-opting production workers to solve management's quality problems. Little work humanization resulted.[9] Don Wells' two case studies of QWL found that implementation was imposed by top management, bringing few improvements in job content. More authority was delegated to a handful of workers and workplace relationships improved, although in one plant these changes came during massive layoffs.[10]

The flagship of the Canadian QWL movement is Shell's chemical plant in Sarnia, Ontario.[11] It is unique because union and management actively collaborated in the socio-technical design of the plant right from the planning stage in 1975. In comparison with existing organizations, such new, or *greenfield*, sites offer greater scope for innovative work arrangements. Shell's goal was a "post-bureaucratic" organization suitable for continuous-process technology, which would also facilitate employee control, learning, and participation. Six teams of twenty workers run the plant around the clock, 365 days of the year. Along with two "coordinators," a single team operates the entire plant during a shift, even hiring new team members when vacancies occur. Teams are supported by technical, engineering, and managerial personnel and a group of maintenance workers, who also teach team members craft skills. The organizational structure is quite "flat," having only three authority levels from top to bottom. Team members have no job titles and rotate tasks regularly. Pay is based on knowledge and skills obtained through job training. It takes about six years of training for an operator to reach the maximum pay level.

This design, in short, empowers workers and allows them to utilize and develop their skills. Continuous-process technology may lend itself more readily to this approach, mainly because of the huge capital investment per worker and the enormous losses to the firm should the system malfunction. There is a clear economic incentive for management to go to considerable lengths to obtain employee commitment. By tapping the talents of its employees, Shell is creating a safer and more productive operation. The restrictive work environment that Shell and the Energy and Chemical Workers' Union sought to erase is captured in one employee's dissatisfaction with his prior job:

> The foreman handed out orders and everyone got away with as much as possible. Here you have freedom, but you have to be responsible. I figure that's a lot better way to operate than having a foreman hovering over me, double-checking every 15 minutes. I'm a responsible person and I don't need that kind of hassle.[12]

According to the director of the union, the Shell plant eliminated authoritarian bureaucracy and provided members with opportunities to improve the quality of their work life.[13] In this application, the socio-technical design seems to have achieved its objectives: a high level of production efficiency, smoothly functioning teams, and mutually beneficial collaboration between union and management.[14]

On the whole, autonomous work teams appear to have the greatest potential for significantly reallocating decision-making power, as well as for creating more interesting, challenging, socially integrated, and skilled work.[15] Why, then, has the Canadian labour movement been a vocal critic of QWL, reluctant to become involved? The drawback for unions is that management has frequently used QWL to circumvent collective agreements, rationalize work processes, and co-opt workers into solving problems of quality and productivity.[16] In short, QWL has often been used to undermine union bargaining power. As well, union officials are often unwilling to assume the quasi-management roles associated with the rhetoric of cooperation. This could require them to downplay the demands of members, pushing aside real work environment problems such as health and safety concerns. Furthermore, in North America, QWL has been a hallmark of labour relations schemes intended to keep firms union-free. From the union movement's perspective, gains in the quality of work life are therefore best achieved via collective bargaining.

In the Shell chemical plant, the union's involvement came only after guarantees that it would be a full partner in the QWL process, and that its ability to represent the interests of employees would not be undermined. It is noteworthy that members of the same union at an adjacent older refinery wanted nothing at all to do with QWL. But the Shell experience appears to be atypical. More common is the stance of the United Auto Workers: "We do not oppose QWL experiments. Contrary to popular conceptions, unions don't spend most of their daily lives dealing with monetary problems; dealing with the 'quality of work life' of our members is already a dominant concern."[17] The union then lays out three pre-conditions (which rarely are met) for its involvement in QWL: management's main goal must be to improve the quality of working life of employees; productivity gains must be a by-product of this, not the overriding concern; and changes must in no way weaken the position of the union.

INDUSTRIAL DEMOCRACY

While some job redesign schemes also emphasize employee participation in decision making, their specific focus is on task content. To the extent that QWL expands worker decision making, it is often restricted to task-related matters, leaving intact the overall structure of power within the organization. Attempts to introduce *industrial democracy*, in contrast, are more broadly concerned with restructuring organizational decision making. Industrial democracy applies the principles of representative democracy found in the political arena to the workplace. Workers have a say directly at the work-group level, as well as indirectly through elected representatives on corporate boards and other key policy-making bodies. Open discussion and consensual decision making involving all employees characterize democratic work environments.

Because industrial democracy challenges traditional management prerogatives, its development within North America has been slow. Approximately one-third of the Fortune 500 corporations now have some form of employee participation. But usually this amounts to joint worker–management consultation committees, special project teams, problem-solving groups reporting to a top executive, and consultation mechanisms designed to open the channels of communication between managers and subordinates.[18]

Industrial democracy is more advanced in Western European countries, particularly Norway, Sweden, Austria, and, to a lesser degree, West Germany. National legislation provides workers with democratically elected representatives on corporate boards, the right to open consultation regarding technological changes, grass-roots control over health and safety matters, and full information and consultation on major corporate policies.[19] Industrial democracy does not require the elimination of bureaucracy, although some reduction in hierarchy may be a by-product. Hierarchy is often retained to allow overall coordination and control of the enterprise. The key feature of a fully participative organization, then, is that through the one-person–one vote principle, all workers maintain control over who holds executive positions, as well as over how income and other rewards are distributed.[20]

In North America, employee share ownership plans (ESOPS) have been promoted as the route to a people's capitalism. ESOPS essentially share profits (and losses in bad times) with employees. Instead of receiving a fixed wage, regardless of a firm's economic health, workers would receive a share of total revenues. Advocates see the schemes as a way of reducing unemployment, controlling inflation, and making workers more productivity conscious. Critics dismiss these stock-ownership and profit-sharing plans as providing no real benefits with respect to job content or decision making. Only a minority of firms with ESOPS have more than 50 percent worker ownership. In Canada, some workers have become share owners in attempts to save their own jobs when firms were threatened with closure. One innovative scheme is the Quebec Federation of Labour's $95 million Solidarity Fund. Since its creation in 1984, the Fund, which is open to all investors, has helped to create or protect 3,000 jobs in viable Quebec companies offering good working conditions.[21]

Firms with ESOPS must be distinguished from organizations, such as cooperatives and collectives, which are both owned and self-managed by all workers. Most Canadians are familiar with cooperatives in the form of wheat pools, co-op food stores, credit unions, and housing co-ops. But generally producer cooperatives are still quite rare. Quebec has the most developed co-op movement in North America.[22] Co-ops are well established in the food processing and logging industries, and the *caisses populaires* provide banking services to a large segment of the public. As Nightingale points out, with the exception of Quebec, North America has not been a hospitable environment for producer cooperatives. And where they have developed, collective ownership has not necessarily been associated with employee control.[23]

We must look abroad for examples of worker control. Central to Yugoslavia's decentralized system of socialism is enterprise-based workers' management. All employees in a firm elect a workers' council through which managers and a managing board are appointed. All major policy decisions are made by the workers' council. In Israel, kibbutz communes operate industries on the basis of collective control through workers' assemblies.[24] Probably the outstanding example of cooperative industry is found in Mondragon, a city in the Basque region of Spain, where over 22,000 worker–owners run a wide range of firms in heavy equipment, consumer goods, and services. Each worker has an economic stake in the enterprise where he or she works and, as a member of the firm's General Assembly, establishes policies, approves financial plans, and elects members to a Supervisory Board, which in turn appoints managers.

Mondragon co-ops have replaced the private ownership of industry with a system of collective ownership and control. By all accounts, these co-ops have achieved high levels of growth, productivity, and employment creation, strong links with the community, harmonious labour relations, a satisfying and non-alienating work environment, and a close integration between workplace and community. Mondragon's success no doubt is tied to the Basque region's unique culture, its struggle for greater autonomy from Spain, the destruction of the area's expanding industrial base during the Spanish Civil War in the 1930s, and the fact that the local Catholic church and unions were supportive of cooperatives. When the first co-op factory opened in 1956, it symbolized the region's independent economic potential. Generally, Mondragon demonstrates the viability of worker-owned-and-operated enterprises.[25]

INDUSTRIAL DEMOCRACY IN ACTION:
THE CASE OF SWEDEN

Sweden is one of the few societies in which industrial democracy has been elevated to a major national goal. The strong political commitment to achieve industrial democracy, social equality, and full employment largely stems from the close, historical alliance between the Social Democratic Party, which has ruled for all but six years since 1932, and the powerful union movement. In fact, the spirit of tripartite cooperation and consultation among large and centralized unions, representing over 85 percent of the work force, the employers' federation, and the state is a hallmark of Swedish democracy. Unions and employers are viewed as *social partners* who play a key role in defining and achieving national social and economic goals.[26] The goals of Sweden's post-World War II economic and labour market policies have been full employment, low inflation, a balance of payments, and an equitable distribution of income. The unions agreed to participate in wage-price stabilization, essential for industrial growth, only if full employment could be maintained without inflation.

The full-employment policy has three key elements: (1) A *wage policy* based on the concept of equal pay for equal work. This removes pay differentials among regions, industries, and firms by pressuring low-wage firms to pay decent wages, and by allowing profitable enterprises to pay less than they would under conventional collective bargaining. Ideally, weaker enterprises either become more efficient or else go out of business. The relatively lower wages in expanding industries should stimulate economic growth. (2) *Active labour market measures* assist those workers displaced from declining industries to find jobs in expanding sectors. Rather than relying on "market mechanisms," concerted efforts are made to relocate and train displaced workers, or to assist new labour force entrants. (3) Finally, *selective employment policies* provide jobs in regions or industries severely hit by structural readjustments in the economy. Sweden's impressive economic performance, high rate of labour force participation, low unemployment, and gradual reduction of the wage gap attest to the model's success. Some observers argue that the capitalist foundation of the Swedish economy is being replaced by a system of democratic socialism at all levels. Others disagree, pointing to emergent counter-trends of fragmentation and decentralization in social and industrial relations.[27]

Basic national agreements between central labour bodies and the employers' federation set the parameters of the employment relationship. But unlike the situation in both Canada and the United States, many significant workplace reforms have been achieved through legislation. Swedish law provides employee representation on corporate boards of directors in firms and central government agencies with more than twenty-five employees. Similar forms of *co-determination* are also found in West Germany, Austria, and Norway. Employee representatives have the same rights and obligations as other board members. However, they cannot participate in discussions regarding industrial disputes, negotiations with unions, and other issues in which possible conflicts of interest exist.

The 1977 Act on Employee Participation in Decision Making has evolved from a landmark agreement signed by the LO (the central labour organization) and the SAF (Swedish Employers' Federation) in 1938. In the 1970s, the labour movement came to view workplace democracy as a central element in the democratization of society. The 1977 act extends employees' rights to negotiation. Employers must initiate negotiations with unions prior to any major decisions regarding firm closures, reorganization, new technologies, expansion, or individual employee transfers. Unions now have access to complete information on the economic status of the firm, its personnel policies, and so forth.

The 1978 Work Environment Act's comprehensive approach involves "achieving working conditions where the individual can regard work as a meaningful and enriching part of existence." It is not enough for work to be free of physical and psychological hazards; it must also provide opportunities for personal involvement, satisfaction, and growth. Work should also encourage employees to be independent and to assume greater responsibility. A basic humanistic assumption underlies the act: that work satisfaction depends on employees having opportunities to participate actively in designing their own workplaces and tasks. In the area of occupational health and safety, for instance, safety stewards and safety committees channel employee input. Safety stewards are elected in all workplaces with more than five employees, and where there are more than fifty, safety committees are formed. These committees are responsible for company-sponsored preventative health programs designed to eliminate physical hazards and psychological stresses. The Work Environment Fund, set up in 1972, sponsors research and development projects leading toward these goals.[28]

Norway's 1977 Work Environment Act actually goes further than this. It advocates a novel approach to organizational life, based on grass-roots industrial democracy principles. Instead of laying out guidelines for how to restructure work, the act defines industrial democracy in terms of employees' own capacity to identify problems and generate solutions. The work experiences of employees provide the basis for initiating changes. Indeed, the whole thrust of the legislation is to legitimize employees' work experiences as useful knowledge. Part of this is a "do it yourself" style of action research whereby workers first develop new definitions of work problems by analyzing their own situations, and then formulate changes based on this information. Learning and a *democratic dialogue* are basic to the whole approach. In short, workers' knowledge becomes a new basis for power, casting them into the roles of experts and leaders in change.[29] This bottom-up approach to organizational reform differs dramatically from the North American top-down, "management knows best" model.

Returning to Sweden, one rather controversial initiative was the introduction of Wage Earner Funds in 1984.[30] Five separate employee investment funds were created through profit sharing (a tax on high profits) and a payroll levy. These funds must invest in manufacturing and related enterprises. Profits from the shares go into employee supplementary pensions. The local trade union in a firm can request 50 percent of the voting rights from the funds' investment. The plan was intended to give employees a share in profits and to encourage restraint in collective bargaining during a period when Swedish industry was faltering internationally. Labour–capital conflict would be reduced by giving workers responsibility for the funds, as well as greater influence in enterprises through co-ownership. Opponents feared that Wage Earner Funds would gradually replace a capitalist, market economy with a worker-run, socialist economy. However, this is unlikely, because the funds can acquire capital only until 1990, at which time they should own 5 to 10 percent of the shares in Swedish firms. Furthermore, employees will not be able to have the controlling voice on corporate boards.

Against this background, it is easy to see why Sweden has been a pioneer in work reforms. The widely publicized Volvo Kalmar plant, which opened in the early 1970s, is based on a socio-technical work design. The assembly line was replaced by battery-powered robot carriers, which automatically move car bodies to different work teams, each responsible for a phase of assembly. Productivity and quality improved, in comparison to assembly-line production methods. But the new factory's potential, especially as embodied in the robot carriers, has not been fully tapped. One of the limitations of the Kalmar plant's socio-technical design is that a computer — not the work teams — controls the movement of the carriers. Task cycles are still fairly short and are largely restricted to direct production. Despite Kalmar's team approach, the elimination of conventional assembly-line production methods, and a pleasant physical environment, the jobs in the plant provide little scope for personal development or for the use of skills and initiative. Workers still complain that their jobs are boring.

A more effective solution to the alienating monotony of assembly-line work can be found in Saab's main auto plant at Trollhattan. The body assembly shop faced problems typical in mass production: high turnover and absenteeism, low quality, widespread dissatisfaction, and a numbing work pace. Reforms initiated in the early 1970s sought to improve the work environment, make jobs more intrinsically satisfying, and boost productivity. As at Volvo, the local union played an active role.

Some remarkable changes have resulted. The assembly-line has been eliminated. Autonomous teams of workers, or *matrix groups*, devote about forty-five minutes to completing an integrated cycle of tasks. In one section of the shop, eighty-five robots have taken over arduous, repetitive welding jobs. Groups of twelve workers control the entire production process in their area. This involves programming the computers and maintaining the robots, ensuring quality control, performing related administrative work, and cleaning up their work space. *Buffer zones* allow teams to build up an inventory of completed bodies, giving greater flexibility over how they use their time. (These buffers, incidentally, were an original feature of the Volvo plant but were later removed.) Skill development, new learning opportunities, and a broader approach to job design provide the teams with what Saab calls "control and ownership" of their contribution to the production process. Far from being victims of work degradation and deskilling through robotics, these Saab employees have reaped the benefits of upgraded job content and decision-making autonomy.[31]

To recap, the prospect for achieving democratic and humane

:es in Canada hinges on changes occurring at several levels.
ɔn enabling employees to reconstruct their work environ-
.... a prerequisite. Within organizations, managers must be
willing to share power with workers and to recognize the necessity of
balancing economic and social goals. Unions are beginning to take
positive steps by devising QWL programs compatible with collective
bargaining. Schemes from Scandinavia offer useful lessons but obviously cannot be transplanted in Canada. Indeed, to do so would be to
ignore the central principle that has contributed to their success:
workers and managers should be active participants in devising
solutions suited to their particular circumstances.

WORK AND WELL-BEING

Health and safety issues have moved into the spotlight during the past
decade. There is growing public awareness that the work we do has a
major impact on our overall well-being. How can we prevent work-
related illness, injury, and death? Should society make a healthy and
safe work environment a basic employee right? Collaboration between employees and their representatives, employers, and governments on these issues is developing in Canada. Indeed, industrial
democracy has recently made some progress in the health and safety
arena. Before considering how employees are involved in programs
designed to protect and promote mental and physical well-being in
their own workplaces, let us provide some background on occupational health and safety problems.

Death and disease are the most serious human costs of industrialization. Breathing polluted air, contact with cancer-producing materials, dangerous machinery and equipment, unsafe work sites, extremely hot, cold, damp, or noisy work environments — historically
these have taken their toll within the working class in terms of shorter
life expectancies and higher illness and disease rates.[32] In 1982, 850
workers in Canada died from work-related injuries or illnesses. Industrial fatalities have been declining, but your chances of being killed on
the job are still greater than your chances of being killed on the road
by a drunk driver. Injury rates, in contrast, have remained fairly
constant since the late 1960s. One in eight workers were injured on
the job in 1982, resulting in a loss of more than 15 million working
days. These figures prompted the federal Minister of Labour to
comment: "Apart from the tragic human consequences of these far
too numerous accidents, the record of working days lost to such
occurrences, which is nearly double that of industrial disputes, is a
national disgrace."[33]

Recognizing that these official statistics minimize the extent of the
problem,[34] a conservative estimate of the direct monetary costs to the

Canadian economy in 1981 of industrial deaths and injuries was $9.5 billion, or 2.9 percent of the gross national product. And according to the Economic Council of Canada, indirect costs — production losses, lower efficiency, decreased employee morale, lost supervisory time — could increase this to $20 billion annually. In addition, the lost productivity, absenteeism, alcoholism, and drug abuse attributable to job-related stresses are costing the national economy $21 million per day.[35] It is, of course, impossible to put a price tag on the human suffering associated with injury, disease, and death. Yet these figures underscore the magnitude of the problem and the urgent need to find solutions.

Workers are at greater risk in some occupations and industries than they are in others. In 1981, about half of the job-related deaths due to occupational diseases, such as asbestosis, pneumoconiosis, and silicosis, were in mining. "Even if a guy does everything right," observed one Sudbury nickel miner (with a twist of fatalism character-istic of high-risk occupations), "he can still get killed. That's one of the hazards of working underground; you can get killed even if you're innocent."[36] Looking at overall fatality rates (per 100,000 workers), the most dangerous industries are fishing, forestry, mining, and construction.[37]

Catastrophes such as the gas leak at Union Carbide's plant in Bhopal, India, or the Chernobyl nuclear reactor malfunction have riveted public attention on the social impact of industrial accidents. While not on this scale, major occupational health disasters have also occurred in Canadian industry. Asbestos, for example, is now recog-nized as one of the most potent known carcinogens. Canada was at one time a leading producer. As medical research uncovered the deadly effects of asbestos fibres in the 1970s, the industry came under intense public scrutiny. The 1980 closure of Johns-Manville's Scar-borough, Ontario, asbestos products plant because of mounting em-ployee deaths led to an Ontario Royal Commission on asbestos. The Commission reported that, by 1983, 68 of the 700 workers at the Johns-Manville plant had died from asbestos-linked diseases.[38]

Noise, an invisible workplace pollutant, is today's most common occupational hazard. In addition to causing hearing impairment, noise can lead to stress, circulatory problems, higher blood pressure, and digestive disorders. In 1984, the Ontario Workers' Compensation Board paid almost $14 million in pensions to workers with job-induced hearing losses. Governments have begun to realize that the reduced medical costs for victims of excessive workplace noise would more than offset the expenses of preventative measures. Ontario's proposed Occupational Health and Safety Act would, for the first time in Canada, designate noise as a hazardous substance that must be carefully monitored and reduced.[39]

There is also mounting evidence, as we noted in Chapter 6, that job stresses take a toll on employees' health. Occupational health legislation and the provincial Workers' Compensation Boards, which administer injury and illness claims, have used a narrow definition of health and illness. Their focus has been on physical injuries and death on the work site. In contrast, stress-induced health problems, which can range from headaches to chronic depression and heart disease, are linked to working conditions in complex ways. Often stress is manifested in deteriorated mental well-being, which employers and compensation boards attribute to an employee's lifestyle and personal situation, not to his or her job.[40]

A study of job stress among 992 Canada Post mail sorters and letter carriers confirmed that highly routine, monotonous, mechanized, and closely supervised jobs are dissatisfying and have negative effects on employees' health. The most stressful job in the post office involved "keying" postal codes using automated machinery. The relentless pace of the machinery, competing demands imposed by management, constant repetition, and lack of challenges and decision-making autonomy were associated with diminished mental and physical health among coders. Also, as a result of these conditions, the use of pain relievers and tranquillizers was significantly higher among the automated coders in comparison to hand sorters. In short, closely supervised, routinized, machine-controlled work is bad for your health.[41]

Micro-electronic technologies have introduced new stresses into white-collar work. A national study of 2,330 unionized male and female office workers, conducted by the Canadian Labour Congress, documents the negative health effects of video display terminals (vDTS). vDT operators, in marked contrast to other occupations in the study, reported more eye and muscle problems, and stress symptoms such as tiredness, poor appetite, irritability, sleeplessness, dizziness, and headaches.[42] There have also been controversial claims about the harmful effects of radiation emitted by vDT screens, ranging from cataracts to increased risk of pregnant vDT operators having miscarriages or babies with birth defects. However, the scientific evidence is inconclusive on these issues and more research needs to be done.[43] A federal government task force on micro-electronics therefore took the cautious route, recommending that, because relatively little is known about the potential hazards of prolonged exposure to low-level radiation, no level should be assumed safe.[44]

As computers spread, electronic surveillance is on the increase, injecting a new source of stress into certain jobs. Bell Canada and Air Canada record employees' telephone calls to evaluate how well they deal with customers, and use computers to monitor productivity. Bell's computerized operator system, introduced in 1977, gives supervisors access to seventy-six pieces of information on an operator's performance at the press of a key. Employees, through their unions, are resisting these intrusions. "You are operating an electronic sweat-shop," observed a union official, "when you know you are being monitored every second of your working day." [45]

ACHIEVING SAFE AND HEALTHY WORKPLACES

Occupational health has always been a politically-charged issue. Governments have had to walk a tightrope, balancing their public health obligations with business pressures to place economic growth and profits first. The Canadian state's involvement in occupational health goes back to the factory acts of the 1880s. These laws required fencing around machines, reasonable ventilation, lunch-rooms and lavatories; they also curbed the employment of women and children on the grounds of protecting their health. Provincial Workers' Compensation Boards, set up around World War I, administered a no-fault system of compensation for employees injured at work.

But legislation has largely dealt with the consequences rather than the root causes, and enforcement of health and safety standards by government inspectors has been ineffective. Furthermore, a *blaming the victim* ideology within industry assumes that workers ultimately are responsible because of carelessness, accident-proneness, or hyper-susceptibility to illnesses.[46] Public policy, however, appears to be shift-ing in the direction of the prevention of accidents and the promotion of health and well-being through improved working conditions.

Worker involvement in health protection and promotion at the workplace increased dramatically in Europe during the 1970s. This sprang from demands for greater industrial democracy and govern-ment reviews of traditional approaches to occupational health and safety.[47] Now joint employee–employer committees develop policies, programs, and protective measures suited to their particular organi-zation. Similar to the Scandinavian legislation already mentioned, the guiding principle is that the experiences and knowledge of employ-ees — those directly exposed to risks and hazards — is an integral part of any solution. Accordingly, employees are directly involved in monitoring, inspection, and education and health promotion at their workplaces.

This new participative approach is slowly being adopted in Canada.[48] The first major initiative to directly involve workers in health and safety issues was the 1972 Saskatchewan Occupational Health Act. This act established workplace health and safety pro-grams premised on the right of workers to participate in the identifi-cation and regulation of hazards. The vehicle for participation is the joint health and safety committee. Committees range from two to twelve members, half of whom must be elected from among non-managerial employees (or appointed by a union if one exists). Such committees are required by law in any workplace employing ten or more persons. The committees monitor the health, safety, and welfare of all persons employed at an establishment. A government agency sets reasonable standards to achieve these objectives. Legislation provides the right of refusal, based on the individual employee's assessment that a particular task presents a genuine risk.

The Saskatchewan act also broke new ground by broadly defining occupational health as "the promotion and maintenance of the highest degree of physical, mental and social well-being of workers." [49] Other provinces have followed Saskatchewan's legislative lead, but none are as comprehensive, especially with regard to empowering committees to identify risks and then solve the underlying problems. Employers' initial apprehensions about the Saskatchewan law have largely been alleviated.[50] Workers have not abused their new responsibilities and the quality of working life and industrial relations have actually improved as a result.

The right of workers to be informed about the potential dangers of the materials with which they work is also being enshrined in legislation. This became part of the Canada Labour Code in 1986, along with joint safety and health committees, and applies to all employees in federal jurisdictions. The *right to know* is backed up by a national Workplace Hazardous Materials Information System. Another recent innovation, adapted from Scandinavia and Britain, is the independent health and safety commission. Now operating in Quebec and New Brunswick, these commissions have equal labour–management representation and a mandate to deal with all issues related to occupational health and safety.[51] In sum, to varying degrees, Canadian workers now have the right to participate in decisions regarding health and safety issues through joint committees, the right to know about the hazards of their jobs, and the right to refuse unsafe work.

Yet Bob Sass, the architect of the Saskatchewan legislation, argues that public policy must

> "stretch" the present legal concept of risk, which covers dust, chemicals, lighting, and other quantifiable and measurable aspects of the workplace to cover all work environment matters: how the work is organized, the design of the job, pace of work, monotony, scheduling, sexual harassment, job cycle, and similar work environment matters of concern to workers.[52]

In short, a health-promoting work site is one that gives employees much greater control over all aspects of their jobs. We must also recognize the organic links between our work and the rest of our lives.

The Canadian Mental Health Association maintains that the workplace must become the focal point for general health promotion.[53] CMHA studies in places as diverse as Yellowknife in the Northwest Territories, St. Catherines in Ontario and Chatham, New Brunswick chronicle a public desire for more flexible lifestyles to optimize personal health and well-being. Canadians, the CMHA argues, want "more freedom to combine employment with education, community service, family involvement, leisure pursuits, and other activities in a way which is more suitable to their own personal development and sense of well-being."[54]

The points raised by Bob Sass and the CMHA challenge us to rethink traditional conceptions of work. They also present an important public policy question: rather than being negatively affected by their jobs, should people be given greater opportunities to reshape the work environment in ways that will enhance their overall enjoyment of life?

THE MICRO-ELECTRONICS REVOLUTION

Industrial capitalist societies are being catapulted into the *information age* by developments in micro-electronic technology made possible by the tiny, inexpensive silicon chip. Information is becoming a key resource, and the ability to acquire, process, and manipulate it a source of power.[55] Have the predictions made by social scientists about an emerging *post-industrial* society come true? Will automation free workers from the drudgery of alienating jobs, as Robert Blauner concluded? Or will new technologies once again further rationalize work for some while forcing others into the ranks of the unemployed? Will the micro-electronics revolution reinvigorate industry, making the economy more competitive and productive? What in fact are the potential advantages of new workplace technologies for employees and society as a whole? How can public policy adapt to the challenges posed by advancing automation, especially in terms of unemployment, education and retraining, and quality-of-working-life concerns? This array of questions requires a careful look at where the *micro-electronics revolution* may be taking us.

The micro-electronics revolution is advancing on several fronts.[56] The office has been the centre of most technological innovation. This is not surprising: given lower capital equipment investment per office employee (compared to industrial workers), potential productivity gains in the office are obviously high. Personal computers are leading the way. Clearly, we have only witnessed the beginning of the micro-electronics revolution in the office. In 1984, for example, only 4 percent of all Canadian office workers had access to a "workstation" terminal (VDT, word processor, or personal computer). Yet it is estimated that by 1990 half will have personal computers.[57] But the information-age office will not emerge until there is a total integration of telecommunications, micro-electronics, and computer technologies. Only a few large corporations now have fully integrated electronic offices.[58]

Automated production systems represent the second major thrust of the micro-electronics revolution. Leading the way are industrial robots and computer-assisted manufacturing (CAM) and computer-assisted design (CAD) technologies.[59] Industrial robots have not been widely installed in Canadian factories, however. Japan and Sweden are world leaders in robotics, having about fifteen times more industrial robots per 10,000 workers in the manufacturing sector.[60]

The clearest picture available of the diffusion of automation in Canada is provided by the Economic Council of Canada. Its survey of a cross section of 946 Canadian establishments revealed that nearly three-quarters of these firms had introduced some form of computerization between 1980 and 1985.[61] In about two-thirds of the cases, this involved office automation — word processors, personal computers, or electronic office communication networks. Another 23 percent involved process automation (mainly computer-assisted manufacturing and design operations). The firms surveyed expected to introduce more sophisticated automation between 1986 and 1990, most of this being targetted for the office, but with growing emphasis on production-related technologies such as robots and CAD-CAM. Regarding employees, the study found that 13 percent of all employees in the sample of firms used automated technologies in their work, with this figure slightly higher among women.

New technologies have stirred heated debates about their potential effects. Proponents of automation argue that how and when to innovate should be a management decision based on the "bottom line" of productivity and profits. But they assume that computers will benefit society by helping build a stronger economy, freeing humans from dull, dirty, and dangerous jobs, and spawning new and more interesting jobs in high-tech areas. Critics, in contrast, voice fears about widespread job losses, increased work routinization and deskilling, and growing social inequalities as women become trapped in electronic job ghettos in offices and stores, while a small cadre of male computer professionals and managers reap the benefits. The first industrial revolution gave birth to the factory system and machine production, while the second introduced mass production assembly-line techniques. In each case, the eventual outcome was one of increased economic growth, job creation, and a higher standard of living. Can we expect the same from this third industrial revolution? Or will the spread of micro-electronic technologies create a fundamentally new kind of workplace and society?

In one important sense, computer technology is following a different trajectory than earlier phases of mechanization. Agriculture and manufacturing were the sectors that experienced technological changes in previous eras. But today micro-electronics is leaving virtually no sector of the economy untouched.[62] In fact, we have probably only begun to witness the potential of computers for information transmission and analysis, production processes, medical care, biotechnology, education and, as many fear, for military purposes. In this crucial respect, it is not an exaggeration to speak of a "micro-electronics revolution."

But concerns about the effects of new technologies on the quality and quantity of work are not unique to our era. In fact, history is full of examples of conflicts between workers and employers over the introduction of labour-saving technologies. At the extreme were the Luddites who, early in the 1800s, rioted and smashed new weaving machines in English mill towns.[63] And recall our discussion in Chapter 1 of the reactions of turn-of-the-century skilled workers in southern Ontario to mechanization. Even though there have not been any Luddite-style reactions to the new technologies of the 1980s, trade unions in particular harbour serious reservations about the benefits flowing to employees.[64]

There is little doubt that automation can significantly increase productivity, often by reducing labour costs. For example, a variety of studies have shown that the average industrial robot replaces between two and seven jobs. In the United States, the hourly cost of labour in the automobile industry was around $24 in 1986 (inclusive of benefits), while a robot working on the line only costs about $6 per hour to operate. A welder on the assembly line might only be able to spend 30 percent of the working day actually welding. But the new breed of "steel collar" worker welds around the clock and, moreover, does not take coffee or lunch breaks, talk back to the foreman, or go on strike. Robots, then, are hailed in some quarters as the ultimate solution to the "labour problem" that has plagued management for the last century.[65]

Researchers also suggest that word processors, computers, and micro-electronic communications systems can easily double the productivity of office workers, thus reducing the clerical staff needed in an organization.[66] In many work settings utilizing new technologies, fewer people are now able to handle an even greater volume of work — despite evidence that many offices underutilize the capabilities of their automated equipment, and that factories frequently encounter start-up problems with their robots and other computerized production systems.[67]

The trend to lower employment is most visible in manufacturing, where many firms responded to the recession of the early 1980s with a three-pronged strategy of reorganizing, automating, and cutting jobs. An extensive overview of recent research on this question concludes that, unlike previous technological innovations, microelectronics will eventually lead to significant job losses. The difference lies in the ability of these technologies to replace mental labour as well as physical labour.[68] But other analysts dismiss such dire predictions, arguing instead that we must consider the unintended and hidden effects of automation. For example, there can be multiplier effects of increased productivity due to automation. Job creation in related industries may result from rising consumer demand for the cheaper and better quality products.[69] Furthermore, office automation is improving the productivity of white-collar workers more slowly than expected.[70] There are numerous reasons for this: managers unwilling to give up their secretaries or learn the typing skills required to use electronic communications networks; a rising demand for word processing services within firms; the creation of "hidden" tasks associated with information processing; disruptions caused by the implementation of automated systems; and inadequate staff retraining. In a systematic study of computer installations in American organizations, Osterman found that clerical and managerial employment could actually increase with automation because the costs of these activities — mainly coordinating and information processing — declines.[71]

In short, predicting future employment patterns is exceedingly complicated given the range of variables that can affect labour supply and demand. However, few observers are willing to predict job creation on a scale sufficient to reduce current rates of unemployment in industrialized countries.[72] Perhaps the best we can expect in Canada is for unemployment to decline slightly into the 1990s, assuming the service sector continues to create new jobs.[73] Yet even if the new "high-tech" or service sector jobs equal the number of employees displaced by automation, a major problem remains. Seldom do individuals displaced from declining industries or obsolete occupations manage to obtain the new jobs created by computerization.[74] Most often, the lack of education and skills appropriate for the new technology becomes an excuse for laying off workers, even though retraining is a viable alternative.

These points are amplified in Heather Menzies' case study of the staffing changes accompanying the introduction of word processing technology in a large Canadian transportation and communications company. In the wake of automation, total staff was reduced by 10 percent and clerical positions declined from 78 to 46 percent of the total. But of the 130 mainly female clerical workers displaced, only two found jobs in the expanding management and professional ranks of the company.[75] Menzies' conclusion that women are most likely to be negatively affected by micro-electronic technology is echoed throughout the literature.[76] Jobs with relatively narrow, fixed, and routine tasks, which are most easily automated, are heavily concentrated in the clerical, sales, and service sectors where female workers are overrepresented.[77] In the manufacturing sectors, where robotic technology is beginning to have an effect, women are more likely to be working in the unskilled and semiskilled jobs that are most vulnerable to automation.[78]

The other prominent concern regarding automation is the *quality of work*. The basis of two contradictory scenarios can be found in Braverman and Blauner. Braverman, you will recall, equates the march of technology with increased managerial control over employees and a general degradation and deskilling of their job content. Blauner's thesis views automation as enhancing employees' job skills and authority, as liberating rather than enslaving. Which of these two assessments fits the new technologies of the 1980s?

Between 1981 and 1985, in Canada, there was a marked shift in employment away from goods-producing industries, where jobs tend to be full-time and better paid, to the service sector with its higher proportion of part-time and low-paid jobs.[79] In addition, service occupations often provide meagre intrinsic rewards.[80] But what about jobs within the dynamic high-tech sector? No doubt the engineers and scientists who design computers are highly skilled and, as a rule, derive great satisfaction from their work.[81] Much the same applies to computer analysts and programmers, although there are signs of fragmentation and routinization creeping into these occupations.[82] On the other hand, making semi-conductors for use in computers is repetitive, low-skill work with possible health risks.[83] Judging from this scattered evidence, there appears to be a segmented labour market within the micro-electronics industry itself.

Automation's potential to eliminate dirty, dangerous, and boring factory jobs has been realized through factory robotics. Robots are ideal for work in cramped spaces, in high temperatures, or in hazardous situations. But frequently the new jobs involved in operating or maintaining robots have not been organized so as to upgrade employee skills and responsibilities. Factory robots are seldom programmed by those running them. In some situations, operators do little more than position the material to be cut, drilled, or welded. In other settings where robots are integrated into an assembly line, operators have experienced an escalation in the pace and intensity of their work.[84] Hence there are only few signs so far that work with industrial robots is any more satisfying or less alienating than the factory jobs that were replaced. The Saab factory described earlier provides an alternative model for how work settings can incorporate robots.

Considerably more has been written about the impact of micro-electronics on office work. The *potential* for clerical workers to obtain new skills in computer programming and operations has often been noted. Such job enlargement should also lead to additional status and power in the office hierarchy. And, as a consequence, job satisfaction should increase, while feelings of powerlessness and the experience of workplace stress should be reduced. To what extent has this occurred in North American work settings? John Naisbett is typical of enthusiasts: " The computer will smash the pyramid; we created the hierarchical, pyramidal, managerial system because we needed it to keep track of people and things people did; with the computer to keep track, we can restructure our institutions horizontally."[85] Critics such as Robert Howard retort that "computer systems are just a way to expand management control," and argue that deskilling rather than worker empowerment is the typical outcome.[86] In fact, some analysts are predicting a revival of Taylorist job rationalization, because advanced forms of office automation require standardized and routi-nized procedures.[87] For example, word processing equipment can further subdivide office tasks if managers make text entry, editing, and printing of the document discrete tasks.[88]

Case studies reveal, however, that the impact of office automation on employees has been both positive and negative. Whether job upgrading or downgrading occurs depends on the circumstances of the particular firm and industry, the size of the organization, the specific type of technology, and managerial decisions about how to reorganize work. Some of the dreary filing and typing chores of office work have disappeared, and opportunities to acquire computer skills have provided more challenging, varied, and interesting jobs for some clerical staff. In other situations, managers have found that it is difficult to replace highly skilled workers with computers, or that the accumulated informal expertise of existing staff is indispensable.[89] Obviously a humanistic approach to implementing office automation could allay concerns about routinization, deskilling, and job displace-ment — especially if clerks and secretaries took an active role in the process.[90]

Clerical workers use automated equipment primarily for data or text entry. As with industrial robots, the programming is looked after by (typically male) computer experts. Opportunities to learn new skills are therefore limited.[91] Often highly skilled personnel are needed during the initial stages of implementing the technology. But then the work can be done by semiskilled staff who have received some retraining.[92] The possibility of clerks moving up into the computer-related technical, professional, or supervisory jobs seems remote. If anything, automation may restrict overall mobility within offices be-cause the middle-level positions, which used to provide a stepping stone, are among the first to be made redundant by office automation.[93]

Automation can also alter social relationships on the job. Work fragmentation via computers may simultaneously increase social isolation in the workplace, reducing social interactions among individuals in different parts of the organization.[94] Micro-electronics opens up new possibilities for people to work out of their own homes. The rise of *electronic cottage industries* could cut employers' overhead costs associated with maintaining large central offices or, depending on the law, paying fringe benefits.[95] Electronic homework would eliminate what for some office employees is a major source of satisfaction, namely socializing with others on the job.[96] But it remains possible that, for some, the electronic decentralization of work sites may be a welcome move. Finally, the social environment of the office can deteriorate, leading to heightened employee stress, if computers are deployed by management to monitor individual productivity — a problem we explored earlier in this chapter.

We must remember that the impact of the micro-electronics revolution depends not on the technology itself, but rather on the manner in which it is adopted. *Technological determinism,* the idea that the developmental pattern and effects of a given technology are universal and unalterable, characterized the theories of post-industrial society and automation popular during the 1960s and 1970s.[97] But with few exceptions, contemporary observers of the micro-electronics revolution argue that *technology is chosen and shaped* for specific social and economic reasons. Micro-electronic technology has the potential to improve the quality of work life but, with some exceptions, it has not been introduced with this goal in mind.[98] Instead, economic goals have been paramount. The major reason for technological innovation in organizations studied by the Economic Council of Canada was to increase productivity, followed by lower labour costs and improved product quality.[99]

Because achieving economic competitiveness through computerization has frequently meant job displacement or downgrading for workers, the labour movements in North America and Britain have opposed the unilateral introduction of new technology by management.[100] But this does not mean that unions oppose technological change in principle. Instead, they have generally insisted that employees be consulted, so that the negative effects can be minimized and opportunities for upgrading jobs and improving working conditions maximized. Unions also wish to see resulting productivity gains shared equitably — for example, a shortening of working hours for the same wages, if productivity increases resulted following computerization.[101]

Few would seriously advocate blocking the diffusion of micro-electronic technology, given the potential it offers for economic prosperity and an improved quality of life for Canadians. Rather, an urgent public policy issue is how our society can ensure orderly technological progress beneficial to all concerned. The spectre of unemployment associated with current methods of technological innovation raises questions about social equity. With fewer people working, material inequality in our society is likely to increase, and reduced purchasing power could curb economic growth.[102] Also, given the concentration of women in clerical, sales, and other service jobs slated for automation, following the present direction of technological change could accentuate gender inequalities.

Involving labour organizations and employees directly in the technological change process would constitute a major step toward striking a balance between economic and social goals.[103] Once again, the Scandinavian experience is instructive. Because Sweden and Norway have strong labour movements, which take an active role in shaping social policy, legislation requires employers to consult with employees prior to automating. Workers have direct input regarding the reorganization of work around new technologies. Widespread layoffs due to technological change have generally been avoided (in cases of redundancy, employers have taken responsibility for retraining and for finding other jobs for those affected within the organization). Canada presently lacks legislation requiring prior consultation with employees on technological change.[104]

Automation appears to be propelling us toward a society in which there will be less work — at least in the conventional sense. However, it is unlikely that we can look forward to a life of leisure.[105] Historically, a major solution to the problem of technologically induced unemployment was a shorter work week.[106] As we have seen in Chapter 2, the apparent shrinking of the average Canadian work week is largely a result of the growing number of low-paying part-time jobs. The possibility of sharing some of the better full-time jobs by reducing working hours has been proposed as a partial solution to unemployment but has not been widely acted upon.[107] If, indeed, there is less work for all of us in the future, then we can expect adjustments in work-related values, behaviours, and institutions. As futurists observe, society will attach greater importance to leisure time and how it is used. Work in the voluntary sector and in the home, which are not now accorded the same status as paid work, could become more central. The primary function of education in our society has generally been one of training people to take their place in the labour force. Education for personal satisfaction and self-development may take on greater significance in the future. In short, it is highly likely that the micro-electronics revolution will trigger a whole series of changes that could ultimately recast the nature and meaning of "work" in society.[108]

INDUSTRIAL RESTRUCTURING

The acceleration of technological change is occurring at a time when the corporate world is undergoing upheavals. The global oil crises of the 1970s, the recession of the early 1980s, and fierce international competition (especially from Japan) have all had a major impact on our economy. The fundamental readjustments taking place in industry are in part facilitated by micro-electronics, but they go beyond technology. This process of *industrial restructuring* is basic to capitalism. The economist Joseph Schumpeter saw restructuring as a process of "creative destruction" — breaking down old ways of running industry and building up more competitive, efficient, and high-tech alternatives.[109] But industrial restructuring can also have consequences, both positive and negative, for the quality of work. Some observers warn that, due to the present restructuring process, workers can expect diminishing employment rights and entitlements as the labour market is "deregulated." Less job security and higher rates of unemployment and underemployment are predicted, along with the growth in part-time and temporary work we have already discussed. There may be a widening gap between haves and have-nots in our society.[110] Thus, industrial restructuring warrants closer scrutiny because of its possible implications for the workplace and for society.

There are several interwoven themes in the industrial restructuring debate. The first is *deindustrialization*. Essentially this refers to the closure or relocation of once prominent manufacturing industries; automotives, steel, textiles, clothing, chemicals, and plastics are examples. Once the mainstay of the Canadian and U.S. economies, these are now sometimes referred to as "sunset industries," no longer competitive or able to adapt to shifting consumer demands. Ailing factories are sold off, shut down, or relocated to areas (the U.S. Sun Belt states, for example, but especially to Third World countries) where labour is cheaper, unions are absent, and employment standards are lax. As Bluestone and Harrison observe, "left behind are shuttered factories, displaced workers, and a newly emerging group of ghost towns."[111]

In some ways, Canada has been more vulnerable than the United States to deindustrialization, primarily because American-owned branch plants account for over 40 percent of our manufacturing. Because they produce for a smaller market, these plants are often less than optimally efficient and, moreover, are often casualties of their multinational parent's global reorganizations. But industries dominated by Canadian capital — the textile industry, for example — have also experienced deindustrialization. Data collected by the Ontario Ministry of Labour reveal that between 1981 and 1983, Ontario experienced 485 plant closures for a loss of 83,213 jobs. Certainly some of these establishments were obsolete money losers. But more typical is the 1983 closure of Canadian General Electric's profitable and high-tech steam turbine plant. The firm's U.S. parent shifted the work to Brazil, leading to layoffs for 429 skilled workers in Ontario.[112]

The second theme in the debate involves a critique of the old formula of Fordism and Taylorism, the cornerstones of industrial production for most of this century. Assembly-line mass production of standardized goods is becoming less socially and economically viable. Attention is focused on Japan, where a new stage of capitalist production known as *flexible specialization* has developed. Analysts such as Robert Reich, however, argue that imitating Japanese management techniques is not the way to reinvigorate North American industry. Rather, we should realize that Japanese industry has surged ahead simply because it is far more responsive and adaptable. Japan, Reich points out, was the first major industrial nation to shift from high volume mass production to flexible, computerized systems.[113]

Flexible production systems, which utilize computers at each stage — from designing a product to selling it — link all aspects of production into a coordinated system. Much smaller product runs are possible, and because computers monitor sales trends and consumer tastes closely, changes in design or product lines can be readily made. High-tech production machinery is versatile in its ability to produce a wide range of goods in industries such as automobiles, furniture, clothing, engineering products, and shoes. Computers also reduce stock control costs ("zero inventory") and improve product quality ("zero defects"). In addition to Japan, firms in West Germany, parts of Scandinavia, and northern Italy have developed this new system. Describing the success of northern Italian consumer goods firms, Piore and Sabel write:

> Flexible specialization is a strategy of permanent innovation: accommodation to ceaseless change, rather than an effort to control it. This strategy is based on flexible (multi-use) equipment; skilled workers; and the creation, through politics, of an industrial community that restricts the forms of competition to those favouring innovation.[114]

Viewed in this light, flexible specialization signals, for Piore and Sabel, a resurgence of the craft forms of production that were eclipsed with the rise of mass production. Despite some predictions of deteriorating working conditions, especially as employers seek more flexible staffing arrangements, Piore and Sabel seem to be proposing the opposite. Indeed, they argue that flexible production systems require more on-the-job training and essentially are skill intensive.

A third issue in discussions of restructuring raises a dominant theme in this book, namely the transition to a service-based economy. With the old manufacturing base in decline, only fractionally offset by job growth in the new micro-electronics industries, the current trend toward service employment can only gather momentum. Does this imply that tomorrow's workers will have to settle for jobs making hamburgers, selling Italian clothes, or servicing Japanese computers? This portrait of future work options is surely overdrawn. Nonetheless, it highlights present concerns about the nature of service sector employment. According to current federal goverment labour force projections, of the twenty jobs contributing most to job growth between 1986 and 1995, the majority will require little or no post-secondary education or training.[115] We should not totally dismiss the possibility that the march of automation will slow job growth in services by the year 2000. But neither should we discount the likelihood that the labour force will become increasingly polarized. This would see large numbers of women and youth in low-skill, dead-end, and unstable service jobs, middle-aged male blue-collar workers laid off from relatively well-paying manufacturing jobs, and a privileged elite of professionals and managers in rejuvenated corporations.

CONCLUSION

Admittedly, we have engaged in much speculation in this chapter. Our intention has been to identify some emergent trends that could have staggering implications for the workplace of the future. The manner in which QWL or industrial democracy are implemented, and in which the micro-electronics revolution and the industrial restructuring process evolve depend on a variety of factors, many of which we know little about. These trends could potentially end up clashing. The quest for more humanized jobs, participatory organizations, healthy work environments, and work arrangements compatible with personal needs could be stalled by industrial restructuring or the spread of low-level service sector employment. An equally plausible scenario would see automation, flexible production systems, and a booming service sector reduce unemployment, provide a shorter work week, and facilitate more rewarding work experiences. As social scientists we cannot predict the future. But with a clearer understanding of the contemporary world of work, we might be better able to influence that future as it unfolds.

NOTES

1. Rinehart (1986): 508. For definitions of QWL, see Mills (1981), Dorian (1981), Cunningham and White (1984); also Kolodny and Stjernberg (1986). Newton (1986:74) broadly defines QWL as encompassing "the total ecology of work,

including the linkages uniting individuals and their social relations, their work organizations and the larger society in which they live."

2. Emery and Thorsrud (1969); Thorsrud (1975); Trist et al. (1963); Herzberg (1966, 1968); Cherns (1976); Gardell (1977, 1982); Gardell and Gustavsen (1980). For background on the development of QWL in Canada, see Newton (1986): 77-80.

3. Miles (1965); see also Perrow (1986:97-99) and Nightingale (1982:47-49) for summaries of this perspective.

4. See Rinehart (1987:197-208) for an overview. An informative collection of essays is found in Hunnius, Garson, and Case (1973). Gorz's work (1967) has been influential for its linking of workers' control of industry with the transition to socialism.

5. These concepts are discussed in Knights, Willmott, and Collison (1985). On quality circles, see Bradley and Hill (1983), and Rinehart's (1984) Canadian case study.

6. Nightingale (1982): 49-50.

7. Cunningham and White (1984).

8. Long (1984).

9. Rinehart (1984).

10. Wells (1986a).

11. This plant is described and evaluated in Davis and Sullivan (1980), Halpern (1984), and the *Globe and Mail* (11 February 1985). For the union's perspective, see Reimer (1979).

12. *Globe and Mail* (11 February 1985).

13. Reimer (1979): 5.

14. See Halpern (1984): 58-59; also the *Globe and Mail* (11 February 1985) for an assessment of the results of this socio-technical prototype.

15. Rinehart (1986): 519; Gardell and Gustavsen (1980): 9.

16. For critiques of QWL, see Stinson (1982), Parrot (1984), Wells, (1986a), Levine (1984), Hunnius (1984), Swartz (1981), and Rinehart (1984, 1986).

17. UAW (1985): 152.

18. Rothschild and Russell (1986).

19. For Canadian perspectives on European approaches to industrial democracy, see Crispo (1978) and Newton (1977). See also, more generally, Spinrad (1984); Zwerdling (1978). Adams (1986) compares the Western European statutory works council model of enterprise decision making with the Canadian approach to collective bargaining. Poole (1982) attempts to outline a theory of industrial democracy. Other useful sources are the journal, *Economic and Industrial Democracy;* Crouch and Heller's collection of essays on organizational democracy (1984); and Wall and Lischeron's (1977) review of the literature on worker participation. As Elden (1981:45) emphasizes, industrial democracy demands a realignment of decision-making powers: "In a democratic work organization, workers instead of managers make decisions about daily work schedules (who works when and where, doing what), personnel administration (hiring, training, rewarding, and disciplining) and those aspects of coordination most immediately affecting the flow of work for which the group is responsible (production management). This is something quite different from human relations training for supervisors. There is no place in a self-managed work group, for example, for the traditional role of a supervisor or 'boss.' "

20. This argument is explored by Abrahamsson (1985). We should point out that, far from having eliminated bureaucracy, socialist societies, with their centralized state planning of the economy, have in many instances created a more unwieldy version of bureaucracy.

21. On the QFL Solidarity Fund, see *Canadian Labour* (May 1987): 11. Rothschild and Russell (1986) note that only 500 of the 6,000 U.S. firms with ESOPs have more than 50 percent employee ownership. A leading advocate of a "share economy" is Weitzman (1984). Nightingale and Long (1984) discuss the relationship between gain and equity sharing programs and the achievement of QWL goals. And for some current Canadian examples of employee ownership (often in a bid to save jobs), see Steed (1985). The use of pension funds to buy shares is on the increase.

22. Nightingale (1982): 227-28.

23. For a good discussion of production co-ops in Canada, see Nightingale (1982): 223-33. See also Long's (1978) analysis of Byers Transport of Edmonton, which ceased being a co-op when employees voted unanimously to sell their shares, for considerable profit, to a new corporate owner.

24. See Tausky (1978:116-29) and Jenkins (1974) on these Yugoslavian and Israeli schemes.

25. Webb (1984) examines Mondragon from a Canadian perspective. More thorough evaluations are provided by Bradley and Gelb (1983) and Thomas and Logan (1982).

26. Sweden is an outstanding model of "corporatism" — institutional arrangements that bring together capital, labour, and the state for national level social and economic planning. Corporatism generally, and Swedish-style, is reviewed in Lash (1985) and Panitch (1986). Details of the Swedish social and economic system are summarized in Erikson et al. (1986-87), Lindbeck (1975), Heckscher (1984), Korpi (1978), and Alestalo and Kuhnle (1986-87).

27. This debate is pursued in Offe (1985), Lash and Urry (1985), and Korpi (1978, 1983).

28. For more details of these legislative initiatives, see Forseback (1980). The information in this section is drawn from various issues of *Working Life in Sweden, Current Sweden, LO News,* and Swedish Trade Union Confederation (1982).

29. See Elden (1986), Gustavsen and Hunnius (1981). Gustavsen (1985:10) notes that 10 to 20 percent of Norwegian workers are now operating under this industrial democracy program.

30. The legislation and its background is summarized in Swedish Ministry of Finance (1984) and Swedish Centre for Working Life (n.d.).

31. On Volvo Kalmar, see Jonsson (1980) and Aguren et al. (1985). On Saab's work reorganization, see Logue (1981) and Helling (1985). These accounts of the Volvo and Saab factories are also based on G. Lowe's personal observations and discussions with union officials, management, and shop-floor workers during visits to both plants, September 1985, as a Guest Researcher at the Swedish Centre for Working Life, Stockholm.

32. For historical examples, see Palmer (1979): 27; Reasons et al. (1981, chapter 11). Good general references on occupational health and safety in Canada are Digby and Riddell (1986); for a critical perspective, see Reasons et al. (1981); for a union perspective, see the Ontario Federation of Labour's (1982) training manual. Also consult the periodicals, *Occupational Health and Safety Canada,* which is oriented toward a broad range of health and safety officials; *At The Source,* published by the

Ontario Federation of Labour's Workers' Occupational Health and Safety Centre; and publications of various provincial governments, such as Alberta's *Occupational Health and Safety Magazine.*

33. Labour Canada, *Information* (12 July 1984). The data in this paragraph are drawn from Labour Canada (1984) and Digby and Riddell (1986).

34. There are four main reasons for under-reporting in accident, illness, and fatality statistics. First, even though employers are legally required to report accidents, because they are assessed Workers' Compensation Board contributions on the basis of their safety record, there clearly are disincentives to accurate reporting. Company doctors are instrumental in keeping the corporate safety record looking good (Walters 1985). Second, provincial compensation boards do not recognize a wide range of illnesses and diseases as job-related. This deflates the incidence of occupational illness, injury, and disease, given that boards' compensation claims provide basic national statistics on these. (See Reasons et al. 1981, chapter 9 for a critical discussion of provincial WCBs.) Third, it is often difficult to clearly establish a direct link between initial exposure to a carcinogen on the job and a medical diagnosis of cancer. And fourth, because numerous new chemicals and other substances are introduced into workplaces annually without knowing the potential carcinogenic or other health-threatening side-effects, it takes years before any resulting illnesses or deaths are considered "occupational."

35. Labour Canada (1984): 4; CUPE, *The Facts* (August 1981): 3.

36. Clement (1981): 219. Leyton (1975) gives moving personal accounts of the ravages of silicosis and lung cancer contracted by fluorspar miners in two Newfoundland communities.

37. Data in this paragraph are from Labour Canada (1984): 9-10.

38. *Globe and Mail* (16 May 1987): D1-2.

39. *Globe and Mail* (15 September 1986): B9.

40. Lowe and Northcott (1986, chapter 1) provide a brief review of the job stress literature.

41. *Ibid.*

42. Canadian Labour Congress (1982).

43. On the health impacts of VDTs, compare the opposing perspectives of the CLC (1987) and Donoghue (1983). For a critical overview of research on the health hazards of VDTs, see DeMatteo (1985).

44. Labour Canada (1982).

45. *Globe and Mail* (22 September 1986); see also Reasons et al. (1981): 55-57; Evans (1982): 173-75; Labour Canada (1982); Howard (1985): 31; Rinehart (1987): 171.

46. Sass (1986b); Reasons et al. (1981, chapter 7).

47. Gevers (1983).

48. See Clark (1982); Sass (1986a, 1986b).

49. Clark (1982): 200.

50. *Ibid.*, 204.

51. Jolley (1986): 19-22. The union movement's criticisms, as articulated by Jolley, concern threats to the equal participation principle because the government — a major employer — appoints the chairperson. Also, unions lack adequate resources to ensure full participation, although Quebec provides unions with funds and personnel to assist them in this role. Political interference in the commissions is also a potential problem.

52. Sass (1986b): 571. Sass was the executive director of Saskatchewan's Occupational

Health and Safety Branch for nearly a decade.

53. Canadian Mental Health Association (1984). The project's report adopts the perspective that "the product of work is people." (CMHA 1984:1, citing Phil Herbst of the Tavistock Institute).

54. *Ibid.*, 172.

55. See Warskett (1981) on the growth of information work in Canada.

56. The literature on this topic is growing almost as quickly as the industry itself. See Jenkins and Sherman (1979), Menzies (1981), Labour Canada (1982), Friedrichs and Schaff (1982), Peitchinis (1983), Hirschhorn (1984), Kaplinsky (1984), Shaiken (1984), Shallis (1984), Gill (1985), Mackenzie and Wajcman (1985), and Howard (1985) for major recent analyses of the social implications of computer technology.

57. *Globe and Mail* (19 October 1984): R1; see also Russell (1981); *Globe and Mail* (May 25, 1984): B10.

58. *Globe and Mail* (19 October 1984):R1.

59. Most industrial robots have little resemblance to the R2D2 variety. A basic industrial robot has a jointed arm with some type of tool (a spray painter, welder, or drill) attached, capable of rotation in a variety of directions according to computerized instructions. The newest generation of industrial robots, mainly intended for assembly purposes, have sensory capacities in addition to the ability to move in response to programmed commands. See Kaplinsky (1984) and Ebel (1986) for useful discussions of industrial robots and computer-assisted manufacturing and design of machinery and products.

60. *Globe and Mail* (6 December 1985); Ebel (1986): 43-44.

61. Betcherman and McMullen (1986).

62. King (1982:14) and Gill (1985:5) both emphasize this point, as well as the fact that micro-electronic technology appeared precisely at a time when the economies of most industrialized countries were doing poorly. Hence, adoption of the technology was seen as a way of regaining international competitiveness. Peitchinis (1983:136) argues that new technologies are not qualitatively different from others that have left their mark on the world, although he also claims that we have yet to see the full impact of computers on our society (p.12).

63. See Jones (1983:20-21) for a short history of the Luddites and their reaction to the mechanization of the weaving industry.

64. Heron and Palmer (1977); Clement (1981) describes the reactions of miners to the extensive automation of Sudbury nickel mines.

65. Ebel (1986): 44. Friedrichs (1982:194) states that one robot generally replaces four people, while one new job maintaining the robot is created. See Peitchinis (1983:136-39) for a review of studies showing displacement of workers by computers and robots. The latest prediction by the Economic Council of Canada indicates that machining jobs, such as metal shaping and forming, will be all but wiped out by 1995 through computerization. (*Globe and Mail*, 8 July 1987): B1-2.

66. Buchanan and Boddy (1982): 6; Eckart (1982); Rumberger (1984): 276; Howard (1985): 20. In an early set of Canadian case studies, Heather Menzies (1981) documented substantial reductions in the number of clerical workers after micro-electronic technology was introduced.

67. See Peitchinis (1983, chapter 4) on "stimulants and barriers" to computerization, and Ebel (1986:44) on start-up problems and large capital investments for robotic technology.

68. Rumberger (1984). See Leontief and Duchin (1986) for a sophisticated econometric model that explores the impact of various future rates of automation in the U.S. A West German study (the Siemens Report) predicted that 40 percent of office work would be automated by 1990, while the Nora/Minc Report prepared for the French government predicted 30 percent staff cuts in the banking and insurance industries (see Peitchinis 1983): 138.

69. Peitchinis (1983): 133-39; Kaplinksy (1984): 140; Ebel (1986): 45.

70. *Economist* (29 March 1986): 55; see also Leontief and Duchin (1986): 79.

71. Osterman (1986).

72. Even Toffler (1980:192), despite his optimism about the future of post-industrial society, is unwilling to make such a prediction.

73. Shallis (1984): 114-29; Gill (1985): 94-96, 114.

74. Eckart (1982): 51; Rumberger (1984): 268; Howard (1985): 50-51. A recent study conducted for the Canadian Auto Workers shows job positions disappearing due to automation, but few people losing their jobs (List 1987). The strength of the union in this case has obviously forced management to rely on attrition for reducing the work force.

75. Menzies (1981): 28.

76. Labour Canada (1982); Friedrichs (1982); Feldberg and Glenn (1983): 74; Kaplinsky (1984): 148; Shallis (1984): 123; Gill (1985): 59.

77. Peitchinis (1983): 98.

78. Ebel (1986): 44.

79. Moloney (1986).

80. Rinehart (1987): 165; see also chapter 2 above.

81. See Tracy Kidder's *The Soul of a New Machine* (1981) for an inside look at this part of the industry.

82. Kaplinsky (1984:137) describes how software companies split up programming tasks across several different individuals to exploit their specific skills, but also to ensure that no single person has access to a complete program.

83. Howard (1985): 140-42; Rinehart (1987): 168.

84. Council for Science and Society (1981): 62-63; Gill (1985): 87; Howard (1985): 36-43; Ebel (1986): 46-47; Rinehart (1987): 170.

85. Naisbett (1982): 282.

86. Howard (1985): 18.

87. Gregory and Nussbaum (1982): 199-200.

88. Rinehart (1987): 170; see also Howard (1985): 24-30.

89. Sullivan and Cornfield (1979); Menzies (1981): 19; Evans (1982): 159-73; Feldberg and Glenn (1983); Kaplinsky (1984): 136; Barker and Downing (1985); Wood (1987): 12-13; Buchanan and Boddy (1982); Crompton and Jones (1984, chapter 2).

90. The argument for involving female clerks — the group most vulnerable to the negative effects of the new technologies — in the change process is made by Driscoll (1982:169-70) and the Organization for Economic Cooperation and Development (OECD 1985): 18-19.

91. Labour Canada (1982); Barker and Downing (1985); Gill (1985): 45; Howard (1985): 55-58.

92. Peitchinis (1983): 129; Howard (1985): 54. The Economic Council of Canada survey (Betcherman and McMullen 1986) offers some Canadian evidence regarding occupational skill changes precipitated by automation. Over 70 percent of the

firms implementing automation had to create new jobs or modify existing ones. Retraining of staff was common when skill requirements changed. About half of these cases involved clerical personnel learning data processing or word processing in short (less than four weeks) on-the-job courses. Only 7 percent of firms sought new recruits, usually highly qualified computer experts and engineers.

93. Menzies (1981): 63; Evans (1982): 179-81; Shallis (1984): 123; Barker and Downing (1985): 160; Gill (1985): 45.

94. Labour Canada (1982); Buchanan and Boddy (1982); Evans (1982): 175-76.

95. Toffler (1980:194-207) is enthusiastic about electronic cottage industry. See Gill (1985:25-27) for a more analytic assessment of this "homework."

96. Naisbett (1982): 42.

97. See especially Blauner (1964); Kerr et al. (1973); Bell (1973). Jones (1983: 210-38) and Mackenzie and Wajcman (1985: 2-25) offer useful critiques of technological determinism.

98. Evans (1982): 157; Peitchinis (1983): 168-70; Gill (1985): 8; Mackenzie and Wajcman (1985); Howard (1985): 35; Rinehart (1987): 172. See Noble (1985) for an interesting account of how a less efficient type of factory automation came to be widely used because it allowed management to have greater control over the labour process.

99. Betcherman and McMullen (1986).

100. Howard (1985): 173-95; Gill (1985): 117-29; Rinehart (1987): 172; Ebel (1986): 49.

101. West German auto workers won a historic concession from management in a 1983 strike — a reduction in the work week from 40 to 38.5 hours for the same pay — on the grounds that new technologies had led to enormous productivity gains for employers (CUPE: *The Facts*, Aug.-Sept. 1984): 11.

102. Peitchinis (1983): 168-70; Rinehart (1987): 164; Leontief (1982).

103. Gill (1985): 47; Howard (1985): 197-210.

104. See Grayson (1985:216-54) for a comparison of Canadian laws regarding plant closures and layoffs with the situation in several European countries. See also Gill (1985:149-60) and Howard (1985:208-9) on the Scandinavian response to microelectronic technology.

105. See Rose (1985:39), who dismisses the predictions that leisure will largely supplant work as "fashionable nonsense."

106. Leontief (1982).

107. Reid (1985).

108. See Jenkins and Sherman (1979), Jones (1983), Handy (1984), Gill (1985:161-84) for insightful discussions of the future of work. See Ross and Usher (1986) for similar comments within an analysis of the potential for community-based economic development in Canada.

109. Schumpeter's views are discussed in Bluestone and Harrison (1982): 9.

110. For a discussion of the implications of restructuring for workers, see Drache (1986). Laxer (1984, chapter 6) and Cohen and Shanon (1984) examine the transition now occurring in the Canadian economy. Mahon (1984) analyzes the restructuring process in the Canadian textile industry.

111. Bluestone and Harrison (1982): 6.

112. *Globe and Mail* (4 October 1986). See also Grayson's (1985) study of factory shutdowns, and Lush (1987) on the economic pressures faced by branch plants in Canada. Mahon's (1984) analysis of restructuring in the Canadian textile

industry pointedly notes that this industry was dominated by Canadian capital.
113. Reich (1983).
114. Piore and Sabel (1984): 17.
115. *Globe and Mail* (23 March 1987): B17. These 20 occupations are expected to account for more than 40 percent of net employment growth to 1995. The five biggest job creators will be commodities sales, food services, bookkeeping, secretaries and stenographers, chefs and cooks. See Kirkland (1985) for a refutation of the argument that service jobs are "bad" jobs.

REFERENCES

Abella, Irving
1974   "Oshawa 1937." In Irving Abella, ed., *On Strike: Six Key Labour Struggles in Canada 1919-1949.* Toronto: James Lewis and Samuel.

Abercrombie, Nicholas, Stephen Hill, and Bryan S. Turner
1980   *The Dominant Ideology Thesis.* London: George Allen and Unwin.

Abrahamsson, Bengt
1985   "On Form and Function in Organization Theory." *Organization Studies* 6:39-53.

Acker, Joan
1978   "Issues in the Sociological Study of Women's Work." In Ann H. Stromberg and Shirley Harkness, eds., *Women Working.* Palo Alto: Mayfield.

Acker, Joan and Donald R. Van Houten
1974   "Differential Recruitment and Control: The Sex Structuring of Organizations." *Administrative Science Quarterly* 19:152-63.

Adam, Barry O. and Douglas E. Baer
1984   "The Social Mobility of Women and Men in the Ontario Legal Profession." *Canadian Review of Sociology and Anthropology* 21:21-46.

Adams, R. J.
1982   "Industrial-Relations Systems in Europe and North America." In John Anderson and Morley Gunderson , eds., *Union-Management Relations in Canada.* Don Mills: Addison-Wesley.
1986   "Two Policy Approaches to Labour-Management Decision Making at the Level of the Enterprise." In W. Craig Riddell, ed., *Labour-Management Cooperation in Canada.* Toronto: University of Toronto Press.

Aguren, Stefan, Christer Bredbacka, Reine Hansson, Kurt Ihregren and K. G. Karlson
1985   *Volvo Kalmar Revisited: Ten Years of Experience.* Stockholm: Efficiency and Participation Development Council.

Akyeampong, Ernest
1986   " 'Involuntary' Part-Time Employment in Canada, 1975-1985." *The Labour Force,* Statistics Canada (December): 143-79.

Albrow, Martin
1970   *Bureaucracy.* London: Macmillan.

Alestalo, Matti and Stein Kuhnle
1986-87 "The Scandinavian Route: Economic, Social and Political Developments in Denmark, Finland, Norway, and Sweden." *International Journal of Sociology* 16: 3-38.

259

Allaire, Yuan and Mihaela E. Firsirotu
1984   "Theories of Organizational Culture." *Organization Studies* 5:193-226.

Althauser, Robert P. and Arne L. Kalleberg
1981   "Firms, Occupations, and the Structure of Labor Markets: A Conceptual Analysis." In Ivar Berg, ed., *Sociological Perspectives on Labor Markets*. London: Academic Press.

Amin, Samir
1976   *Unequal Development*. New York: Monthly Review.

Anderson, Grace M. and Liviana M. Calzavara
1986   "Networks, Education and Occupational Success." In K. L. P. Lundy and B. Warme, eds., *Work in the Canadian Context: Continuity Despite Change* . 2nd ed. Toronto: Butterworths.

Anderson, John and Morley Gunderson
1982a   "The Canadian Industrial-Relations System." In John Anderson and Morley Gunderson, eds., *Union-Management Relations in Canada*. Don Mills: Addison-Wesley.
1982b   "Strikes and Disputes Resolution." In John Anderson and Morley Gunderson, eds., *Union-Management Relations in Canada*. Don Mills: Addison-Wesley.

Anisef, Paul and Etta Baichman
1984   *What Jobs Pay: The Complete Guide to Careers and Salaries in Canada*. Edmonton: Hurtig.

Anisef, Paul, J. Gottfried Paasche, and Anton H. Turrittin
1980   *Is the Die Cast?: Educational Achievements and Work Destinations of Ontario Youth*. Toronto: Ontario Ministry of Colleges and Universities.

Anthony, P. D.
1977   *The Ideology of Work*. London: Tavistock Publications.

Antoniou, Andreas and Robin Rowley
1986   "The Ownership Structure of the Largest Canadian Corporations, 1979." *Canadian Journal of Sociology* 11:253-68.

Antos, Joseph R., Mark Chandler, and Wesley Mellow
1980   "Sex Differences in Union Membership." *Industrial and Labor Relations Review* 33:162-69.

Apostle, Richard, Don Clairmont, and Lars Osberg
1985   "Segmentation and Wage Determination." *Canadian Review of Sociology and Anthropology* 22:30-56.
1986   "Economic Segmentation and Politics." *American Journal of Sociology* 91:905-31.

Archibald, W. Peter
1976   "Using Marx's Theory of Alienation Empirically." In R. Felix Geyer and David R. Schweitzer, eds., *Theories of Alienation*. The Hague: Martinus Nijhoff.
1978   *Social Psychology as Political Economy*. Toronto: McGraw-Hill Ryerson.

Armstrong, Pat
1984   *Labour Pains: Women's Work in Crisis*. Toronto: The Women's Press.

Armstrong, Pat and Hugh Armstrong
1983   *A Working Majority: What Women Must Do for Pay.* Ottawa: Canadian Advisory
        Council on the Status of Women.
1984   *The Double Ghetto: Canadian Women and their Segregated Work.* 2nd ed. Toronto:
        McClelland and Stewart.

Aronowitz, S.
1973   *False Promises: The Shaping of American Working Class Consciousness.* New York:
        McGraw-Hill.

Asch, Michael
1977   "The Dene Economy." In Mel Watkins, ed., *Dene Nation: The Colony Within.*
        Toronto: University of Toronto Press.

Ashton, David
1986   *Unemployment Under Capitalism: The Sociology of British and American Labour
        Markets.* Brighton, England: Wheatsheaf Books.

Aston, T. H. and C. H. E. Philpin, eds.
1985   *The Brenner Debate: Agrarian Class Structure and Economic Development in Pre-
        Industrial Europe.* Cambridge: Cambridge University Press.

Attenborough, Susan
1982   *Bargaining For Equality.* Ottawa: National Union of Provincial Government
        Employees.

At The Source (published by the Ontario Federation of Labour's Workers' Occupa-
        tional Health and Safety Centre).

Averitt, Robert
1968   *The Dual Economy.* New York: Norton.

Avery, Donald
1979   *Dangerous Foreigners: European Immigrant Workers and Labour Radicalism in Can-
        ada, 1896-1932.* Toronto: McClelland and Stewart.

Babcock, Robert H.
1974   *Gompers in Canada: A Study in American Continentalism Before the First World War.*
        Toronto: University of Toronto Press.

Baer, Doug, Edward Grabb, and William A. Johnston
1987   "Class, Crisis and Political Ideology in Canada: Recent Trends." *Canadian
        Review of Sociology and Anthropology* 24:1-22.

Bain, George S.
1970   *The Growth of White Collar Unionism.* Oxford: Oxford University Press.
1978   *Union Growth and Public Policy in Canada.* Ottawa: Labour Canada.

Bain, George S. and H. A. Clegg
1974   "A Strategy for Industrial Relations Research in Britain." *British Journal of
        Industrial Relations* 12:91-113.

Baker, Maureen and Mary-Ann Robeson
1986   "Trade Union Reactions to Women Workers and Their Concerns." In K. L. P.
        Lundy and B. Warme, eds., *Work in the Canadian Context.* 2nd ed. Toronto:
        Butterworths.

Baldamus, W.
1961   *Efficiency and Effort: An Analysis of Industrial Administration.* London: Tavistock Publications.

Barbash, Jack
1979   "Collective Bargaining and the Theory of Conflict." *Relations industrielles/ Industrial Relations* 34:646-59.

Barker, Jane and Hazel Downing
1985   "Word Processing and the Transformation of Patriarchal Relations of Control in the Office." In Donald Mackenzie and Judy Wajcman, eds., *The Social Shaping of Technology.* Milton Keynes, England: Open University Press.

Batstone, Eric, Ian Boraston, and Stephen Frenkel
1978   *The Social Organization of Strikes.* Oxford: Basil Blackwell.

Beaud, Michel
1983   *A History of Capitalism 1500-1980.* New York: Monthly Review.

Becker, Gary S.
1964   *Human Capital.* Chicago: University of Chicago Press.

Beckett, Elizabeth.
1984   *Unions and Bank Workers: Will the Twain Ever Meet?* Ottawa: Labour Canada, Women's Bureau.

Bell, Daniel
1973   *The Coming of Post-Industrial Society.* New York: Basic Books.

Bendix, Reinhard
1974   *Work and Authority in Industry.* Berkeley: University of California Press.

Bercuson, David J.
1974   *Confrontation at Winnipeg: Labour, Industrial Relations, and the General Strike.* Montreal: McGill-Queen's University Press.
1978   *Fools and Wise Men: The Rise and Fall of One Big Union.* Toronto: McGraw-Hill Ryerson.
1981   "Through the Looking Glass of Culture: An Essay on the New Labour History and Working-Class Culture in Recent Canadian Historical Writing." *Labour/ Le Travailleur* 7:95-112.

Berger, Chris J., C. A. Olson, and J. W. Boudreau
1983   "Effects of Unions on Job Satisfaction: The Role of Work-Related Values and Perceived Rewards." *Organizational Behavior and Human Performance* 32:289-324.

Berger, Thomas R.
1977   *Northern Frontier, Northern Homeland: The Report of the Mackenzie Valley Pipeline Inquiry,* vol. 1. Ottawa: Supply and Services Canada.

Berle, Adolf A. and Gardiner C. Means
1968   *The Modern Corporation and Private Property.* Rev. ed. New York: Harcourt, Brace and World.

Betcherman, Gordon and Kathryn McMullen
1986   *Working With Technology: A Survey of Automation in Canada.* Ottawa: Economic

Council of Canada.

Beynon, H.
1984 *Working For Ford.* 2nd ed. Harmondsworth, England: Penguin Books.

Beynon, H. and R. M. Blackburn
1972 *Perceptions of Work: Variations Within a Factory.* Cambridge: Cambridge University Press.

Bielby, William T. and James N. Baron
1986 "Men and Women at Work: Sex Segregation and Statistical Discrimination." *American Journal of Sociology* 91:759-99.

Black, Don and John Myles
1986 "Dependent Industrialization and the Canadian Class Structure: A Comparative Analysis of Canada, the United States and Sweden." *Canadian Review of Sociology and Anthropology* 23:157-81.

Blackburn, Mckinley L. and David E. Bloom
1985 "What is Happening to the Middle Class?" *American Demographics* 7:18-25.

Blackburn, R. M. and Michael Mann
1979 *The Working Class in the Labour Market.* London: Macmillan.

Blau, Francine D. and Marianne A. Ferber
1986 *The Economics of Women, Men and Work.* Englewood Cliffs, N.J.: Prentice-Hall.

Blau, Peter M.
1963 *The Dynamics of Bureaucracy.* 2nd ed. Chicago: University of Chicago Press.

Blau, Peter M. and Otis Dudley Duncan
1967 *The American Occupational Structure.* New York: John Wiley and Sons.

Blau, Peter M. and W. Richard Scott
1963 *Formal Organizations: A Comparative Approach.* London: Routledge and Kegan Paul.

Blauner, Robert
1964 *Alienation and Freedom: The Factory Worker and His Industry.* Chicago: University of Chicago Press.

Bleasdale, Ruth
1981 "Class Conflict on the Canals of Upper Canada in the 1840s." *Labour/Le Travailleur* 7:9-39.

Blishen, Bernard R. and Hugh A. McRoberts
1976 "A Revised Socioeconomic Index for Occupations in Canada." *Canadian Review of Sociology and Anthropology* 13:71-79.

Bluestone, Barry and Bennett Harrison
1982 *The Deindustrialization of America.* New York: Basic Books.

Bluestone, Barry, W. M. Murphy, and M. Stevenson
1973 "Low Wages and the Working Poor." Policy Paper in *Human Resources and Industrial Relations* 22. Ann Arbor: Institute of Labor and Industrial Relations, University of Michigan.

Blumstein, Philip and Pepper Schwartz
1983   *American Couples.* New York: William Morrow.

Boulet, Jac-Andre and Laval Lavallee
1984   *The Changing Economic Status of Women.* Ottawa: Supply and Services Canada (Economic Council of Canada).

Bowles, Roy T., ed.
1982   *Little Communities and Big Industries: Studies in the Social Impact of Canadian Resource Extraction.* Toronto: Butterworths.

Boyd, Monica
1985   "Revising the Stereotype: Variations in Female Labour Force Interruptions." Paper presented at the annual meetings of the Canadian Sociology and Anthropology Association and the Canadian Population Society, Montreal.
1986   "Socioeconomic Indices and Sexual Inequality: A Tale of Scales." *Canadian Review of Sociology and Anthropology* 23:457-80.

Boyd, Monica, J. Goyder, F. E. Jones, H. A. McRoberts, P. C. Pineo, and J. Porter
1981   "Status Attainment in Canada." *Canadian Review of Sociology and Anthropology* 18:657-73.
1985   *Ascription and Achievement: Studies in Mobility and Status Attainment in Canada.* Ottawa: Carleton University Press.

Boyd, Monica and Elizabeth Humphreys
1979   "Labour Market and Sex Differences in Canadian Incomes." Ottawa: Economic Council of Canada, Discussion Paper No. 143.

Bradbury, Bettina
1984   "Women and Wage Labour in a Period of Transition: Montreal, 1861-1881." *Histoire sociale/Social History* 17:115-31.

Bradley, Keith and Alan Gelb
1983   *Cooperation at Work: The Mondragon Experience.* London: Heinemann Educational Books.

Bradley, Keith and Stephen Hill
1983   "After Japan: The Quality Circle Transplant and Productive Efficiency." *British Journal of Industrial Relations* 21: 291-311.

Bradwin, Edmund
1972   *The Bunkhouse Man: A Study of Work and Pay in the Camps of Canada.* Toronto: University of Toronto Press [originally published in 1928].

Braverman, Harry
1974   *Labor and Monopoly Capital: The Degradation of Work in the Twentieth Century.* New York: Monthly Review Press.

Breton, Raymond
1972   *Social and Academic Factors in the Career Decisions of Canadian Youth.* Ottawa: Queen's Printer.

Brinkerhoff, Merlin B. and David J. Corry
1976   "Structural Prisons: Barriers to Occupational and Educational Goals in a Society of 'Equal' Opportunity." *International Journal of Comparative Sociology* 17:261-74.

Briskin, Linda and Lynda Yantz, eds.
1983 *Union Sisters: Women in the Labour Movement.* Toronto: Women's Press.

Brown, Richard
1976 "Women as Employees: Some Comments on Research in Industrial Sociology."
      In D. L. Barker and S. Allen, eds., *Dependence and Exploitation in Work and
      Marriage.* London: Longman.

Buchanan, David A. and David Boddy
1982 "Advanced Technology and the Quality of Working Life: The Effects of Word
      Processing on Video Typists." *Journal of Occupational Psychology* 55:1-11.

Bulmer, Martin
1975 *Working Class Images of Society.* London: Routledge and Kegan Paul.

Burawoy, Michael
1978 "Toward a Marxist Theory of the Labour Process: Braverman and Beyond."
      Politics and Society 8:247-312.
1979 *Manufacturing Consent: Changes in the Labor Process under Monopoly Capitalism.*
      Chicago: University of Chicago Press.
1984 "Karl Marx and the Satanic Mills: Factory Politics under Early Capitalism in
      England, the United States, and Russia." *American Journal of Sociology* 90: 247-82.
1985 *The Politics of Production: Factory Regimes under Capitalism and Socialism.* London:
      Verso.

Burnham, James
1941 *Managerial Revolution.* Harmondsworth, England: Penguin.

Burns, T. and G. M. Stalker
1961 *The Management of Innovation.* London: Tavistock Publications.

Burrell, Gibson and Gareth Morgan
1979 *Sociological Paradigms and Organizational Analysis: Elements of the Sociology of
      Corporate Life.* London: Heinemann.

Burstein, M., N. Tienharra, P. Hewson, and B. Warrander
1975 *Canadian Work Values: Findings of a Work Ethic Survey and a Job Satisfaction Survey.*
      Ottawa: Information Canada.

Business Week

Butler, Peter M.
1980 "Establishments and the Work-Welfare Mix." *Canadian Review of Sociology and
      Anthropology* 17:138-53.

Campbell, Richard T.
1983 "Status Attainment Research: End of the Beginning or Beginning of the End?"
      Sociology of Education 56: 47-62.

Canada
1969 *Canadian Industrial Relations: The Report of the Task Force on Labour Relations.*
      Ottawa: Queen's Printer.
1984 *Report of the Commission on Equality in Employment* [The Abella Report]. Ottawa:
      Supply and Services Canada.

Canada, Department of Labour
1958   *Survey of Married Women Working for Pay in Eight Canadian Cities.* Ottawa: Queen's Printer.

Canadian Labour

Canadian Labour Congress
1982   *Toward a More Humanized Technology: Exploring the Impact of Video Display Terminals on the Health and Working Conditions of Canadian Office Workers.* Ottawa: CLC.
1987   "Fighting the Radiation Hazards of VDTs." *Health and Safety Bulletin,* no.3: CLC.

Canadian Mental Health Association
1984   *Work and Well-Being: The Changing Realities of Employment.* Toronto: Canadian Mental Health Association.

Caplan, R. D., S. Cobb, J. R. P. French, R. van Harrison, and S. R. Pinneau
1980   *Job Demands and Workers' Health: Main Effects and Occupational Differences.* Ann Arbor: Survey Research Center, Institute for Social Research, University of Michigan.

Caragata, Warren
1979   *Alberta Labour: A Heritage Untold.* Toronto: James Lorimer.

Carey, Alex
1967   "The Hawthorne Studies: A Radical Criticism." *American Sociological Review* 32:403-16.

Carroll, William K., John Fox, and Michael D. Ornstein
1982   "The Network of Directorate Links among the Largest Canadian Firms." *Canadian Review of Sociology and Anthropology* 19:44-69.

Chaison, Gary N.
1982   "Unions: Growth, Structure and Internal Dynamics." In John Anderson and Morley Gunderson, eds., *Union-Management Relations in Canada.* Don Mills: Addison-Wesley.

Chaison, Gary N. and P. Andiappan
1982   "Characteristics of Female Union Officers in Canada." *Relations industrielles/ Industrial Relations* 37:765-78.

Chaison, Gary N. and Joseph B. Rose
1981   "The Structure and Growth of the Canadian National Unions." *Relations industrielles/Industrial Relations* 36:530-51.

Chandler, Alfred D., Jr.
1962   *Strategy and Structure: Chapters in the History of the American Industrial Enterprise.* Cambridge, Mass.: MIT Press.
1977   *The Visible Hand: The Managerial Revolution in American Business.* Cambridge, Mass.: Harvard University Press.

Chelte, Anthony F., James Wright, and Curt Tausky
1982   "Did Job Satisfaction Really Drop During the 1970s?" *Monthly Labor Review* 105(11):33-36.

Chen, Mervin Y. T. and Thomas G. Regan
1985   *Work in the Changing Canadian Society.* Toronto: Butterworths.

Cherns, A.
1976 "The Principles of Socio-Technical Design." *Human Relations* 29:783-92.

Child, John
1972 "Organizational Structure, Environment and Performance: The Role of Strategic Choice." *Sociology* 6:2-22.

Chinoy, Ely
1955 *Automobile Workers and the American Dream.* Boston: Beacon Press.

Clairmont, Don and Richard Apostle
1986 "Work: A Segmentation Perspective." In K. L. P. Lundy and B. Warme, eds., *Work in the Canadian Context* . 2nd ed. Toronto: Butterworths.

Clairmont, Donald, R. Apostle, and R. Kreckel
1983 "The Segmentation Perspective as a Middle-Range Conceptualization in Sociology." *Canadian Journal of Sociology* 8:245-71.

Clairmont, Donald H., Martha Macdonald, and Fred C. Wein
1980 "A Segmentation Approach to Poverty and Low-Wage Work in the Maritimes." In John Harp and John R. Hofley, eds., *Structured Inequality in Canada.* Scarborough: Prentice-Hall.

Clark, R. D.
1982 "Worker Participation in Health and Safety in Canada." *International Labour Review* 121:199-206.

Clark, S. D.
1971 "The Position of the French-Speaking Population in the Northern Industrial Community." In R. J. Ossenberg, ed., *Canadian Society: Pluralism, Change and Conflict.* Scarborough: Prentice-Hall.

Clement, Wallace
1975 *The Canadian Corporate Elite: An Analysis of Economic Power.* Toronto: McClelland and Stewart.
1981 *Hardrock Mining: Industrial Relations and Technological Changes at Inco.* Toronto: McClelland and Stewart.
1986 *The Struggle to Organize: Resistance in Canada's Fishery.* Toronto: McClelland and Stewart.

Coburn, David and Virginia L. Edwards
1976 "Objective and Subjective Socioeconomic Status: Intercorrelations and Consequences." *Canadian Review of Sociology and Anthropology* 13:178-88.

Cohen, Dian and Kristin Shannon
1984 *The Next Canadian Economy.* Montreal: Eden Press.

Copp, Terry
1974 *The Anatomy of Poverty: The Condition of the Working Class in Montreal, 1897-1929.* Toronto: McClelland and Stewart.

Cornfield, Daniel B.
1985 "Economic Segmentation and Expressions of Labor Unrest: Striking versus Quitting in the Manufacturing Sector." *Social Science Quarterly* 66:247-65.

Coser, Lewis A.
1971   *Masters of Sociological Thought: Ideas in Historical and Social Context.* New York: Harcourt Brace Jovanovich, Inc.

Council for Science and Society
1981   *New Technology: Society, Employment and Skill.* London: CSS.

Craven, Paul
1980   *'An Impartial Umpire': Industrial Relations and the Canadian State, 1900-1911.* Toronto: University of Toronto Press.

Crispo, John
1967   *International Unionism: A Study of Canadian-American Relations.* Toronto: McGraw-Hill Ryerson.
1978   *Industrial Democracy in Western Europe: A North American Perspective.* Toronto: McGraw-Hill Ryerson.

Crompton, Rosemary and Gareth Jones
1984   *White-Collar Proletariat: Deskilling and Gender in Clerical Work.* London: Macmillan.

Crouch, Colin
1982   *Trade Unions: The Logic of Collective Action.* Glasgow: Fontana.

Crouch, Colin and Frank A. Heller, eds.
1984   *International Yearbook of Organizational Democracy. Vol. II: International Perspectives on Organizational Democracy.* Chichester, England: John Wiley.

Crozier, Michel
1964   *The Bureaucratic Phenomenon.* Chicago: University of Chicago Press.

Cuneo, Carl and James E. Curtis
1975   "Social Ascription in the Educational and Occupational Status Attainment of Urban Canadians." *Canadian Review of Sociology and Anthropology* 12:6-24.

Cunningham, J. B. and T. H. White, eds.
1984   *Quality of Working Life: Contemporary Cases.* Ottawa: Labour Canada.

Current Sweden (published regularly by the Swedish Institute, Stockholm).

Curtis, James E. and William G. Scott
1979   "Introduction: The Substance of Social Stratification." In James E. Curtis and William G. Scott, eds., *Social Stratification in Canada.* 2nd ed. Scarborough: Prentice-Hall.

D'Amico, Ronald and Timothy Brown
1982   "Patterns of Labor Mobility in a Dual Economy: The Case of Semi-Skilled and Unskilled Workers." *Social Science Research* 11:153-75.

Daft, Richard L.
1986   *Organization Theory and Design.* 2nd ed. St. Paul: West Publishing Co.

Dalton, Melville
1959   *Men Who Manage: Fusions of Feeling and Theory in Administration.* New York: John Wiley and Sons.

Davis, Kingsley and Wilbert E. Moore
1945 "Some Principles of Stratification." *American Sociological Review* 10:242-49.

Davis, Louis E. and Charles Sullivan
1980 "A Labour Management Contract and Quality of Working Life." *Journal of Occupational Behaviour* 1:29-41. [Reprinted in G. S. Lowe and H. J. Krahn, eds., *Working Canadians*. Toronto: Methuen, 1984.]

DeMatteo, Bob
1985 *Terminal Shock: The Health Hazards of Video Display Terminals.* Toronto: NC Press.

Denton, Margaret A. and Alfred A. Hunter
1982 *Equality in the Workplace: Economic Sectors and Gender Discrimination in Canada.* Ottawa: Labour Canada.

Dex, Shirley
1985 *The Sexual Division of Work: Conceptual Revolution in the Social Sciences.* Brighton, England: Wheatsheaf Books.

Dhingra, Harbans L.
1983 "Patterns of Ownership and Control in Canadian Industry: A Study of Large Non-Financial Private Corporations." *Canadian Journal of Sociology* 8:21-44.

Digby, Caroline and W. Craig Riddell
1986 "Occupational Health and Safety in Canada." In W. Craig Riddell, ed., *Canadian Labour Relations.* Toronto: University of Toronto Press.

Donaldson, Lex
1985 *In Defence of Organization Theory: A Reply to the Critics.* Cambridge: Cambridge University Press.

Donoghue, Shauney L.
1983 "Dealing with the Video Display Terminal." *Canadian Journal of Public Health* 74:179-82.

Dorion, Raynald, ed.
1981 *Adapting to a Changing World: A Reader on Quality of Working Life.* Ottawa: Labour Canada.

Downie, Bryan.
1982 "Union-Management Cooperation." In John Anderson and Morley Gunderson, eds., *Union-Management Relations in Canada.* Don Mills: Addison-Wesley.

Drache, Daniel
1986 "Industry and Humanity." *Policy Options* 7:41-45.

Driscoll, James W.
1982 "How to Humanize Office Automation." *Office: Technology and People* 1:167-76.

Dunlop, John T.
1948 "The Development of Labor Organization: A Theoretical Framework." In R. A. Lester and J. Shister, eds., *Insights into Labor Issues.* New York: Macmillan.
1971 *Industrial Relations Systems.* Carbondale, Ill.: Southern Illinois University Press [originally published in 1958].

Durkheim, Emile
1960   *The Division of Labour in Society.* New York: Free Press [originally published in 1897].

Ebel, Karl H.
1986   "The Impact of Industrial Robots on the World of Work." *International Labour Review* 125:39-51.

Eckart, Dennis R.
1982   "Microprocessors, Women and Future Employment Opportunities." *International Journal of Women's Studies* 5:47-57.

Economic Council of Canada
1976   *People and Jobs: A Study of the Canadian Labour Market.* Ottawa: Economic Council of Canada.
1982   *In Short Supply: Jobs and Skills in the 1980s.* Ottawa: Economic Council of Canada.

Economist, The (London).

Edwards, Richard C.
1979   *Contested Terrain: The Transformation of the Workplace in the Twentieth Century.* New York: Basic Books.

Elden, Max
1981   "Political Efficacy at Work: The Connection between More Autonomous Forms of Workplace Organization and a More Participatory Politics." *American Political Science Review* 75:43-58.
1986   "Sociotechnical Systems Ideas as Public Policy in Norway: Empowering Participation through Worker-Managed Change." *Journal of Applied Behavioral Science* 22:239-55.

Eldridge, J. E. T.
1971   *Sociology and Industrial Life.* Don Mills: Thomas Nelson and Sons.

Elias, Peter Douglas
1975   *Metropolis and Hinterland in Northern Manitoba.* Winnipeg: Museum of Man and Nature.

Emery, F.E. and Einar Thorsrud
1969   *Form and Content in Industrial Democracy.* London: Tavistock Publications.

Engels, Friedrich
1971   *The Condition of the Working Class in England.* Oxford: Basil Blackwell [originally published in 1845].

Erikson, Robert et al., eds.
1986-87 Special issue on "The Scandinavian Model." *International Journal of Sociology* 16.

Etzioni, Amitai
1975   *A Comparative Analysis of Complex Organizations.* 2nd ed. New York: Free Press.

Etzioni, Amitai and Edward W. Lehman
1980   *A Sociological Reader on Complex Organizations.* 3rd ed. New York: Holt, Rinehart and Winston.

Evans, John
1982   "The Worker and the Workplace." In G. Friedrichs and A. Schaff, eds.,
        Microelectronics and Society: For Better or for Worse. Oxford: Pergamon Press.

Facts, The (published by the Canadian Union of Public Employees) [CUPE].

Farber, Henry S. and Daniel H. Saks
1980   "Why Workers Want Unions: The Role of Relative Wages and Job
        Characteristics." *Journal of Political Economy* 88:349-69.

Feldberg, Roslyn L. and Evelyn Nakano Glenn
1979   "Male and Female: Job versus Gender Models in the Sociology of Work." *Social
        Problems* 26:524-38.

Feuchtwang, Stephen
1982   "Occupational Ghettos." *Economy and Society* 11:251-91.

Financial Post, The (Toronto).

Financial Times, The (Toronto).

Fine, Gary Alan
1984   "Negotiated Orders and Organizational Cultures." *Annual Review of Sociology*
        10:239-62.

Finn, Ed
1983   "Decline of the Middle Class." *The Facts,* CUPE (November): 4-7.
1984   "Ten Labour Myths." In G. S. Lowe and H. J. Krahn, eds., *Working Canadians:
        Readings in the Sociology of Work and Industry.* Toronto: Methuen.

Fireman, Bruce and William A. Gamson
1979   "Utilitarian Logic in the Resource Mobilization Perspective." In Mayer N.
        Zald and John D. McCarthy, eds., *The Dynamics of Social Movements.* Cam-
        bridge, Mass.: Winthrop.

Fisher, E. G.
1982   "Strike Activity and Wildcat Strikes in British Columbia: 1945-1975." *Relations
        industrielles/Industrial Relations* 37: 284-312.

Flanders, Allen
1970   *Management and Unions: The Theory and Reform of Industrial Relations.* London:
        Faber and Faber.

Foot, David K. and Jeanne C. Li
1986   "Youth Employment in Canada: A Misplaced Priority?" *Canadian Public Policy*
        12:499-506.

Forcese, Dennis
1986   *The Canadian Class Structure.* 3rd ed. Toronto: McGraw-Hill Ryerson.

Form, William
1983   "Sociological Research on the American Working Class." *Sociological Quarterly*
        24: 163-84.
1985   *Divided We Stand: Working Class Stratification in America.* Urbana: University of
        Illinois Press.

Forseback, L.
1980 *Industrial Relations and Employment in Sweden.* Stockholm: Swedish Institute.

Forsey, Eugene
1982 *Trade Unions in Canada, 1812-1902.* Toronto: University of Toronto Press.

Frank, David
1986 "Contested Terrain: Workers' Control in the Cape Breton Coal Mines in the 1920s." In Craig Heron and Robert Storey, eds., *On the Job: Confronting the Labour Process in Canada.* Toronto: McGill-Queen's University Press.

Franke, Richard Herbert and James D. Kaul
1978 "The Hawthorne Experiments: First Statistical Interpretation." *American Sociological Review* 43:623-43.

Fraser, T. M.
1983 *Human Stress, Work and Job Satisfaction: A Critical Approach.* Occupational Safety and Health Series, no. 50. Geneva: International Labour Office.

Freedman, Marcia
1976 *Labor Markets: Segments and Shelters.* Montclaire, N.J.: Allanheld, Osmun and Co.

Freeman, Bill
1982 *1005: Political Life in a Union Local.* Toronto: James Lorimer.

Freeman, R. B. and J. L. Medoff
1984 *What Do Unions Do?* New York: Basic Books.

Friedman, Andrew L.
1977 *Industry and Labour: Class Struggle at Work and Monopoly Capitalism.* London: Macmillan.

Friedrichs, Gunter
1982 "Microelectronics and Macroeconomics." In G. Friedrichs and A. Schaff, eds., *Microelectronics and Society.* Oxford: Pergamon Press.

Friedrichs, Gunter and Adam Schaff, eds.
1982 *Microelectronics and Society: For Better or for Worse.* Oxford: Pergamon Press.

Fromm, Delee and Marjorie Webb
1985 "The Work Experience of University of Alberta Graduates." *Alberta Law Review* 23:366-77.

Furnham, Adrian and Alan Lewis
1986 *The Economic Mind: The Social Psychology of Economic Behaviour.* Brighton, England: Wheatsheaf Books.

Gabin, Nancy
1979-80 "Women Workers and the UAW in the post-World War II Period: 1945-1954." *Labor History* 21:5-30.

Galbraith, John Kenneth
1967 *The New Industrial State.* New York: Mentor.

Gallie, Duncan
1978 *In Search of the New Working Class: Automation and Social Integration within the Capitalist Enterprise.* Cambridge: Cambridge University Press.

1983   *Social Inequality and Class Radicalism in France and Britain.* Cambridge: Cambridge University Press.

Gardell, B.
1977   "Autonomy and Participation at Work." *Human Relations* 30:515-33.
1982   "Scandinavian Research on Stress in Working Life." *International Journal of Health Services* 12:31-41.

Gardell, B. and B. Gustavsen
1980   "Work Environment Research and Social Change: Current Developments in Scandinavia." *Journal of Occupational Behaviour* 1:3-17.

Garnsey, E., J. Rubery, and F. Wilkinson
1985   "Labour Market Structure and Work-Force Divisions." In R. Deem and G. Salaman, eds., *Work, Culture and Society.* Milton Keynes and Philadelphia: Open University Press.

Gartrell, C. David
1982   "On the Visibility of Wage Referents." *Canadian Journal of Sociology* 7:117-43.

Getman, Julius G., Stephen B. Goldberg, and Jeanne B. Herman
1976   *Union Representation Elections: Law and Reality.* New York: Russell Sage.

Gertler, Len and Ron Crowley
1979   *Changing Canadian Cities: The Next 25 Years.* Toronto: McClelland and Stewart.

Gevers, J. K. M.
1983   "Worker Participation in Health and Safety in the EEC: The Role of Representative Institutions." *International Labour Review* 122: 411-28.

Gill, Colin
1985   *Work, Unemployment and the New Technology.* Cambridge: Polity Press.

Glaberman, Martin
1983   "Building the Japanese Car." *Canadian Dimension* 17(1):17-19. [Reprinted in G. S. Lowe and H. J. Krahn, eds., *Working Canadians.* Toronto: Methuen, 1984.]

Glenn, Evelyn Nakano and Roslyn L. Feldberg
1977   "Degraded and Deskilled: The Proletarianization of Clerical Work." *Social Problems* 25:52-64.

Glenn, Norval D. and Charles N. Weaver
1982   "Further Evidence on Education and Job Satisfaction." *Social Forces* 61:46-55.

Globe and Mail, The (Toronto).

Goldthorpe, John H., D. Lockwood, F. Bechhofer, and J. Platt
1969   *The Affluent Worker in the Class Structure.* Cambridge: Cambridge University Press.

Gordon, David M., Richard Edwards, and Michael Reich
1982   *Segmented Work, Divided Workers: The Historical Transformation of Labor in the United States.* New York: Cambridge University Press.

Gorz, Andre
1967   *Strategy for Labor: A Radical Proposal.* Boston: Beacon Press.

Gouldner, Alvin W.
1954   *Patterns of Industrial Bureaucracy.* New York: Free Press.
1955   *Wildcat Strike.* New York: Free Press.

Goyder, John
1984   "Social Mobility or Status Attainment?" *Canadian Review of Sociology and Anthropology* 21:331-43.

Grabb, Edward G.
1984   *Social Inequality: Classical and Contemporary Theorists.* Toronto: Holt, Rinehart and Winston.

Grandjean, Burke D.
1981   "History and Career in a Bureaucratic Labor Market." *American Journal of Sociology* 86:1057-92.

Grant, Gail
1983   *The Concrete Reserve: Corporate Programs for Indians in the Urban Work Place.* Montreal: Institute for Research on Public Policy.

Grayson, J. Paul
1985   *Corporate Strategies and Plant Closures: The SKF Experience.* Toronto: Our Times.

Gregory, J. and K. Nussbaum
1982   "Race Against Time: Automation of the Office." *Office: Technology and People* 1:197-236.

Gunderson, Morley
1982   "Union Impact on Wages, Fringe Benefits and Productivity." In John Anderson and Morley Gunderson, eds., *Union-Management Relations in Canada.* Don Mills: Addison-Wesley.

Gustavsen, Bjorn
1985   "Workplace Reform and Democratic Dialogue." *Economic and Industrial Democracy* 6:461-79.

Gustavsen, Bjorn and Gerry Hunnius
1981   *New Patterns of Work Reform: The Case of Norway.* Oslo: Universitetsforlaget.

Haber, Samuel
1964   *Efficiency and Uplift: Scientific Management in the Progressive Era, 1890-1920.* Chicago: University of Chicago Press.

Hacker, Sally
1981   "The Culture of Engineering: Woman, Workplace and Machine." *Women's Studies International Quarterly* 4:341-53.

Hackett, Robert
1982   "Is TV News Biased Against Labour?" *Canadian Labour* 28(5): 12-15.

Hall, Richard H.
1986   *Dimensions of Work.* Beverly Hills: Sage.

Halpern, Norman
1984   "Sociotechnical Systems Design: The Shell Sarnia Experience." In J. B. Cunningham and T. H. White, eds., *Quality of Working Life: Contemporary Cases.*

Ottawa: Labour Canada.

Hamilton, Richard F. and James D. Wright
1986   *The State of the Masses.* New York: Aldine.

Handy, Charles
1984   *The Future of Work: A Guide to a Changing Society.* Oxford: Basil Blackwell.

Hearn, Jeff and P. Wendy Parkin
1983   "Gender and Organizations: A Selective Review and a Critique of a Neglected Area." *Organization Studies* 4:219-42.

Heckscher, Gunnar
1984   *The Welfare State and Beyond.* Minneapolis: University of Minnesota Press.

Helling, Jan
1985   *Innovations in Work Practices at Saab-Scania* (Saab-Scania Personnel Division). Paper delivered at the U.S.–Japan Automotive Industry Conference, Ann Arbor, Mich., March 5-6.

Henry, Frances and Effie Ginzberg
1985   *Who Gets the Work? A Test of Racial Discrimination in Employment.* Toronto: The Urban Alliance on Race Relations and the Social Planning Council of Metropolitan Toronto.

Heron, Craig
1980   "The Crisis of the Craftsmen: Hamilton's Metal Workers in the Early Twentieth Century." *Labour/Le Travailleur* 6:7-48. [Reprinted in G. S. Lowe and H. J. Krahn, eds., *Working Canadians.* Toronto: Methuen, 1984.]

Heron, Craig and Bryan Palmer
1977   "Through the Prism of the Strike: Industrial Conflict in Southern Ontario, 1910-14." *Canadian Historical Review* 58:423-58. [Reprinted in G. S. Lowe and H. J. Krahn, *Ibid.*]

Heron, Craig and Robert Storey, eds.
1986a   *On the Job: Confronting the Labour Process in Canada.* Montreal: McGill-Queen's University Press.

Heron, Craig and Robert Storey
1986b   "On the Job in Canada." In Craig Heron and Robert Storey, eds., *On The Job: Confronting the Labour Process in Canada.* Montreal: McGill-Queen's University Press.

Herzberg, Frederick
1966   *Work and the Nature of Man.* New York: World.
1968   "One More Time: How Do You Motivate Employees?" *Harvard Business Review* 46:53-62.

Hill, Richard Child and Cynthia Negrex
1987   "Deindustrialization in the Great Lakes." *Urban Affairs Quarterly* 22:580-97.

Hill, Stephen
1981   *Competition and Control at Work.* London: Heinemann.

Hilton, Rodney, ed.
1976   *The Transition from Feudalism to Capitalism.* London: New Left Books.

Himelfarb, Alex
1976   *The Social Characteristics of One-Industry Towns in Canada.* Royal Commission on Corporate Concentration, Report no. 30. Ottawa: Supply and Services Canada.

Hirsch, Eric
1980   "Dual Labor Market Theory: A Sociological Critique." *Sociological Inquiry* 50:133-45.

Hirschhorn, Larry
1984   *Beyond Mechanization: Work and Technology in a Postindustrial Age.* Cambridge: MIT Press.

Hirschman, A. O.
1970   *Exit, Voice and Loyalty.* Cambridge, Mass.: Harvard University Press.

Hodson, Randy
1978   "Labor in the Monopoly, Competitive, and State Sectors of Production." *Politics and Society* 3-4:429-80.
1984   "Corporate Structure and Job Satisfaction: A Focus on Employer Characteristics." *Sociology and Social Research* 69:22-49.
1985   "Workers' Comparisons and Job Satisfaction." *Social Science Quarterly* 66:266-80.

Hodson, Randy and Robert L. Kaufman
1982   "Economic Dualism: A Critical Review." *American Sociological Review* 47:727-39.

Hollinger, Richard and John Clark
1982   "Employee Deviance: A Response to the Perceived Quality of the Work Experience." *Work and Occupations* 9:97-114.

Homans, George C.
1950   *The Human Group.* New York: Harcourt, Brace and World.

Horan, Patrick M.
1978   "Is Status Attainment Research Atheoretical?" *American Sociological Review* 43:534-41.

Horvat, Andrew
1983   "Work Comes Before Pleasure for Japanese." *Edmonton Journal* (June 15): F6.

House, J. D.
1980   *The Last of the Free Enterprisers: The Oilmen of Calgary.* Toronto: Macmillan.

House, J. S.
1981   *Work, Stress and Social Support.* Reading, Mass.: Addison-Wesley.

Howard, Robert
1985   *Brave New Workplace: America's Corporate Utopias — How They Create Inequalities and Social Conflict in Our Working Lives.* New York: Penguin.

Hull, F., N. S. Friedman, and T. F. Rogers
1982   "The Effect of Technology on Alienation from Work: Testing Blauner's Inverted U-Curve Hypothesis." *Work and Occupations* 9:31-57.

Humphries, Jane
1977 "Class Struggle and the Persistence of the Working Class Family." *Cambridge Journal of Economics* 1:241-58.

Hunnius, Gerry
1984 "Co-Determination — A Capitalist Innovation." In G. S. Lowe and H. J. Krahn, eds., *Working Canadians.* Toronto: Methuen.

Hunnius, Gerry, G. D. Garson, and J. Case, eds.
1973 *Workers' Control: A Reader on Labor and Social Change.* New York: Vintage Books.

Hunter, Alfred A.
1986 *Class Tells: On Social Inequality in Canada.* 2nd ed. Toronto: Butterworths.

Hunter, Alfred A. and Michael C. Manley
1986 "On the Task Content of Work." *Canadian Review of Sociology and Anthropology* 23:47-71.

Huxley, Christopher
1979 "The State, Collective Bargaining and the Shape of Strikes in Canada." *Canadian Journal of Sociology* 4:223-39.

Hyman, Richard
1975 *Industrial Relations: A Marxist Introduction.* London: Macmillan.
1978 *Strikes.* 2nd ed. Glasgow: Fontana.

Hyman, Richard and Ian Brough
1975 *Social Values and Industrial Relations.* Oxford: Basil Blackwell.

Iaffaldano, Michelle T. and Paul M. Muchinsky
1985 "Job Satisfaction and Job Performance: A Meta-Analysis." *Psychological Bulletin* 97:251-73.

Industrial Canada (Toronto).

Ingham, G. K.
1974 *Strikes and Industrial Conflict: Britain and Scandinavia.* London: Macmillan.

Institute for Research on Public Policy
1986 *Towns, Wheels or Wings for Resource Development?: An Annotated Bibliography.* Victoria: Institute for Research on Public Policy, Western Resources Program.

Jacobs, Jerry
1983 "Industrial Sector and Career Mobility Reconsidered." *American Sociological Review* 48:415-21.

Jacoby, Sanford M.
1985 *Employing Bureaucracy: Managers, Unions, and the Transformation of Work in American Industry, 1900-1945.* New York: Columbia University Press.

Jamieson, Stuart Marshall
1971 *Times of Trouble: Labour Unrest and Industrial Conflict in Canada, 1900-66.* Ottawa: Queen's Printer.

Jasso, Guillermina and Peter H. Rossi
1977 "Distributive Justice and Earned Income." *American Sociological Review* 42:639-51.

Jelinek, M., L. Smircich, and P. Hirsch, eds.
1983   Special Issue on "Organization Culture." *Administrative Science Quarterly* 28.

Jenkins, Clive and Barrie Sherman
1979   *The Collapse of Work*. London: Eyre Methuen.

Jenkins, David
1974   *Job Power: Blue and White Collar Democracy*. Baltimore, MD: Penguin Books.

Johnson, Laura C.
1986   *Youth and Employment: Baseline Report on Young People's Work Experience and Attitudes*. Toronto: Joint Task Force on Youth and Employment and the Social Planning Council of Metropolitan Toronto.

Johnson, Laura C. and Robert E. Johnson.
1982   *The Seam Allowance: Industrial Home Sewing in Canada*. Toronto: Women's Press.

Johnson, Leo A.
1974   "The Political Economy of Ontario Women in the Nineteenth Century." In Janice Acton, Penny Goldsmith, and Bonnie Shepard, eds., *Women at Work: Ontario, 1850-1930*. Toronto: Canadian Women's Educational Press.
1979   "Precapitalist Economic Formations and the Capitalist Labour Market in Canada, 1911-1971." In James E. Curtis and William G. Scott, eds., *Social Stratification in Canada*. Scarborough: Prentice-Hall.
1980   "The Development of Class in Canada in the Twentieth Century." In John Harp and John R. Hofley, eds., *Structured Inequality in Canada*. Toronto: Prentice-Hall.

Johnson, Terry
1980   "Work and Power." In Geoff Esland and Graeme Salaman, eds., *The Politics of Work and Occupations*. Toronto: University of Toronto Press.

Johnson, Walter, ed.
1983   *Working in Canada*. 2nd ed. Montreal: Black Rose Books.

Johnston, Richard
1986   *Public Opinion and Public Policy in Canada: Questions of Confidence*. Toronto: University of Toronto Press.

Johnston, William A. and Michael D. Ornstein
1985   "Social Class and Political Ideology in Canada." *Canadian Review of Sociology and Anthropology* 22: 369-93.

Jolley, Linda
1986   "H. & S. Commissions." *The Facts*, CUPE (Nov.-Dec.):19-22.

Jones, Barry
1983   *Sleepers, Wake! Technology and the Future of Work*. 2nd ed. Oxford: Oxford University Press.

Jones, Frank E.
1980   "Skill as a Dimension of Occupational Classification." *Canadian Review of Sociology and Anthropology* 17:176-83.

Jonsson, Berth
1980   "The Volvo Experiences of New Job Design and New Production Technology." *Working Life in Sweden* 18 (Sept.).

Kaliski, Stephen F.
1986   "Trends, Changes and Imbalances: A Survey of the Canadian Labour Market." In W. Craig Riddell, ed., *Work and Pay: The Canadian Labour Market.* Toronto: University of Toronto Press.

Kalleberg, Arne
1977   "Work Values and Job Rewards: A Theory of Job Satisfaction." *American Sociological Review* 42:124-43.

Kalleberg, Arne and Ivar Berg
1987   *Work and Industry: Structures, Markets and Processes.* New York: Plenum.

Kalleberg, Arne and Larry J. Griffin
1978   "Positional Sources of Inequality in Job Satisfaction." *Sociology of Work and Occupations* 5:371-401.

Kalleberg, Arne and Karyn A. Loscocco
1983   "Ageing, Values and Rewards: Explaining Age Differences in Job Satisfaction." *American Sociological Review* 48:78-90.

Kamata, Satoshi
1983   *Japan in the Passing Lane: An Insider's Account of Life in a Japanese Factory.* New York: Pantheon.

Kanter, Rosabeth Moss
1977   *Men and Women of the Corporation.* New York: Basic Books.

Kaplinsky, Raphael
1984   *Automation: The Technology and Society.* Harlow, England: Longman.

Karasek, R. A.
1979   "Job Demands, Job Decision Latitude and Mental Health Implications for Job Redesign." *Administrative Science Quarterly* 24:285-308.

Kasl, S. V.
1978   "Epidemiological Contributions to the Study of Work Stress." In C. L. Cooper and R. Payne, eds., *Stress at Work.* New York: Wiley.

Katz, D. and R. L. Kahn
1978   *The Social Psychology of Organizations.* New York: John Wiley.

Kaufman, Robert L., Randy Hodson, and Neil D. Fligstein
1981   "Defrocking Dualism: A New Approach to Defining Industrial Sectors." *Social Science Research* 10:1-31.

Kealey, Gregory S.
1980   *Toronto Workers Respond to Industrial Capitalism, 1867-1892.* Toronto: University of Toronto Press.
1981a   "Labour and Working-Class History in Canada: Prospects in the 1980s." *Labour/Le Travailleur* 7:67-94.
1981b   "The Bonds of Unity: The Knights of Labour in Ontario, 1880-1900." *Histoire sociale/Social History* 14:369-411.

1984   "1919: The Canadian Labour Revolt." *Labour/Le Travail* 13:11-44.
1986   "Work Control, the Labour Process, and Nineteenth-Century Printers." In
        Craig Heron and Robert Storey, eds., *On the Job: Confronting the Labour Process
        in Canada.* Montreal: McGill-Queen's University Press.

Keddie, V.
1980   "Class Identification and Party Preference among Manual Workers." *Canadian Review of Sociology and Anthropology* 17: 24-36.

Keenoy, Tom
1985   *Invitation to Industrial Relations.* Oxford: Basil Blackwell.

Kelly, John E.
1982   *Scientific Management, Job Redesign and Work Performance.* London: Academic
        Press.

Kelvin, Peter and Joanna E. Jarrett
1985   *Unemployment: Its Social Psychological Effects.* Cambridge: Cambridge University
        Press.

Kerckhoff, Alan C., Richard D. Campbell, and Idee Winfield-Laird
1985   "Social Mobility in Great Britain and the United States." *American Journal of
        Sociology* 91:281-308.

Kerr, Clark, J. T. Dunlop, F. H. Harbison, and C. A. Myers
1973   *Industrialization and Industrial Man.* London: Penguin.

Kerr, Clark and Abraham Siegel
1954   "The Interindustry Propensity to Strike — An International Comparison." In
        Arthur Kornhauser et. al., eds., *Industrial Conflict.* New York: McGraw-Hill.

Kessler, Ronald C.
1983   "Methodological Issues in the Study of Psychosocial Stress." In Howard B.
        Kaplan ed., *Psychosocial Stress: Trends in Theory and Research.* New York: Academic Press.

Kessler-Harris, Alice
1975   "Stratifying by Sex: Understanding the History of Working Women." In
        Richard C. Edwards, Michael Reich, and David M. Gordon, eds., *Labor Market
        Segmentation.* Lexington, Mass.: D.C. Heath.

Kidder, Tracy
1981   *The Soul of a New Machine.* Boston: Little, Brown and Company.

King, Alexander
1982   "Introduction: A New Industrial Revolution or Just Another Technology?" In
        Gunter Friedrichs and Adam Schaff, eds., *Microelectronics and Society: For Better
        or For Worse.* Oxford: Pergamon Press.

Kirkland, Richard I., Jr.
1985   "Are Service Jobs Good Jobs?" *Fortune* (June 10):38-43.

Knights, David, Hugh Willmott, and David Collison, eds.
1985   *Job Redesign: Critical Perspectives on the Labour Process.* Aldershot, England:
        Gower.

Knottnerus, J. David
1987   "Status Attainment Research and its Image of Society." *American Sociological Review* 52:113-21.

Kochan, Thomas A.
1979   "How American Workers View Labor Unions." *Monthly Labor Review* 102 (April):23-31.

Kohn, Melvin L.
1976   "Occupational Structure and Alienation." *American Journal of Sociology* 82:111-30.

Kohn, Melvin L. and Carmi Schooler
1983   *Work and Personality: An Inquiry into the Impact of Social Stratification.* Norwood, N. J.: Ablex.

Kolodny, Harvey and Torbjorn Stjernberg
1986   "The Change Process of Innovative Work Designs: New Design and Redesign in Sweden, Canada and the U.S." *Journal of Applied Behavioral Science* 22:287-301.

Korpi, Walter
1978   *The Working Class in Welfare Capitalism.* London: Routledge and Kegan Paul.
1983   *The Democratic Class Struggle.* London: Routledge and Kegan Paul.

Krahn, Harvey and John W. Gartrell
1983   "Labour Market Segmentation and Social Mobility in a Canadian Single-Industry Community." *Canadian Review of Sociology and Anthropology* 20:322-45.

Krahn, Harvey and Graham S. Lowe
1984   "Public Attitudes towards Unions: Some Canadian Evidence." *Journal of Labor Research* 5:149-64.

Kreckel, Reinhard
1980   "Unequal Opportunity Structure and Labour Market Segmentation." *Sociology* 14:525-49.

Kumar, Krishan
1984   "The Social Culture of Work: Work, Employment, and Unemployment as Ways of Life." In Kenneth Thompson, ed., *Work, Employment and Unemployment: Perspectives on Work and Society.* Milton Keynes, England: Open University Press.

Kumar, Pradeep
1986   "Union Growth in Canada: Retrospect and Prospect." In W. Craig Riddell, ed., *Canadian Labour Relations.* Toronto: University of Toronto Press.

Kuttner, Bob
1983   "The Declining Middle." *Atlantic Monthly* (July):60-72.

Labour Canada
1982   *In the Chips: Opportunities, People, Partnerships.* Report of the Labour Canada Taskforce on Microelectronics and Employment. Ottawa: Labour Canada.
1984   *Employment Injuries and Occupational Illnesses, 1972-81.* Ottawa: Labour Canada.

1986   *Women in the Labour Force, 1985-86 Edition.* Ottawa: Labour Canada, Women's
        Bureau, Cat. no. L38-30/1986.
        Information (news bulletin).
        Strikes and Lockouts in Canada. Ottawa: Labour Canada, Cat. no. L45-2895.

Lacroix, R.
1986   "Strike Activity in Canada." In W. Craig Riddell, ed., *Canadian Labour
        Relations.* Toronto: University of Toronto Press.

Land, Hillary
1980   "The Family Wage." *Feminist Review* 6:55-77.

Landes, David S.
1986   "What Do Bosses Really Do?" *Journal of Economic History* 46:585-623.

Lash, Scott
1984   *The Militant Worker: Class and Radicalism in France and America.* London:
        Heinemann.
1985   "The End of Neo-Corporatism?: The Breakdown of Centralized Bargaining in
        Sweden." *British Journal of Industrial Relations* 23:215-39.

Lash, Scott and John Urry
1985   *The End of Organized Capitalism.* Cambridge: Polity Press.

Laxer, Gordon
1985   "Foreign Ownership and Myths about Canadian Development." *Canadian
        Review of Sociology and Anthropology* 22:311-45.

Laxer, James
1984   *Rethinking the Canadian Economy.* Toronto: NC Press.

Laxer, Robert
1976   *Canada's Unions.* Toronto: James Lorimer.

Leon, Joel
1985   "The Effects of Labor Market Segmentation on Economic Resources in
        Retirement." *Social Science Research* 14:351-73.

Leontief, Wassily
1982   "The Distribution of Work and Income." *Scientific American* 247(3):188-204.

Leontief, Wassily and Faye Duchin
1986   *The Future Impact of Automation on Workers.* New York: Oxford University Press.

Lenski, Gerhard
1966   *Power and Privilege: A Theory of Social Stratification.* New York: McGraw-Hill.

Levine, Gilbert
1984   "Industrial Democracy is Workers' Control." In G. S. Lowe and H. J. Krahn,
        eds., *Working Canadians.* Toronto: Methuen.

Levy, Frank
1987   "Changes in the Distribution of American Family Incomes, 1947 to 1984."
        Science 236 (May 22): 923-27.

Leyton, Elliott
1975   *Dying Hard: The Ravages of Industrial Carnage.* Toronto: McClelland & Stewart.

Li, Peter
1982   "Chinese Immigrants on the Canadian Prairie, 1910-47." *Canadian Review of Sociology and Anthropology* 19:527-40.

Lincoln, James R. and Arne L. Kalleberg
1985   "Work Organization and Workforce Commitment: A Study of Plants and Employees in the U.S. and Japan." *American Sociological Review* 50:738-60.

Lindbeck, Assar
1975   *Swedish Economic Policy.* London: Macmillan.

Linhart, Robert
1981   *The Assembly Line.* London: John Calder.

Lipset, Seymour Martin
1987   "Comparing Canadian and American Unions." *Society* 24(2):60-70.

Lipset, Seymour Martin and Reinhard Bendix
1959   *Social Mobility in Industrial Society.* Berkeley: University of California Press.

Lipset, Seymour Martin, Martin Trow, and James Coleman
1956   *Union Democracy: The Internal Politics of the International Typographical Union.* Garden City, N. J.: Anchor Books.

Lipton, C.
1968   *The Trade Union Movement of Canada, 1827-1959.* Montreal: Canadian Social Publications.

List, Wilfred
1987   "Technology Hits Jobs More Than Workers in Auto Industry." *Globe and Mail* (May 19): B5.

Littler, Craig R.
1982   *The Development of the Labour Process in Capitalist Societies.* London: Heinemann.

Littler, Craig R. and Graeme Salaman
1982   "Bravermania and Beyond: Recent Theories of the Labour Process." *Sociology* 16:251-69.

Locke, Edwin A.
1976   "The Nature and Causes of Job Satisfaction." In Marvin B. Dunnette, ed., *Handbook of Industrial and Organizational Psychology.* Chicago: Rand-McNally.

Lockwood, David
1966   "Sources of Variation in Working Class Images of Society." *Sociological Review* 14:249-67.

Logan, Harold
1948   *Trade Unions in Canada: Their Development and Functioning.* Toronto: Macmillan.

Logue, John
1981   "Saab/Trollhattan: Reforming Work Life on the Shop Floor." *Working Life in Sweden* 23 (June).

Loher, Brian T., R. A. Noe, N. L. Moeller, and M. P. Fitzgerald
1985   "A Meta-Analysis of the Relation of Job Characteristics to Job Satisfaction."

Journal of Applied Psychology 70:280-89.

LO *News* (published by the Swedish Trade Union Confederation [LO], Stockholm).

Long, Richard J.
1978   "The Effects of Employee Ownership on Organizational Identification, Employee Job Attitudes and Organizational Performance: A Tentative Framework and Empirical Findings." *Human Relations* 31:29-48.
1984   "Introducing Employee Participation in Ownership and Decision Making." In J.B. Cunningham and T.H. White, eds., *Quality of Working Life: Contemporary Cases.* Ottawa: Labour Canada.

Looker, Dianne E. and Peter C. Pineo
1983   "Social Psychological Variables and their Relevance to the Status Attainment of Teenagers." *American Journal of Sociology* 88:1195-219.

Loveridge, Ray
1983   "Sources of Diversity in Internal Labour Markets." *Sociology* 17:44-62.

Lowe, Graham S.
1981   "Causes of Unionization in Canadian Banks." *Relations industrielles/Industrial Relations* 36:865-92.
1984   "The Rise of Modern Management in Canada." In G. S. Lowe and H. J. Krahn, eds., *Working Canadians.* Toronto: Methuen.
1986   "The Administrative Revolution in the Canadian Office: An Overview." In K. L. P. Lundy and B. Warme, eds., *Work in the Canadian Context.* 2nd ed. Toronto: Butterworths.
1987   *Women in the Administrative Revolution: The Feminization of Clerical Work.* Toronto: University of Toronto Press.

Lowe, Graham S. and Harvey J. Krahn, eds.
1984   *Working Canadians: Readings in the Sociology of Work and Industry.* Toronto: Methuen.

Lowe, Graham S. and Harvey Krahn
1985   "Where Wives Work: The Relative Effects of Situational and Attitudinal Factors." *Canadian Journal of Sociology* 10: 1-22.

Lowe, Graham S. and Herbert C. Northcott
1986   *Under Pressure: A Study of Job Stress.* Toronto: Garamond Press.

Loxley, John
1981   "The 'Great Northern' Plan." *Studies in Political Economy* 6:151-82.

Lucas, Rex A.
1971   *Minetown, Milltown, Railtown.* Toronto: University of Toronto Press.

Lush, Patricia
1987   "Going, Going, Gone." *Report on Business Magazine* (January): 36-40.

Luxton, Meg
1980   *More Than a Labour of Love.* Toronto: Women's Press.

Macarov, David
1982   *Worker Productivity: Myths and Reality.* Beverly Hills: Sage.

MacFarlane, David
1984 "Moving the Mail." In G. S. Lowe and H. J. Krahn, eds., *Working Canadians*. Toronto, Methuen.

Mackenzie, Donald and Judy Wajcman, eds.
1985 *The Social Shaping of Technology*. Milton Keynes, England: Open University Press.

MacKinnon, Malcolm H.
1981 "The Industrial Worker and the Job: Alienated or Instrumentalized?" In K. L. P. Lundy and B. Warme, eds., *Work in the Canadian Context*. Toronto: Butterworths.

Maclean's (Toronto).

Mahon, Rianne
1984 *The Politics of Industrial Restructuring: Canadian Textiles*. Toronto: University of Toronto Press.

Malcolmson, Robert W.
1981 *Life and Labour in England 1700-1780*. London: Hutchinson.

Mann, Michael
1970 "The Social Cohesion of Liberal Democracy." *American Sociological Review* 35:423-39.

Marchak, M. Patricia
1974 "Women Workers and White-Collar Unions." *Aspects of Canadian Society*, Special Edition of the *Canadian Review of Sociology and Anthropology*:187-200.
1975 "Class, Regional, and Institutional Sources of Social Conflict in B.C." *B.C. Studies* 27:30-49.
1981 *Ideological Perspectives on Canada*. 2nd ed. Toronto: McGraw-Hill Ryerson.

Marglin, Stephen A.
1976 "What Do Bosses Do? The Origins and Functions of Hierarchy in Capitalist Production." In Andre Gorz, ed., *The Division of Labour*. New York: Humanities Press.

Mars, Gerald
1982 *Cheats at Work: An Anthropology of Workplace Crime*. London: Unwin Paperbacks.

Marsden, Lorna R.
1986 "The Unemployment of Young Canadians Is Not Only About Jobs." *Atkinson Review of Canadian Studies* 3(2):3-7.

Marshall, G.
1982 *In Search of the Spirit of Capitalism: An Essay on Max Weber's Protestant Ethic Thesis*. London: Hutchinson.

Martin, Jurek
1984 "Japanese Working Habits Weighed." *Globe and Mail* (November 4): B5.

Marx, Karl
1967 *Capital*. vol. 1. New York: International Publishers [originally published in 1867].

Marx, Karl and Friedrich Engels
1962 *Selected Works*. Moscow: Progress Publishers.

Matras, Judah
1980 "Comparative Social Mobility." *Annual Review of Sociology* 6:401-31.

Matthews, Roy A.
1985 *Structural Change and Industrial Policy: The Redeployment of Canadian Manufacturing, 1960-80*. Ottawa: Supply and Services Canada.

Mayo, Elton
1945 *The Social Problems of an Industrial Civilization*. Cambridge, Mass.: Harvard University Press.

McCormack, A. Ross
1978 *Reformers, Rebels and Revolutionaries: The Western Canadian Radical Movement, 1899-1919*. Toronto: University of Toronto Press.

McKay, Ian
1983 "Strikes in the Maritimes." *Acadiensis* 13: 3-46.

McLean, A.
1979 *Work Stress*. Reading, Mass.: Addison-Wesley.

McNally, Fiona
1979 *Women for Hire: A Study of the Female Office Worker*. London: Macmillan.

Meissner, Martin
1969 *Technology and the Worker: Technical Demands and Social Processes in Industry*. San Francisco: Chandler.
1971 "The Long Arm of the Job: A Study of Work and Leisure." *Industrial Relations* 10:239-60. [Reprinted in G. S. Lowe and H. J. Krahn, eds., *Working Canadians*. Toronto: Methuen, 1984.]

Meissner, Martin, E. W. Humphreys, S. M. Meis, and W. J. Scheu
1975 "No Exit for Wives: Sexual Division of Labour and the Cumulation of Household Demands." *Canadian Review of Sociology and Anthropology* 12:424-39.

Menzies, Heather
1981 *Women and the Chip: Case Studies of the Effects of Informatics on Employment in Canada*. Montreal: Institute for Research on Public Policy.

Merkle, Judith A.
1980 *Management and Ideology: The Legacy of the International Scientific Management Movement*. Berkeley: University of California Press.

Merton, Robert K.
1952 "Bureaucratic Structure and Personality." In Robert K. Merton, A. P. Gray, B. Hockey, and H.C. Selvin, eds., *Reader in Bureaucracy*. New York: Free Press.
1957 *Social Theory and Social Structure*. New York: Free Press.

Meyer, Stephen
1981 *The Five Dollar Day: Labor Management and Social Control in the Ford Motor Company, 1908-1921*. Albany, N. Y.: State University of New York Press.

Michels, Robert
1959   *Political Parties: A Sociological Study of the Oligarchical Tendencies of Modern Democracy*. New York: Dover Publications [originally published in 1915].

Miles, Raymond E.
1965   "Human Relations or Human Resources." *Harvard Business Review* 43 (July-August): 148-63.

Milkman, Ruth, ed.
1985   *Women, Work, and Protest: A Century of Women's Labor History*. London: Routledge and Kegan Paul.

Miller, Delbert C. and William H. Form
1980   *Industrial Sociology: Work in Organizational Life*. 3rd ed. New York: Harper and Row.

Miller, Joanne
1980   "Individual and Occupational Determinants of Job Satisfaction: A Focus on Gender Differences." *Sociology of Work and Occupations* 7:337-66.

Miller, Joanne, C. Schooler, M. L. Kohn, and K. A. Miller
1979   "Women and Work: The Psychological Effects of Occupational Conditions." *American Journal of Sociology* 85:66-94.

Miller, Joanne, K. M. Slomczynski, and M. L. Kohn
1985   "Continuity of Learning-Generalization: The Effect of Job on Men's Intellective Process in the United States and Poland." *American Journal of Sociology* 91:593-615.

Mills, Ted
1981   *What is Quality of Working Life?* Ottawa: Labour Canada.

Mills, C. Wright
1948   *The New Men of Power*. New York: Harcourt-Brace.
1956   *White Collar: The American Middle Classes*. New York: Oxford University Press.

Milton, David
1986   "Late Capitalism and the Decline of Trade Union Power in the United States." *Economic and Industrial Democracy* 7:319-49.

Mirus, Rolf and Roger S. Smith
1985   "Canada's Irregular Economy." *Canadian Public Policy* 8:444-53.

Moloney, Joanne
1986   "Recent Industry Trends in Employment: Canada and the Provinces." Statistics Canada, *The Labour Force* (November): Cat. no. 71-001, monthly.

Monthly Labor Review

Moodie, Susanna
1962   *Roughing it in the Bush*. Toronto: McClelland and Stewart [originally published in 1852].

Morgan, Gareth
1986   *Images of Organization*. Beverley Hills: Sage.

Mortimer, Jeylan, R. Hall, and R. Hill
1978   "Husband's Occupational Attributes as Constraints on Wive's Employment."
        Sociology of Work and Occupations 5:285-313.

Morton, Desmond
1982   "The History of Canadian Labour." In John Anderson and Morley Gunder-
        son, eds., *Union-Management Relations in Canada.* Don Mills: Addison-Wesley.

Mottaz, Clifford
1986   "Gender Differences in Work Satisfaction, Work-Related Rewards and Values,
        and the Determinants of Work Satisfaction." *Human Relations* 39:359-78.

Moulton, David
1974   "Ford Windsor 1945." In Irving Abella, ed., *On Strike: Six Key Labour Struggles
        in Canada 1919-1949.* Toronto: James Lewis and Samuel.

Murray, Michael A. and Tom Atkinson
1981   "Gender Differences in Correlates of Job Satisfaction." *Canadian Journal of
        Behavioural Science* 13:44-52.

Naisbett, John
1982   *Megatrends: Ten New Directions Transforming our Lives.* New York: Warner.

National Council of Welfare
1984a   *Better Pensions for Homemakers.* Ottawa: Supply and Services Canada.
1984b   *1984 Poverty Lines.* Ottawa: Supply and Services Canada.
1985   *Poverty Profile 1985.* Ottawa: Supply and Services Canada.
1986   *1986 Poverty Lines.* Ottawa: Supply and Services Canada.

Naylor, R. T.
1972   "The Rise and Fall of the Third Commercial Empire of the St. Lawrence." In
        Gary Teeple, ed., *Capitalism and the National Question in Canada.* Toronto:
        University of Toronto Press.

Nelson, Daniel
1980   *Frederick W. Taylor and the Rise of Scientific Management.* Madison: University of
        Wisconsin Press.

Newfoundland and Labrador Federation of Labour
1978   *Now That We've Burned Our Boats: Report of the People's Commission on Unemploy-
        ment in Newfoundland and Labrador.* St. John's: Newfoundland and Labrador
        Federation of Labour.

Newton, Keith
1977   "The Theory and Practice of Industrial Democracy: A Canadian Perspective."
        Economic Council of Canada, Discussion Paper No. 94.
1986   "Quality of Working Life in Canada: A Survey." In W. Craig Riddell, ed.,
        Labour-Management Cooperation in Canada. Toronto: University of Toronto
        Press.

Nightingale, Donald
1982   *Workplace Democracy: An Inquiry into Employee Participation in Canadian Work
        Organizations.* Toronto: University of Toronto Press.

Nightingale, Donald V. and Richard J. Long
1984 *Gain and Equity Sharing*. Ottawa: Labour Canada.

Nightingale, Donald V. and Jean-Marie Toulouse
1978 "Alienation in the Workplace: A Comparative Study in French and English-Canadian Organizations." *Canadian Journal of Behavioural Science* 10(4):271-82.

Noble, David F.
1985 "Social Choice in Machine Design: The Case of Automatically Controlled Machine Tools." In Donald Mackenzie and Judy Wajcman, eds., *The Social Shaping of Technology*. Milton Keynes, England: Open University Press.

Nolan, Peter and P. K. Edwards
1984 "Homogenise, Divide and Rule: An Essay on Segmented Work, Divided Workers." *Cambridge Journal of Economics* 8: 197-215.

Northcott, Herbert C. and Graham S. Lowe
1987 "Job and Gender Influences in the Subjective Experience of Work." *Canadian Review of Sociology and Anthropology* 24:117-31.

Occupational Health and Safety Canada.

Occupational Health and Safety Magazine (published by the province of Alberta).

O'Connor, James
1973 *The Fiscal Crisis of the State*. New York: St. Martin's Press.

Offe, Claus
1985 *Disorganized Capitalism: Contemporary Transformations of Work and Politics*. Cambridge: Polity Press.

Olson, Mancur
1965 *The Logic of Collective Action*. Cambridge, Mass.: Harvard University Press.

Ontario Federation of Labour
1982 *Occupational Health and Safety: A Training Manual*. Toronto: Copp Clark Pitman.

Oppenheimer, Valerie K.
1970 *The Female Labor Force in the United States*. Berkeley: Institute of International Studies, University of California.

Organization for Economic Cooperation and Development (OECD)
1985 *The Integration of Women into the Economy*. Paris: OECD.
1986 *OECD Employment Outlook*. Paris: OECD

Ornstein, Michael D.
1983a "The Development of Class in Canada." In J. Paul Grayson, ed., *Introduction to Sociology: An Alternative Approach*. Toronto: Gage.
1983b "Class, Gender, and Job Income in Canada." In D. J. Treiman and R. V. Robinson, eds., *Research in Social Stratification and Mobility*, vol. 2. Greenwich, Conn.: JAI Press Inc.

Osberg, L., D. Clairmont, and R. Apostle
1981 "A Segmentation Approach to Low Wage Work in the Maritimes — An Interim Report." Halifax: Proceedings of the Canadian Industrial Relations

Association.

Osterman, Paul, ed.
1984   *Internal Labor Markets.* Cambridge, Mass.: MIT Press.

Osterman, Paul
1986   "The Impact of Computers on Employment of Managers and Clerks." *Industrial and Labor Relations Review* 39: 175-86.

Ostry, Sylvia
1968   *The Female Worker in Canada.* Ottawa: Queen's Printer.

Ostry, Sylvia and Mahmood A. Zaidi
1972   *Labour Economics in Canada.* 2nd ed. Toronto: Macmillan of Canada.

O'Toole, James, ed.
1974   *Work and the Quality of Life: Resource Papers for Work in America.* Cambridge, Mass.: MIT Press.
1977   *Work, Learning and the American Future.* San Francisco: Jossey-Bass.

Ouchi, William
1981   *Theory Z: How American Business Can Meet the Japanese Challenge.* Reading, Mass.: Addison-Wesley.

Ouchi, William G. and Alan L. Wilkins
1985   "Organizational Culture." *Annual Review of Sociology* 11:457-83.

Pahl, R. E.
1984   *Divisions of Labour.* Oxford: Basil Blackwell.

Palmer, Bryan
1975   "Class, Conception and Conflict: The Thrust for Efficiency, Managerial Views of Labor and the Working Class Rebellion, 1902-22." *Radical Review of Political Economics* 7:31-49.
1979   *A Culture in Conflict: Skilled Workers and Industrial Capitalism in Hamilton, Ontario, 1860-1914.* Montreal: McGill-Queen's University Press.
1983   *Working-Class Experience: The Rise and Reconstitution of Canadian Labour, 1800-1980.* Toronto: Butterworths.
1986   *The Character of Class Struggle: Essays in Canadian Working Class History, 1850-1985.* Toronto: McClelland and Stewart.

Panitch, Leo
1986   "The Tripartite Experience." In Keith Banting, ed., *The State and Economic Interests.* Toronto: University of Toronto Press.

Panitch, Leo and Donald Swartz
1985   *From Consent to Coercion: The Assault on Trade Union Freedoms.* Toronto: Garamond Press.

Parker, Robert Nash
1981   "Structural Constraints and Individual Career Earning Patterns." *American Sociological Review* 46:884-92.

Parliament, Jo-Anne
1987   "Increases in Long-Term Unemployment." *Canadian Social Trends* (Spring): 16-19.

Parrot, Jean Claude
1984 "Why We Continue to Struggle." In G. S. Lowe and H. J. Krahn, eds., *Working Canadians*. Toronto: Methuen.

Peitchinis, Stephen G.
1983 *Computer Technology and Employment: Retrospect and Prospect*. London: Macmillan.

Penn, Roger
1982 " 'The Contest Terrain': A Critique of R. C. Edwards' Theory of Working Class Fractions and Politics." In Graham Day, ed., *Diversity and Decomposition in the Labour Market*. Aldershot, England: Gower.

Penn, Roger and Hilda Scattergood
1985 "Deskilling or Enskilling? An Empirical Investigation of Recent Theories of the Labour Process." *British Journal of Sociology* 36:611-30.

Penner, Norman, ed.
1973 *Winnipeg 1919: The Strikers' Own History of the Winnipeg General Strike*. Toronto: James Lewis and Samuel.

Pentland, H. Claire
1979 "The Canadian Industrial Relations System: Some Formative Factors." *Labour/Le Travailleur* 4:9-23.
1981 *Labour and Capital in Canada, 1650-1860*. Toronto: James Lorimer.

Perlman, Mark, ed.
1958 *Labor Union Theories in America: Background and Development*. Evanston, Ill.: Row, Peterson.

Perlman, Selig
1928 *A Theory of the Labor Movement*. New York: Macmillan.

Perrow, Charles
1986 *Complex Organizations: A Critical Essay*. 3rd ed. New York: Random House.

Peters, Thomas J. and Robert H. Waterman Jr.
1982 *In Search of Excellence*. New York: Warner.

Pettigrew, Andrew M.
1979 "On Studying Organizational Culture." *Administrative Science Quarterly* 24:570-81.

Petty, M. M., G. McGee, and J. Cavender
1984 "A Meta-Analysis of the Relationship between Individual Job Satisfaction and Individual Performance." *Academy of Management Review* 9:712-21.

Phillips, Paul
1982 *Regional Disparities*. 2nd ed. Toronto: James Lorimer.

Phillips, Paul and Erin Phillips
1983 *Women and Work: Inequality in the Labour Market*. Toronto: James Lorimer.

Picot, W. Garrett
1987 "The Changing Industrial Mix of Employment, 1951-1985." *Canadian Social*

Trends (Spring): 8-11.

Pineo, Peter C. and John Porter
1967   "Occupational Prestige in Canada." *Canadian Review of Sociology and Anthropology* 4:24-40.

Pineo, Peter C., John Porter, and Hugh A. McRoberts
1977   "The 1971 Census and the Socioeconomic Classification of Occupations." *Canadian Review of Sociology and Anthropology* 14:91-102.

Piore, Michael J.
1975   "Notes for a Theory of Labor Market Segmentation." In Richard Edwards, M. Reich, and D. Gordon, eds., *Labor Market Segmentation*. Lexington: D.C. Heath and Company.

Piore, Michael J. and Charles F. Sabel
1984   *The Second Industrial Divide: Possibilities for Prosperity.* New York: Basic Books.

Piva, Michael J.
1979   *The Condition of the Working Class in Toronto, 1900-1921.* Ottawa: University of Ottawa Press.

Piven, Frances Fox and Richard A. Cloward
1971   *Regulating the Poor: The Functions of Public Welfare.* Toronto: Random House.

Polanyi, Karl
1957   *The Great Transformation.* Boston: Beacon Press.

Pollard, Sidney
1968   *The Genesis of Modern Management.* Harmondsworth: Penguin.

Pomfret, Richard
1981   *The Economic Development of Canada.* Toronto: Methuen.

Ponak, Alan and Larry F. Moore
1981   "Canadian Bank Unionism: Perspectives and Issues." *Relations industrielles/ Industrial Relations* 36:3-30.

Ponting, J. Rick and Roger Gibbins
1980   *Out of Irrelevance: A Socio-political Introduction to Indian Affairs in Canada.* Toronto: Butterworths.

Poole, Michael
1981   *Theories of Trade Unionism.* London: Routledge and Kegan Paul.
1982   "Theories of Industrial Democracy: The Emerging Synthesis." *Sociological Review* 30:181-207.

Porter, John
1965   *The Vertical Mosaic: An Analysis of Social Class and Power in Canada.* Toronto: University of Toronto Press.
1985   "Canada: The Societal Context of Occupational Allocation." In M. Boyd, J. Goyder, F. E. Jones, H. A. McRoberts, P. C. Pineo, and J. Porter, *Ascription and Achievement: Studies in Mobility and Status Attainment in Canada.* Ottawa: Carleton University Press.

Porter, John, Marion Porter, and Bernard R. Blishen
1982   *Stations and Callings: Making it Through the School System.* Toronto: Methuen.

Porter, Marion, John Porter, and Bernard R. Blishen
1979   *Does Money Matter?* Toronto: Macmillan.

Prandy, Kenneth
1979   "Alienation and Interests in the Analysis of Social Cognitions." *British Journal of Sociology* 30:442-74.

Prentice, Alison and Susan Mann Trofimenkoff, eds.
1985   *The Neglected Majority: Essays in Canadian Women's History,* vol. 2. Toronto: McClelland and Stewart.

Presthus, Robert
1978   *The Organizational Society.* 2nd ed. New York: St. Martin's Press.

Pugh, D. S., D. J. Hickson, and C. R. Hinings
1985   *Writers on Organizations.* Beverly Hills: Sage.

Purcell, Kate
1979   "Militancy and Acquiescence amongst Women Workers." In Sandra Burman, ed., *Fit Work for Women.* London: Croom Helm.

Quinn, Robert P. and Linda J. Shepard
1974   *The 1972-73 Quality of Employment Survey.* Ann Arbor: Institute for Social Research, University of Michigan.

Ranson, Stewart, Bob Hinings, and Royston Greenwood
1980   "The Structure of Organizational Structures." *Administrative Science Quarterly* 25:1-17.

Ray, Carol Axtell
1986   "Corporate Culture: The Last Frontier of Control?" *Journal of Management Studies* 23:287-97.

Reagan, Barbara B. and Martha Blaxall
1976   "Occupational Segregation in International Women's Year." In M. Blaxall and B.B. Reagan, eds., *Women and the Workplace.* Chicago: University of Chicago Press.

Reasons, Charles E., Lois L. Ross, and Craig Paterson
1981   *Assault on the Worker: Occupational Health and Safety in Canada.* Toronto: Butterworths.

Reich, Robert
1983   *The Next American Frontier.* New York: Times Books.

Reid, Frank
1982   "Wage-and-Price Controls in Canada." In John Anderson and Morley Gunderson, eds., *Union-Management Relations in Canada.* Don Mills: Addison-Wesley.
1985   "Reductions in Work Time: An Assessment of Employment Sharing to Reduce Unemployment." In W. Craig Riddell, ed., *Work and Pay: The Canadian Labour Market.* Toronto: University of Toronto Press.

Reimer, Neil
1979   "Oil, Chemical and Atomic Workers International Union and the Quality of
        Working Life — A Union Perspective." *Quality of Working Life: The Canadian
        Scene* (Winter): 5-7.

Reiter, Esther
1986   "Life in a Fast-Food Factory." In Craig Heron and Robert Storey, eds., *On the
        Job*. Montreal: McGill-Queen's University Press.

Riddell, W. Craig
1985   "Work and Pay: The Canadian Labour Market: An Overview." In W. Craig
        Riddell, ed., *Work and Pay: The Canadian Labour Market*. Toronto: University of
        Toronto Press.
1986a   "Canadian Labour Relations: An Overview." In W. Craig Riddell, ed., *Canadian
        Labour Relations*. Toronto: University of Toronto Press.
1986b   "Labour-Management Cooperation in Canada: An Overview." In W. Craig
        Riddell, ed., *Labour-Management Cooperation in Canada*. Toronto: University of
        Toronto Press.

Rinehart, James
1978   "Contradictions of Work-Related Attitudes and Behaviour: An
        Interpretation." *Canadian Review of Sociology and Anthropology* 15:1-15. [Re-
        printed in G. S. Lowe and H. J. Krahn, eds., *Working Canadians*. Toronto:
        Methuen, 1984.]
1984   "Appropriating Workers' Knowledge: Quality Control Circles at a General
        Motors Plant." *Studies in Political Economy* 14:75-97.
1986   "Improving the Quality of Working Life through Job Redesign: Work Hu-
        manization or Work Rationalization?" *Canadian Review of Sociology and
        Anthropology* 23:507-30.
1987   *The Tyranny of Work: Alienation and the Labour Process*. 2nd ed. Toronto:
        Harcourt Brace Jovanovich.

Robin, Martin
1968   *Radical Politics and Canadian Labour: 1880-1930*. Kingston: Queen's University
        Industrial Relations Centre.

Roethlisberger, F. J. and W. J. Dickson
1939   *Management and the Worker*. Cambridge, Mass.: Harvard University Press.

Rose, Joseph B. and Gary N. Chaison
1985   "The State of Unions: United States and Canada." *Journal of Labor Research*
        6:97-111.

Rose, Michael
1985   *Re-Working the Work Ethic: Economic Values and Socio-Cultural Politics*. London:
        Batsford.

Ross, David P. and Peter J. Usher
1986   *From the Roots Up: Economic Development as if Community Mattered*. Toronto:
        James Lorimer.

Rothschild, Joyce and Raymond Russell
1986   "Alternatives to Bureaucracy: Democratic Participation in the Economy."
        Annual Review of Sociology 12:307-28.

Rowbotham, Sheila
1973   *Hidden from History: 300 Years of Women's Oppression and the Fight Against It.*
        London: Pluto Press.

Roy, Donald
1952   "Quota Restriction and Goldbricking in a Machine Shop." *American Journal of
        Sociology* 57:427-42.
1954   "Efficiency and the Fix: Informal Intergroup Relations in a Piecework Ma-
        chine Shop." *American Journal of Sociology* 60:255-66.
1959-60 " 'Banana Time': Job Satisfaction and Informal Interaction." *Human Organi-
        zation* 18:158-68.

Rumberger, Russell W.
1984   "High Technology and Job Loss." *Technology in Society* 6:263-84.

Russel, Robert Arnold
1981   *Office Automation: Key to the Information Society.* Montreal: Institute for Research
        on Public Policy.

Salaman, Graeme
1979   *Work Organizations: Resistance and Control.* London: Longman.

Sangster, Joan
1978   "The 1907 Bell Telephone Strike: Organizing Women Workers." *Labour/Le
        Travailleur* 3:109-30.

Sass, Robert
1986a   "The Workers' Right to Know, Participate and Refuse Hazardous Work: A
        Manifesto Right." *Journal of Business Ethics* 5:129-36.
1986b   "Workplace Health and Safety: Report from Canada." *International Journal of
        Health Services* 16: 565-82.

Seager, Allen
1985   "Socialists and Workers: The Western Canadian Coal Miners, 1900-21."
        Labour/Le Travail 16: 25-39.

Seeman, Melvin
1959   "On the Meaning of Alienation." *American Sociological Review* 24:783-91.
1967   "On the Personal Consequences of Alienation in Work." *American Sociological
        Review* 32:273-85.
1975   "Alienation Studies." *Annual Review of Sociology* 1:91-125.

Selye, Hans
1976   *Stress in Health and Disease.* Boston: Butterworths.

Sennett, Richard and Jonathon Cobb
1972   *The Hidden Injuries of Class.* New York: Knopf.

Shaiken, Harley
1984   *Work Transformed: Automation and Labor in the Computer Age.* New York: Holt,
        Rinehart and Winston.

Shallis, Michael
1984   *The Silicon Idol: The Micro Revolution and its Social Implications.* Oxford: Oxford
        University Press.

Sheppard, Harold L. and Neal Q. Herrick
1972   *Where Have All the Robots Gone? Worker Dissatisfaction in the 1970s.* New York: Free Press.

Shorter, Edward and Charles Tilly
1974   *Strikes in France, 1830-1968.* Cambridge, Mass.: Cambridge University Press.

Smith, Adam
1976   *The Wealth of Nations.* Chicago: University of Chicago Press [originally published in 1776].

Smith, D. Randall
1983   "Mobility in Professional, Occupational-Internal Labor Markets: Stratification, Segmentation and Vacancy Chains." *American Sociological Review* 48:289-305.

Smith, Michael R.
1978   "The Effects of Strikes on Workers: A Critical Analysis." *Canadian Journal of Sociology* 3:457-72.

Smucker, Joseph
1980   *Industrialization in Canada.* Scarborough: Prentice-Hall.

Social Planning Council of Metropolitan Toronto
1984   "Hidden Unemployment." *Social INFOPAC* 3 (February).

Sonnenfeld, Jeffrey A.
1985   "Shedding Light on the Hawthorne Studies." *Journal of Occupational Behaviour* 6:111-30.

Spencer, Metta
1985   *Foundations of Modern Sociology.* 4th ed. Scarborough: Prentice-Hall.

Spenner, Kenneth I.
1983   "Deciphering Prometheus: Temporal Change in the Skill Level of Work." *American Sociological Review* 48:824-37.

Spilerman, Seymour
1977   "Careers, Labor Market Structure, and Socioeconomic Achievement." *American Journal of Sociology* 83:551-93.

Spinrad, William
1984   "Work Democracy: An Overview." *International Social Science Journal* 36:195-215.

Staines, Graham L.
1980   "Spillover versus Compensation: A Review of the Literature on the Relationship between Work and Non-Work." *Human Relations* 33: 111-29.

Statistics Canada
1973   Corporations and Labour Unions Returns Act (CALURA). *Report for 1970.* Part II Labour Unions (cat. no. 71-202).
1974   *Report for 1971.*
1979   *Report for 1977.*
1986   *Report for 1983.*

The Labour Force (cat. no. 71-001, monthly).

1984   *Charting Canadian Incomes 1951-1981* (cat. no. 13-581E).

1985a   *Income Distributions by Size in Canada* (cat. no. 13-207).

1985b   *Self-Employment in Canada. Labour and Household Surveys Analysis Division* (cat. no. 71-582).

Steed, Judy

1985   "The Rewards of Running Your Own Show." *Report on Business Magazine* (March):22-28.

1986   "The Middle Class Is Under Pressure and Losing Ground as the Rich Get Richer and the Poor Get More Numerous." *Globe and Mail* (October 4): D5.

Stern, Robert N.

1976   "Intermetropolitan Pattern of Strike Frequency." *Industrial and Labor Relations Review* 29:218-35.

Stewart, A. and R. M. Blackburn

1975   "The Stability of Structured Inequality." *Sociological Review* 23:481-508.

Stewart, A., K. Prandy, and R. M. Blackburn

1980   *Social Stratification and Occupational Structure.* London: Macmillian.

Stinson, Jane

1982   "The QWL Delusion." *CUPE: The Facts* (June-July): 14-16.

Stokes, Henry Scott

1982   "Sweatshops Undercut Image of Satisfied Japanese Worker." *Globe and Mail* (July 21).

Storey, Robert

1983   "Unionization versus Corporate Welfare: 'The Dofasco Way.' " *Labour/Le Travailleur* 12:7-42.

Stymeist, David H.

1975   *Ethnics and Indians: Social Relations in a Northwestern Ontario Town.* Toronto: Peter Martin.

Sufrin, Eileen

1982   *The Eaton Drive: The Campaign to Organize Canada's Largest Department Store, 1948 to 1952.* Toronto: Fitzhenry and Whiteside.

Sullivan, Teresa A. and Daniel B. Cornfield

1979   "Downgrading Computer Workers: Evidence from Occupational and Industrial Redistribution." *Sociology of Work and Occupations* 6:184-203.

Sunahara, Ann Gomer

1981   *The Politics of Racism: The Uprooting of Japanese Canadians During the Second World War.* Toronto: James Lorimer.

Swartz, Donald

1981   "New Forms of Worker Participation: A Critique of Quality of Working Life." *Studies in Political Economy* 5:55-78.

Swedish Centre for Working Life

  Employee Investment Funds. Working Paper (no date).

Swedish Ministry of Finance
1984   *Employee Investment Funds.* Stockholm.

Swedish Trade Union Confederation (LO)
1982   *Co-Determination Through Collective Agreements and Legislation.* Stockholm: LO.

Tanner, Julian
1984   "Skill Levels of Manual Workers and Beliefs about Work, Management, and Industry: A Comparison of Craft and Non-Craft Workers in Edmonton." *Canadian Journal of Sociology* 9:303-18.

Tanner, Julian and Rhonda Cockerill
1986   "In Search of Working-Class Ideology: A Test of Two Perspectives." *Sociological Quarterly* 27: 389-402.

Tanner, Julian, Graham S. Lowe, and Harvey Krahn
1984   "Youth Unemployment and Moral Panics." *Perception* 7(5):27-29.

Tausky, Curt
1978   *Work Organizations: Major Theoretical Perspectives.* 2nd ed.   Itasca, Ill.: F. E. Peacock Publishers.

Taylor, Frederick W.
1919   *Shop Management.* New York: Harper.

Teeple, Gary
1972   "Land, Labour and Capital in Pre-Confederation Canada." In Gary Teeple, ed., *Capitalism and the National Question in Canada.* Toronto: University of Toronto Press.

Tentler, Leslie Woodcock
1979   *Wage-Earning Women: Industrial Work and Family Life in the United States, 1900-1930.* New York: Oxford University Press.

Thomas, Henk and Chris Logan
1982   *Mondragon: An Economic Analysis.* London: George Allen and Unwin.

Thompson, Paul
1983   *The Nature of Work: Introduction to Debates on the Labour Process.* London: Macmillan.

Thorsrud, Einar
1975   "Collaborative Action Research to Enhance the Quality of Working Life." In L.E. Davis and A.B. Cherns, eds., *The Quality of Working Life,* vol. 1. New York: Free Press.

Thurow, Lester C.
1975   *Generating Inequality: Mechanisms of Distribution in the U.S. Economy.* New York: Basic Books.

Tilly, Charles
1979   *From Mobilization to Revolution.* Reading, Mass.: Addison-Wesley.

Tilly, Louise A. and Joan W. Scott
1978   *Women, Work and Family.* New York: Holt, Rinehart and Winston.

Toffler, Alvin
1980   *The Third Wave.* New York: Bantam.

Tolbert, Charles M., II
1982   "Industrial Segmentation and Men's Career Mobility." *American Sociological Review* 47:457-77.

Trice, Harrison M. and Janice M. Beyer
1984   "Studying Organizational Cultures through Rites and Ceremonials." *Academy of Management Review* 9:653-69.

Trist, E. L. and K. W. Bamforth
1951   "Some Social and Psychological Consequences of the Longwall Method of Coal-Getting." *Human Relations* 4:3-38.

Trist, E. L., G. W. Higgins, E. Murray, and B. Pollock
1963   *Organizational Choice.* London: Tavistock Publications.

Trofimenkoff, Susan Mann and Alison Prentice, eds.
1977   *The Neglected Majority.* Toronto: McClellend and Stewart.

Turrittin, Anton H.
1974   "Social Mobility in Canada: A Comparison of Three Provincial Studies and Some Methodological Questions." *Canadian Review of Sociology and Anthropology* (Special issue on the occasion of the Eighth World Congress of Sociology): 163-86.

Tyree, Andrea, H. Semyonov, and R.W. Hodge
1979   "Gaps and Glissandos: Inequality, Economic Development, and Social Mobility in 24 Countries." *American Sociological Review* 44:410-24.

United Auto Workers
1985   "Can Capital and Labour Cooperate?" In Daniel Drache and Duncan Cameron, eds., *The Other Macdonald Report.* Toronto: James Lorimer.

Useem, Michael and Jerome Karabel
1986   "Pathways to Top Corporate Management." *American Sociological Review* 51:184-200.

Vallas, Steven Peter and Michael Yarrow
1987   "Advanced Technology and Worker Alienation: Comments on the Blauner/ Marxism Debate." *Work and Occupations* 14: 126-42.

van Cleef, Danny
1985   "Persons Working Long Hours." *The Labour Force,* Statistics Canada (May): 87-94.

Van Kirk, Sylvia
1980   *'Many Tender Ties': Women in Fur-Trade Society, 1670-1870.* Winnipeg: Watson and Dwyer.

Veevers, Richard
1986   "Results from the Annual Work Patterns Survey: 1984 and 1985." *The Labour Force,* Statistics Canada (March): 93-104.

Veltmeyer, Henry
1983   "The Development of Capitalism and the Capitalist World System." In J. Paul Grayson, ed., *Introduction to Sociology: An Alternative Approach.* Toronto: Gage.

Walker, C. R. and R. H. Guest
1952   *Man on the Assembly Line.* Cambridge, Mass.: Harvard University Press.

Wall, T. D. and J. A. Lischeron
1977   *Worker Participation: A Critique of the Literature and Some Fresh Evidence.* London: McGraw-Hill.

Wallace, Michael and Arne L. Kalleberg
1982   "Industrial Transformation and the Decline of Craft: The Decomposition of Skill in the Printing Industry, 1931-1978." *American Sociological Review* 47:307-24.

Walters, Vivienne
1985   "The Politics of Occupational Health and Safety: Interviews with Workers' Health and Safety Representatives and Company Doctors." *Canadian Review of Sociology and Anthropology* 22:57-79.

Wanner, Richard A. and Lionel S. Lewis
1983   "Economic Segmentation and the Course of the Occupational Career." *Work and Occupations* 10:307-24.

Warskett, George
1981   "Information, Competition and Cybernetic Work." *Studies in Political Economy* 5:107-25.

Washington Post, The (Washington).

Watkins, Mel
1963   "A Staple Theory of Economic Growth." *Canadian Journal of Economics and Political Science* 29:141-58.
1977   "From Underdevelopment to Development." In Mel Watkins, ed., *Dene Nation: The Colony Within.* Toronto: University of Toronto Press.
1982   "The Innis Tradition in Canadian Political Economy." *Canadian Journal of Political and Social Theory* 6 (Winter-Spring):12-34.

Watson, Tony J.
1987   *Sociology, Work and Industry.* 2nd ed. London: Routledge and Kegan Paul.

Webb, Sidney and Beatrice Webb
1894   *The History of Trade Unionism.* London: Longmans, Green.

Webb, Tom
1984   "Workers' Industry." In G. S. Lowe and H. J. Krahn, eds., *Working Canadians.* Toronto: Methuen.

Weber, Max
1946   *From Max Weber: Essays in Sociology.* Trans. and ed. by H. H. Gerth and C. W. Mills. New York: Oxford University Press.
1947   *The Theory of Social and Economic Organization.* Trans. by A. M. Henderson and T. Parsons. New York: Free Press.
1958   *The Protestant Ethic and the Spirit of Capitalism.* New York: Scribner.

1964 *The Theory of Social and Economic Organization*. New York: Free Press.

Weeks, Wendy
1980 "Part-Time Work: The Business View on Second-Class Jobs for Housewives and Mothers." *Atlantis* 5:69-86. [Reprinted in G. S. Lowe and H. J. Krahn, eds., *Working Canadians*. Toronto: Methuen, 1984.]

Weiss, Donald D.
1976 "Marx versus Smith on the Division of Labour." *Monthly Review* 28(3):104-118.

Weitzman, Martin L.
1984 *The Share Economy*. Cambridge, Mass.: Harvard University Press.

Wells, Don
1986a *Soft Sell: "Quality of Working Life" Programs and the Productivity Race*. Ottawa: Canadian Centre for Policy Alternatives.
1986b "Autoworkers on the Firing Line." In Craig Heron and Robert Storey, eds., *On The Job*. Montreal: McGill-Queen's University Press.

Whitaker, R.
1979 "Scientific Management Theory as Political Ideology." *Studies in Political Economy* 2:75-108.

White, Julie
1980 *Women and Unions*. Report for the Canadian Advisory Council on the Status of Women. Ottawa: Supply and Services Canada.

White, Terrence H.
1981 "The Relative Importance of Work as a Factor in Life Satisfaction." *Relations industrielles/Industrial Relations* 36:179-91.

Whitehead, T. N.
1936 *Leadership in a Free Society*. Cambridge, Mass.: Harvard University Press.

Wholey, Douglas R.
1985 "Determinants of Firm Internal Labor Markets in Large Law Firms." *Administrative Science Quarterly* 30:318-35.

Wilensky, Jeanne L. and Harold L. Wilensky
1951 "Personnel Counseling: The Hawthorne Case." *American Journal of Sociology* 57:265-80.

Wilkinson, Frank, ed.
1982 *The Dynamics of Labour Market Segmentation*. New York: Academic Press.

Williams, Claire
1983 "The 'Work Ethic', Non-Work and Leisure in an Age of Automation." *Australian and New Zealand Journal of Sociology* 19:216-37.

Wood, Stephen, ed.
1982 *The Degradation of Work?: Skill, Deskilling and the Labour Process*. London: Hutchinson.

Wood, Stephen
1987 "The Deskilling Debate, New Technology and Work Organization." *Acta Sociologica* 30:3-24.

Woodward, Joan
1980   *Industrial Organization: Theory and Practice. 2nd ed.* Oxford: Oxford University Press.

Working Life in Sweden
        New York: Swedish Information Service, Swedish Consulate General.

Worsley, Peter
1984   *The Three Worlds: Culture and World Development.* London: Weidenfeld and Nicolson.

Wright, Eric Olin, C. Costello, D. Hachen, and J. Sprague
1982   "The American Class Structure." *American Sociological Review* 47:709-26.

Wright, James D. and Richard F. Hamilton
1979   "Education and Job Attitudes among Blue-Collar Workers." *Sociology of Work and Occupations* 6:59-83.

Wylie, William N. T.
1983   "Poverty, Distress, and Disease: Labour and the Construction of the Rideau Canal, 1826-1832." *Labour/Le Travailleur* 11:7-30.

Zeitlin, Irving M.
1968   *Ideology and the Development of Sociological Theory.* Englewood Cliffs, N. J.: Prentice-Hall.

Zeitz, Gerald
1983   "Structural and Individual Determinants of Organization Morale and Satisfaction." *Social Forces* 61:1088-108.

Zey-Ferrell, Mary and Michael Aiken, eds.
1981   *Complex Organizations: Critical Perspectives.* Glenview, Ill.: Scott, Foresman and Company.

Zimbalist, Andrew, ed.
1979   *Case Studies on the Labor Process.* New York: Monthly Review Press.

Zucker, Lynne G. and Carolyn Rosenstein
1981   "Taxonomies of Institutional Structure: Dual Economy Reconsidered." *American Sociological Review* 46:869-84.

Zwerdling, Daniel
1978   *Workplace Democracy: A Guide to Workplace Ownership, Participation, and Self-Management Experiments in the United States and Europe.* New York: Harper and Row.

INDEX

Abella Commission (Royal Commission on
    Equality in Employment), 142-44
Absenteeism, 160
Administrative revolution, 19
Affluent Worker Study, 156-57
Agriculture
    and rise of capitalism, 12-13
Alienation, 106, 169-72
    Blauner's theory of, 166
    definition of, 169-70, 180n.110
    and job dissatisfaction, 169, 171
    Marx's theory of, 22, 155
    social psychological perspective on, 171
    structural perspective on, 170
American Federation of Labour, 188
Anisef, P., 76
Anthony, P.D., 149
Arkwright, R., 11
Armstrong, P. (and H. Armstrong), 141
Aspirations
    educational, 75-76
    occupational, 76
    sex differences in, 77
Assembly-line technology, impact on
    workers, 106, 169
Automation
    impact on skills, 256-57n.92; see also
        Micro-electronics technology; Robots
Automobile workers
    and work orientations, 156-58
Autonomous work teams, 227-29
    and buffer zones, 235
    matrix groups, 235

Babbage, Charles, 25
Batstone, E., 217
Bell, Daniel, 32-33
Bendix, R., 79, 101
Blackburn, R., 157, 161
Blaming the victim, 239
Blau, P., 100
    and O. Duncan, 80
    and W. Scott, 110
Blauner, R., 166, 171-72
Blishen, B., 71
Blishen scores (of occupational status), 71-
    72, 94n.18
Bluestone B., (and B. Harrison), 91, 249
Bourgeoisie, 21
Braverman, H., 82-84
    criticisms of his Labor and Monopoly
        Capital, 114-15
British Columbia Solidarity Movement, 221
Burawoy, M, 111-12, 116-17

Bureaucracy, 26-28, 225-27
    and alienation, 170
    problems of, 99-101
    and rational-legal value systems, 100
    under socialism, 253n.20
    within unions, 209
Bureaucratic personality, 100
Burger King, 106
Burns, T. (and G. Stalker), 102
Business unionism, 186

Caisse populaires, 231
Calvinism
    impact on capitalism, 150
Canada
    early industrialization, 15-16
    pre-industrial economy, 14-15
Canada Labour Code, 240
Canadian Auto Workers Union, 199; see also
    United Auto Workers
Canadian Congress of Labour, 190
Canadian Job Satisfaction survey, 151, 153-
    154, 161, 163-65
Canadian Labour Congress (CLC), 190,
    201, 219
Canadian Mental Health Association, 241
Canadian Paperworkers Union, 199
Canadian Work Ethic Study, 151, 153-54,
    158-59
Capitalism
    definition of, 7-8
    transition from feudalism to, 14-15
    work in early period of, 10-14
Capitalist work relations
    and alienation, 170
Carey, A., 108
Census, Canadian, 38
Chandler, A., 103
Chaplin, C., 104
Charter of Rights and Freedoms, 222
    effects of Section 15 on women, 144
Chinoy, E., 157
Class conflict
    in Marxian theory, 21; see also Conflict;
        Militancy
Class consciousness, 218
Class structure
    in Canada, 46-48
    in pre-industrial societies, 9-10
    see also Social class
Clement, W., 116
Clerical work
    and automation, 242, 246-47
    deskilling of, 82-83

Clerical work *(continued)*
  feminization of, 130, 132, 141
  growth of, 19-20
Co-determination, 233
Collective action
  and unions, 208-10
Communication Workers of Canada, 199
Comparable worth legislation, 143
Compliance
  of employees within work organizations,
    107; *see also* Consensus; Cooperation;
    Normative control
Concession bargaining, 203
Conflict
  in employment relations and work or-
    ganizations, 2, 110, 115, 119
  F. W. Taylor's view on, 105
  in industrial relations, 181-85, 212
  institutionalization of, 205n.34
  unorganized versus organized, 211
  view of in Human Relations theory, 109
Conflict perspective
  in industrial sociology, 3, 23
Congress of Industrial Organizations, 189
Consensus
  in work organizations, 113, 119; *see also*
    Cooperation; Compliance; Norma-
    tive control
Consensus perspective
  in industrial sociology, 3, 23, 26
Consent
  manufactured, 112
Consciousness
  dual, 218
  explosions of, 218
Contingency theory, 101
Control
  absence/presence of in job, 111, 169-70
  bureaucratic, 117
  conflict over in industrial relations, 183-
    84
  direct, 116
  managerial, 114-15
Cooperation
  management theories' emphasis on,
    105, 109
  within work organizations, 111-12, 115
  in industrial relations, 182, 184-85, 203-
    204
  see also Compliance; Consensus;
    Normative control
Cooperatives
  in Canada, 231; *see also* Worker coopera-
    tives
Cost accounting, 103
Core sector of economy, 117
Corporate capitalism, 28
Corporate concentration, 18-19, 36n.26
Corporate welfare programs (industrial
    betterment), 20, 107, 202

Corporatism, 253n.26
Counter-culture in organizations, 113
Craft work
  decline of in Canada, 16-17
  ideal of, 24-25
Craft unions
  early developments, 188
  merger with industrial unions, 190
  responses to women in the labour force,
    200

Dalton, M., 112
Deferential workers, 156
Deindustrialization, 91-92, 249-50
Despotic organization of work, 116
Deskilling, 82-84
Discrimination
  and female earnings, 137
  against women, 88, 143
  against visible minorities, 89
Division of labour, 24-26, 184
  Durkheim's theory of, 36n.38
Dofasco, 202
Domestic work, 124
Dual economy theory, 84-85; *see also* Labour
    market segmentation theory
Durkheim, Emile, 7, 25-26, 113

Economic Council of Canada, 242, 247
Edmonton Area Study, 158-60
Edwards, R., 117
Effort bargaining, 217
Electronic cottage industries, 247
Employee participation schemes: *see*
    Industrial democracy; Quality of
    working life
Employee share ownership plans, 231
Employment
  future trends, 61-63
  industrial distribution of, 41-43
  involuntary part-time, 54-55
  of Native Canadians, 65n.41
  occupational distribution of, 42-44
  part-time, 54-55
  regional differences in, 48-53
  sex differences in occupational
    distribution, 44-46
Employment equity
  definition of, 142-43
Energy and Chemical Workers Union, 199,
    229
Engels, Friedrich, 22
England
  development of capitalism in, 11-12
Equal pay
  different concepts of, 143
Europe
  origins of capitalism in, 8-9

Factories in early capitalism, 12

Family wage
  ideology of, 124
Faulkner, W., 173
Federal Task Force on Labour Relations, 183-84, 215
Feldberg, R. (and E. Glenn), 138
Female labour force participation, 125-27
  comparative data on, 126
  factors influencing, 126-27
  and family responsibilities, 127-29
Female job ghettos, 130, 200
Feminism, 126, 144
Feudalism
  decay of, 10
  work relations in, 9-10
Flanders, A., 209
Flexible specialization, 250
Ford, Henry, 106-107
Fordism, 106, 116, 119, 226, 250
France
  development of capitalism in, 11
Freeman, R. (and J. Medoff), 187
Free-rider problem for unions, 209
Friedman, A., 116
Fringe benefits, 70
Frontier of control, 116

Gainers strike, 181, 184, 203, 222
Gallie, D., 172, 218-19
Gallup polls on union attitudes, 186
Gender division of labour, 124
  materialist model of, 141
Gender inequalities
  major research questions on, 123
Gender role socialization, 129-30, 140
General Motors, 106, 228
  1937 Oshawa strike, 189
Goldthorpe, J., 156
Gordon, D. (and R. Edwards and M. Reich), 90-91
Gouldner, A., 100
Gunderson, M., 137

Hargreaves, J., 11
Hawthorne effect, 108
Hawthorne studies, 108-10
Hegemonic organization of work, 116
Heron, C. (and R. Storey), 118
Herzberg, F., 164, 226
Hewlett-Packard, 113, 202
Hidden economy, 39-40
Hill, S., 184-85
Hirschman, A., 209
Hodson, R., 166
Household division of labour, 128-29, 145n.14
  class differences in, 129
Human capital theory, 67-68, 73-74
  comparisons with labour market seg-

mentation theory, 92-93
  critical assessment, 77-78, 82
  similarities with functionalist theory of stratification, 94n.20
  status attainment research, 95n.37
  occupational sex segregation, 137-39
Human relations theory, 106-10, 226
  compared with scientific management, 107
  and job satisfaction, 164
Human resource management theory, 226
Hyman, R., 183

IBM, 113
  and unions, 202
Immigration and Canadian industrialization, 14-15
Income
  occupational distribution of, 68-70
  of corporate executives, 93n.7
  sex differences in, 68-70
Industrial capitalism
  origins of, 8-13
Industrial democracy, 230-36
  definition of, 230, 252n.19
  European legislation on, 230-31
  in Volvo and Saab factories, 235
Industrial disputes
  over union recognition, 201
Industrial Disputes Investigation Act, 190-91
Industrialization
  definition of, 7-8
  in Canada, 14-21
Industrial restructuring, 249-51
Industrial relations
  definition of, 183
  future of, 202-204
  major sociological questions about, 181-82
  role of state in, 190-91
  as a zero-sum or a win-win situation, 184
Industrial Relations and Disputes Act, 191
Industrial Revolution, 8-9, 13
Industrial society
  definition of, 7-8
Industrial unions, 189-90
Inequality, 2
Informal system of production, 111
Innis, Harold, 49
Institutionalization of industrial conflict, 191, 211
International Brotherhood of Electrical Workers, 200
International Nickel Company (INCO), 116
International Typographical Union, 182
International unions, 188
International Workers of the World ("Wobblies"), 189
Instrumentalism, 160, 172-73

Instrumentalism *(continued)*
and alienation, 171; *see also* Orientations
to work
Internal labour market, 84, 87-88, 117, 139
Iron law of oligarchy, 185
Irregular economy, 63n.5

Japan
industrial relations in, 152-53, 216
corporate cultures, 113
production systems, 250
Job dissatisfaction
and employee deviance, 167
exit and voice methods of dealing with,
209
and quitting, 167
and unions, 167
Job enlargement, 227
Job enrichment, 227
Job ghettos, 87, 129, 133-34, 139
Job redesign, 225-30
Job regulation
concept of in industrial relations, 183
Job rewards
definition of, 168; *see also* Job satisfaction; Job security; Fringe benefits;
Income; Occupational status
Job rotation, 227
Job satisfaction, 159-68
effects of age and education on, 161-62
gender differences in, 162-63
Herzberg's theory of, 164
from a labour market segmentation
perspective, 166
impact of work content and organiza-
tional characteristics, 163-67
measures of, 160-61, 178n.79
and productivity, 167
Job security, 70-71
Job stress:*see* Stress.
Johnston, W., 220
Joint occupational health and safety
committees, 239-40

Kalleberg, A., 165
Kalleberg, A. (and L. Griffin), 161
Kanter, R.M., 129, 140-42
Kealey, G., 188
Kelvin, P. (and J. Jarrett), 153
Kerr, C. (and A. Seigel), 216
Kibbutz, 231
King, W.L.M., 190
Knights of Labour, 189
Kohn, M., 174

Labour force participation
definition of, 39
rates in Canada, 40-41
Labour Force Survey, Canada, 39

Labour legislation
investigation of in Canada by International Labour Organization, 222; *see
also* specific acts
Labour market
definition of, 38
Labour markets
barriers to entry/discrimination in, 88-
90
internal, 84, 87-88, 117, 139
and poverty in the Maritimes, 90
related institutions, 67
segmented, 84-87
Labour market segmentation
Gordon, et al's research on, 90-91
and unions, 96n.52
Labour market segmentation theory, 84-92
criticisms of, 92
of Edwards et. al., 117
and occupational sex segregation, 139-
40
Labour market shelters, 129
Labour movement
theories of, 182-83
Labour problem, 105, 118
Labour process
literature on, 3
rationalization of, 104-05
research and debates, 114-18
Labour radicalism, 18; *see also* Militancy
Labour unrest
in early 19th century, 190
Lash, S., 219
Lenin, V., 185
Lenski, G., 31-32, 34
Levels of analysis
macro and micro, 2-3
Li, P., 89
Life chances, 129
Lipset, S.M., 79
Lockout: *see* Strikes
Lockwood, D., 155-56
Logic of industrialism thesis, 30-31, 33
Luddites, 11-12, 243
Leisure and work
compensatory and spillover hypotheses,
174
Luther, M.
and work values, 149
MacKinnon, M., 157-58
Management
barriers for women, 141
and employee conflict, 104
goals of, 103-104, 112-13
ideologies of, 101, 103, 148, 202
panacea fallacy regarding control of
employees, 122n.75
rights of, 202
Managerial revolution, 28-30, 103

Mann, M., 157, 218
Market economy
    definition of, 13
Marx, Karl, 7, 113-14, 154-55, 169-70, 172, 184
    on social class, 46
    theory of alienation, 169-70
    theory of social change, 21
Masonic Order, 112
Mayo, E., 109
Means of production, 21
Meissner, M., 129, 174
Menzies, H., 244-45
Meritocracy, 79
Michels, R., 185
Micro-electronics revolution, 241
Micro-electronics technology, 241-49
    computer-assisted manufacturing and computer-assisted design, 242
    debate over impact, 242-48
    in offices, 241-42
    and job loss or creation, 244
    robots, 242
    see also Automation; Robots
Militancy, 217-22
    and societal or industrial radicalism, 219; see also Class conflict; Conflict; Labour radicalism; Strikes
Mills, C.W., 24
Mode of production, 21
Mondragon cooperative, 231-32
Morgan, G.
    definition of bureaucracy, 99
Motivation
    of employees, 105, 107, 109; see also Management ideologies

Naisbett, J., 33
National War Labour Order (P.C. 1003), 191
New Democratic Party, 219
Nightingale, D., 166, 227-28
Nine Hour Movement, 188, 211
Normative controls of employees, 107, 113; see also Compliance; Consensus; Cooperation
Norway Work Environment Act, 234

Occupational choice, 74-75
Occupational health and safety, 236-41
    Canadian statistics on, 236-37
    legislation on, 237-41
    problems with official statistics on, 254n.34
    worker participation in regulation of, 239-40
Occupational mobility
    Blau and Duncan study, 80
    Canadian Mobility Study, 80

ethnic and immigrant differences in, 81-82
    gender differences in, 81
    see also Social mobility
Occupational sex segregation, 129-33
    definition of, 129
    explanations of, 138-42
    impact of family roles on, 140
    impact of unionization, 200
    and sex labelling, 130
    trends in, 130-33
    within specific occupations, 133-35
    see also Job ghettos; Women's work
Occupational self-direction, 174-75
Occupational status, 71-72
Occupational trends
    international comparisons, 44-45
Office automation, 241-42
Olson, M., 209
One Big Union, 189
Ontario Royal Commission on Asbestos, 237
Organizational culture, 112-14
Organizational goals, 101
Organization for Economic Cooperation and Development (OECD), 130
Organizations
    informal aspects, 110-12
    major research questions on, 98
    organic model of, 101
    post-bureaucratic, 228
    reification of, 102
    social psychology of, 120n.17
    strategic choice perspective on, 102
    see also Bureaucracy
Orientations to work, 148, 155-59, 173
    gender differences in, 163
    job satisfaction, 165
    see also Instrumentalism
Ornstein, M., 220
Osterman, P., 244
Ouchi, W., 113

Palmer, B., 104, 221
Participative management: see Industrial democracy; Quality of working life
Patriarchy, 128
Pay equity legislation, 143-44
Peasants during early capitalism, 12
Pensions
    gender differences in, 146n.30
Pentland, H.C., 190
Perlman, S., 182
Perrow, C., 110
Personnel management, 109-10
Petite bourgeoisie, 21-22
Piecework, 111-12
Pocklington, P., 181-84
Polanyi, Karl, 13
Poole, M., 182

Porter, J., 75
Positive labour relations, 202
Post-industrial society, 32-34, 241
Poverty
    official definition of, 145n.29
Power
    in employment relations and work or-
        ganizations, 2-3, 109-11, 114, 119
    in industrial relations, 182, 209
Powerlessness, 170-71
Privatized workers, 156; see also Instrumen-
    talism
Proctor and Gamble, 113
Production bonuses, 105, 111-12
Productivity
    and automation, 241, 243, 247
    as considered by management theories/
        goals, 105, 108, 111, 184
    determinants of, 167-68
    impact of quality of work life programs,
        179n.95
    and job satisfaction, 159-60, 167-68
    and unions, 187, 204
    see also Micro-electronics technology
Profit sharing, 231
Proletarian workers, 155
Proletariat, 21
Protestant work ethic, 150-51, 153-54; see also
    Work ethic
Public Service Staff Relations Act, 191, 198
Purcell, K., 199
Putting out system, 11

Quality control circles, 227-28
Quality of work life (QWL), 110, 116, 226-
    30
    benefits of, 228-29
    criticisms of, 228-30
    definition of, 226, 251n.1
    and productivity, 228
    and unions, 228-30
    and worker alienation, 155
Quit rates, 160

Rand formula, 214
Reagan, B. (and M. Blaxall), 139
Reich, R., 250
Resource industries
    working conditions in, 17-18
Resource towns
    decline of, 64n.25; see also Single
        industry communities
Responsible autonomy, 116
Riddell, C., 203-204
Rinehart, J., 158, 160
Robots, 242-43, 255n.59; see also Automa-
    tion; Micro-electronics technology
Roy, D., 111, 140
Royal Commission on Equality of Employ-
    ment (Abella Commission), 142-44

Saab auto plant
    and industrial democracy, 235
Sabel, C. (and M. Piore), 250
Salaries: see Income
Saskatchewan Occupational Health Act,
    239-40
Sass, R., 241
Scientific management, 20, 104-106
    artisans' opposition to, 188
    assembly-line technology, 106
    Canadian applications of, 105
    in the service sector, 106
    see also Taylor, F.W.; Taylorism
Secondary labour market, 117
    women's employment, 139-40; see also
        Labour market segmentation
Secretary as office wife, 141-42
Self-employment, 47, 64n.18
Sennett, R. (and J. Cobb), 157
Service sector
    employment in, 42-43
    and industrial restructuring, 251
    and new technologies, 245
Shell chemical plant, Sarnia, 228-29
Simple control, 117
Single industry communities
    occupational structure of, 51-53; see also
        Resource towns
Skill
    and deskilling, 114-15, 118
    impact of office automation on, 242,
        246-47, 256-57n.92
    and industrial restructuring, 250
Smith, Adam, 24-25
Smith, M., 220
Smucker, J., 103, 201
Social class
    definition of, 46
    effects on educational aspirations and
        attainment, 75-76
    structure of in Canada, 46-48
    see also Class structure
Social integration, 2-3
Social mobility, 78-79; see also Occupational
    mobility
Social relations of production, 21
Socio-economic status
    scales of, 71-72; see also Blishen scores
Sociology of work and industry
    definition of, 1
Socio-technical work design, 102, 226, 235
Solidarity Fund of Quebec Federation of
    Labour, 231
Sonnenfeld, J., 109
Staple theory of economic growth, 49-50
Stewart, A., 161
Stress, 106, 173, 238
    in assembly-line work, 169
    determinants of, 168-69
Strikebreaking, 181, 222

Strikes, 160, 170
    Air Canada ticket agents in 1985, 203
    Bell Telephone operators in 1907, 200
    Canadian trends, 212-15
    class consciousness, 218-22
    as collective action, 217
    definition of, 211
    explanations of, 216-17
    Ford Motor Company, Windsor in 1945,
        214
    Gainers, Edmonton in 1986, 181, 184,
        203, 222
    international trends, 215-16
    isolation hypothesis of, 216-17
    labour legislation prohibitions, 185
    by letter carriers in 1987, 222
    by skilled crafts workers in early 1900s,
        17
    Toronto printers in 1872, 188, 211
    wildcat, 211
    Winnipeg in 1919, 189, 213-14
    see also Class conflict; Conflict; Militancy;
        Labour radicalism
St. Thomas Aquinas
    view of work, 149
Surplus value
    Marx's theory of, 22
Sweden
    industrial democracy in, 232-36
    industrial relations in, 216
    Wage Earner Fund, 234-35
Swedish Act on Employee Participation in
    Decision Making, 233
Swedish Work Environment Act, 233
Swedish Work Environment Fund, 234
Syndicalism, 189

Tavistock Institute of Human Relations,
    102, 226
Taylor, F.W., 20, 104-107
Taylorism, 109, 114, 116, 119, 225-27, 246,
    250,
    and job satisfaction, 164; see also Scientific
        management
Technical control, 117
Technological determinism, 172, 247
Technology
    and alienation, 166, 172
    as a cause of stress, 106, 238-39
    job redesign, 228-29
    in theories of social change, 30-32
    worker opposition to, 243
    work relations, 102, 111, 117, 121n.54
    see also Microelectronics technology;
        Robots; Technological determinism
Thorsrud, E., 226
Tilley, C., 210
Tokenism
    problem for women managers, 142

Toyota Corporation, 227
Trades and Labour Congress, 188
Trade Union Act, 188, 191
Trist, E.L. (and K.W. Bamforth), 102
Unemployment
    among Native Canadians, 57
    among women, 57
    among youth, 58
    changing rates of, 55-56
    discouraged workers, 58-59
    explanations of, 59-60
    international trends, 60-61
    regional variations in, 56-57
    voluntary, 59
Union democracy, 185
Union dues check-off, 214
Union-management relations: see Industrial
    relations
Unionism
    rational choice model of, 208, 223n.8
Unionization
    explanation of, 208-10
    of 19th-century skilled craftworkers, 187-
        88
    problems among white-collar workers,
        201
Unions
    Canadianization trend, 198-99
    decertification of at Eaton's stores, 200
    emergence in Canada, 187-90
    goals and strategies, 186
    impact of Charter of Rights and
        Freedoms on, 222
    impact of industry deregulation on, 203
    industrial democracy in Sweden, 232-36
    international comparisons of member-
        ship, 193-94
    male domination of, 200
    management opposition to, 201-202
    as managers of discontent, 185, 205n.14
    membership growth trends, 192-94
    membership variations by sex, industry,
        occupation, region, 195-99
    and politics in Canada, 219
    providing collective goods, 209
    public opinion about, 186-87
    as social movements, 209-10
    socio-economic impact of, 186-87
    and technological change, 247-48
    ten largest in Canada, 196-98
    and women workers, 199-201
Union shop, 214
United Auto Workers, 189, 195, 230; see also
    Canadian Auto Workers Union
United Steel Workers, 195
Unpaid work, 2
U.S. National Labour Relations Act
    (Wagner Act), 191
U.S. Quality of Employment Survey, 164-65

Values
    definition of, 148
Volvo Kalmar plant, 235

Wage bonuses, 117
Wage gap: see Wages, gender inequalities in
Wages
    gender inequalities in, 135-38
Watt, J., 11
Webb, S. (and B. Webb), 182
Weber, Max, 7, 129, 150-51, 153
    on bureaucracy 26-27, 99-101
Wells, D., 228
Western Federation of Miners, 189
West Germany
    industrial relations in, 216
Welfare work: see Corporate welfare
    programs
Winnipeg General Strike, 189, 213-14
Wisconsin model of status attainment,
    95n.39
Wives and two-person career, 129
Women
    as household managers, 125
    impact of microelectronics/automation
        on, 242, 245
    in non-traditional areas of employment,
        134, 200
    union membership, 199-201
Women's movement, 123
Women's work
    employment of married women, 124,
        128
    historical trends, 123-25
    ideological basis of, 130
    impact of family income on, 14n.10
    job and gender models of the
        workplace, 138
    managerial and administrative occupa-
        tions, 133-34
    and poverty, 135
    in pre-industrial Canada, 124
    teaching profession, 133
    see also Occupational sex segregation
Woods, H.D., 215
Woodward, J., 102
Work
    _approaches to, 3

changing meaning of historically, 148-49
definition of, 1-2
Durkheimian, Marxist and Weberian
    humanization of, 225-30
macro and micro approaches to, 225
Workers' compensation boards, 237-39
Worker cooperatives, 231-32
    in Mondragon, Spain, 231-32
Workers' management in Yugoslavia, 231
Workers' rights, 181
Work ethic
    Canadian data on, 151, 153-154
    decline of, 151-54
    of Japanese workers, 151-53
    see also Protestant work ethic
Work groups
    informal norms of, 108
Work hours, 53-54
    reduction of, 257n.101
    and technology, 248
Working class
    ideologies of males in, 220
    and political ideologies in Canada, 220-
        21
    political action, 218-22
Working class communities, and unions,
    188
Working class consciousness, 155
Working class images of society
    D. Lockwood's theory of, 155-56
    and strikes, 176n.28
Working class radicalism, 189
Working class women
    work in late 19th century, 125
Working conditions
    impact on non-work activities, 174
    impact on personality, 174-75
Work orientations: see Orientations to work
Workplace Hazardous Materials System, 240
Work values, 148
    humanistic tradition, 154-55, 160
Wright, Eric Olin
    theory of class, 47-48

Xerox Corporation, 202

Zeitlin, I., 23